C#
Black Book

Matt Telles

President and CEO
Roland Elgey

Publisher
Al Valvano

Associate Publisher
*Katherine R.
Hartlove*

Acquisitions Editor
*Jawahara
Saidullah*

Development Editor
Jessica Choi

**Product Marketing
Manager**
Tracy Rooney

Project Editor
*Marta Justak,
Justak Literary
Services*

Technical Reviewer
Sumit Pal

Designer
Laura Wellander

CD-ROM Developer
*Michelle
McConnell*

C# Black Book

Limits of Liability and Disclaimer of Warranty

The author and publisher of this book have used their best efforts in preparing the book and the programs contained in it. These efforts include the development, research, and testing of the theories and programs to determine their effectiveness. The author and publisher make no warranty of any kind, expressed or implied, with regard to these programs or the documentation contained in this book.

The author and publisher shall not be liable in the event of incidental or consequential damages in connection with, or arising out of, the furnishing, performance, or use of the programs, associated instructions, and/or claims of productivity gains.

Trademarks

Trademarked names appear throughout this book. Rather than list the names and entities that own the trademarks or insert a trademark symbol with each mention of the trademarked name, the publisher states that it is using the names for editorial purposes only and to the benefit of the trademark owner, with no intention of infringing upon that trademark.

The Coriolis Group, LLC
14455 N. Hayden Road
Suite 220
Scottsdale, Arizona 85260

(480) 483-0192
FAX (480) 483-0193
www.coriolis.com

Library of Congress Cataloging-in-Publication Data
Telles, Matthew A.
    C# black book / by Matthew Telles.
        p.   cm.
    ISBN 1-58880-192-6
    1. C# (Computer program language)   I. Title.
QA76.73.C154 T45 2001
005.13'3–dc21

2001047679
CIP

Printed in the United States of America
10   9   8   7   6   5   4   3   2   1

⊙ CORIOLIS™

The Coriolis Group, LLC • 14455 North Hayden Road, Suite 220 • Scottsdale, Arizona 85260

A Note from Coriolis

Coriolis Technology Press was founded to create a very elite group of books: the ones you keep closest to your machine. In the real world, you have to choose the books you rely on every day *very* carefully, and we understand that.

To win a place for our books on that coveted shelf beside your PC, we guarantee several important qualities in every book we publish. These qualities are:

- *Technical accuracy*—It's no good if it doesn't work. Every Coriolis Technology Press book is reviewed by technical experts in the topic field, and is sent through several editing and proofreading passes in order to create the piece of work you now hold in your hands.

- *Innovative editorial design*—We've put years of research and refinement into the ways we present information in our books. Our books' editorial approach is uniquely designed to reflect the way people learn new technologies and search for solutions to technology problems.

- *Practical focus*—We put only pertinent information into our books and avoid any fluff. Every fact included between these two covers must serve the mission of the book as a whole.

- *Accessibility*—The information in a book is worthless unless you can find it quickly when you need it. We put a lot of effort into our indexes, and heavily cross-reference our chapters, to make it easy for you to move right to the information you need.

Here at The Coriolis Group we have been publishing and packaging books, technical journals, and training materials since 1989. We have put a lot of thought into our books; please write to us at **ctp@coriolis.com** and let us know what you think. We hope that you're happy with the book in your hands, and that in the future, when you reach for software development and networking information, you'll turn to one of our books first.

Coriolis Technology Press
The Coriolis Group
14455 N. Hayden Road, Suite 220
Scottsdale, Arizona
85260

Email: ctp@coriolis.com
Phone: (480) 483-0192
Toll free: (800) 410-0192

Look for these related books from The Coriolis Group:

C# Core Language Little Black Book
by Bill Wagner

.NET Content Management Systems Development
by Stephen Fraser

Visual Studio .NET: The .NET Framework Black Book
by Julian Templeman and David Vitter

Visual Basic .NET Programming with Peter Aitken
by Peter Aitken

Visual Basic .NET Black Book
by Steven Holzner

Also published by Coriolis Technology Press:

C++ Black Book
by Steven Holzner

Java 2 Network Protocols Black Book
by Al Williams

Java 2 Black Book
by Steven Holzner

Software Project Management: From Concept to Deployment
by Kieron Conway

This book is dedicated to my friends Carol, Louise, and Denise, without whom I would be much worse than I am now. And, of course, for my children, Jenny, Rachel, and Sarah, without whom my world would be a much more dismal place. Thank you all.

About the Author

Matt Telles is a 15-year veteran of the software development wars. In his time, he has seen FORTRAN, COBOL, and other dinosaur languages come and go. Currently a senior software engineer for Microsoft Corporation, his days are spent finding and fixing bugs that other people have created. Besides trying to be tactful, he also enjoys working with other developers to teach the techniques he has mastered over his career. With expertise in programming, designing, documenting, and debugging applications, he has reached the pinnacle of a programmer's existence—the ability to write his own blurbs for books. The author of seven books on software and programming, Matt lives in Lakewood, Colorado, and pines away for his beloved DEC 10.

Acknowledgments

I would like to acknowledge my employer, Microsoft Corporation, for allowing me the time and space to work on this book. In addition, I would like to acknowledge my friends and family, who ignored the ranting and raving that came out of my office from time to time during the production of this tome. Finally, no book could be written without a considerable amount of behind-the-scenes work. Marta Justak and Becky Whitney worked tirelessly to turn the inane words I wrote into something vaguely resembling English.

Contents at a Glance

Table of Contents

Chapter 8
The Common Language Runtime Libraries 307

Introduction

Thanks for buying the *C# Black Book*!

The new C# programming language was created by Microsoft to respond to some specific and important needs in the programming community. The C# language answers the problems that exist in many other languages. Security, garbage collection, interoperability with other languages, and cross-platform compatibility are just a few reasons you should consider switching to this new language.

If you are a C++ programmer, you will find C# at once familiar and more powerful than the language you have used in the past. If you are accustomed to working with Visual Studio, you will find the new Visual Studio.NET to be a powerful yet comfortable tool that extends rather than replaces your existing programming environment.

If you are a Java programmer, you will find C# to be a language as well thought out as Java, but with extensions and built-in components that Java does not yet have. From the intuitive drag-and-drop programming environment of C# to its use of delegates and event handlers, Java programmers will find it to be a natural upgrade path in programming.

Finally, if you are a Visual Basic programmer moving up to C#, you will see that the language provides all the simple drag-and-drop functionality you have used in the past and also allows you to use true object-oriented programming techniques to move you into a whole new realm of programming.

Is This Book for You?

The *C# Black Book* was written with intermediate or advanced users in mind. Some topics covered in this book are shown in this list:

- Garbage collection
- Graphics
- Multithreading
- The new Windows forms library
- Custom controls

How to Use This Book

The *Black Book* series was created to be both an introduction to and immersion in a topic as well as a reference series that can be used day in and day out. In this book, you can jump around from chapter to chapter without worrying about needing information from previous chapters. In each chapter that uses information from a previous chapter, a cross-index table refers you back to the information you may need.

Each chapter in the book is split into two separate pieces. First, the chapter begins with an extensive look at the chapter topic. This In Depth section explains all the components of that topic and walks you through any information you need in order to understand that topic. Next, the chapter contains an Immediate Solutions section, which contains specific examples that illustrate exactly how to solve a specific problem you may encounter in your professional efforts.

The *Black Book* Philosophy

Written by experienced professionals, books in the Coriolis *Black Book* series provide immediate solutions to global programming and administrative challenges, helping you complete specific tasks, especially critical ones that are not well documented in other books. The *Black Book*'s unique two-part chapter format—thorough technical overviews followed by practical immediate solutions—is structured to help you use your knowledge, solve problems, and quickly master complex technical issues to become an expert. By breaking down complex topics into easily manageable components, this format helps you quickly find what you're looking for, with the diagrams and code you need to make it happen.

I welcome your feedback on this book. You can email either The Coriolis Group, at **ctp@coriolis.com**, or me directly, at **matttelles@sprynet.com**. Errata, updates, and more information are available at **www.coriolis.com**.

Chapter 1

The Data Types

In Depth

The basis for any language is the data type it supports. C# supports a rich and varied selection of data types, from built-in types, such as integers or strings, to user-defined types, such as enumerations, structures, and classes. In this section, you examine those data types as well as the modifiers that can be applied to them, such as arrays.

The C# language begins with a rich set of built-in types. When dealing with these data types, remember these two facts about the C# environment:

- All variables, whether user-defined or intrinsic (built-in), are first-class variables. That is, they can be used as objects anywhere in the system.

- All variables in the system are automatically initialized to default values by the system when they are declared.

The other important thing to remember about C# variables is that they all break down into two simple organizational structures: value types and reference types. *Value* types are variables that can be assigned a value directly. *Reference* types are variables that must be interfaced to through methods or functions to be able to access their internal data. In object-oriented parlance, a *reference type* supports data hiding, and a *value type* does not. Reference types are different also in that two reference variables may refer to the same object, whereas simple value types are always discrete entities.

The Value Types

Take a look at the value types first and see what they can be used for and how they are referenced. To see simply how to use each type directly without the underlying discussion on how the types work or what their limitations and capabilities are, please refer to the "Immediate Solutions" section later in this chapter. Table 1.1 shows all the available types and what they represent.

When I talk about the basic value types, I am talking about the bread and butter of the C# programmer. These types are where data is stored and used in the application. You need to understand the types of variables available to you and what they can be used for. In addition, the conversions needed to make one type into another are important.

Table 1.1   **C# basic value data types.**

Value Type	What It Represents
sbyte	8-bit signed integral type.
short	16-bit signed integral type.
int	32-bit signed integral type.
long	64-bit signed integral type.
byte	8-bit unsigned integral type.
ushort	16-bit unsigned integral type.
uint	32-bit unsigned integral type.
ulong	64-bit unsigned integral type.
float	Single-precision floating-point type.
double	Double-precision floating-point type.
bool	Boolean type; a **bool** value is either true or false.
char	Character type, a **char** value is a Unicode character.
decimal	Precise decimal type with 28 significant digits.

The Integral Types

The integral types of the C# system break down into signed and unsigned value types. *Signed* value types may contain negative or positive values, and *unsigned* value types may contain only positive values. Unlike with C++, converting between the two types usually requires an explicit cast. This requirement is one more way in which C# prevents you from making silly mistakes in your code that are hard to track down.

The Sbyte and Byte Types

The **sbyte** and **byte** types represent a single byte (or character, in the old non-Unicode world). Bytes can be used to store very small numbers, such as the day of the month, or to read individual elements from a file. **Byte** values are often used for flags, signal values, and serialization efforts. C# has no true notion of pointers, so bytes are often used to "index into" a string and write it out. Of course, because a **byte** value is restricted to only 8 bits of precision, a long string could overflow the index.

The Short Value

The **short** value is used to represent small integers in the programming world. **Short** values can range from –32767 through 32767 and can hold all values in between. Unsigned **short** values can range from 0 through 65535. Although you certainly would not use a **byte** value to represent a person's age, you would be quite safe in using an unsigned **short** value. (After all, even with life extension, how many of us are likely to live 65,000 years?)

The Floating-Point Type

Similarly, the floating-point numbers break down into two types: single and double floats. *Single* floats, familiar to C++ developers as the **float** data type, hold values up to 10^{308}. *Double* data types, also similar to the C++ **double** type, hold values up to 10^{308}. Obviously, both are good for scientific programming.

The Boolean and Decimal Types

The other two important value types are the **Boolean** type and the **Decimal** type. *Booleans* are simple true or false values. Unlike in C++, they cannot be assigned to any other type, nor can they be used in any sort of computation. The result of an expression in C# is not a Boolean expression, unless you specifically assign it as true or false. The following code

```
int x = 3;
If ( x ) {
}
```

does not work in C# because you can use Boolean values in only Boolean expressions. For the preceding example, you must write something like this:

```
int x = 3;
if ( x != 0 )
{
}
```

These two code snippets are functionally equivalent in C++ or Java, but do not behave the same (in fact, the first does not compile) in C#. This difference between C# and the other two languages is important and is one that avoids problems noticed in the past by programmers.

The other data type, **Decimal**, is equivalent to a long integer that behaves as if it were a floating-point number. Decimal values are intended to be used for monetary computations or other calculations in which truncation beyond the decimal point is not desired behavior.

The Reference Types

C# also provides types that are, by their nature, passed by reference. These types are the classes and structures, which are the user-defined types of C#. Although all variables in C# are first-class objects and may be treated the same way, classes and structures have special abilities, such as constructors and destructors. You look in depth at classes in Chapter 2. For now, I talk a little about the rationale for objects in C#.

In C#, all classes, and even all value types, are really objects. All objects derive from a single base class, called **object**. It allows all objects to be "understood" by the system and to be treated in the same way. When you pass an object to a function, you can find out what kind of object you are dealing with by using the **as** keyword. I discuss this subject more in Chapter 6, when I discuss reflection.

All applications in C# are based on a class. Unlike with C++ or C, you cannot have a simple function that acts on its own. This concept is more in the Java mold of programming. All C# console applications, for example, contain a single static method, called **Main**, that must be present. The following is a minimal C# application:

```
Class Foo
{
    static void Main()
    {
        System.Console.WriteLine("Hello world from C#");
    }
}
```

In this example, you have defined a simple class, called **Foo**, that would normally reside in a file named Foo.cs. When compiled, it would form an executable named Foo.exe that could run from the command line. C# applications do not form native executables. These executable files are really stubs that load the C# runtime environment and load in the precompiled code that makes up the program you wrote. In the preceding example, the stub would load the interpreter, which would then fetch the **Console** object from the **System** namespace and invoke the static **WriteLine** method of that object. The string "**Hello world from C#**" would be passed in, and the method would then output that string to the console device. That is, in a nutshell, how C# works.

Structures are quite similar to classes, but are not available for running applications. A *structure* is intended to be a collection of value types (or other user-defined types, if you like) that is encapsulated to represent some real-world entity. For example, if you want to define a structure to model a point in C#, you might write something like this:

```
struct Point
{
    public int x;
    public int y;
};
```

```
class Foo
{
    static void Main()
    {
        Point p;
        p.x = 1;
        p.y = 2;
        System.Console.WriteLine("P.x = {0} P.y = {1}", p.x, p.y);
    }
}
```

C# and either Java or C++ have quite a few differences between them, as you can tell. For one thing, the default for structure elements in C# is protected, not public, as it would be in C++. For another, you must specifically designate each element of a structure as public in order for a method outside the structure to use it directly. Structures, as in C++, can have methods, constructors, and destructors. In addition, C# structures can contain properties, which I discuss in Chapter 2. Another important difference is that C# does not initialize structure elements to a given value. Class elements automatically default to an initialized value of 0 for all value types, with the exception of character data, which take on a character null value.

One other difference between C# and the other languages is that C# structures can be created on the heap or on the stack. C# classes, however, can be created only on the heap (via the **new** keyword). Given the preceding declaration, for example, in C# you cannot write:

```
Foo f;
```

Instead, you must write:

```
Foo f = new Foo();
```

The first example line does not compile in C#; only the second line is considered syntactically correct by the compiler.

Arrays

All modern programming languages support arrays of value types or reference types, and C# is certainly no exception to that rule. A few things make C# somewhat unique in the handling of arrays, however. First, arrays in C# cannot be created on the stack. That is, you cannot create an array statically in a method as you would in C++ or Java. In these languages, you can write something like the following code snippet:

```
int x[10];
```

This code would create a static array of 10 elements, each of which was properly sized to hold one integer. In C#, the array is an actual type, much like integers. Arrays must be allocated on the heap. The following line is the equivalent array statement of the preceding C++ or Java code line:

```
int[] x = new int[10];
```

As you can see, an array is much more than a simple modifier, as it would be in C++ or Java. Because arrays are first-class objects, just as all other types are in C#, you can also inspect them for certain attributes. The most obvious attribute is that of the "size" of the array, which is also the number of elements that can be stored in the array. This attribute is inspected via the **Length** property, which is used as a property rather than as a method. You access the length of an array by writing:

```
int len = x.Length;
```

C# also supports multidimensional arrays, which must be allocated on the heap as well. Unlike C++ or Java, C# uses the old-style FORTRAN syntax for declaring multiple dimensions, by having comma-delimited dimensions in an array definition, as in:

```
int multix[,] = new int[5,5];
```

This line creates an array that represents a 5×5 matrix. You can create arrays of many different dimensions, such as 3×3×3. Unfortunately, the **Length** property of the array returns the total number of elements. That's a nice situation, but when you have something like this

```
Int fivebyfive[5,5] = new int[5,5];
System.Console.WriteLine("Length of fivebyfive = {0}", fivebyfive.Length);
```

this snippet produces the following output:

```
Length of fivebyfive = 25
```

That's certainly useful in that you know the total size of the array, but determining what each row has in the way of number of columns is difficult. For this reason,

C# provides two other methods of the array class: **GetLowerBound** and **GetUpperBound**. Given the preceding 5×5 matrix, for example, you could find out its boundaries by writing something like this:

```
System.Console.WriteLine("Lower Bound = {0}, Upper Bound = {1}",
    fivebyfive.GetLowerBound(0), fivebyfive.GetUpperBound(0) );
```

This snippet produces the following output:

```
Lower Bound = 0, Upper Bound = 4
```

As you can see, the array elements are valid from 0 through 4, which are five total elements for the first row.

C# also allows for "jagged" arrays. You don't have to create all the elements of the array if you don't want to. Consider, for example, the need to store only a "triangle's" worth of data in a 5×5 array. You could create a 5×5 array as you did previously, but that would waste lots of space. If your array is in the thousands of elements and memory is tight, this problem could be serious. Instead, you might do something like this:

```
class CH1_ID3
{
    public static void Main()
    {
        int[][] jagged = new int[5][];
        for ( int i=0; i<5; ++i )
            jagged[i] = new int[i];
    }
}
```

As you can see, the syntax for jagged arrays is slightly different from that of "normal" arrays and is more familiar to C++ or Java programmers. You are defining an array of arrays, which is perfectly legitimate in C#. The only real difference between an array of arrays and a standard array is that a standard array is a fixed size. An array of arrays permits you to make each row a different number of columns wide (permitting jagged arrays). You should note that the rank of such a construct is simply the number of ranks in the first array element. In the example, the rank is 1 because a single-dimensional array is used for the first array. The **Length** property can be used on the second array element. So you can write something like this:

```
for ( int i=0; i<5; ++i )
        System.Console.WriteLine("Rank of {0} = {1}",
i, jagged[i].Length);;            .
```

With the preceding jagged array definition, this line would be printed as:

```
Rank of 0 = 0
Rank of 1 = 1
Rank of 2 = 2
Rank of 3 = 3
Rank of 4 = 4
```

Collections

Although arrays are useful constructs, programmers often need to do other things, such as insert into and delete from a collection of elements. C# provides a rich set of collection classes, as shown in Table 1.2.

Collections in C# are used in a simple, intuitive manner, after you get the hang of them. Collections may have elements inserted into them, using either the **Add** or **Insert** methods, and collections can be deleted from, using the **RemoveAt** method. Finally, collections can be iterated over, using the **foreach** statement of the language.

C# maintains the collections, allocating or compacting as needed to maintain the number of elements in the most efficient manner. If, for example, you begin with an **ArrayList** of 10 elements and add 11 elements, you find that the array

Table 1.2 **C# collection classes.**

Collection Class	Description
ArrayList	A dynamically sized array that can contain any sort of object.
BitArray	A compact array of bit values whose value can be either true or false.
HashTable	A hash table that maps given keys to values allowing for buckets of segmented data. A hash table maintains a sorted list of key/value pairs that can be accessed by key value.
Queue	Represents a first-in, first-out collection of objects.
SortedList	Maintains a sorted list of key/value pairs that can be accessed by either key or index.
Stack	Represents a single list of objects in a last-in, first-out manner.
StringCollection	Maintains a collection of strings, much like an array does.

automatically grows as required. Here's a simple example of using such a collection in C#:

```
ArrayList a = new ArrayList(10); // Create a new array list with an initial
    allocation of 10 items.
// Add 20 items to the array in ascending order. The array grows as needed
For ( int I=0; I<20; ++I )
    a.Add( I );
// Remove a few elements
a.RemoveAt(0);
a.RemoveAt(2);
a.RemoveAt(4);
```

Finally, you can look at how to iterate through the elements of an array collection. Arrays can be accessed in two ways. The standard way uses the indexer property of the class, which makes the **ArrayList** collection look just like a "normal" array:

```
for ( int I=0; I<a.Count; ++I )
    System.Console.WriteLine("Element {0} = {1}", I, a[I] );
```

The alternative, and preferred, method of iterating through the array is to use the **foreach** statement. To iterate through the **ArrayList**, for example, you would use a statement like the following:

```
foreach ( int i in a )
{
    System.Console.WriteLine("Element {0}", a[i] );
}
```

You can find other examples of using the various collection types in the "Immediate Solutions" section later in this chapter.

Conversions

The final topic of your whirlwind, in-depth tour of the C# data type world centers on conversions. One typical job a programmer must do is convert one data type to another. Conversions come in two forms: explicit and implicit. *Explicit* conversions are done by the programmer in the code itself. Examples of explicit conversions are those required by the language, such as the following:

```
Single s = 123.45;
Int I = (int)Single;
```

Implicit conversions are conversions the language does for you, behind the scenes, in a type-safe manner. The preceding example, showing the truncating of a floating-point number, is not a type-safe conversion because it can potentially lose significance. For this reason, C# requires that you explicitly convert one to the other. On the other hand, converting an integer to a floating-point number is perfectly safe and can be done implicitly, like this:

```
Int I = 123;
Single s = I;
```

All these conversions, however, are done in the old-style C++ or Java way. C# introduces the notion of built-in conversions from type to type. Table 1.3 lists the available conversion methods that are built into the data types in C#.

The C# way of converting a given type into any other type is to use one of the conversion functions on the type itself. For example, to convert an integer to a string, you would do something like this:

```
string s = anInteger.ToString();
```

Table 1.3 **C# conversion methods.**

Conversion Method	Description
ToBoolean	Converts this type to a Boolean value, if possible
ToByte	Converts this type to a byte
ToChar	Converts this type to a single character (Unicode), if possible
ToDateTime	Converts types (mostly integers and string) to date-time structures
ToDecimal	Converts types (floating point or integer) to decimal values
ToDouble	Converts virtually any type safely to a double
ToInt16	Converts virtually any type safely to an int
ToInt32	Converts virtually any type to a long integer
ToInt64	Converts virtually any type to a big integer
ToSbyte	Converts a given type to a signed byte field, if possible
ToSingle	Converts virtually any type to a small floating-point number
ToString	Converts virtually any type to a string
ToType	Converts a type to another specified type, if possible
ToUInt16	Converts a type to an unsigned int, if possible
ToUInt32	Converts virtually any type to an unsigned long
ToUInt64	Converts virtually any type to an unsigned big integer

Any type in C# can be converted safely to a string. Other type conversions are somewhat more negotiable. For example, a type conversion from a floating-point number to a byte could easily overflow the result and cause a bad answer. To protect against this situation, C# provides the exception mechanism, which I talk about in Chapter 2.

At this point, you should have a firm grasp on the fundamentals of the data types involved in programming in C#. After you understand the basic building blocks, it is generally a short trip to being able to do anything you want. At this point, take a look at the "Immediate Solutions" section in this chapter so that you can learn how to do the tasks you need to do to get your job done.

Immediate Solutions

Creating a Simple **Hello World** Framework

Every programmer requires that you show her how to create and run a simple program in the programming language she is trying to use. In this case, I use the standard **Hello World** application to show how to compile, link, and run a C# application as well as to describe the basic structure of a C# program. Listing 1.1 shows a standard C# application that simply prints the literal string **"Hello World!"** to the console output device.

Listing 1.1   A simple Hello World framework in C#.

```
// A "Hello World!" program in C#
class Hello {
   public static void Main()
   {
      System.Console.WriteLine("Hello World!");
   }
}
```

A few things are worth noting in this simple program. First, notice that the entire program is wrapped in a **class** statement. C# is a true object-oriented language, unlike C++. In that respect, everything in C# is an object, and all code must reside in classes. In a C# application, the "main" class (that is, the one from which the program begins) must contain a method called **Main**, which must be declared as static. A *static* method is one that requires no object to call it, much like in C++.

Another important concept in the class is the use of the **public** keyword. I discuss access specifiers later in this chapter; for now, assume that this method is accessible to objects outside the class itself. Because the class framework needs access to the **Main** method to launch the application, the **Main** method must be declared public.

Notice that unlike some examples in the documentation for the system, you do not include any namespaces. Namespaces, which you look at in Chapter 4, would take the form of a **using** statement, such as the following:

```
using System;
```

This line is not necessary because the compiler knows where to find the **Console.WriteLine** method because you fully qualified it with the **System** object tag. If you had placed the **using** statement at the head of the code, you could have written the code as:

```
Console.WriteLine("Hello World");
```

Related solution:	*Found on page:*
Creating a Simple Class	55

Declaring a Variable

To do anything useful with an application, you need to have variables to work with. Input variables are necessary in order to transfer information from the outside world (from the program's standpoint) into the application, and output variables are used to store output results and display data for the user. In Listing 1.2, you can see how to declare a variable, give it a value, and then print the result to the output console device. The shaded lines in the listing show the declarations of three simple value types in the application.

Listing 1.2   Declaring a variable.

```
class CH1_2 {
    public static void Main()
    {
    short x;
    int   y;

    double z = 0;

    x = 6;
    y = 10;
    z = x + y;
    System.Console.WriteLine("X = {0} Y = {1} Z = {2}", x, y, z);
    }
}
```

One curious note in the preceding example is the **WriteLine** method call from the **System.Console** object. Notice how all the objects are placed into the method call following the formatting string, which begins with "**X = {0}**". The parameters are pulled off the stack in the order they are placed into the method. In other words, the x parameter is number 0; the y parameter, number 1; and the z parameter, number 2. Furthermore, notice that, because C# treats everything as a first-class object, you need no information to determine what kind of parameters they are.

Initializing a Variable

If you have a variable declared in your application, you often want to initialize it. Variables can be initialized in several different ways: at the time they are declared, within the application with a constant value, or by copying the value of another variable into them. Sometimes, the final version requires explicit coercion on the part of the programmer. Listing 1.3 shows the code that does all these initializations.

Listing 1.3   Initializing a variable.

```
using System;

class CH1_1 {
   public static void Main()
   {
       // Initialize a variable at declaration
       short x = 5;

        // Initialize a variable as a copy of another
        int   y = x;

        double z = y + 10.25;

        int a = (int)z;

        Console.WriteLine("X = {0} Y = {1} Z = {2}", x, y, z);
        Console.WriteLine("A = {0}", a);
   }
}
```

The two shaded lines are the most interesting aspects of the preceding program. Also, please note that in this example you import the namespace System (via the **using System** statement), which allows you to write **Console.WriteLine** rather than to have to fully qualify the **System.Console.WriteLine** statement. In the first shaded line, you are assigning an integer value to a floating-point value. Note that no coercion is necessary because this cast cannot lose precision; it can only gain it. In the second shaded line, you are converting a floating-point number to an integer. This case requires an explicit cast because it can (and does) lose precision in its execution. Imagine that you had written this line as:

```
int a = z;
```

In the preceding line of code, the compiler would generate an error message:

```
Microsoft (R) C# Compiler Version 7.00.8905 [NGWS runtime 2000.14.1812.10]
Copyright (C) Microsoft Corp 2000. All rights reserved.

CH1_3.cs(14,10): error CS0029: Cannot implicitly convert type 'double'
    to 'int'
```

In this way, C# protects you as a developer from making mistakes without understanding what it is that you are doing. By forcing you to specifically cast the floating-point number to an integer, the compiler makes sure that you understand the consequences of your actions. It's hard to overestimate the number of occasions in which invalid conversions in applications have led to bugs that caused serious damage and were difficult to track down.

If you don't believe that this statement is true, consider the C++ application shown in Listing 1.4. It compiles with no errors or warnings under Visual C++.

Listing 1.4   Coercion in C++.

```
#include <stdio.h>
#include <string.h>
#include <stdlib.h>

double DoubleIt( int temp )
{
     double d = temp * 2.0;
     return d;
}

int main(void)
{
     double temp = 0;
     double x = 99.65;
     double y = 10.45;

     double z = x + y;
     printf("Z = %lf\n", z );
     temp = z + 10.0;

     printf("Temp = %lf\n", temp );
     printf("DoubleIt = %lf\n", DoubleIt( temp ) );
     return 0;
}
```

If you add 99.65 and 10.45, you get a result of 120.1. In fact, the output from this function is:

```
Z = 110.100000
Temp = 120.100000
DoubleIt = 240.000000
```

Note that the doubling function does not appear to work. In fact, the shaded line in the listing is the entire problem. You are passing in a double value (a floating-point number), but accepting an integer. No warnings of this coercion come from the compiler, and no errors are generated. You just get an incorrect answer when you are finished with the application. Imagine trying to track down something like this in a large-scale application.

Scoping Variables

One of the ways in which C# makes life easier for the developer is to remove the ability to have global variables. It does, however, have multiple levels of variables, including different scopes for different kinds of variables. We revisit this issue in Chapter 2, when I discuss classes and structures, but in this section you simply look at some examples of how variable scope works in C#. Listing 1.5 shows a simple example of two variables of the same name but in a different scope.

Listing 1.5   Scoping in C#.

```csharp
using System;

class CH1_4 {
    // Class level x variable
  static int x = 10;

  public static void Main()
  {
    // Locally defined copy of x
    int x = 5;
    int   y = x;
    double z = y + 10.25;

    int a = (int)z;

    // Output X. Which one gets written?
    Console.WriteLine("X = {0} Y = {1} Z = {2}", x, y, z);
    Console.WriteLine("A = {0}", a);
```

```
      // Force the output of the class level x variable
      Console.WriteLine("Class Level X = {0}", CH1_4.x);
  }
}
```

The output from this small application is:

```
X = 5 Y = 5 Z = 15.25
A = 15
Class Level X = 10
```

In short, it is exactly what you would expect to see if you were reading the code. (C# is about minimal astonishment.) What you see is really what you should get when you run the program.

In C and C++, you can do much more complicated tasks. For example, you would think, as a C++ programmer, that you could do the following to create a local variable of the same name:

```
using System;

class CH1_4 {
      // Class level x variable
   static int x = 10;

   public static void Main()
   {
      // Locally defined copy of x
      int x = 5;
      int   y = x;
      double z = y + 10.25;

      int a = (int)z;

      {
         int x = 15;
         Console.WriteLine("Inside Braces, X = {0}", x);
      }

       // Output X. Which one gets written?
      Console.WriteLine("X = {0} Y = {1} Z = {2}", x, y, z);
      Console.WriteLine("A = {0}", a);

      // Force the output of the class level x variable
      Console.WriteLine("Class Level X = {0}", CH1_4.x);
   }
}
```

Surprisingly, this code doesn't work. In fact, the compiler is smart enough to catch it and tell you what you are doing wrong:

```
Microsoft (R) C# Compiler Version 7.00.8905 [NGWS runtime 2000.14.1812.10]
Copyright (C) Microsoft Corp 2000. All rights reserved.

CH1_4.cs(17,9): error CS0136: A local variable named 'x' cannot be declared
in this scope because it would give a different meaning to 'x', which is
already used in a 'parent or current' scope to denote something else
```

This example illustrates, one more time, how C# makes programming safer by not allowing you to make silly mistakes.

Creating a Simple Array

The C# language supports both single-dimensional and multidimensional arrays. In all cases, the arrays are dynamic. In addition, consider the notion of a *jagged* array, which contains an irregular number of columns or rows. C# has no notion of a simple static array, such as you might find in C or C++. Listing 1.6 shows a simple application that defines and uses both single- and multidimensional arrays.

Listing 1.6   Single- and multidimensional arrays in C#.

```csharp
using System;

class CH1_5 {

    public static void PrintOneDArray( int[] arr, int dim )
    {
        for ( int i=0; i<dim; ++i )
        Console.WriteLine( "OneDArray Row {0} = {1}", i, arr[i]);
    }

    public static void PrintTwoDArray( int[,] arr, int dim1, int dim2 )
    {
        for ( int row = 0; row < dim1; ++row )
        for ( int col=0; col<dim2; ++col )
        Console.WriteLine( "TwoDArray Row {0} Col {1} = {2}",
            row, col, arr[row,col]);
    }

    public static void Main()
    {
        // A dynamic array of 10 elements
        int[] x = new int[10];
```

```
            for ( int i=0; i<10; ++i )
            x[i] = i;

            // A multidimensional array
            int[,] y = new int[10,20];
            for ( int k=0; k<10; ++k )
            for ( int i=0; i<20; ++i )
            y[k,i] = i*k;

            Console.WriteLine("One Dimensional Array\n");
            PrintOneDArray( x, 10 );
            Console.WriteLine("\nTwo Dimensional Array\n");
            PrintTwoDArray( y, 10,20 );
    }
}
```

As you can see from the listing, C# arrays are somewhat different from those in
C++ or Java. For one thing, you cannot simply create an array on the stack using
a line such as:

```
int x[10];
```

The equivalent line in C# looks like this:

```
int[] x = new int[10];
```

Another interesting thing about C# arrays is that they cannot be treated as simply
pointers, the way you could in C++. You cannot, for example, write a single function to handle both single- and multidimensional arrays. The number of dimensions of the array defines the type itself.

Enumerating an Array

If you have an arbitrary array and want to know how big it is, to iterate through it,
you would have a problem in C++. C++ does not maintain any state information
about the length of an array. Likewise, if you have a multidimensional array in
Java, knowing how many dimensions it has is impossible without looking at the
source code. Worrying about something like this might seem absurd, unless you
are writing a component that deals with reflection or serialization, topics I discuss later in this book in Chapter 6.

In the following application, you examine how to print an array of one dimen-
sion with an unknown number of columns in it. Listing 1.7 also shows how to

determine the number of dimensions of an array. The number of dimensions, as you might guess from reading the source code, determines the *rank* of the array.

Listing 1.7   Array sizes and dimensions.

```
using System;

class CH1_6 {

    public static void PrintArray( int[] arr )
    {
        for ( int i=0; i<arr.Length; ++i )
            Console.WriteLine( "OneDArray Row {0} = {1}", i, arr[i]);
    }

    public static void PrintArrayRank( int[,] arr )
    {
        Console.WriteLine( "PrintArrayRank: {0} dimensions", arr.Rank );
    }


    public static void Main()
    {
        // A dynamic array of 10 elements
        int[] x = new int[10];
        for ( int i=0; i<10; ++i )
            x[i] = i;
        PrintArray( x );

        // A multiply dimensioned array
            int[,] y = new int[10,20];
            for ( int k=0; k<10; ++k )
        for ( int i=0; i<20; ++i )
            y[k,i] = i*k;

        PrintArrayRank( y );

    }
}
```

One thing that came to mind when I was reading about the length and rank features of C# initially was how helpful they would have been when I was writing matrix functions in FORTRAN. Reading about these features told me two things: C# is ideally suited for mathematical coding, and I am getting old if I remember the old FORTRAN days.

Creating a Simple Function Returning a Boolean

C# doesn't really have the concept of functions. Instead, everything is a method. You can, however, have methods that don't require objects (which I talk about in Chapter 2). These methods, known as *static* methods, can be used without having to have an object. In that respect, they are much like the C or C++ concept of a function. In this example, you create a simple "function" that inspects an input value and returns a true or false response depending on whether the value is acceptable. This method is shown in Listing 1.8.

Listing 1.8   A static method that returns a Boolean value.

```
using System;

class CH1_7 {

    public static Boolean TestInput( int val )
    {
        if ( val < 1 || val > 10 )
            return false;
        return true;
    }

    public static void Main()
    {
        Console.WriteLine( "TestInput(0) = {0}", TestInput(0));
        Console.WriteLine( "TestInput(1) = {0}", TestInput(1));
        Console.WriteLine( "TestInput(5) = {0}", TestInput(5));
        Console.WriteLine( "TestInput(11) = {0}", TestInput(11));
    }
}
```

The output from this program is:

```
TestInput(0) = False
TestInput(1) = True
TestInput(5) = True
TestInput(11) = False
```

This example illustrates a couple of things: first, how to create the equivalent of a function for C++ programmers and, second, how to have that function return a value to the calling application. As you see in Chapter 2, values can be returned in other ways, including passing something to a method by reference. Finally, this example shows you that C# recognizes Boolean values and knows not only how to pass them around but also how to print them. Remember, in C#, everything is an object—even a simple variable type, like a Boolean.

Identifying the System Maximums and Minimums

One thing that makes C# such a well-designed language to work with is that it was so well thought out by its designers. Little things, like worrying about overflows in numeric values while doing computations, form the core of the system. In the spirit of this design, the implementers gave each data type in the system its own, unique maximum and minimum value that could be assigned to it. This technique allows the system to do internal checking for validity and allows the application programmer to check whether values would be within system norms. In Listing 1.9, you see that the programmer can view not only the maximum allowable value for each data type but also the minimum value. Both overflows and underflows for data types can then be checked.

Listing 1.9   System maximums and minimums.

```
using System;

class CH1_8 {

    public static void Main()
    {
        // First, print out the minimum values
        Console.WriteLine("System Minimums\n");
        Console.WriteLine( "MinSByte {0}", System.SByte.MinValue);
        Console.WriteLine( "MinByte {0}", System.Byte.MinValue);
        Console.WriteLine( "MinInt16 {0}", System.Int16.MinValue);
        Console.WriteLine( "MinUInt16 {0}", System.UInt16.MinValue);
        Console.WriteLine( "MinInt32 {0}", System.Int32.MinValue);
        Console.WriteLine( "MinUInt32 {0}", System.UInt32.MinValue);
        Console.WriteLine( "MinInt64 {0}", System.Int64.MinValue);
        Console.WriteLine( "MinUInt64 {0}", System.UInt64.MinValue);
        Console.WriteLine( "MinChar {0}", System.Char.MinValue);
        Console.WriteLine( "MinSingle {0}", System.Single.MinValue);
        Console.WriteLine( "MinDouble {0}", System.Double.MinValue);
        // Console.WriteLine( "MinBoolean {0}", System.Boolean.MinValue);
        Console.WriteLine( "MinDecimal {0}", System.Decimal.MinValue);

        Console.WriteLine("\nSystem Maximums\n");
        Console.WriteLine( "MaxSByte {0}", System.SByte.MaxValue);
        Console.WriteLine( "MaxByte {0}", System.Byte.MaxValue);
        Console.WriteLine( "MaxInt16 {0}", System.Int16.MaxValue);
        Console.WriteLine( "MaxUInt16 {0}", System.UInt16.MaxValue);
        Console.WriteLine( "MaxInt32 {0}", System.Int32.MaxValue);
        Console.WriteLine( "MaxUInt32 {0}", System.UInt32.MaxValue);
        Console.WriteLine( "MaxInt64 {0}", System.Int64.MaxValue);
        Console.WriteLine( "MaxUInt64 {0}", System.UInt64.MaxValue);
        Console.WriteLine( "MaxChar {0}", System.Char.MaxValue);
```

```
            Console.WriteLine( "MaxSingle {0}", System.Single.MaxValue);
            Console.WriteLine( "MaxDouble {0}", System.Double.MaxValue);
            Console.WriteLine( "MaxDecimal {0}", System.Decimal.MaxValue);
        }
    }
```

Notice the two shaded lines, which would normally print the minimum and maximum values for the Boolean type. Because C# is a strongly typed language, data types can be used and compared only when doing so makes sense. For example, you cannot compare directly a character string to a number. You must first convert the string to a numeric value. Likewise, you cannot assign anything other than true or false to a Boolean type. Because no acceptable definition exists for whether true is greater than false or vice versa, the language does not provide a minimal or maximal value for this data type.

The output from this program is as follows, at least on a Windows 2000 system:

```
System Minimums

MinSByte -128
MinByte 0
MinInt16 -32768
MinUInt16 0
MinInt32 -2147483648
MinUInt32 0
MinInt64 -9223372036854775808
MinUInt64 0
MinChar
MinSingle -3.40282347E38
MinDouble -1.7976931348623157E308
MinDecimal -79228162514264337593543950335


System Maximums

MaxSByte 127
MaxByte 255
MaxInt16 32767
MaxUInt16 65535
MaxInt32 2147483647
MaxUInt32 4294967295
MaxInt64 9223372036854775807
MaxUInt64 18446744073709551615
MaxChar ?
MaxSingle 3.40282347E38
MaxDouble 1.7976931348623157E308
MaxDecimal 79228162514264337593543950335
```

All the numbers shown are what you would expect them to be, given the allowable range of the data types. One thing worth noting in the listing is that the data type minimums and maximums are objects themselves and can be compared or printed as any other sort of object.

Related solution:	Found on page:
Enumerating Files in a Directory	325

Creating a Collection

One of the most useful features of the C# Common Language Runtime (CLR) that is available to both C# developers and any other developers of a .NET language is the use of prebuilt collection classes. C# provides quite a few types of collection classes. Although you explore this subject to a greater degree in Chapter 8, it's helpful to see up front an example of how to do this, while you are trying to explore the basics of the language. Listing 1.10 shows an example of how to create a simple hash table and then look up values in it.

Listing 1.10   The use of a simple hash table in C#.

```
using System;
using System.Collections;

class CH1_9 {

    public static void Main()
    {
        // Create a hashtable with a default comparison operator
        // and initially 10 elements.

        Hashtable ht = new Hashtable(10);

        // Add ten strings to the hashtable associated with a
        // key value (integer).

        ht.Add( 100, "Science");
        ht.Add( 200, "Math");
        ht.Add( 300, "English");
        ht.Add( 400, "History");
        ht.Add( 500, "Gym");

        // How many elements does the table contain?
        Console.WriteLine("The hashtable contains {0} elements", ht.Count);
```

```
    // Does it contain the entry for Gym? How about Recess?
    Console.WriteLine("The hashtable contains 500? {0}",
        ht.Contains(500));
    Console.WriteLine("The hashtable contains 600? {0}",
        ht.Contains(600));

    // What is the value for 400? 800?
    Console.WriteLine("The value for 400 is {0}", ht[400]);
    Console.WriteLine("The value for 800 is {0}", ht[800]);

    // See if the values are null
    if ( ht[400] == null )
        Console.WriteLine( "Entry 400 is null" );
    else
        Console.WriteLine( "Entry 400 is NOT null" );

    if ( ht[800] == null )
        Console.WriteLine( "Entry 800 is null" );
    else
        Console.WriteLine( "Entry 800 is NOT null" );

    }
}
```

Besides being a good example of how to use a hash table, the preceding listing has several noteworthy items. Although most are issues that we look at in more depth later in this book (in Chapters 2 and 4), take a short look at them now.

The first noteworthy item is the shaded line **using System.Collections**. When I discuss namespaces and assemblies, you'll understand this statement much better. For now, just say that it is the C# equivalent of a C++ **include** statement or a Java **import** statement. Similarly to those languages, C# requires that you include the levels of the namespaces you want to use. When you use the **System** namespace, therefore, you do not automatically get everything below the **System** namespace. You must include each one by itself. This situation is both good and bad. It means that you don't get severely bloated code because you aren't getting any more than you want. At the same time, however, it means that you often have to do some digging into the documentation or the Class Viewer (which you look at in Chapter 8) to find out where a given class is defined.

The second notable issue is the use of the **[ ]** notation to retrieve a value from a hash table. A hash table is not an array and cannot really be treated as one, yet it shares many of the same properties as an array. For this reason, the C# library developers chose to implement the hash table access via an *indexer*, which I discuss in Chapter 2. This statement won't mean much to you now, but you must see how indexers are used so that you can use the language efficiently and get up to speed quickly. You don't always have to understand something in order to use it.

The third notable item in the listing is the hash table, which—like most of the C# collection classes—does not throw an exception if you look for something that isn't in it. Instead, it simply returns a null object. The exception to this rule is in arrays, which throws an index-out-of-bounds exception.

Enumerating a Collection

When you have a collection, such as a hash table, how do you go about finding out what is in it? For the hash table, you can use a pick-and-choose sort of approach, looking for each element you know about and then finding out whether the hash table contains that element. But sometimes you just want to go through all the elements in the collection at one time and do something with them, such as save them to a persistent device. In this case, you need to enumerate the collection.

C# uses the **foreach** process for enumerating collections and arrays. In Listing 1.11, you look at how to use the **foreach** statement to iterate through a hash table and how to look at the individual components of the hash table entries.

Listing 1.11   Enumerating a hash table collection.

```
using System;
using System.Collections;

class CH1_10 {

    public static void Main()
    {
        Hashtable ht = new Hashtable(10);

        // Add strings to the hashtable associated with a
        // key value (integer).

        ht.Add( 100, "Science");
        ht.Add( 200, "Math");
        ht.Add( 300, "English");
        ht.Add( 400, "History");
        ht.Add( 500, "Gym");

        foreach ( DictionaryEntry de in ht )
        {
```

```
        Console.WriteLine( "Entry Key {0} Value {1}", de.Key,
            de.Value );
        }

    }
}
```

As you can see, the **foreach** statement is simple enough to use. What is important here is that each entry in a hash table is a separate data type used to store the key and value pairs. In this case, the class is called **DictionaryEntry** and contains two properties called **Key** and **Value**. They are first-class objects of their own, so they can be printed or modified as you see fit. Note that modifying a **Key** value in a hash table is considered to be a bad idea. However, you can feel free to modify the **Value** entry for a given Key. Normally, you would do it via the indexer methodology:

```
Ht["Key"] = NewValue;
```

The collections of C# and the CLR are powerful devices that can save you immense time and effort in your own application development. You should seriously consider using them instead of inventing your own collection classes.

Inserting into a Collection

If you have a collection, the most natural thing in the world to do is to insert items into that collection. One huge advantage that C# collections have over arrays is that you can extend them easily and insert items into them at arbitrary locations. For example, if you want to insert an element at the beginning of a "standard" array object, you would have to either copy the entire array into a new array of a larger size and then put the new element at the beginning or remove an existing element.

With C# collection classes, the grunt work is already done for you. To insert at the beginning or end of an array, you need only use the **ArrayList** class to have immediate access to that functionality. The **ArrayList**, like most of the C# collection classes, automatically extends itself to the proper size to accommodate all the elements in the array, and it allows you to quickly and easily insert and remove elements from the array.

In Listing 1.12, you can see how to create an **ArrayList** object and then insert elements at either the beginning or end. Arbitrary insertions are also illustrated. Finally, the array is printed so that you can see where everything ends up in the final result.

Listing 1.12   Inserting into a collection.

```
using System;
using System.Collections;

class CH1_11 {

    public static void Main()
    {
        ArrayList al = new ArrayList(5);

        // Add three elements to the end of the array
        al.Add( 10 );
        al.Add( 9 );
        al.Add( 8 );

        // Now, insert three elements in the front of the array
        al.Insert( 0, 1 );
        al.Insert( 0, 2 );
        al.Insert( 0, 3 );

        // Finally, insert into some random spots
        al.Insert( 2, 4 );
        al.Insert( 4, 5 );
        al.Insert( 6, 6 );


        // Enumerate the array
        foreach ( int i in al )
        {
            Console.WriteLine( "Entry {0}", i );
        }


    }
}
```

The output from this program is:

```
Entry 3
Entry 2
Entry 4
Entry 1
Entry 5
Entry 10
Entry 6
Entry 9
Entry 8
```

As you can see, adding or inserting elements into a C# **ArrayList** object involves no real effort. The designers and implementers have made it as simple as possible to do the things you need to do to get your job done.

Deleting from a Collection

If you can insert items into a collection and enumerate over the contents of that collection, the last thing you need to be able to do is to remove things from the collection when you don't want them any more. For example, if you were keeping track of the programming languages a company uses and the company decided not to use several of them any more (because C# replaced them all, of course), you would need to remove them from the collection that held the usable languages.

Removing an item from a collection is a twofold process. First, you need to be able to find the item you want to remove. Then, you need to remove the item and reconfigure the rest of the items so that they take up the optimal amount of space. Fortunately, C# does all this for you automatically when you use the collection classes built into the CLR. In Listing 1.13, you look at a simple example of adding some items to a dictionary and then removing a few of them. The dictionary is printed both before and after the removal so that you can see what the results are.

Listing 1.13   Deleting from a collection.

```
using System;
using System.Collections;

class CH1_12 {
    public static void Main()
    {
        Dictionary dict = new Dictionary();

        dict.Add(1, "C++");
        dict.Add(2, "C");
        dict.Add(3, "Ada");
        dict.Add(4, "APL");
        dict.Add(5, "VB");
        dict.Add(6, "C#");
        dict.Add(7, "Java");
        dict.Add(8, "FORTRAN");

        // Print out the list
        Console.WriteLine("Before Deleting Anything");
        foreach ( DictionaryEntry de in dict )
        {
```

```
        Console.WriteLine( "Entry Key {0} Value {1}", de.Key,
            de.Value );
    }

    dict.Remove( 4 );
    dict.Remove( 7 );

    Console.WriteLine("\nAfter Deletions");
    foreach ( DictionaryEntry de in dict  )
    {
        Console.WriteLine( "Entry Key {0} Value {1}", de.Key,
            de.Value );
    }

    }
}
```

The output from this program is:

```
Before Deleting Anything
Entry Key 8 Value FORTRAN
Entry Key 7 Value Java
Entry Key 6 Value C#
Entry Key 5 Value VB
Entry Key 4 Value APL
Entry Key 3 Value Ada
Entry Key 2 Value C
Entry Key 1 Value C++

After Deletions
Entry Key 8 Value FORTRAN
Entry Key 6 Value C#
Entry Key 5 Value VB
Entry Key 3 Value Ada
Entry Key 2 Value C
Entry Key 1 Value C++
```

Creating a Literal

Literal strings are the bread and butter of software programs. After all, without some form of text, users would have no clue what you were asking for or telling them. Literal strings are important in any programming language, and C# is certainly no exception. Unlike C, or C++, C# has quite a few different ways to define a literal string. On the other hand, like C and C++, C# gives you numerous different ways to output special characters, such as linefeeds, carriage returns, extended ASCII characters, and the like. C# was built from the ground up to be portable and international, so it supports the Unicode standard. It also works quite nicely with ASCII.

One of the more interesting things in C# is that someone finally noticed that programmers truly hate to have to "escape" (that is, preface characters with a \) special characters, like the \ character. If you place the @ sign in front of a string, the compiler interprets the entire string as literally what it says it is rather than use the \ character to escape each special character you want to use.

Listing 1.14 shows an application that illustrates how you can use various methods to create literal strings in C#. Note that even with the @"<*string*>" format, you may not embed a double-quote (") in your string. Doing so terminates the string, and it results in a compiler error.

Listing 1.14   Creating a literal.

```
using System;

class CH1_13 {

    public static void Main()
    {
        // Create a simple string literal
        string s1 = "This is a test";

        // Create a string literal with an escaped character
        string s2 = "This is a \"real\" test";

        // Create a string literal with the @ sign
        string s3 = @"This is a \real\ test";

         // You can't do this:
        // string s4 = @"This is a "real" test";

        // Output them
        Console.WriteLine("String 1 = {0}", s1 );
        Console.WriteLine("String 2 = {0}", s2 );
        Console.WriteLine("String 3 = {0}", s3 );
    }
}
```

The output from this application is:

```
String 1 = This is a test
String 2 = This is a "real" test
String 3 = This is a \real\ test
```

Literal strings in C# are also Unicode strings by default. You can pass them to any function that expects a Unicode string within the CLR. To pass strings back and forth between C# and other languages, like C++, you need to convert them into byte arrays and treat them as such on the other side because of their multibyte nature.

Creating an Alias

As you have probably noticed by now, C# uses namespaces to demark the area where code is defined and exported from. The convention for these namespaces is to use a high-level section, such as System, followed by one or more sublevels that define where the actual class lives. This process can result in very long names you would have to fully qualify to find if these names conflicted with other general names. Imagine that you have some legacy code that you had ported to C# and that implemented a database structure. The class name **Database** is almost certainly used within a C# class library, so you would put the class within a namespace of your own. If that namespace contained another namespace, you would then have to deal with writing something like this:

```
CompanyDatabase.Database.CallThisMethod
```

Listing 1.15 shows a contrived, but reasonable, example of a possible scenario, as just described. In this case, you have a series of namespaces for your company, one of which happens to be **Company.InternalClasses**. Within that namespace is a **Database** namespace that contains some number of classes defined to deal with databases. One such class, **Table**, deals with an individual table in a database.

Listing 1.15   Using the alias keyword to refer to a nested namespace.

```
// define an alias to represent a namespace
using CmpDb = Company.InternalClasses.Database.Table;

namespace Company.InternalClasses {
    public class DBInterface {
        public static void Open() {
            System.Console.WriteLine("Opening database");
```

```
        }
    }
    // Define a nested namespace within InternalClasses
    namespace Database {
        public class Table {
            public static void Open( string tblName )
                {
                        System.Console.WriteLine("Opening table {0}", tblName );
                }
        }
    }
}


public class CH1_14 {
    public static void Main() {
        CmpDb.Open("fred");
    }
}
```

Notice how, after you define an alias for the long namespace string, you can then refer to that long string by the simple alias name (**CmpDb**, in this case) from that point on in the application or class. That makes dealing with complex namespaces much easier. Note, however, that you may not define an alias, which would conflict with a namespace that already exists. In other words, you cannot define your own **System** alias and then use both that alias and the **System** namespace within the same application. The compiler would have no way of knowing which namespace you meant in case of a conflict.

Converting a String to a Number Explicitly

One common experience a programmer faces in writing applications is the need to convert input, in the form of textual data, into a numeric format so that computations can be performed on it. Obvious examples include reading lines from a text file and converting them into numbers and reading input from users via forms and then converting those input text strings into numbers so that they can be compared and used for calculations.

In C++, you would do this task via one of the many text-conversion functions, such as **atof** or **atoi**, which convert alphanumeric strings to floating-point numbers or integers, respectively. In Java, you would use the **parseInt** or **valueOf** methods of the **Integer** or **Float** classes, respectively. Leaving aside the annoyance of having the two methods with similar functions named completely differently, the problem is that these methods are static methods of the classes. You must therefore convert whatever form of string you have into the proper form and then pass it to this static method and retrieve the result as the returned value of the method. In short, the conversion functions are little more than wrappers for the **atoi** and **atof** functions.

In C#, however, objects "understand" how to convert themselves into other objects. To convert a string to something else, you use one of the conversion functions built into the string class itself. In this example, you can see how to trivially convert a string into either an integer or a floating-point number. Similar conversion functions (as discussed in the "In Depth" section, earlier in this chapter) convert strings to virtually all other variable types. Listing 1.16 shows you how to use the **toInt16** and **toSingle** methods of the string class to convert to integers or floating-point numbers.

Listing 1.16   Using the built-in conversion methods of the string class.

```
using System;

class CH1_15 {

    public static void Main()
    {
        string s1 = "123.45";
        string s2 = "123";

        // Convert them both to floating-point numbers
        Single sngl1 = s1.ToSingle();
        Single sngl2 = s2.ToSingle();

        // Print them out
        Console.WriteLine( "Single 1 = {0}", sngl1 );
        Console.WriteLine( "Single 2 = {0}", sngl2 );

        // Convert them both to integers
        int i1 = (int)s1.ToSingle();
        int i2 = s2.ToInt16();

        // Print those out
        Console.WriteLine( "Integer 1 = {0}", i1 );
        Console.WriteLine( "Integer 2 = {0}", i2 );
    }
}
```

One curious note in the preceding example is shown in the shaded line of the code listing. Here, you do not convert the string from its natural format into an integer directly, using the **ToInt16** function, but instead convert it to a floating-point number and then cast it to an integer. Why do you do this? The simple explanation is that the **ToInt16** function appears to have a problem with invalid formats, which it considers a floating point (123.45) to be. As a result, it would throw an exception of type **InvalidFormat**, and the application would die. Rather than have this happen, you convert the string to a "safer" format, the floating-point format, and then allow the natural truncation to occur in the explicit conversion from floating-point format to integer format.

Converting One Number Type to Another Implicitly or Explicitly

The business of converting numbers from one type to another is a complex one. Sometimes, you want to simply truncate a given type to get only the whole number portion of it. At other times, you might want to convert from strings to numbers. Finally, you might want to convert one type to another directly, in a type-safe manner. C# has taken all these factors into account in providing methods to work with numbers. Previously, you have used the C method of conversion, which is to simply cast one type to another. This method, provided primarily for backward compatibility with C programmers, is not the best way to do things.

If you convert one type to another in a non-type-safe manner, such as a direct cast, you are taking full responsibility for your actions. The compiler cannot really check to verify that the types you are converting are legitimate versions of one another. If, for example, you were to convert a very big floating-point number into an integer, you would find that an overflow occurred in a place where you were not expecting it to happen. These types of errors are generally difficult to track down and can cause nasty side effects in an application. Imagine a banking transaction that suddenly converts your account value from $100 to -$1,234,567. That would certainly make your day a bit dimmer, wouldn't it?

The C# method of converting data types is to use one of the built-in conversion methods of the class you are working with. As you have seen in the "In Depth" section earlier in this chapter, quite a few of these legitimate conversions exist. In this example, you see how to use some of those conversions as well as the object-oriented method of doing multiple conversions in a single statement. Listing 1.17 contains the code for an application that converts a string first to a floating-point number and then to an integer, without relying on any casting.

Listing 1.17 Conversions the C# way.

```
using System;

class CH1_16 {

    public static void Main()
    {
        // Start with a string representing a floating point
        string s1 = "123.45";
        // Convert it to a real floating point
        Single sng11 = s1.ToSingle();
        // Convert that to an integer
        int i1 = sng11.ToInt16();
        // And print it out
        Console.WriteLine( "Single 1 = {0}", sng11 );
        Console.WriteLine( "Integer 1 = {0}", i1 );

        // Now, do it the "neat" way
        int i2 = s1.ToSingle().ToInt16();
        Console.WriteLine( "Integer 2 = {0}", i2 );

    }
}
```

Chapter 2

User-Defined Types

In Depth

The true measure of a new programming language is determined by how well it allows you to extend it to cover situations the original designers and developers might not have thought about. For modern programming languages, that extensibility comes in the form of user-defined types. A *user-defined* type is created, as its name suggests, by the developer to solve a specific problem. User-defined types might include such things as new models for real-world data types (such as a complex variable) or ways to model existing real-world entities (such as a traffic light controller, a component used in a city model). C# has a rich variety of available user-defined types that you can create and use to extend the reach of the system. In this chapter, I describe a few of these types, including classes, interfaces, and properties.

Enumerations

The most basic user-defined type is the *enumeration,* which is simply the process of making a list of possible values for a given type. For example, you might have a program that models a traffic light. Traffic lights, obviously, have three possible states: the green (or go) light, the yellow (or warning) light, and the red (or stop) light. For a given traffic light, the condition of that light can be one and only one of those states. It cannot be 3, for instance, nor can it be Stop. It can be only Red, Yellow, or Green.

The C# model of an enumeration is to define a new user-defined type. For the traffic light, for example, you would write something like this:

```
enum TrafficLight
{
    Red,
    Green,
    Yellow
};
```

To use the enumerated type, you could then declare a variable of the new type by simply typing something like this:

```
TrafficLight tl;
```

As you can see, by creating an enumerated type called **TrafficLight**, I have created a new way to define variables in the language. The other nice aspect of this functionality is that I have defined a bound type. For example, I can type something like this:

```
tl = TrafficLight.Red;
//…
tl = TrafficLight.Yellow;
```

I cannot, however, do something like this:

```
tl = 3;
```

Enumerations default to beginning with the value of 0 for the first entry in the enumeration. You can modify this value, however, by entering a different value for the first value, such as:

```
enum TrafficLight
{
    Red=1,
}
```

The reason is that a traffic light, as mentioned, is a bound value. It can take on only values that exist in the enumeration itself. That's the good news. The bad news is that C# is far from perfect in its implementation of enumerations. Here are a few of the "catches" you may encounter when working with enumerations:

- First, the enumeration type does not "know" how to display itself as anything other than the integer value it really is. That is, if you print a **TrafficLight** enumerated value, such as **Red**, you see the value **0** displayed on the console or form.

- Enumerations seemingly do not allow you to assign invalid values to a type. However, because enumeration is nothing more than a wrapper around an integer and the integer type can be cast to anything you like, you can write something like **tl=(TrafficLight)4** in your code and have it work. It doesn't mean anything, of course, but the compiler does not catch the invalid cast.

Enumerations are not perfect. If you want to make absolutely sure that your values fall within a given range, you should define a class to handle it instead. With that in mind, let's take a look at classes in C#.

Classes

C# provides the class mechanism as a way to support object-oriented development and design. *Classes* allow you to define a self-contained environment where you control all the functions that can be applied to a given set of data as well as how that data can be accessed. Classes also give you the ability to extend the environment and allow the developer to reuse existing functionality in a new way. Combined with interfaces, which I discuss a bit later in this chapter, classes form the core of the power of C#.

Classes in C# have these powerful features:

- Syntax
- Methods
- Variables
- Inheritance
- Properties
- Events
- Constructors and destructors
- Operators
- Overloading

In the next few sections, I describe these features one at a time and discuss what they mean to you as a developer.

Syntax

The basic syntax of the class structure is:

```
class <className> [ : Base Class or Interface ]
{
    <access-modifier> [static] <return-type> MethodName( <signature>);
    <access-modifier> [static] <variable type> variablename;
}
```

In the interest of deconstructing the nightmare the preceding syntax provides, let's look at a simple example of a class:

```
// A class derived from another class
Class Foo : BaseFoo
{
    // A method, the main entry point for this application.
    public static void Main()
    {
    }
    // A variable
    private int fAge;
}
```

If you are accustomed to working with C++ or Java, you find few surprises in working with C#. Built on the technologies of these two other languages, it supports nearly all the same constructs and statement types as they do.

Of course, after you have defined a class, you need to add functionality to it. A class without functionality is like a morning without coffee. (Okay, maybe it's not quite that bad, but it's close.) The C# implementation of functionality is its methods, properties, and member variables. I describe those next.

Methods

A *method* is a small bit of functionality that performs a given task in a class. You can think of a method as an instruction to a class to do something. Methods can be either static or nonstatic. *Static* methods require no object to operate on, and *nonstatic* methods use the built-in state of the method to operate on the object as a whole. A static method is equivalent to a function in C or C++. Think of a static method as a generalized instruction to the system, and a nonstatic (or member) method as a modification to the internal data of an object. Here is a simple example of a class with a static method and the use of that method in another class:

```
class StaticMethodFoo
{
    public static void DoSomething()
    {
    }
}
class Foo
{
    public static void Main()
    {
        StaticMethodFoo.DoSomething();
    }
}
```

The shaded line shows a couple of interesting concepts. First, it illustrates how to "scope" a call from one class to another. Second, the line shows you that no object was required to call the **static** method. Let me illustrate how to create an object and how it is used to call a method of a class for that object:

```
public class Foo
{
    void CallAFunctionForThisObject()
    {
        Console.WriteLine("This is an object {0}", this );
    }
```

```
public static void Main()
{
    Foo f = new Foo();
    f.CallAFunctionForThisObject();
}
}
```

This code listing shows off a few aspects of the class structure and its use in C#. First, I create an object, which is an instance of the class **Foo**. This object is then used to call a method of that class, named **CallAFunctionForThisObject**. This method, which is nonstatic, requires that I have an object to call it with. I use the object I created—called **f**, in this case—to call the method. Within the method, the **System.Console.WriteLine** method (a static method) is used to print the object itself by using a special keyword, named **this**, that represents the object being called for the method. (Lots of stuff is in that simple example.)

Methods have three parts that need to be understood. First, the return type value is returned from the method to the calling application. Next, there are the arguments to the method. C++ programmers should not be surprised to know that C# allows arguments to be of any of the following types: input, output, or both. Java programmers may be somewhat surprised to find out that you can return multiple values from a C# method (as shown in the section "Creating a Method with a Reference Argument," later in this chapter). In C#, you can also pass a variable number of arguments to a method, even varying in type or size. I examine this topic in the section "Creating a Method with a Variable Number of Arguments," later in this chapter.

The final segment of methods is the access level of the method. In C#, as in C++ and Java, methods can be private, public, or protected. Private methods can be used only within methods of the class in which they are defined. Protected methods can be used within either the class in which they are defined or derived classes. Public methods can be called from any other method, regardless of whether they exist in the same class.

Variables

A *variable*, a storage element in C#, can store one or more values of a certain type. A variable can be local or class level. *Local* variables exist within the scope of a given method in a class, whereas *class* variables exist for the entire lifetime of the object instance of a class. Class variables can be used in any method of a class and can be public, private, or protected, just as methods are. If a class variable is public, it can be read or written to from any class method, whether or not that method resides within the same class. Local variables cannot be defined as public or private because they are not accessible outside the method in which they are defined.

C# also uses static class variables, which can be used in static class methods. A single instance of the static class variable exists for all instances of a given class. You can see an example of how to create and use a static class variable in the section "Creating a Static Class-Level Variable," later in this chapter.

Variables can be of either simple or array types (refer to Chapter 1 if you need a refresher on the simple value types available in C#). To create an array of integers, for example, you would do something like this:

```
int[] arr = new int[10];
```

Variables, however, are not restricted to simple value types or arrays of those types. You can also define variables that are user-defined types. For example, you could create an enumeration, as I have discussed earlier in this chapter. Alternatively, you could create a class instance (object) by writing:

```
Foo f = new Foo();
```

In fact, you can even create an array of enumerations or objects:

```
TrafficLight[] tla = new TrafficLight[10];
Foo[] fooarray = new Foo[10];
```

The first line creates an array of an enumerated type. The second one appears to create an array of objects, but in fact does nothing of the sort. This concept is confusing in C# and is worth mentioning because if you were to use that second line of code, you would not end up with an array containing 10 **Foo** objects. Instead, an array-size block of memory would be allocated that is big enough to hold 10 **Foo** objects. To then create them all, you would do something like this:

```
Foo[] fooarray = new Foo[10];
for ( int I=0; I<10; ++I )
    Fooarray[I] = new Foo();
```

If you don't create all the array elements, the program crashes as soon as you try to access the actual objects in the array because they are not yet initialized.

Inheritance

One major purpose of object-oriented programming is to promote the reuse of code and to eliminate redundant code. To accomplish this, the object-oriented languages promote the use of inheritance to reuse existing functionality, code, and concepts. *Inheritance* allows you to use an existing class and extend it in a customizable way.

C# supports *single inheritance*, in which you may have a maximum of one base class for each class you define. This rule is not strictly adhered to, however, because the language also allows you to inherit multiple interfaces. The simple rule is that you may have one base class and as many interfaces supported by your class as you want. For example, to have a class named **Derived**, which is derived from the base class **Base** and supports the interfaces **IPersistent**, **IEnhanced**, and **IPrintable**, you use the following syntax when defining your class. Note that it makes no difference in what order you add the interfaces or base classes:

```
Class Derived : Base, IPersistent, IEnhanced, IPrintable
{
}
```

The convention used in the C# programming system is that classes normally begin with a descriptive noun that explains what they do, and interfaces begin with the capital letter *I* followed by a descriptive name. Thus, when you see something that says **I<*name*>**, you can reasonably assume that it is an interface.

Inheriting from a base class means that you automatically get all the functionality of the base class in the derived class. For example, if the base class has methods named **Print**, **Copy**, and **Delete**, you could call these methods from the derived class and be sure that they would work, albeit from the perspective of the derived class. To change the way the base class methods work, you would have to override the methods in the class. You would use the **virtual** and **override** keywords, as you can see in the section "Overriding a Method," later in this chapter. Note that you can override only a virtual method in C#, exactly as is true in both C++ and Java. However, unlike in these languages, you must explicitly tell the compiler that you mean to override the method in the derived class with the **override** keyword.

Properties

C# is one of the first languages to offer direct support for properties. The C++ Builder and Delphi languages offered this feature as an extension to the languages they supported (C++ and Object Pascal, respectively), but were not considered "standard" features. In C#, properties are a standard part of the language itself, and they can be a part of any class defined in the system. This statement begs the question, of course: What is a property? A *property* is a way for you to expose an internal data element of a class in a simple and intuitive manner while retaining control over the way the data is used.

To the user of a class, a property looks like a public variable that she can read or write, just by using it. A property can look like the following:

```
// Set the color property
Foo.Color = Color.White;
// Get the color property
Color c = Foo.Color;
```

Properties, however, are implemented with type-safe **get** and **set** functions. You create a property by defining an externally available name and then writing the **set** and **get** functions. You decide whether to allow the user to modify the property, depending on the input the caller of the property method gives you. The general format involved in writing a property is shown here:

```
// Define the property accessors
public <type> <PropertyName>
{
    get
    {
        return <var>;
    }
    set
    {
        // Validate the input, found in value
        if ( IsValid(value) )
            <var> = value;
    }
}
```

For the specifics of implementing a property in your class, check out the section "Implementing a Property for a Class," later in this chapter. The important thing to notice is the **value** keyword that appears in the listing. The value type is of the same type as the property itself, found on the **public** *<type> <PropertyName>* line. You are defining on this line the name of the property as the outside user sees it and the type of that property. Note that you need not have the same type of property as the internal member variable (denoted in the preceding listing by *<var>*). You can do whatever conversions you like in the **set** and **get** functions to make the value passed into the specific accessor the right internal format.

A Few Notes on How the System Works Internally

After encountering a property declaration in your class, the compiler automatically generates two methods for the class: **set_*<propertyname>*** and **get_*<property_name>***. The code for these two methods is the same as the code within the **set** and **get** blocks in your class declaration. One rather annoying issue about the integrated nature of a C# class declaration is that you have no way to show someone the public portion of the class without showing that person the entire definition. That is, you have no way to do the following:

```
class Foo
{
    public int Age
    {
        set;
        get;
    }
}
Foo.Age.set()
{
}
Foo.Age.get()
{
}
```

It's a flaw in an otherwise good system, but one you must get used to if you are accustomed to separate declarations and implementations, such as you would find in C++.

Events

The C# language is one of the first to offer support for events built into the language as well. Similar to the concept of listeners in Java, *events* are a way to notify external objects that something has happened that they might be interested in. Changes to values, modifications of structures, and deletions of elements are obvious situations in which some external functionality might be involved in dealing with the change.

To fully understand events, you must first understand delegates, which I discuss in Chapter 5. Because the event mechanism is so closely tied to classes, however, you can immediately see how to implement a simple event-handling system; see the section "Creating an Event," later in this chapter.

Constructors and Destructors

If you have worked in C++ or Java, you are accustomed to the idea of constructors and destructors. A *constructor* is called when an object is first created. A *destructor* (or finalizer) is called when the object is finally destroyed and the garbage collected. The constructor and destructor are named as they are in C++. The constructor is called the same name as the class, and the destructor is the class name prefaced with a tilde (~). The constructor is normally used to initialize the object and set any parameters you want. In addition, constructors can be written to accept arguments. Here are a few simple examples of constructors and a destructor for a class named **Foo**:

```
Foo() {};
Foo( string s )
Foo( int I, string s );
~Foo();
```

Destructors are a bit strange in C#. For one thing, you have no guarantee of when or if they will be called in the application. Because C# has a garbage-collection mechanism that works when the runtime environment finds it necessary and because an object isn't destroyed until its reference count drops to 0, you have no way of telling when an object will be destroyed and, hence, when the destructor will be called. You can, however, implement a method that allows the programmer to control when the object is destroyed. In the section "Creating a Simple Class," later in this chapter, you learn how to implement this function and use it.

Operators

The C# language lets you define your own operators for classes. For example, to use a more "natural" way to add complex numbers, you might have a class that implements complex numbers and adds a **+** operator to that class. This technique is much like the C++ method of doing things. One common task to do for a class is to add an equality operator.

Here's a simple example of a class with two data values that contains equality and inequality operators:

```
class TwoDataValues
{
    int value1;
    double value2;
    public static bool operator==(TwoDataValues v1, TwoDataValues v2)
    {
        if ( v1.value1 == v2.value1 )
            if ( v1.value2 == v2.value2 )
                return true;
        return false;
    }
    public static bool operator!=(TwoDataValues v1, TwoDataValues v2)
    {
        if ( v1.value1 == v2.value1 )
            if ( v1.value2 == v2.value2 )
                return false;
        return true;
    }
}
```

You should hesitate before overloading operators in a class. Unless you have a compelling reason to do so, all you are doing is making the class more complex and the job of debugging the code that much harder. Operator overloading is something developers new to a language often do when they are enamored with a "cool new feature."

Overloading Methods

In C#, you can *overload* methods, or define several methods with the same name and different arguments. For example, you might use methods to print a given variable type. One method might accept an integer, and another might accept a floating-point number. A third method might accept and print a string. Because they all perform the print functionality, you could call them all **Print** but overload each one to have a different signature.

Here's a simple example. Note that you can create overloaded methods as either member methods or static methods of a class, as you can see in this simple C# code listing:

```
using System;

class Test
{
    public static void Print( int i )
    {
        Console.WriteLine("Integer {0}", i );
    }
    public static void Print( double d )
    {
        Console.WriteLine("Double {0}", d );
    }
    public static void Print( string s )
    {
        Console.WriteLine("String {0}", s );
    }
    public static void Main()
    {
        Print(10);
        Print(10.0);
        Print("Hello");
    }
}
```

If you were to compile and run the preceding program, you would get the following output, indicating that the overloading worked properly:

```
Integer 10
Double 10
String Hello
```

I hope this example gives you a good foundation in the concept of classes in C#. If you have programmed in C++, Java, or even Visual Basic, you should already understand the concept of class programming and how to design and build classes. If you have not previously worked with classes, you should pick up a good book on fundamental object-oriented programming.

Interfaces

Interfaces in C# are almost exactly the same as interfaces in Java, but are more flexible in their implementation. If you are accustomed to C++, an *interface* is the equivalent of an abstract base class. You cannot instantiate an object through an interface, but you can offer, through an interface, a set of functionality that is common to several different classes. When you define an interface, you are collecting a set of functionality that implements a specific task. As a simple example, consider the idea of objects that know how to save themselves to disk. This functionality could be called **Persistence**. An interface that implements **Persistence** would be called **IPersistent**, in keeping with the convention of interfaces in COM or Java. Such an interface might look something like this:

```
public interface IPersistent
{
    boolean Save();
    boolean Load()
    boolean IsLoaded();
}
```

As you can see from this example, interfaces may have the same access modifiers as a class. In many ways, an interface is just a class skeleton with no code defined.

Interfaces in C# provide an additional benefit that does not exist in C++ or Java: Multiple interfaces can have the same method names, and you can then qualify them in your class by using the full interface name (**IPersistent.Save**, for example). This feature makes it easier to create interfaces, by allowing designers to use descriptive names, not long, unwieldy names caused by artificial constraints. An example is in the section "Accessing an Interface from a Class," later in this chapter.

Exception Handling

Exception handling forms the core of error handling in C#. Although you can still do it the "old-fashioned way" of returning error codes or setting flags in objects, exception handling is the preferred method of dealing with exceptional conditions in C#. Exception handling consists of three parts: throwing, catching, and anticipating exceptions.

Use the **throw** statement to perform the throwing of an exception. The **throw** statement takes only a single argument: the exception you want to pass up the call chain. When a **throw** statement is encountered, the method terminates and returns the error to the calling method to be handled or passed further up the chain. Exceptions are always derived from the **System.Exception** class. Here's a simple example of throwing an exception in C#:

```
throw new DivideByZeroException("Divide By 0 error!");
```

In this example, I am throwing a predefined exception type, **DivideByZero-Exception**. As you might guess, this exception is defined for math errors where the user attempts to divide by zero. As you can see, you may attach your own information to the exception, with the **string** field added to the exception.

Anticipating an exception is done with the **try** block statement. A **try** block is wrapped around a section of code that might throw an exception. If an exception is generated, the **try** block allows the code to catch the exception, cleaning up the stack and heap and making sure that the system is in a consistent state before allowing the program to continue, if possible. The **try** block looks something like this:

```
try
{
    // Do something that might cause an exception
}
```

A **try** block must always be followed by one or more **catch** blocks and then (optionally) a **finally** block. The **catch** block can be implemented in one of three ways. You may catch a specific exception, catch a generic **Exception** (the base class for all exceptions), or have a blank catch handler catch any error.

In general, the whole picture looks like this, using the divide-by-zero error as an example:

```
try
{
    int y = 0;
```

```
    int x = 5 / y;
}
catch
{
    Console.WriteLine("Exception!");
}
finally
{
    Console.WriteLine("Finally!!");
}
}
```

Exception handling isn't a complicated affair in C#, nor should it be. By making error handling as simple as possible in your application, the language makes it more likely that you will do things the right way the first time.

Exceptions are all derived from the base **Exception** class in the C# CLR. You can use the simple **Exception** class to pass error descriptions back and forth, or you can derive your own, customized exception class from **Exception** to pass errors more efficiently to calling functions.

Serialization

Serialization is the process of saving an object persistently on disk or in memory from an object. C# provides extensive support for serialization in the form of the **ISerialize** interface, which is built into the basic object support for C# classes. To serialize an object to disk, memory, or another stream, you simply create a stream and a formatter, and you call the **serialize** method of the formatter for a given object. The formatter uses reflection, which I discuss in Chapter 6, to determine the elements of the class and what types need to be saved to disk.

Serialization uses one of the various stream classes to save the objects to a persistent storage device. *Streams* are simply conduits that transfer data from one area to another. A stream might connect a program with a file or a program with a network socket.

Because the overall problem of serializing an object is standard, let's look at a simple example of how to do it. You can then "clone" the following example into whatever applications you have that require objects to be serialized:

```
using System;
using System.IO;
using System.Runtime.Serialization;
using System.Runtime.Serialization.Formatters.Binary;
```

```
class SerializeExample
{
    int x;
    int y;
    int z;

    SerializeExample()
    {
        x = 5;
        y = 10;
        z = 20;
    }
    static public void Main()
    {
        SerializeExample se = new SerializeExample();

        // Set up something to serialize into
        FileStream fs = new FileStream("serialize.txt",
            FileMode.OpenOrCreate, FileAccess.Write);
        BinaryFormatter t = new BinaryFormatter();

        t.Serialize(fs, se);
    }
}
```

The important aspects of this listing are the required import namespaces (**Serialization** and **Serialization.Formatters.Binary**) and the use of the **FileStream** class to provide a conduit for the object to be written. The process is simple: Create the stream to which you want the object to be written, create a formatter that knows how to serialize an object, and use the formatter to write the object to the stream.

That sums up the general class support offered by the C# language. I explore some more exotic parts of the language support in later chapters, including reflection (see Chapter 6). For now, though, let's jump into the "Immediate Solutions" portion of this chapter, giving you a chance to look at some real-world code to solve your problems.

Immediate Solutions

Creating a Simple Class

As you have seen in the "In Depth" section, a *class* is made up of several different components. A constructor, destructor, and methods are all parts of a class, whether you define them or not. The constructor is always called as soon as the object is created. The destructor is called when the object goes out of scope and garbage is collected. These concepts are similar in both C++ and Java. Unlike in C++, however, an object need not be deleted to get rid of it. After the object has gone out of scope and no further references exist for it, it is destroyed. Unlike in Java, the C# methodology allows for a way to get rid of an object when you, the programmer, want to do so, rather than only when the system wants it to go away.

One last note on constructors: You can create private constructors for a class that can be called only from within the class methods. For example, you might create a factory method in a class that implements a way to create and track elements of that class.

In this example, I describe the basic structure of a class. This class contains a constructor, a destructor, a method that can be called by the user, and a method for cleaning itself up. This class could be used as a template for all classes created in C# because it follows all the rules needed for classes. Listing 2.1 shows the class code along with some highlighted pieces I discuss after the listing.

Listing 2.1   A simple, but complete, C# class.

```
using System;

class CH2_1
{
    CH2_1()
    {
        Console.WriteLine("CH2_1 Constructor Called");
    }

    ~CH2_1()
    {
        Console.WriteLine("CH2_1 Destructor Called");
    }
    void PrintAMessage( string msg )
    {
```

```
        Console.WriteLine("PrintAMessage: {0}", msg);
    }
    void Dispose()
    {
        Finalize();
        GC.SuppressFinalize(this);
    }

    static void Main()
    {
        Console.WriteLine("Top of function main");
        CH2_1 app = new CH2_1();
        app.PrintAMessage( "Hello from class");
        Console.WriteLine("Bottom of function main");
        app.Dispose();
    }
}
```

The preceding code listing shows that the system has a primary entry point, called **Main**. This function is used by the C# runtime environment to load the program. The first thing the **Main** function does is to output a message to the console indicating that it has been loaded. The program then creates a new instance of the primary class for the application (CH2_1, in this case). The system then calls the constructor for the class, which outputs a message telling you that it has been called. The **Main** function then calls a method of that class for the object it has created. This message also prints a message. Finally, the program displays a diagnostic, indicating that it is finished, and "deletes" the object by calling the **Dispose** method of the class.

Dispose is an important method for any class that maintains any sort of resources. If memory is allocated, it should be freed. If files are opened, they should be closed. The **Dispose** method calls the **Finalize** method to accomplish these cleanup tasks, which is called by the system in the garbage-collection routine if it has not already been called. The **Finalize** method is a part of the base **Object** class from which all classes in C# are derived. How do you indicate to the system that the method has already been called? You call the **SuppressFinalize** method of the garbage-collection system, as shown in the **Dispose** method.

Here is the output from running this application:

```
Top of function main
CH2_1 Constructor Called
PrintAMessage: Hello from class
Bottom of function main
CH2_1 Destructor Called
```

Creating a Derived Class

If the only thing you could do with a language was create new classes and use them, the language would be valuable, but would suffer from the issue of nonreusability. Each time you had a new problem that was similar to an existing problem, you would need to duplicate a ton of code to solve the same issues. This method is hardly a cost-effective way of doing development work. Instead, you want to be able to create new classes and reuse the existing functionality of old classes. C# uses inheritance to give you this ability.

Inheritance lets you create classes derived from other classes. Derived classes get all the functionality of the base class, but allow you to customize the functionality or extend it. A classic example of inheritance is to have a base **Transportation** class and then have inherited classes that override some of the functionality to implement custom classes, such as **Bicycle**, **Train**, or **Automobile**. In this example, you can see how to create one or more derived classes from a base class. Listing 2.2 shows the base class, **Transportation**, along with a few methods and two derived classes, **Automobile** and **Bicycle**, to show you how to work with derived classes.

Listing 2.2   Creating derived classes in C#.

```
using System;
class Transportation
{
    private int fNumWheels;
    private int fDoors;
    private float fMaxSpeed;

    public Transportation()
    {
        // Default values
        fNumWheels = 4;
        fDoors     = 2;
        fMaxSpeed  = (float)55.0; // MPH
    }
    public int getNumberOfWheels()
    {
        return fNumWheels;
    }
    public void setNumberofWheels(int nw)
    {
        fNumWheels = nw;
    }
```

```
            public int getNumberOfDoors()
            {
                return fDoors;
            }
            public void setNumberOfDoors(int nd)
            {
                fDoors = nd;
            }
            public float getMaxSpeed()
            {
                return fMaxSpeed;
            }
            public void setMaxSpeed(float ms)
            {
                fMaxSpeed = ms;
            }
        }
        class Bicycle : Transportation
        {
            public Bicycle()
            {
                setNumberofWheels(2);
                setNumberOfDoors(0);
                setMaxSpeed((float)15.5);
            }
        }
        class Automobile : Transportation
        {
            public Automobile()
            {
                setNumberofWheels(4);
                setNumberOfDoors(4);
                setMaxSpeed((float)65.5);
            }
        }
        class CH2_2
        {
            public static void Main()
            {
                Transportation t1 = new Transportation();
                Transportation t2 = new Bicycle();
                Transportation t3 = new Automobile();

                Console.WriteLine(
                    "T1: # Wheels = {0}, # Doors = {1}, Max Speed = {2}",
```

```
        t1.getNumberOfWheels(), t1.getNumberOfDoors(),
        t1.getMaxSpeed());
    Console.WriteLine(
        "T2: # Wheels = {0}, # Doors = {1}, Max Speed = {2}",
        t2.getNumberOfWheels(), t2.getNumberOfDoors(),
        t2.getMaxSpeed());
    Console.WriteLine(
        "T3: # Wheels = {0}, # Doors = {1}, Max Speed = {2}",
        t3.getNumberOfWheels(), t3.getNumberOfDoors(),
        t3.getMaxSpeed());
    }
}
```

Please note that you can use better ways to implement some parts of the system in this example. In this example, the simplest method was chosen to make the purpose of the code clearer. The output is:

```
T1: # Wheels = 4, # Doors = 2, Max Speed = 55
T2: # Wheels = 2, # Doors = 0, Max Speed = 15.5
T3: # Wheels = 4, # Doors = 4, Max Speed = 65.5
```

As you can see, the powerful tool of inheritance can do quite a bit behind the scenes for users.

Creating a Constructor

Constructors, used to initialize internal data or to allocate memory to be used in the running of objects, are present by default. Constructors are the first thing called after an object of a class is created. If you do not create a constructor for a class, the compiler generates one automatically, which is similar to how things work in C++ and Java. Constructors may or may not take arguments. You can have overloaded versions of constructors that take different numbers or types of arguments.

In this example, I show a class with two constructors. The first constructor has no arguments and selects its own internal default values for use. The other constructor allows the user to pass in values to be used. Each constructor creates an internal array of a number of elements. The example also illustrates how you must specify a protection level (in this case, public) so that a constructor or other method can be used from outside the object. Listing 2.3 shows the class with constructors as well as a simple test driver for the class.

Listing 2.3   Creating a constructor.

```
using System;

class TestConstructor
{
    int[] anArray;

    // This is the default constructor (no arguments)
    public TestConstructor()
    {
        anArray = new int[6];
        for( int i=0; i<6; ++i )
            anArray[i] = i;
    }


    // This is the "normal" constructor for the class
    public TestConstructor(int arraySize)
    {
        anArray = new int[arraySize];
        for( int i=0; i<arraySize; ++i )
            anArray[i] = i;
    }
    public int getElement(int index)
    {
        if ( index < 0 || index > anArray.Length-1 )
            return -1;
        return anArray[ index ];
    }
}

class CH2_3 {
    public static void Main()
    {
        // Create an object with 10 elements
        TestConstructor tc = new TestConstructor(10);

        // print out every other element to test
        for ( int i=0; i<12; i+=2 )
            Console.WriteLine("Element {0} = {1}", i, tc.getElement(i));

        // Create an object with no set # of arguments
        TestConstructor tc1 = new TestConstructor();
```

```
        // print out every other element to test
        for ( int i=0; i<12; i+=2)
            Console.WriteLine("Element {0} = {1}", i, tcl.getElement(i));


    }
}
```

Here is the output from this program:

```
Element 0 = 0
Element 2 = 2
Element 4 = 4
Element 6 = 6
Element 8 = 8
Element 10 = -1
Element 0 = 0
Element 2 = 2
Element 4 = 4
Element 6 = -1
Element 8 = -1
Element 10 = -1
```

As you can see, constructors form an important part of the life span of a C# object. Be sure to initialize all your member variables and memory allocations within the constructor so that the object is in a valid state for users to use immediately.

Creating a Destructor

The destructor, or finalizer method, for a class is the last chance you get to clean up anything a class does during its lifetime. Destructors are good places to close files, de-allocate blocks of memory that might have been allocated, free resources, or decrement reference counts. Unless you specifically invoke a destructor, the runtime environment calls it when the object is finished being used. You have no particular guarantee that this process occurs when you want it to, especially if your destructor requires that other things be destroyed before or after it is executed.

For this reason, you should always create a destructor and create a **Dispose** method for the programmer using your class to call. In the first case, the system itself calls the destructor if nobody else does. If the programmer wants to destroy your objects, however, he can do so explicitly. This situation is the best of both worlds: It employs the flexibility of C++ with the protection of Java. In short, it is the C# way.

In Listing 2.4, you see how to create a destructor and the order in which things are called in a C# application. This example demonstrates how to implement a reference-counting function in a class and how to use the constructor and destructor for the class to manage that reference count.

Listing 2.4   Creating a destructor.

```
using System;
class Disposal
{
    static int refCount=0;

    public Disposal()
    {
        System.Console.WriteLine( "Disposal Constructor" );
        refCount++;
    }
    ~Disposal()
    {
        System.Console.WriteLine(
            "Disposal Destructor. RefCount = {0}", refCount );I
        refCount--;
    }
    public void Dispose()
    {
        Finalize();
        GC.SuppressFinalize(this);
    }
}

class CH2_4 {
    public static void Main()
    {
        Disposal d1 = new Disposal();
        Disposal d2 = new Disposal();
        Disposal d3 = new Disposal();

        d1.Dispose();
        d2.Dispose();
        d3.Dispose();
    }
}
```

Creating a Method with a Variable Number of Arguments

If you are an experienced C or C++ programmer, you have probably run across functions written to take a variable number of arguments, that are usually with the **va_start**, **va_arg**, and **va_end** macros. In C++, for example, I could write a function that looks like the one shown in Listing 2.5.

Listing 2.5   Variable argument list to a function in C++.

```
#include <stdarg.h>
#include <string.h>
#include <stdio.h>

int PrintParams( int count, ... )
{

   va_list va;
   va_start(va,count);

   for ( int i=0; i<count; ++i )
   {
      int num = va_arg(va, int);
     printf("Number %d = %d\n", i, num );
   }

   va_end(va);
   return 0;

}


int main(void)
{
   PrintParams( 3, 1, 2, 3);
   return 0;
}
```

This program suffers from numerous problems, however. First, you have to know, in the function receiving the variable number of arguments, what kind of arguments you will receive. Second, if an invalid argument was passed, you would never know it. Finally, the use of macros is fraught with danger because they are non-type-safe entries. C#, on the other hand, employs the use of a new keyword, **params**, to deal with these issues. Listing 2.6 shows a similar function to print variable arguments in C#. Note the use of the **params** keyword to indicate that the input element is of variable length. The system converts all arguments to the method into a single object array when the **params** keyword is used.

Listing 2.6   Variable arguments to a method in C#.

```
using System;

class CH2_5 {
   public static void PrintParams( params object[] list )
   {
      for ( int i=0; i<list.Length; ++i )
         Console.WriteLine("Object {0} = {1} ({2})", i, list[i],
list[i].GetType());
   }

   public static void Main()
   {
      PrintParams ( 1,2,"a", "b", 23.4);
   }
}
```

Creating a Method with a Reference Argument

One nice thing about C++ compared to Java is its ability to return multiple values
from a given function or method. Java allows only a single return value, and it
must be returned as the simple return value from a function. Parameters passed
into a method of a Java class are one-way only, for simple types. You cannot pass
in an integer, for example, and have it modified in the method. Java passes only
simple arguments by value and only for methods. C++, on the other hand, lets you
use two different methods for passing things by reference into a method or function. You can pass the address of a variable and treat it as a pointer in the method
or function, or you can accept a reference to a variable and modify it in the method
or function. A simple example is:

```
int PassByPointer( int* x )
{
   *x = 3;
}
int main(void)
{
   int x = 10;
   PassByPointer(&x);
   // x is now 3
}
```

Alternatively, you can do this in a "cleaner" but less obvious way:

```
int PassByReference( int& x )
{
    x = 3;
}
int main(void)
{
   int x = 10;
   PassByReference(x);
   // x is now 3
}
```

The problem with both these approaches is that they are dangerous. In the first example, you could pass in a NULL pointer. Dereferencing that pointer would crash the program. In the second example, it is not obvious to the programmer calling the function that it modifies the incoming data, which can lead to obscure errors that are difficult to track down.

C# solves both these problems by using the **ref** keyword. This keyword has two parts to it. You must declare a method to use the reference type. In addition, you must pass the variable in and specify that you are sending it by reference. In this way, both the developer of the method and the programmer using the method are protected. You cannot pass a NULL reference. Attempting to pass NULL to a reference argument results in a compile-time error. By requiring that you explicitly indicate that you are sending a value by reference, you understand that it is likely to change. Listing 2.7 shows an application in C# that uses both nonreference passed variables (by value) and reference passed variables so that you can see the results for both.

Listing 2.7   Creating a method with a reference argument.

```
using System;
class CH2_6
{
    static void Main()
    {
       int x = 10;

       Console.WriteLine("Before calling non-ref function, x = {0}", x );
       NonRefFunction( x );
       Console.WriteLine("After calling non-ref function, x = {0}", x );
       RefFunction( ref x );
       Console.WriteLine("After calling ref function, x = {0}", x );
    }
```

```
static void NonRefFunction( int x )
{
    Console.WriteLine( "Top of NonRefFunction. X = {0}", x );
    x = x + 10;
    Console.WriteLine( "Bottom of NonRefFunction. X = {0}", x );
}

static void RefFunction( ref int x )
{
    Console.WriteLine( "Top of RefFunction. X = {0}", x );
    x = x + 10;
    Console.WriteLine( "Bottom of RefFunction. X = {0}", x );
}
}
```

The two important lines in this application are shaded. The first shaded line indicates how you pass a reference parameter to a method. The second shaded line shows how the method accepts the parameter into itself.

The output from this application is:

```
Before calling non-ref function, x = 10
Top of NonRefFunction. X = 10
Bottom of NonRefFunction. X = 20
After calling non-ref function, x = 10
Top of RefFunction. X = 10
Bottom of RefFunction. X = 20
After calling ref function, x = 20
```

Implementing a Property for a Class

Properties are a somewhat new concept in C#. Originally found in languages like Delphi and C++ Builder, *properties* allow you to make access to internal data for a class more intuitive and less cumbersome. Rather than have to write code that first calls a **set** function followed by one that uses a **get** function, properties allow programmers to refer to properties by useful names in a direct fashion.

Most of the work of properties is done behind the scenes by the compiler in a way you don't have to understand in order to use the property concept. When you create a property, the compiler automatically generates class methods to set and get the property value and makes calls to these methods automatically when the programmer uses the property in the functionality of an application. Listing 2.8 shows a simple property that does some checking for the validity of its input.

Listing 2.8   Implementing a property for a class.

```
using System;

class CH2_7
{
    // Define the actual data member
    protected int fAge;

    CH2_7()
    {
        fAge = 21;
    }

    // Define the property accessors
    public int Age
    {
        get
        {
            return fAge;
        }
        set
        {
            // Validate that the age is between 18 and 65
        if ( value >= 18 && value <= 65 )
            fAge = value;
        }
    }

    public static void Main()
    {
        CH2_7 obj = new CH2_7();
        Console.WriteLine("Initially, age = {0}", obj.Age);
        obj.Age = 13;
        Console.WriteLine("After first set, age = {0}", obj.Age);
        obj.Age = 35;
        Console.WriteLine("Finally, age = {0}", obj.Age);
    }
}
```

The output from this small application is:

```
Initially, age = 21
After first set, age = 21
Finally, age = 35
```

As you can see from this example, properties allow you to safely yet conveniently set data in a class by an application programmer while retaining complete control over the validation of that data.

Creating a Static Class-Level Variable

A *static class-level* variable can be used from any object of a given class or any derived class. Static variables are useful for such tasks as implementing reference counting, maintaining unique identifiers for objects, and doing other things that require you to know about every object created for a given class. The most curious thing about static variables is that each class has exactly one static variable. No matter how many objects of a class are created, only one static variable exists in that class.

One potential problem with static variables is that they are not thread-safe. If, for example, you create a static variable that maintains a list of all the objects created for a given class and you access that variable from two objects at one time, you run into the standard problems with multithreaded applications. For this reason, you should create a static member function to use static variables. Listing 2.9 shows an example of a static member variable being used from a static member function of a class. Note that although static variables are the only sort that can be used in a static member function, other member functions can use any sort of variable.

Listing 2.9   Creating a static, class-level variable.

```
using System;

class CH2_8
{
    static int ReferenceCount;

    private static void IncrementReferenceCount()
    {
        // Here we would do any synchronization needed
        // for multithreaded apps.
        ReferenceCount++;
        Console.WriteLine("IncrementReferenceCount {0}", ReferenceCount);
        // Here we would release the synchronization flag
    }
    private static void DecrementReferenceCount()
    {
        // Here we would do any synchronization needed
        // for multithreaded apps.
        ReferenceCount--;
```

```
        Console.WriteLine("DecrementReferenceCount {0}", ReferenceCount);
        // Here we would release the synchronization flag
    }

    public CH2_8()
    {
        IncrementReferenceCount();
    }
    ~CH2_8()
    {
        DecrementReferenceCount();
    }
    void Dispose()
    {
        Finalize();
        GC.SuppressFinalize(this);
    }


    public static void Main()
    {
        CH2_8 app = new CH2_8();
        app.Dispose();
    }
}
```

The output from this program is (not surprisingly):

```
IncrementReferenceCount 1
DecrementReferenceCount 0
```

As you can see, a static method and a static member variable for a class can be used to accomplish tasks across object boundaries. Reference counting is an excellent concept to add to your objects to verify that you are creating the number of objects you are expecting and to check to see how many objects of a given class are active at any given time.

Creating an Array of Objects

Arrays of objects in C# are a bit different from object arrays in C++ or Java. An *array* of objects is an object itself. It must first be created, and then the individual elements of the array must be created. This situation is different from C++, where creating an array of objects automatically calls the constructor and creates each individual element of the array. Likewise, Java permits you to create arrays of objects directly. In C#, this task is not possible. The basic reason was that C#'s original developers wanted to keep the language as simple as possible.

In Listing 2.10, I examine a simple example of the two-step process of creating an array of objects in C#. First, the array object is created. Then, each element of the array is created. Finally, the individual elements are given values, and those values are printed to show how to refer to the individual array objects.

Listing 2.10   Creating an array of objects.

```
using System;

class CH2_9
{
    private int fValue;
    public CH2_9()
    {
        fValue = 0;
    }
    public void setValue(int value)
    {
        fValue = value;
    }
    public int getValue()
    {
        return fValue;
    }

    public static void Main()
    {
        CH2_9[] arr = new CH2_9[10];
        for ( int i=0; i<10; ++i )
            arr[i] = new CH2_9();

        for ( int i=0; i<10; ++i )
            arr[i].setValue(i);

        for ( int i=0; i<10; ++i )
            Console.WriteLine("Object {0}. Value = {1}",
                i, arr[i].getValue ());

    }
}
```

The important piece of this application is shown in the shaded lines. This section creates the array object itself and then creates each individual part of the array.

Creating an Interface

Interfaces provide a way to create common functionality among classes in C#. In general, a C# interface contains a set of methods that would implement a particular task. For example, an interface might provide logging functionality. Interfaces provide only the actual definitions of the functionality for that task—they do not implement any specific code to do the task. That job is left to the class that implements the interface. Interfaces are a roundabout method of providing a form of multiple inheritance in C#, a language that otherwise allows for only single inheritance.

Listing 2.11 shows a typical implementation and use of an interface in C#. Notice that the interface definition itself contains no code—only the actual method signatures. The implementation of the methods is left to the class that inherits the interface, as you can see from the listing.

Listing 2.11   Creating an interface.

```
using System;
public interface ILog
{
    int OpenLogFile( string fileName );
    int CloseLogFile();
    void LogString( string strToLog );
}
public class MyLog : ILog
{
    public int OpenLogFile( string fileName )
    {
        Console.WriteLine("Opening File {0}", fileName );
        return 0;
    }
    public int CloseLogFile()
    {
        Console.WriteLine("Closing log file");
        return 0;
    }
    public void LogString( string strToLog )
    {
        Console.WriteLine("Logging String {0}", strToLog );
    }
}
class CH2_10
{
    public static void Main()
    {
```

```
        MyLog app = new MyLog();
        app.OpenLogFile("AFile");
        app.LogString("Hello world");
        app.CloseLogFile();
    }
}
```

Creating an Abstract Class

Interfaces are a powerful method for creating functionality you can abstract into other classes. Sometimes, however, you don't want to reuse the interface as much as you want to reuse the functionality inherent in a given class. C# provides two methods of completing this task: simple inheritance and abstract inheritance. In the case of simple inheritance, you start with a base class, which can have objects instantiated for it, and derive a new class, which also allows object instantiation.

Abstract classes are similar to base classes, but do not allow application programmers to create instances of themselves. Listing 2.12 shows another version of the **Logging** interface I presented in Listing 2.11. This time, however, the logging functionality is presented not as an interface, but rather as an abstract class.

Listing 2.12   Creating an abstract class.

```
using System;

abstract public class ILog
{
    public int OpenLogFile( string fileName )
    {
        Console.WriteLine("Opening File {0}", fileName );
        return 0;
    }
    public int CloseLogFile()
    {
        Console.WriteLine("Closing log file");
        return 0;
    }
    public void LogString( string strToLog )
    {
        Console.WriteLine("Logging String {0}", strToLog );
    }
}
```

```
public class MyLog : ILog
{
    public MyLog()
    {
    }
    public void LogAString(string s)
    {
        OpenLogFile( "AFile" );
        LogString( s );
        CloseLogFile();
    }
}

class CH2_11
{
    public static void Main()
    {
        MyLog app = new MyLog();
        app.LogAString("Why Not?");
        app.OpenLogFile("AFile");
        app.LogString("Hello world");
        app.CloseLogFile();
    }
}
```

Abstract interfaces and classes can be public or private, just as any other type in C# can be.

Overriding a Method

One basic concept behind object-oriented programming is that you can create virtual methods that can be overridden in a derived class to change the functionality of the base class in a way that fits with the derivation. You can do this in C# with the **override** and **virtual** keywords.

Virtual methods must be defined in the base class explicitly by the programmer who writes the base class. You cannot simply create a derived class and derive whatever you like, willy-nilly. You use the **virtual** keyword to indicate that you want to have a base method overridden in a derived class. Likewise, you cannot simply override a method in a derived class by reimplementing it. You must specifically tell the compiler that you are intending to override an existing virtual method by using the **override** keyword. Listing 2.13 shows an example of several of these features.

Listing 2.13   Overriding a method.

```
using System;
public class Person
{
   private int fAge;

   public Person()
   {
      fAge = 21;
   }
   public virtual void setAge(int age)
   {
      fAge = age;
   }
   public virtual int getAge()
   {
      return fAge;
   }
}

public class AdultPerson : Person
{
   public AdultPerson()
   {
   }
   override public void setAge(int age)
   {
      if ( age > 21 )
         base.setAge(age);
   }
}

class CH2_12
{
   public static void Main()
   {
      Person p = new Person();
      p.setAge(18);
      AdultPerson ap = new AdultPerson();
      ap.setAge(18);
      Console.WriteLine("Person Age: {0}", p.getAge());
      Console.WriteLine("AdultPerson Age: {0}", ap.getAge());
   }
}
```

The interesting parts of this example are shown in the shaded block of code in the listing. First, you can see how to override an existing virtual method. Note that you don't need to override a method if you are happy with the way it performs. An example is shown in the **getAge** method of the base class. Another interesting feature is the way in which you can call the existing base class method from the derived class via the **base** keyword. The **base** keyword allows you to invoke a method from the base class directly in a derived class, without causing the infinite loop that would occur if you simply called the same method name again.

Creating an Event

An *event* is something that happens in a program. For a C# class, events may be defined to handle any sort of circumstance, from an exceptional condition to a change in a value. C# allows you to define at the class level your own event handlers, which can be used to monitor what is going on with a given object. For example, you might have a property that is important to the remainder of your application within a given object. For that object, you want to be notified when the property changes. In C#, you can define a specific event handler for that property change and be notified when that event occurs.

Events can be useful for items like persistent objects. Imagine that some objects have a **dirty flag** property that knows when an object's internal state has changed. If you defined an event handler for all objects of that class that were triggered by a change in the dirty flag, you would be able to safely and easily store all the objects that are changed persistently. In Listing 2.14, I explore the idea of events and event handlers for a given class.

Listing 2.14   Creating an event.

```
using System;
public delegate void AgeChangeHandler( int age, object obj,
                ref bool dontdoit );

class Person
{
    public event AgeChangeHandler AgeChange;
    int fAge;
    public int Age
    {
        set
        {
            Boolean dontdoit = false;
        AgeChange( value, this, ref dontdoit);
```

```
        if ( !dontdoit )
          fAge=value;
        }
        get
        {
          return fAge;
        }
      }
    public Person()
    {
      fAge = 0;
    }
  }
  class CH2_13
  {
    private static void MyAgeChangeHandler( int age, object obj,
            ref bool dontdoit )
    {
      Console.WriteLine(
          "MyAgeChangeHandler called with age {0} obj.age = {1}",
            age, ((Person)obj).Age );
      if ( age < 0 || age > 99 )
        dontdoit = true;
    }

    public static void Main()
    {
      Person p = new Person();
      // Set up our handler
      p.AgeChange += new AgeChangeHandler(MyAgeChangeHandler);
      p.Age = 21;
      p.Age = 33;


    }
  }
```

A few things worth noting about this example are evident in the preceding listing. First, notice that you must define a delegate to act as the go-between for the object that is firing the event and the event handler. (I talk more about delegates in Chapter 5 and explore events and event handling in depth in that chapter.) In addition, because you can pass the object itself to the event handler, you can then write a generic event handler for all objects of a given class.

The last thing to note in this example is the odd syntax of the shaded line of code. Note how the += operator is used to add a new event handler to the object event. The reason is simple: A default event handler always exists for an event. You are adding a new event handler to the chain of events for that particular trigger event. You can add more event handlers for the event as well. For example, I could add the following code to the system

```
private static void MyAgeChangeHandler2( int age, object obj,
        ref bool dontdoit )
{
    Console.WriteLine("MyAgeChangeHandler2 called with age {0}",
        age);
}
```

and then add the following line to the **Main** function:

```
p.AgeChange += new AgeChangeHandler(MyAgeChangeHandler2);
```

This process would create a second handler for the same event for the object. In fact, the output from this program would be:

```
MyAgeChangeHandler called with age 21 obj.age = 0
MyAgeChangeHandler2 called with age 21
MyAgeChangeHandler called with age 33 obj.age = 21
MyAgeChangeHandler2 called with age 33
```

Events and event handlers are an integral part of the GUI-handling process in C#, but are also a powerful technique for handling changes to the object system.

Related solution:	Found on page:
Creating a Delegate	195

Using an Indexer

An *indexer* allows you to treat any object as though it were an array and to "index into" that object by using whatever keys you want to use. You can, for example, use the indexer property to provide a different interface to properties in your object or to allow you to get back different attributes of the object. An interesting use of an indexer is to provide a VB-like way of setting and getting properties by name rather than by some kind of integer value.

In this example, I provide two different ways of indexing the same object. The first method uses a string to allow you to retrieve properties by name, à la Visual Basic. The second method uses the more standard integer property to give you access to the same information in a somewhat less convenient, but more familiar, way. Listing 2.15 shows the two different methods along with a simple driver that illustrates how the application programmer uses them.

Listing 2.15   Using an indexer.

```
using System;
class Book
{
    private string fTitle;
    private string fAuthor;
    private string fSubject;
    private string fDescription;

    public Book( string title, string author, string subj,
                        string descr )
    {
        fTitle = title;
        fAuthor = author;
        fSubject = subj;
        fDescription = descr;
    }
    public Book()
    {
    }

    // Define an indexer.
    public string this[string index]
    {
        get
        {
            if ( index == "Title" )
            return fTitle;
        if ( index == "Author" )
            return fAuthor;
        if ( index == "Subject" )
            return fSubject;
        if ( index == "Description" )
            return fDescription;
        return "Unknown";
        }
        set
        {
            if ( index == "Title" )
            fTitle = value;
        if ( index == "Author" )
            fAuthor = value;
        if ( index == "Subject" )
```

```
            fSubject = value;
        if ( index == "Description" )
            fDescription = value;
            }
        }
    public string this[int index]
    {
        get
        {
            if ( index == 1 )
            return fTitle;
        if ( index == 2 )
            return fAuthor;
        if ( index == 3 )
            return fSubject;
        if ( index == 4 )
            return fDescription;
        return "Unknown";
        }
        set
        {
            if ( index == 1 )
            fTitle = value;
        if ( index == 2 )
            fAuthor = value;
        if ( index == 3 )
            fSubject = value;
        if ( index == 4 )
            fDescription = value;
        }
    }
}


class CH2_14
{
    static public void Main()
    {
        Book b = new Book("C# Black Book", "Matt Telles",
                    "C# programming", "A great book");

        Console.WriteLine("Book Title: {0}", b["Title"]);
        Book b2 = new Book();
        b2["Title"] = "The Second Volume";
        b2[2] = "Another Author";
        Console.WriteLine("Book Title: {0}", b2["Title"]);
    }
}
```

Accessing an Interface from a Class

Interfaces provide a way for a developer to create multiple inheritance in a class by deriving from more than one interface for a given class. This capability can lead to problems, however, especially when two interfaces have a method name in common. How do you determine which one you are calling? More importantly, how does the compiler know which interface you are referring to? Fortunately, C# addresses this problem by allowing you to scope the interface you are implementing and calling. In this example, I explore the idea of two interfaces with a method name in common and describe how to access the one you want.

Listing 2.16 shows how to scope an interface method name so that both you and the compiler know which method you really mean to call in your application usage of the class.

Listing 2.16   Accessing an interface from a class.

```
using System;

public interface Channel
{
   void Next();
   void Previous();
}

public interface Book
{
   void Next();
   void Chapter();
}

public class CH2_15 : Channel, Book
{
   void Channel.Next()
   {
      Console.WriteLine("Channel Next");
   }
   void Book.Next()
   {
      Console.WriteLine("Book Next");
   }
   public void Previous()
   {
      Console.WriteLine("Previous");
   }
```

```
public void Chapter()
{
   Console.WriteLine("Chapter");
}

public static void Main()
{
   CH2_15 app = new CH2_15();
   ((Book)app).Next();
   app.Previous();
   app.Chapter();
}
}
```

Notice how, in the listing, I completely scope the name of the method I am implementing in the class, telling the compiler which interface this method is implementing. This concept is important because it allows both the human reader and the compiler to understand what you are trying to do. Notice that to call the proper interface method, you must cast the object itself to the right kind of interface object. You might think that you could write something like this:

```
app.Book.Next ();
```

The compiler, however, has other ideas and does not allow it, for a variety of reasons. The primary reason is that the language would become overly complex by forcing the compiler to use the scope (.) operator for two different purposes. The class has no element called **Book**, so it would have to be a special case. (C# is about simplicity, not special cases.)

Throwing an Exception

Exceptions form the core of the C# error-handling system. *Exceptions* indicate a problem that cannot be solved in the normal path of a program's execution. A common mistake made by beginning programmers who work with languages that support exception handling is that the programmers use the exception-handling mechanism for all errors that crop up in the program. This mistake is a bad one because the cost of exception handling is high. The system must unwind the stack and make sure that all objects are properly destructed and all garbage collected. The system must also make sure that the program is in the proper state to continue normally after the error is handled. This task is difficult and time consuming.

To use exception handling properly, you must be sure that the error is occurring and that the method or class you are working with cannot handle the error in a reasonable manner. If an error that results in a program crash is not handled, it is an ideal candidate for exception handling. Listing 2.17 shows how to throw an exception in such a case.

Listing 2.17   Throwing an exception.

```
using System;
class CH2_16
{
    public static int AnExceptionFunction( int value )
    {
        if ( value == 0 ) // Can't divide by zero
            throw new DivideByZeroException("Divide By 0 error!");

        int x = 20/value;
        return x;
    }

    public static void Main()
    {
        int value = 0;
        value = AnExceptionFunction(10); // This works ok
        Console.WriteLine("Value = {0}", value );
        AnExceptionFunction(0); // This doesn't
        Console.WriteLine("Value = {0}", value );
    }
}
```

The output from this little program is:

```
Value = 2

Exception occurred: System.DivideByZeroException: Divide By 0 error!
   at CH2_16.AnExceptionFunction(Int32)
   at CH2_16.Main()
```

As you can see, the exception-handling mechanism works to prevent what would have been a bad situation. Of course, it also terminates the program in an abnormal fashion. This outcome obviously isn't the desired result of error handling. In the next example, you see how to catch this error to handle it without crashing the program.

Handling a Possible Exception with a **try/catch** Block

A dirty truth about programming in any language is that you need to clean up after your own messes. Nowhere is this more true than in error handling. When you call a function that can throw an exception, you must make sure that any exceptions that are thrown are caught and dealt with, if possible. No matter what might go wrong, you should never allow an error that isn't handled to bubble itself up a layer to an unsuspecting audience of code.

In C#, the method for handling exceptions is a **try/catch** block: You "try" a block of code and then "catch" any exceptions generated within that block. You may elect to catch individual error types separately or catch all possible errors in one small error-handling area. In any case, you may elect to pass the error further up the call tree to whoever called your function, or you might handle the error directly and pass the appropriate information to the caller.

Listing 2.18 shows how to throw an exception in a function and then catch that exception in the calling function. The program does not terminate when an exception is generated, but continues doing what it was supposed to do.

Listing 2.18   Handling a possible exception.

```
using System;
class CH2_17
{
    public static int AnExceptionFunction( int value )
    {
       if ( value == 0 ) // Can't divide by zero
          throw new DivideByZeroException("Divide By 0 error!");

       int x = 20/value;
       return x;
    }

    public static void Main()
    {
       int value = 0;
       try
       {
       value = AnExceptionFunction(10); // This works ok
       Console.WriteLine("Value = {0}", value );
       AnExceptionFunction(0); // This doesn't
       Console.WriteLine("Value = {0}", value );
       }
```

```
        catch (Exception e)
        {
            Console.WriteLine("Caught an exception {0}. Continuing", e);
        }
        Console.WriteLine("Done");
    }
}
```

The output from this function, unlike the previous example, is somewhat more comforting to developers. Here is what it prints when you run it:

```
Value = 2
Caught an exception System.DivideByZeroException: Divide By 0 error!
    at CH2_17.AnExceptionFunction(Int32)
    at CH2_17.Main(). Continuing
Done
```

Note that the program is continuing past the point of the exception and continues to work properly, displaying the **Done** message. Unlike an exception that isn't handled, the **try/catch** block lets you gracefully recover from what could be a catastrophic error. For a way to deal with multiple types of errors and to move past them correctly, check out the example in the next section, which talks about working with the **finally** statement.

Moving Past an Exception with finally

One problem with exception handling is that it often leaves you in a position in which you aren't sure where you should go next. Suppose that you run a block of code that might throw an exception. You want to catch that exception and pass it up the chain to the caller, but you also want to do some cleanup and reinitialization before you do that. How can you accomplish both these tasks without duplicating lots of code in several places?

The answer turns out to be the C# **finally** statement. This statement is processed within a **try/catch** block when the last of the error-handling statements is processed. No matter that an error occurred or did not occur—the **finally** code is always executed. Listing 2.19 shows how the **try/catch/finally** block works.

Listing 2.19 Moving past an exception with **finally**.

```
using System;
class CH2_18
{
   public static void CallExceptionFunction()
   {
      throw new Exception("This is an exception");
   }

   public static void Main()
   {

   try
   {
     // Call a function that throws an exception
     try
     {
       CallExceptionFunction();
       Console.WriteLine("This should never be printed");
       throw new Exception("Bad Error Exception");
     }
     catch( Exception e)
     {
       Console.WriteLine("Catching the BadError Exception"); // #1
         throw new Exception("Rethrowing", e);
     }
         finally
         {
             Console.WriteLine("Finally Statement #1"); // #2
         }
       }
       catch ( Exception e)
   {
     Console.WriteLine("Catching Exception #2 {0}", e ); // #3
   }
       finally
   {
     Console.WriteLine("We are at the last outside nested block"); // #4
   }
   try
   {
     Console.WriteLine("No error will occur here"); // #5
   }
   catch ( Exception e )
```

```
{
    Console.WriteLine("Caught an exception in a BAD place {0}", e );
        // #6
}
finally
{
    Console.WriteLine("This is the last finally block"); // #7
}
}
}
```

Before I get into how the code works, take a quick look at the output from the program. Tracing through the code by using the output statements is instructive:

```
Catching the BadError Exception
Finally Statement #1
Catching Exception #2 System.Exception: Rethrowing ---> System.
Exception: This i
s an exception
    at CH2_18.CallExceptionFunction()
    at CH2_18.Main()
    at CH2_18.Main()
We are at the last outside nested block
No error will occur here
This is the last finally block
```

As you can see, the error is caught in the error handler for the function call. This block is the one marked **#1** in the listing. Notice that even though I am rethrowing the error up to the next level (block **#3**), the **finally** block that occurs after the rethrow is still executed. Even though no error occurs in that outer block, the **finally** blocks (**#4** and **#7**) are executed anyway. You can think of **finally** blocks as living outside the normal stream of events that occur with error handling.

Chapter 3

Language Features

In Depth

The C# programming language offers a rich set of functionality and powerful constructs that allow you to quickly and easily create new applications with a minimum of fuss and coding. In this chapter, I explore a few of those features and look at the differences between C# and languages such as C++ and Java. If you are learning the C# language after using other languages, this chapter should prove to be invaluable in showing you some differences and similarities between these languages. If you are using C# as your first language, you will learn to appreciate the power and flexibility built into this language—features that give it an advantage over other, older languages, like Java and C++.

C# is a *derivative* language in that it contains many familiar constructs and syntax elements. By understanding these differences and the reasons they exist, you can write better C# code immediately and get up to speed more quickly. The major elements of C# that I examine in this chapter include:

- Attributes
- Expressions
- Garbage collection
- Structs
- Enums
- New keywords

Attributes

Rather than begin with an item in C# that is similar to those used in C++, C, or Java, let's start with one that is completely different from anything that exists in those languages. The concept of attributes is one that simply doesn't "map" to anything in the other languages. Much like a binary comment, an *attribute* is a piece of data that sticks with the binary component of a class in C#, even after the compile process is done. Unlike "regular" comments in C++, or even the notion of Javadoc-like comments in Java, attributes are available not only at compile and link times but also at runtime from the pure-binary object.

Attributes can be used to denote information about a class, such as its author, version number, type of component, and description of the way in which the author intended the class to be used. Attributes are classes in and of themselves, which allows them to contain information of any type you can dream up. Unlike COM components, which can contain only descriptions and type information, attributes are unlimited in their scope of information.

This simple example of a class implements an attribute (you see this example used more thoroughly in the section "Immediate Solutions" later in this chapter):

```
[AttributeUsage(AttributeTargets.Class|AttributeTargets.Struct)]
public class Creator : System.Attribute
{
    public Creator(string name, string date)
    {
        this.name = name;
        this.date = date;
        version = 0.1;
    }
    string date;
    string name;
    public double version;
}
```

As you can see, this code listing appears to be a standard C# class, with several member variables, a constructor, and a **public** security level. Looking just a bit further, however, you can see the two elements that make this class into an attribute as well as a regular C# class. First, notice that the class derives from the **System.Attribute** CLR class. This class implements the basic functionality necessary to use attributes in the C# runtime system.

The second important part of the attribute definition is the **AttributeUsage** statement that appears just above the actual class definition. This statement is a modifier to the class declaration itself. By adding an **AttributeUsage** statement, I am declaring to the compiler that this class can and will be used as an attribute to other classes. The **AttributeUsage** statement defines how the attribute can be used in the system. The argument to the **AttributeUsage** statement is an **AttributeTargets** element. If you do not specify for which targets you want to allow the attribute to be used, the default is used for all of them. Table 3.1 lists the available targets and shows how these attributes are used in the sample code.

Note that multiple types can be combined for any given attribute. In the preceding example, I have specified that the attribute can be applied to any value type, which allows me to use any user-defined type and apply this attribute to it.

After I have defined the attribute, I need to use it to give it meaning. The following simple class contains this attribute. Note that you may have more than one

Table 3.1   Attribute targets.

Attribute Target	How It Is Applied
All	To any element
Assembly	To any assembly
Class	To any class
ClassMembers	To a class, a structure, an enumeration, a constructor, a destructor, a method, a property, a field, an event, a delegate, or an interface
Constructor	To only class constructor
Delegate	To any delegate
Enum	To any enumeration
Event	To any event
Field	To any field in a class
Interface	To any interface for class derivation
Method	To any method within a class
Module	To any module-level entity
Parameter	To one or more parameters to a method
Property	To any property of a class
Return Value	To a return value of a method
Struct	To a structure

attribute for a class. In this case, you simply add the attributes in the order that you want to see them viewed. The class (ch3_1) is:

```
[Creator ("Matt Telles", "05/01/2001", version=1.1)] class CH3_1
{
    Foo ()
    {
    }
}
```

By writing the preceding statements, I have attached information about the class to that class in a binary persistent manner. This class can then be viewed at runtime, and the information about it can be retrieved and displayed. You see specifically how to do this in the section "Displaying Attributes for a Class," later in this chapter. These are not specified by the user of the class, but by the class author.

Expressions

C# has most of the same sorts of expressions as any other language you might have worked with. Rather than dwell on the **assignment** statement, the comparison operators, the various kinds of conditionals, and the like, focus instead on the differences between C# and other languages you might have used in the past.

Assignments

For the most part, C# **assignment** statements are the same as in any other language. You can assign a value to a value or a reference type. One major difference, however, is that C# is a type-safe language. Any attempt to assign a value of the wrong type to a variable is flagged as an error. Although C# supports both implicit and explicit conversions, no unsafe conversion is permitted without an explicit cast. For example, in C++, you could write something like this:

```
float x = 10.45;
int  I = x;
```

This statement would result, in most C++ compilers, in a warning that a loss of precision is possible. In C#, this statement is an error. You cannot assign a floating-point number to an integer without casting it to that integer or using one of the built-in conversion methods. This limitation protects you from ignoring statements with warnings. As in C++ or Java, the C# compiler does have an option to mark all warnings as errors.

Another interesting thing about C# assignments is that if they are not made, the variable is automatically assigned a default value and a warning is issued to the developer. Likewise, if a variable is not used after having a value assigned to it, the compiler automatically warns you. This warning prevents *dead code*, which results in bloated programs and difficult debugging problems.

If Statements

C# contains basic if-statement logic that allows you to take conditional paths based on the value of a given expression. Unlike C++ or Java, however, C# allows you to use an **if** statement for only a true Boolean expression. This situation is different from C++, which would permit something like this:

```
int x = 10;
if ( x )
{
}
```

C#, though, would not permit this **if** statement, requiring you instead to write:

```
If ( x > 0 )
{
}
```

This example works as simply another safety net for expressions that have been problematic in the past in coding efforts. In general, C# errs on the side of caution. C++ tends to err on the side of allowing programmers to do whatever they want to do. Java is somewhere in between.

Loops

The C# language allows you to use several loop types, including the **for** loop from C++, the **while** loop from both C++ and Java, and the **do** loop, which existed in C, C++, and Pascal. All these loop variables work the same way as they do in other languages, with one exception: The scope of the indexing variable in a **for** loop is restricted to the loop itself. This standard is the one proposed for C++ and the regular standard for Java. In other words, in the old-style C++, you could write:

```
for ( int I=0; I<10; ++I )
{
}
// Now, you can still use I
int z = I
```

C#, as well as Java and the new C++ standard, do not support this technique. After the outer edge of the **for** loop (the closing brace) is reached, the variable ceases to have a valid scope. In C#, the variable **I** would be undefined after I got past the closing brace. In C++, as I am accustomed to, I can continue to use that variable.

Like the **if** statement, the **while** and **do** loops require a Boolean expression. This concept is different from other languages. The designers of C# found that more mistakes were made writing a statement than could be justified, such as:

```
if ( x = 2 )
{
}
```

As a result, the statement must resolve to a distinct Boolean value.

Garbage Collection

One big difference between C# and its predecessor, C++, is, certainly, that C# implements true garbage collection in its runtime environment. To you, the programmer, the language no longer requires you to remember to clean up your allocations when you are done with them. This situation is a huge benefit over older languages, such as C and C++, because garbage collection eliminates many bugs in code. Memory leaks and corrupted memory are both problems of the past in C#.

Java also implements garbage collection, but in a slightly different way. In Java, you must let the system decide when to collect orphaned memory. This requirement leads to problems with the system's slowing down and then bogging down a time-critical section of code that is being executed. In addition, because Java waits until doing the collection is absolutely necessary, gathering up all the memory being freed can take some time, resulting in a wait for allocations.

C# gets around these problems by allowing programmers to decide whether they want to force the issue of collecting the garbage or decide on a good time to do so. You see how to make this decision in the section "Forcing Garbage Collection," later in this chapter.

C# works better with garbage collection because that process was well thought out to begin with. C# implements the idea of "generations" in the code, which allow the classes to segment themselves so that garbage collection is done more easily. You see how to do this by implementing a **Dispose** method in the "Forcing Garbage Collection" section just mentioned.

Most of the work done by the garbage-collection mechanism is done through the **System.GC** object. This object contains a large number of methods that allow you to do such things as force immediate garbage collection throughout the system (**GC.Collect**). You can suppress the call to **Finalize** for a given object (probably because it was called immediately) in the **GC.SuppressFinalize** method. Finally, you can call **ReRegisterForFinalize**, which allows you to undo the result of **SuppressFinalize** for a given object.

Structs

Primarily offered for backward compatibility with C++ programmers, the **struct** statement creates a structure of elements. Unlike in C++, structs in C# are much more closely related to classes than C structures. All elements of a structure are private by default, and a structure initializes its elements to the default value for each data type if none is specified and a structure is created on the heap. Finally, although a structure may contain methods of its own, it is not required to do so.

One big difference between structures and classes in C# is that a C# structure can be created on the stack. C# classes can be created on the heap by using only the new operator.

Here is a simple example of a structure in C#:

```
using System;

public struct X
{
    public int x;
    public int y;
    public int z;
}

class Foo
{
    public static void Main()
    {
        X x;

        x.x = 1;
        x.y = 2;
        x.z = 3;

        Console.WriteLine("X = {0}, Y = {1}, Z = {2}", x.x, x.y, x.z);

        X x1 = new X();
        Console.WriteLine("X = {0}, Y = {1}, Z = {2}", x1.x, x1.y, x1.z);

    }
}
```

You can see several differences between a struct and a class. For one thing, the struct has no methods. For another, you can create structures either on the stack or on the heap, as shown in the example. Take a look at the following output:

```
X = 1, Y = 2, Z = 3
X = 0, Y = 0, Z = 0
```

You can also see in this example that heap-based struct items are automatically initialized to default values (**0**, in this case). Finally, you can see that you are required to put an access modifier on each structure element, just as you would with a class. You can always add accessor methods to a structure, if you like, just as you can add any other sort of method. Structures can have constructors and destructors, just as they do in C++. The final complement to structures is that they may contain properties, just as classes do. As you can see, a structure is a powerful thing.

Enumerations

I talked briefly about enumerations in Chapter 2, so now let's look at some differences between enumerations in C# and those in C++. Java doesn't use the concept of an enumeration, so no differences exist there.

C# considers enumerations to be an extension of the integer type. Virtually any integer, therefore, can be assigned to an enumeration, whether or not the conversion makes any sense. In this regard, enumerations are a bad thing because they violate type safety. For this reason, you need to always validate an enumeration when you are using it. One thing to consider is the use of enumerations as a property within a class, which allows you to control whether valid values are assigned to the enumeration. For example, you could do something like this:

```
using System;

public enum _Color
{
   Red,
   Green,
   Blue
};

class EnumTest
{
   private _Color clr;

   public _Color Color
   {
      set
      {
         if ( value >= _Color.Red && value <= _Color.Blue )
         clr = value;
      }
      get
      {
         return clr;
      }
   }
   EnumTest()
   {
      clr = _Color.Red;
   }
```

```
    public static void Main()
    {
        EnumTest app = new EnumTest();
        Console.WriteLine( "Color = {0}", app.Color );
        app.Color = (_Color)5;
        Console.WriteLine( "Color = {0}", app.Color );
    }
}
```

You can see in the shaded line how you can do comparisons of enumerations to enumerated values, and in the sample **Main** function, how you can cast any integer, valid or not, to an enumeration.

Enumerations are a powerful force in C#—one you should seriously consider using when looking at data types. Also, here's one other feature worth mentioning about enumerations: You can select the type of enumeration by using the derivation function in C#. That is, you can do something like this:

```
public enum _MyColor : byte
{
    Green,
    Yellow
};
```

This snippet of code illustrates how to define the size of your enumeration, which also sets the size of the object used to store it and defines how many entries you may have in a given enumeration. You may not derive one enumeration from another and therefore extend it. In other words, you can't do this:

```
public enum _MyColor : _Color
{
}
```

In addition, enumerations may not be of user-defined types. Only system-defined types are permissible.

New Keywords

The C# language introduces a host of new keywords. Let's take a look at them, exploring what each one does and when you might use them. They turn up in examples throughout this book, where they are further explained. For now, however, you have to understand only what they mean and how to use them.

foreach

The **foreach** keyword is used to iterate through a collection. You simply define a variable to hold the individual elements in the collection and then do whatever you want in the loop within the **foreach** statement to process that element. For example, to process a simple array, you enter:

```
int[] array = new array[10];
// ..
foreach ( int I in array )
{
    System.WriteLine( "Element = {0}", I );
}
```

checked

The **checked** keyword (used in the section "Checking for Overflows," later in this chapter) allows you to check for underflows or overflows in a given numeric expression. Rather than worry about whether two numbers being added or multiplied would exceed the maximum allowable value for a given data type, you can use the **checked** keyword to throw an exception if the result in a given section of code exceeds the allowable maximum for that value type.

lock

The **lock** keyword is used for synchronization in threaded applications. A **lock** statement implements a critical section for that block of code. Only when the block has been exited is the next thread allowed into the block.

base

The **base** keyword is used to access base class members or methods within a derived class. Because C# has no notion of a scooping operator (::), as C++ does, C# must rely on the Java-like **base** keyword. When you call a base method using **base.<*methodname*>**, you are directly calling the class that your class is derived from. Because C# has only single-level inheritance, you may have only a single base class for a given class. Of course, that base class can be derived from another class and so forth. It is a simple linear inheritance, rather than a tree; you cannot mistake one base class for another. Note that **base** does not work for interfaces; you must specifically call the interface name you want to use.

this

The **this** keyword, used to refer to the current object in a method, can be used to differentiate between an input argument to a method and a member variable. The

this keyword can also be used to pass to a static method of a class the pointer to the actual object you are working with.

out

The **out** keyword is used to specify that an argument will be passed out of a method and not into it. Arguments returned to the caller are **out** arguments.

abstract

The **abstract** keyword is used to indicate that a class is not instantiable and can be used only as a base class for other classes. This keyword is akin to using a pure virtual method in C++. Abstract base classes are the foundation of most class libraries in the world, and the C# designers took this factor into account by giving those class library writers a method of creating abstract base classes.

event

The **event** keyword allows you to define events for a class. An *event* is a change that can be fired and caught asynchronously in another class or method, to make you aware of changes that occur in an object. For example, events can be used to notify a caller of when a property of a class changes. You should always have events for all properties you implement because this technique permits users to know if something changes in one of their objects. The **event** keyword serves to eliminate many classes of errors that would otherwise occur. Here is a simple rule: If you add a property, add an event for that property.

override

The **override** keyword is used to indicate that you are overriding a virtual function in a base class. Unlike in C++ or Java, you must explicitly tell the compiler that you want to override a base class virtual function. This keyword provides protection to the writers of the class by forcing them to understand the implications of what they do in their own derived classes. In addition, the compiler then becomes smarter about the code that is generated, by not having to worry about going through the code twice to determine which method the caller meant to call. This process makes the language much more efficient.

readonly

The **readonly** keyword is a reserved word in C# and cannot be used. It apparently can be used as a modifier for properties to define them as nonwritable, but that functionality is easier to obtain by simply not defining a **set** accessor function for the property. See the section "Creating a Read-Only Property," later in this chapter, for an example.

sealed

The **sealed** keyword is used to indicate that a class may not be used as a base class. When the **sealed** keyword is applied to a class as a modifier, that class is final. This concept is akin to the Java **final** keyword.

Hopefully, at this point in our whirlwind tour of C#, you have gained a good understanding of what all those funny things in the language are. Obviously, given the scope of this book, this discussion is not intended as an in-depth tutorial on how to use the language. Instead, you are being shown how to get into the depths of the language to do the things your job requires.

At this point, I launch into some immediate solutions you can use to quickly and easily find fast answers to specific problems that are likely to come up as you increasingly work with C#.

Immediate Solutions

Creating an Attribute

Attributes, a new concept in C#, are descriptive tags you can use for internal documentation or external display that are not a part of the actual "code" for a class or object. Attributes can be found by reflection and can be displayed in an object browser or form property sheet. One simple use for an attribute is keeping track of the author and design notes for a component. Another use might be to track the versioning information for that component.

Although attributes are not a part of the actual code for a class, they do appear in the definition for the class as modifiers. In Listing 3.1, you can see two elements of the attribute subsystem. First, the actual definition of the attribute contains the name of the writer of the class, the date the class was first created, and the current version number of the class. Next, the **Creator** attribute I just defined is used for a new class to provide information about that class for programmers browsing the library.

Listing 3.1   Creating and using a class attribute.

```
using System;
using System.Reflection;

[AttributeUsage(AttributeTargets.Class|AttributeTargets.Struct)]
public class Creator : System.Attribute
{
    public Creator(string name, string date)
    {
        this.name = name;
        this.date = date;
        version = 0.1;
    }
    string date;
    string name;
    public double version; // to illustrate how to use named attributes

}

[Creator("Matt Telles", "05/01/2001", version=1.1)] class CH3_1
{
```

```
static public void Main(String[] args)
{
   for ( int i=0; i<args.Length; ++i )
      System.Console.WriteLine("Args[{0}] = {1}", i, args[i]);


}
}
```

The important aspects of this code example are shown in the shaded portion of the listing. First, the code uses a definition of an attribute. As you can see, an attribute is nothing more than a "standard" C# class with some information attached at the beginning. The second important portion of the example is the actual use of the attribute in front of the **CH3_1** class declaration. In this case, I simply attach the attribute to the class that follows with the proper information to construct the attribute object.

Related solution:	*Found on page:*
Creating a Constructor	59

Displaying Attributes for a Class

Reflection, which I discuss in depth in Chapter 5, can show you information about classes, including the methods, variables, and constructors for the class. Now, however, let's concern ourselves with only the attributes for classes. In this example, you see how to explore all the attributes associated with a class and how to display them so that a user can view them. With a bit of work, this stripped-down example could be easily expanded to be a complete class browser.

Listing 3.2 shows a simple custom attribute and several classes that use that attribute. Then the program displays the attributes for the various classes using some reflection techniques built into the class libraries.

Listing 3.2   Displaying attributes for a class.

```
using System;
using System.Reflection;

[AttributeUsage(AttributeTargets.Class|AttributeTargets.Struct)]
public class Creator : System.Attribute
{
   public Creator(string name, string date)
   {
      this.name = name;
```

```
         this.date = date;
         version = 0.1;
      }
      public void Dump()
      {
         Console.WriteLine("Name {0}", name );
         Console.WriteLine("Date {0}", date );
         Console.WriteLine("Version {0}", version );
      }
      string date;
      string name;
      public double version; // to illustrate how to use named attributes

}

[Creator("Matt Telles", "05/01/2001", version=1.1)] class ATestClass1
{
    ATestClass1()
    {
    }
}

[Creator("Irving Berlin", "04/01/2000", version=1.5)] class ATestClass2
{
    ATestClass2()
    {
    }
}

[Creator("Anonymous", "12/31/2000", version=2.5)] class ATestClass3
{
    ATestClass3()
    {
    }
}


class CH3_2
{
    public static void PrintAttributeInformation(Type classType)
    {
        Console.WriteLine("Attributes for class {0}", classType );
        object[] attr = classType.GetCustomAttributes();
        foreach ( object o in attr )
```

```
    {
        Console.WriteLine("Attribute {0}", o );
    if ( o is Creator )
        ((Creator)o).Dump ();
    }
}
public static void Main()
{
    PrintAttributeInformation( typeof(ATestClass1) );
    PrintAttributeInformation( typeof(ATestClass2) );
    PrintAttributeInformation( typeof(ATestClass3) );
}
}
```

The output from this program is:

```
Attributes for class ATestClass1
Attribute Creator
Name Matt Telles
Date 05/01/2001
Version 1.1
Attributes for class ATestClass2
Attribute Creator
Name Irving Berlin
Date 04/01/2000
Version 1.5
Attributes for class ATestClass3
Attribute Creator
Name Anonymous
Date 12/31/2000
Version 2.5
```

As you can see from the shaded portion of the listing, which does the actual work of finding and displaying the custom attributes for the class, reflection makes it possible to put lots of information into the binary components in C# and retrieve them easily. In this case, I am simply retrieving all the custom attributes and displaying the ones I know something about. As you see in Chapter 5 (reflection), I could easily get back the actual elements of all the classes without knowing a thing about them.

Related solutions:	Found on page:
Using a Delegate in a Method	198
Obtaining Member Information from a Class	235

3. Language Features

Creating a Read-Only Property

In Chapter 2, I explored some features of C# classes. One thing that doesn't fit into that chapter is the concept of read-only properties. Java has an equivalent concept, as do the nonstandard extensions of C++Builder and Delphi. You can certainly emulate this functionality in C++, but it has no built-in way of doing it. In C#, creating a read-only property is easy.

As you may recall from Chapter 2, properties are implemented using an internal member variable along with **set** and **get** methods. By simply not implementing one of the accessor members, such as the **set** functionality, you create a property that has no way to assign values to it. This property is read-only. Likewise, you could create a property that is *write-only*, which has only the ability to be assigned to. Oddly enough, you have good reasons to have a write-only property: You could use it for such tasks as updating a global state, for example.

Listing 3.3 shows a class that contains a read-only property. Note the line that is commented out at the end of the listing. Removing that line is instructive. Try it and see what error you get from the compiler.

Listing 3.3   Creating a read-only property.

```
using System;

public class ClassWithReadOnlyProperty
{
    int fAge;

    public int Age
    {
        get
        {
            return fAge;
        }
    }
    public ClassWithReadOnlyProperty()
    {
        fAge = 21;
    }
}

class CH3_1
{
    static public void Main()
    {
```

```
        ClassWithReadOnlyProperty crp = new ClassWithReadOnlyProperty();
        Console.WriteLine("Age {0}", crp.Age );
        // Can't do this:
        // crp.Age = 22;
    }
}
```

Did you give it a try? If you remove the comment from the shaded line, you get the following error from the compiler:

```
Microsoft (R) C# Compiler Version 7.00.8905 [NGWS runtime 2000.14.1812.10]
Copyright (C) Microsoft Corp 2000. All rights reserved.

CH3_3.cs(27,7): error CS0200: Property or indexer
'ClassWithReadOnlyProperty.Age
' cannot be assigned to -- it is read only
```

As you can see, read-only properties were well thought out in C#.

Related solution:	Found on page:
Creating an Abstract Class	72

Synchronizing a Method for Multithreading

One common problem in modern programming is that of multithreading issues. Having more than one thread running at the same time means that you need to worry about multiple ways in which your data can be updated at the same time. This situation can cause problems with concurrency and with items being out of sync. For example, if a method performs three separate tasks and that method is called from more than one thread, in some cases the different threads are at different places in the method. This placement can cause issues when the data is not written out correctly.

C# provides a built-in method for helping you to avoid such multitasking issues. The primary weapon that you, the programmer, have in the war against multithreading problems is the **lock** statement. It gives the application a "critical section" capability. Simply, the **lock** statement stops a section of code from being entered until the lock is released at the end of the statement. In Listing 3.4, you see an example of a multithreaded application in C#, along with a locked method that prevents the other threads from competing in a small area, until the first thread to reach that area is finished.

Listing 3.4   Synchronizing a method for multithreading.

```
using System;
using System.Threading;

public class CH3_4
{
    Thread[] threads;
    int      whichThread;
    int      runCount;

    public void CheckThread()
    {
        lock(this)
        {
            // Kill them as they come in
            runCount ++;
            Console.WriteLine("Run Count {0}", runCount );
            if ( runCount > 4 )
            {
                Console.WriteLine("Which Thread {0}", whichThread );
                threads[whichThread].Stop();
                runCount = 0;
                whichThread++;
            }
        }
    }

    public void RunThread()
    {
        Boolean done = false;
        while ( !done )
        {
            CheckThread();
        }
    }

    public void StartThreads()
    {
        threads =  new Thread[5];
        runCount = 0;
        whichThread=0;

        for ( int i=0; i<5; ++i )
        {
            threads[i] = new Thread( new ThreadStart(RunThread) );
            threads[i].Start();
```

```
    }
     }

    public static void Main()
    {
        CH3_4 app = new CH3_4();

    app.StartThreads();
     }
}
```

The output from this program, with the **lock** statement in place, is:

```
Current Thread 0
Run Count 1
Current Thread 0
Run Count 2
<snip for space reasons>
Run Count 4
Current Thread 3
Run Count 5
Current Thread 3
Run Count 6
Stopping thread 3
Current Thread 4
Run Count 1
Current Thread 4
Run Count 2
Current Thread 4
Run Count 3
Current Thread 4
Run Count 4
Current Thread 4
Run Count 5
```

This output shows what you would think would happen. However, if you remove the **lock** statement highlighted in the code listing, you get a different output, and one that is more difficult to explain. The output would read like this:

```
Current Thread 0
Run Count 4
<snip for space>
Current Thread 5
Exception occurred:
```

```
Exception occurred: Run Count 5

Exception occurred: System.IndexOutOfRangeException
    at CH3_4.CheckThread()
    at CH3_4.RunThread()System.IndexOutOfRangeException
    at CH3_4.CheckThread()
    at CH3_4.RunThread()System.IndexOutOfRangeException
    at CH3_4.CheckThread()
```

Why did this occur? For the simple reason that too many threads were incrementing the same memory blocks at the same time. As a result, the **whichThread** variable got incremented too many times and the attempt to stop the thread killed the system because it used an array index out of range for the **threads** array.

The general rule of thumb for threads is to lock things if you aren't sure if they are thread-safe.

Forcing Garbage Collection

One of the most incredible and annoying features of Java is garbage collection. How can a feature be both incredible and annoying? It's fairly easy. Garbage collection is, in theory, a wonderful concept—no more worrying about allocated memory being orphaned, resulting in "leaks" that eventually bring the system to its knees. No more worrying about allocating something once and deleting it twice, thereby corrupting the memory-management system and crashing the application in strange, unpredictable places. Garbage collection once seemed like the greatest thing since sliced bread.

Of course, in practice, even a wonderful theory can turn into a nightmare. Garbage collection works by waiting until it is needed (Just in Time) and then scavenging up objects that are no longer being used, de-allocating their memory and de-initializing their internal structures. The problem, as you might guess, is that sometimes garbage collection doesn't happen as quickly as you want. Imagine that a file object gets closed when the object is destroyed. In the C++ world, this object immediately closes the file when the object goes out of scope (in the case of a stack-based object) or is deleted explicitly by the programmer (in the case of a heap-based object). In Java, this same object could remain for quite some time, leaving the file open. Of course, a well-written object requires that you explicitly close the file, but then you're right back at the "forgetting to do something" stage.

Enter C#. The designers of C# recognized that garbage collection, as a failsafe mechanism, is a wonderful thing. You don't have to worry about the system's running out of memory in the long term because anything you allocate in your application is (at worst) freed up at some point when the application terminates. The problem is, of course, that this process doesn't help the file object. It is still holding on to that open file and preventing the user from, say, copying it in the outer operating system layer. C#, however, was designed for programmers. As a result, you have a simple and easy way to force the garbage-collection system to run. Listing 3.5 shows an application that forces garbage collection, illustrating its point by printing a message in the object destructor to show that things happened as expected.

Listing 3.5   How to force garbage collection.

```
using System;

class CH3_5
{
    CH3_5()
    {
        Console.WriteLine("CH3_5 Constructor called");
    }
    ~CH3_5()
    {
        Console.WriteLine("CH3_5 Destructor called");
    }

    public static void Main()
    {
        CH3_5 app = new CH3_5();

        app.Finalize();

        GC.SuppressFinalize(app);
    }

}
```

The output from this small program is:

```
CH3_5 Constructor called
CH3_5 Destructor called
```

Of course, calling the **finalize** method of an object always invokes the destructor. However, in this case, I also call the **GC.SuppressFinalize** method, which stops this object from being cleaned up when the final garbage collection has taken place. I have, in short, forced an object to be deleted, as if I were using C++ and had called **delete app**.

Checking for Overflows

One dangerous problem in software development is the issue of hidden conversion errors. Data types in all languages, including C#, can hold only a certain maximum value. For example, the **short** data type can hold only a maximum of 32767 before it overflows. An overflow can easily occur in a short conversion, especially in an expression that contains several terms. C# helps the programmer to avoid this trap by providing runtime errors, checking for overflow and underflow conditions. These checks are provided by the use of the **checked** keyword in the code.

To verify that something is working correctly, you must enclose that statement in a **checked** keyword call. This action allows the runtime environment to verify that the result of the statement is valid for the data type you are trying to assign it to. If the result would end up with a number that is not in range or that would "wrap around" the data type range, an exception is thrown to the application. Of course, this exception happens only if you use the **checked** keyword. Otherwise, the "hidden danger" remains.

Listing 3.6 shows a simple application that contains two methods. The first method uses the **checked** keyword to verify the result of adding two short integers. The second method does not use any boundary checking. Take a look at the code and then try to guess the result of the application. The output is shown following the code listing.

Listing 3.6   Checking for overflows.

```
using System;
public class CH3_6
{
    public int CheckedAddition( short s1, short s2)
    {
        int z = 0;
        try
        {
    z =   checked((short)(s1 + s2));
        }
        catch ( OverflowException )
        {
            Console.WriteLine("Overflow Exception, Returning 0");
        }
        return z;
    }
    public int UncheckedAddition( short s1, short s2 )
    {
```

```
      int z = ((short)(s1 + s2));
      return z;
   }

   public static void Main()
   {
      CH3_6 app = new CH3_6();
      short s1 = 32767;
      short s2 = 32767;

      Console.WriteLine("Checked Addition is: {0}",
        app.CheckedAddition(s1,s2));
      Console.WriteLine("Unchecked Addition is: {0}",
        app.UncheckedAddition(s1,s2));
   }
}
```

The result of running this application is the following output to the console window:

```
Overflow Exception, Returning 0
Checked Addition is: 0
Unchecked Addition is: -2
```

As you can see, the difference between using checked and unchecked math statements can be dramatic. Imagine if you were using this functionality in a banking transaction. Would you want your account to "go negative" because someone picked the wrong data type?

Creating an Enumeration

Enumerated types are an important aspect of the software development world. Enumerations allow you to show people exactly what kinds of values a given variable was intended to have, without allowing them the excessive freedom to assign values that make no sense in the context of the application. Obvious examples of enumerations include items like traffic lights (Red, Green, Yellow) and gender (Male, Female). Because neither of these objects would make any sense with any other values (perhaps Unknown for both), an enumerated type does the job of showing a developer what values are available for the variable, without allowing the developer to assign values that make no sense.

In this example, I create a simple enumerated type that represents the days of the week. I can then create a variable of that type and show how you can use that enumeration without worrying about invalid values. A C# flaw allows you to cast any integer value to an enumeration, whether or not it makes sense. This example illustrates that process and the problems it can cause. Listing 3.7 shows how to create enumerations and use them.

Listing 3.7 Creating an enumeration.

```
using System;

enum DayOfTheWeek
{
    Monday,
    Tuesday,
    Wednesday,
    Thursday,
    Friday,
    Saturday,
    Sunday
};

class CH3_7
{

    static public string DayName( DayOfTheWeek day )
    {
        switch ( day )
        {
            case DayOfTheWeek.Monday:
          return "Monday";
            case DayOfTheWeek.Tuesday:
          return "Tuesday";
            case DayOfTheWeek.Wednesday:
          return "Wednesday";
            case DayOfTheWeek.Thursday:
          return "Thursday";
            case DayOfTheWeek.Friday:
          return "Friday";
            case DayOfTheWeek.Saturday:
          return "Saturday";
            case DayOfTheWeek.Sunday:
          return "Sunday";
      default:
            return "Huh??";
        }
    }
```

```
static public void Main()
{
    DayOfTheWeek day = DayOfTheWeek.Monday;
    Console.WriteLine("First day is {0}", DayName(day));
    DayOfTheWeek huhday = (DayOfTheWeek)8;
    Console.WriteLine("Eighth day is {0}", DayName(huhday));
}
}
```

The output from this little program is:

```
First day is Monday
Eighth day is Huh??
```

As you can see, enumerations are really not true types, but instead are just a novel way of working with simple integer values.

Getting the Current Object

Sometimes, you need to work with an object in a method, but you aren't really sure which one you have. For this purpose, C# provides the **this** keyword for working with the current object of a method. Why would you need to do something like this? Really, you have several reasons. One possible reason is that a static array in a class keeps track of all the objects of a given class. In a case like this one (a cache, for example), you need to know what object you are working with so that you can mark it as dirty in the cache itself—and you would use the **this** keyword.

The other, more natural case for needing the **this** keyword is when a variable that is either passed into the method or defined in the method happens to have the same name as a member variable of the class. In this case, distinguishing between the input variable and the class member variable is impossible. The program in Listing 3.8 illustrates how to use the **this** keyword to indicate to the compiler which version of a variable you mean.

Listing 3.8   Getting the current object.

```
using System;
class CH3_8
{
    string name;
    string date;
    int    age;
```

```
public CH3_8(string name, string date, int age)
{
    this.name = name;
    this.date = date;
    this.age = age;
}
string getName() { return name; }
string getDate() { return date; }
int    getAge()  { return age; }

void   setName( string name ) { this.name = name; }
void   setDate( string date ) { this.date = date; }
void   setAge ( int age )     { this.age = age; }

public static void Main()
{
    CH3_8 app = new CH3_8("Matt Telles", "05/01/2001", 39 );

    Console.WriteLine("Name {0}, Date {1}, Age {2}",
        app.getName(), app.getDate(), app.getAge() );
}
}
```

As you can see, the **this** keyword indicates to the compiler that you mean the member variable. The **this** keyword can be used to modify internal data or return data to the caller. You cannot directly modify the **this** pointer itself because that would change the underlying object memory, which is likely to cause a program crash.

Allocating Memory

Unlike C++, C# has no generic block of memory that can be allocated. You can allocate arrays, and you can allocate objects, but C# has no simple **blob** (Binary Large Object Block) type to allocate. The language does support the byte type, and you can create large arrays of bytes in which to store data. A byte array can be used to store virtually anything. *Streams*, for example, are little more than large chunks of bytes that can hold any kind of information you want.

In Listing 3.9, you can see an example of a large buffer, made up of an array of bytes that is used to store a series of strings. The example stores two strings and then prints the resulting byte array.

Listing 3.9   Allocating memory in C#.

```
using System;
class CH3_9
{
    Byte[] blob;
    int    nPos;

    CH3_9()
    {
        blob = new Byte[1000];
        nPos = 0;
    }
    public void storeString(string s)
    {
        for ( int i=0; i<s.Length; ++i )
        {
            blob[nPos] = (Byte)s[i];
     nPos ++;
        }
    }
    public void printBlob()
    {
        for ( int i=0; i<nPos; ++i )
            Console.Write("{0}", (char)blob[i]);
    }
    public static void Main()
    {
        CH3_9 app = new CH3_9();
        app.storeString( "Hello world");
        app.storeString( "And goodbye");
        app.printBlob();
    }
}
```

The output from this application is:

```
Hello worldAnd goodbye
```

Compiling a Simple Command-Line Application

Having an immediate solution this far into the book to handle the compiling of a simple command-line application might seem strange, but in this case I examine some options you might not be aware of for compiling a C# program into an executable. The simple listing is shown in Listing 3.10.

Listing 3.10   A simple C# program for examining compile options.

```
using System;

class CH3_10
{
    public static void Main()
    {
        Console.WriteLine("Hello world");
    }
}
```

The first thing you can do is to simply compile the module without generating an executable. You might do this to verify that a single module compiles, for example, in a large-scale C# application. To compile with no executable generated, use the **/nooutput+** option:

```
C:\>csc /nooutput+ ch3_10.cs
Microsoft (R) Visual C# Compiler Version 7.00.9030 [CLR version
    1.00.2204.21]
Copyright (C) Microsoft Corp 2000. All rights reserved.
```

If the program has compile errors, they are displayed here. The next option is to generate an automated XML documentation file for the program. You do this with the **/doc** command:

```
C:\>csc /doc:rpt ch3_10.cs
Microsoft (R) Visual C# Compiler Version 7.00.9030 [CLR version
    1.00.2204.21]
Copyright (C) Microsoft Corp 2000. All rights reserved.
```

This command generates a simple documentation file, using the XML file format for this program. The resulting DOC file looks like this:

```
C:\Books\C-Sharp>type rpt
<?xml version="1.0"?>
<doc>
    <assembly>
```

```
        <name>CH3_10</name>
    </assembly>
    <members>
    </members>
</doc>
```

As you can see, that document file does not have a ton of information, but it does contain the assembly and all the classes found for that assembly. *Assemblies*, if you have not already discovered them, are the basic compilation unit of C#, used to maintain a module.

The assembly is the most basic unit available to the C# programmer. An assembly consists of one or more files that contain the functionality you want to expose to the application developer.

Entering **csc** with no arguments can help you to discover the final interesting options. If you do this, you get a complete listing of the possible commands. Here is the first screen output you see:

```
Microsoft (R) Visual C# Compiler Version 7.00.9030 [CLR version
    1.00.2204.21]
Copyright (C) Microsoft Corp 2000. All rights reserved.


                    Visual C# Compiler Options

                        - OUTPUT FILES -
/out:<file>             Output file name (derived from first source file
                        if not specified)
/target:exe             Build a console executable (default) (Short form:
                        /t:exe)
/target:winexe          Build a windows executable (Short form: /t:winexe)
/target:library         Build a library (Short form: /t:library)
/target:module          Build a module that can be added to another assembly
                        (Short form: /t:module)
/nooutput[+|-]          Only check code for errors; do not emit executable
/define:<symbol list>   Define conditional compilation symbol(s) (Short
                        form: /d)
/doc:<file>             XML Documentation file to generate

                        - INPUT FILES -
/recurse:<wildcard>     Include all files in the current directory and
                        subdirectories according to the wildcard
                        specifications
/main:<type>            Specifies the type that contains the entry point
                        (ignore)
```

3. Language Features

As you can see, the command-line compiler is powerful and is capable of doing anything the integrated environment can do. You should find that you increasingly migrate toward the command-line compiler as you become more accustomed to working with the language.

Creating a New Resource

One exciting thing about Windows programming was its introduction of the concept of resources. Resources are—besides things like memory, disk space, or drawing tools—files that can be loaded dynamically by the application. These files contain such information as string tables that allow you to map constant elements to string values, which suddenly made the job of customization and internationalization much easier.

C# was designed from the ground up to be easy to use and to extend. It is no surprise, therefore, that resource files were built into the system from the ground up. What is a surprise, however, is that the C# library designers chose to expose to the application programmer the functionality of writing new resource files. Before then, you had to create a resource template file (usually, an RC file), run it through the resource compiler, and then bind the resulting resource file into your application. C# allows you to follow that same road with the Resgen utility, which ships with the Visual Studio.NET system, but it also permits you to write your own resource files from within your application.

The possibilities offered by the dynamic creation of resource files are almost endless. You can use a resource file to store commonly used strings within an application, for example. Perhaps, in your application domain, a company always displays certain information in its printed documents. This information (the company name, address, phone number, and contact name, for example) can easily be stored and retrieved in a resource file. For agencies that deal with a number of different companies, you can have a single resource file dedicated to each one. By using a resource file to store all this information, you get to take advantage of all the built-in functionality and error checking of the CLR system.

In Listing 3.11, you see exactly how to create or open an existing resource file, how to write strings and floating-point numbers to that resource file, and then how to close the file. When you run the application, you find a file named English.resources in your directory. This resource file contains the information the application will write out. In the next example, I can then use this file to read in that information.

Listing 3.11 Writing a resource file programmatically.

```
using System;
using System.Resources;

class CH311
{
    public static void WriteEnglishResources()
    {
        ResourceWriter rw = new ResourceWriter("English.resources");
        rw.AddResource("PgmName", "CH3_11");
        rw.AddResource("PgmVer", 1.0 );
        rw.AddResource("PgmAuthor", "Matt Telles");
        rw.Write();
        rw.Close();
    }

    public static void Main()
    {
        WriteEnglishResources();
    }
}
```

Note that any valid object type may be written out using the **AddResource** method of the **ResourceWriter** class. If you want to store user-defined objects, you can use this method to write them out as well. Finally, C++ may use this method in unmanaged code to write out character strings or **blob** objects by using the **char** * or **byte[]** overloaded versions of the method. Check the documentation for the CLR for details on what types are permitted.

Reading Resources

Resources are the second-best things since sliced bread. You can load them into applications as part of the executable, or you can treat them as external files to be loaded dynamically at runtime.

In the preceding example, I showed how you can generate a simple resource file from an application. In this example, I examine how to use that resource file as well as how to embed a resource file in your application and use it directly from memory. The resource subsystem involves two different kinds of objects: the **ResourceManager** and the **ResourceReader**. The **ResourceManager** class features the ability to work with resources embedded in your application. The **ResourceReader**, as its name indicates, works with external resource files and reads them into your application.

The initial step of generating a resource file is illustrated in the preceding section, "Creating a New Resource." If that example were run again and modified to generate a different resource file, named English1.resources, you could see how to create both an internal and external resource. In the directory for this example, you can find both resource files, or you can take the time to generate a new one. In either case, Listing 3.12 shows you the application I work with to use both the internal and external resources.

Listing 3.12   Reading resources.

```
using System;
using System.Resources;
using System.Collections;

public class CH3_12
{
    public static void DumpResources( string resName )
    {
        // Open the resource file for reading.
        ResourceReader reader = new ResourceReader(resName);

        // Get an enumerator so we can step through all of the
        // resources in this file
        IDictionaryEnumerator en = reader.GetEnumerator();
        while (en.MoveNext())
        {
            Console.WriteLine("Resource Name: [{0}] = {1}", en.Key, en.Value );
        }
        reader.Close();
    }

    public static void DumpAResource( string resName, string keyName )
    {
        try
        {
        ResourceManager rMgr = new ResourceManager( resName,
            System.Reflection.Assembly.GetExecutingAssembly() );
            Console.WriteLine("Resource: {0}", rMgr.GetString( keyName ));
        }
        catch ( Exception e )
        {
            Console.WriteLine("Exception creating manager {0}", e );
    return;
        }
    }
```

```
public static void Main(string[] args)
{
    for ( int i=0; i<args.Length; ++i )
        DumpAResource( "English", args[i] );
    DumpResources("English1.resources");
}
}
```

A few tricks are involved in getting a resource into the application. For one thing, you need to change the compile step for the application to let the compiler "know" about the new resource that needs to be bound into the program. To do this, enter the following compile command on the command line:

```
C:\ >csc /res:English.resources ch3_12.cs
Microsoft (R) Visual C# Compiler Version 7.00.9030 [CLR version
    1.00.2204.21]
Copyright (C) Microsoft Corp 2000. All rights reserved.
```

This command compiles the C# program and also binds into it the resource file (in the **/res:** portion), named English.resources. The resource manager uses that internal resource to load the data I am looking for. Also, note that users are allowed to specify on the command line which resource string they are looking for. Here's a sample run of the program, showing the command line as well as the dump of the external resource file:

```
C:\ >ch3_12 PgmAuthor
Resource: Matt Telles
Resource Name: [PgmAuthor] = Matt Telles
Resource Name: [PgmVer] = 1
Resource Name: [PgmName] = CH3_11
```

Internal resource files are bound into the program and deployed with the executable that you deliver to the user. *External* resource files are separate files that can be loaded at run-time from any external file or files. You may have as many external resources as you like shipping with an application. For internal resources, there is no practical limit to the number, but each must be uniquely named.

As you can see, working with resources is really easy. To load internal resources, just create a new **ResourceManager** instance for your application and use the **GetString** method to retrieve the string you are interested in by the key which identifies that string. To work with external resources, load the file with a **ResourceReader** object and then retrieve a dictionary interface to the file. From there, you can enumerate the individual keys to retrieve a specific key by using the built-in functionality of the dictionary.

Using a Resource in Your Application

Having a resource is all well and good, but using one makes the whole resource system worth using. When a resource file is in your application, you can select from different languages to load in strings for users to view. Imagine being able to select your language and then have the system automatically switch to the correct greeting for your nationality.

In the example in this section, a series of resource files contain information in various languages—I want to greet users in the languages most comfortable to them. Of course, they do have to indicate what language they speak. (Mind reading isn't covered until the advanced class in C#—just kidding.) First, I need to write out the resource files. In Visual Studio, you can either directly create three resource files with the information listed here or use the following little program to do it quickly and easily. Listing 3.13 shows the application for generating the resource file.

Listing 3.13   Resource file generator application.

```
using System;
using System.Resources;
class LanguageResourceWriter
{
    public static void WriteEnglishResources()
    {
        ResourceWriter rw = new ResourceWriter("Eng.resources");
        rw.AddResource("Greeting", "Hello");
        rw.AddResource("Program Name", "CH3 Example 13" );
        rw.AddResource("Author", "Matt Telles");
        rw.Write();
        rw.Close();
    }
    public static void WriteSpanishResources()
    {
        ResourceWriter rw = new ResourceWriter("Span.resources");
        rw.AddResource("Greeting", "Hola");
        rw.AddResource("Program Name", " ejemplo 13 Chaperto el capitulo 3"
);
        rw.AddResource("Author", "Matt Telles");
        rw.Write();
        rw.Close();
    }
    public static void WriteFrenchResources()
    {
        ResourceWriter rw = new ResourceWriter("French.resources");
        rw.AddResource("Greeting", "Bonjour");
```

```
    rw.AddResource("Program Name", "Esample l'exemple 13 Chaperte le
        chapitre 3" );
    rw.AddResource("Author", "Matt Telles");
    rw.Write();
    rw.Close();
    }

    public static void Main()
    {
        WriteEnglishResources();
        WriteSpanishResources();
        WriteFrenchResources();
    }
}
```

Listing 3.14, on the other hand, shows the application I use to greet new users in the language of their choice.

Listing 3.14   The Greeting application.

```
using System;
using System.Resources;
using System.Collections;

public class CH3_13
{
    public static void DisplayGreeting( string resName )
    {
        try
        {
            ResourceReader reader = new ResourceReader(resName+".resources");
            IDictionaryEnumerator dict = reader.GetEnumerator();
            while ( dict.MoveNext() )
            {
                string s = (string)dict.Key;
                if ( s == "Greeting" )
                        Console.WriteLine("{0}", dict.Value);
            }
        }
        catch ( Exception e )
        {
            Console.WriteLine("Exception creating manager {0}", e );
        return;
        }
    }
```

```
public static void Main(string[] args)
{
    DisplayGreeting(args[0]);
}
}
```

As you can see from this application, using an external resource file, rather than one bound into the application, has one serious limitation (see the section "Reading Resources," earlier in this chapter): You cannot simply jump to a given resource in the resource file without stepping through all the resources individually. Also, note the need to cast the **Key** property of the enumerator to a string before comparing it. If you do not do this, the comparison will fail because the **Key** type is an object rather than a string.

Creating a New Resource Reader

Sometimes, you want to have all the functionality of a resource reader but not have to go through the hassle of creating a resource file—especially when you want to be able to use a resource file directly within your application, but need to be able to load into the reader different strings from different places. You could certainly create your own private class to manage your string information, but why would you want to do that when the power of the CLR **ResourceReader** class is at your beck and call?

In this example, you look at how to build your own **ResourceReader**-based class that allows you to treat it as though it were a "regular" resource-reading class in C#. Listing 3.15 shows how to derive from an interface, something you learned about in Chapter 2.

Listing 3.15   Creating a new resource reader.

```
using System;
using System.Resources;
using System.Collections;

public class MyResourceReader : IResourceReader, IEnumerable
{
    private Dictionary dict;
    private string fResName;

    void IResourceReader.Close()
    {
```

3. Language Features

```
        // We would do any resource cleanup here
    }

    IDictionaryEnumerator IResourceReader.GetEnumerator()
    {
        return dict.GetEnumerator();
    }

    IEnumerator IEnumerable.GetEnumerator()
    {
        return dict.GetEnumerator();
    }

    public MyResourceReader(string resName)
    {
        fResName = resName;
        dict = new Dictionary();
        dict.Add("Greeting", "Hello");
        dict.Add("Program", "My Program");
        dict.Add("Test Resource", "Fred");
    }
}

class CH3_14
{
    public static void Main()
    {
        MyResourceReader reader = new MyResourceReader("MyResources");
        IDictionaryEnumerator dict =
((IResourceReader)reader).GetEnumerator();
        while ( dict.MoveNext() )
        {
            string s = (string)dict.Key;
            if ( s == "Greeting" )
                Console.WriteLine("{0}", dict.Value);
        }
    }
}
```

As you can see from the listing, to implement the interface in the class, you need to implement not only all the **IResourceReader** member functions but also the **IEnumerable** member functions—which is why you have to implement the same method name (**GetEnumerator**) twice.

Deriving a Class from C# in Another Language

One fundamental philosophy of the .NET initiative is that everything can be used anywhere you like. The Common Language Runtime (CLR) is therefore available to any language written to access the .NET interface, and all languages are more or less interchangeable. To illustrate this concept, I can create a component in C# and then use that component as the base class for a class in another .NET language, such as managed C++ or VB.NET.

First, I need to create a component. As with all other Windows programming languages, C# implements components in the form of a dynamic link library (DLL). Fortunately, C# makes it easy to implement a DLL, by simply making you change your compile options slightly. Listing 3.16 illustrates the class I use to compile into a DLL.

Listing 3.16   A class in C# to make into a DLL.

```
namespace CSharpVBInterface
{
    using System;

    public class CH3_15
    {
        public CH3_15() {} // Constructor

        public int DaysInMonth( string monName )
        {
            if ( monName == "September" ||
            monName == "April" ||
            monName == "June" ||
            monName == "November" )
            return 30;

            if ( monName == "February" )
            return 28;

            return 31;
        }
        public string DayName( int dayNo )
        {
            switch ( dayNo )
        {
          case 0:
            return "Sunday";
          case 1:
```

```
      return "Monday";
   case 2:
      return "Tuesday";
   case 3:
      return "Wednesday";
   case 4:
      return "Thursday";
   case 5:
      return "Friday";
   case 6:
      return "Saturday";
}
      return "Unknown";
   }
   }
}
```

To build this class into a DLL file, use the following command-line argument:

```
C:\> csc /target:module CH3_15.cs
```

When the compile process is finished, you should have in your directory a file named CH3_15.DLL that you use to import into other languages. Note the use of the **target** switch in the compile line to specify that you want to build a DLL module rather than an executable.

You can now use this class in another language by importing the DLL (using **CsharpVBInterface.CH3_15**) and then deriving from it just as you would with any other local class.

Chapter 4

Programming Concepts

In Depth

Understanding how the syntax of a language works is the first step toward understanding how the language is best incorporated into your application development environment. The next step in learning how the system works is to understand the tools built into the language that you can use to develop your applications. These tools take the form of programming concepts that all languages support, such as controlling flow, naming, interfacing to other systems, and extending the language. Nearly all modern programming languages can do all these things. C# is certainly no exception to the rule. In this chapter, I examine all the built-in components that make the language successful. When you finish this chapter, you should know everything you need to know to write C# applications that do everything you want them to do. From this point on in this chapter, I explore the special extensions of the language that make specific programming problems easier to solve.

Besides either writing code that sets variable values or making calls to functions, people who develop software spend the majority of their time creating control structures that determine what functionality is called and in what order. Rarely does an application simply require you to do straight-line programming with no loops or conditionals or without reusing code. For this reason, you must understand how C# gives you control over all these aspects of your programming job. In the next section, take a look at what each aspect is and what C# offers you as well as any "gotchas" you might encounter while working with a particular feature.

Flow Control

The determination of which way a program executes based on certain criteria is called *flow control*, which consists of three different areas:

- Selection
- Iteration
- Conditional logic

The C# flow-control mechanisms are similar to those of other languages, but have a few unique twists and turns of their own. Although C# has all the standard elements you would expect—**if** statements, loops, and **switch** statements—it also contains several new mechanisms that are either borrowed from other languages or unique to the C# language. In this section, I examine the various flow-control mechanisms.

Selection

Selection allows you to take a variety of paths based on a given input value. For section handling, the main method C# allows is the **switch** statement, which has this general form:

```
switch ( expression )
{
    case value:
            statement
            break;
    case other-value:
            ...
    default:
}
```

Any programmer familiar with either C++ or Java should recognize this syntax. The differences for C# lie in the types of variables you can use in the expression statement, the way in which you break out of cases, and the way in which you jump from one case to another.

In C++ or Java, the **switch** statement can be used with integer or Boolean values. You may elect to test a value using the **switch** statement for virtually any data type, but the result must be an integer result. In C#, this restriction is not valid. You may elect to have a string variable in the **switch** statement or a floating-point value or anything in between. You can use strings in a **switch** statement or use enumerated values. The one thing you cannot put in a **switch** statement is an object that does not equate to an integral value. (You have to have some limits, I suppose.)

As a simple example of what you can do with **switch** statements in C#, consider this trivial program:

```
using System;

enum Color
{
    Red,
    Green,
    Blue,
    Yellow
}

class EnumSwitchTest
{
```

```
public static void Main()
{
    Color clr = Color.Red;

    switch ( clr )
    {
         case Color.Red:
        Console.WriteLine("Red");
        break;
         case Color.Blue:
        Console.WriteLine("Blue");
        break;
         case Color.Green:
        Console.WriteLine("Green");
        break;
         default:
        Console.WriteLine("Unknown");
        break;
    }
    String s = "hello";
    switch ( s )
    {
        case "Hello":
          Console.WriteLine("Hello yourself!");
          break;
        case "Goodbye":
          Console.WriteLine("Goodbye, come again!");
          break;
        default:
          Console.WriteLine("I don't understand {0}", s );
          break;
    }

    }
}
```

In this example, you can see where the language permits not only simple integer values but also enumerations and strings to be used in **switch** statements. The most interesting thing about this example is what it prints. The first **switch** statement obviously prints **Red** because that is the value of the enumeration. The second **switch** statement, however, prints **"I don't understand hello"** rather than **"Hello yourself"**, as you might expect. Careful inspection of the code shows why this happens: In the string being compared, the case does not match any of the **switch** statement cases. As a result, the string does not match. Strings are not compared in a case-insensitive manner in C# **switch** statements.

You can also move around in **switch** statements. The **break** statement examined in these examples allows you to terminate the processing of a case. However, unlike with C++ or Java, you cannot intentionally omit a **break** statement and have the code drop through to the next **case** label. What you can do is intentionally jump to a given **case** label in a **switch** statement. This feature is one that virtually no other language allows directly. You can jump to labels in other languages, but not to **case** statements. For example, you could do this:

```
switch ( I )
{
    case 0:  // Do some processing, then handle same as case 3
        DoSomething();
        goto case 3;
    case 1:
        DoSomethingElse();
        break;
    case 2:
        DoSomethingEntirelyDifferent();
        break;
    case 3:
        ProcessMore();
        break;
}
```

As you can see, the **switch** statement in C# has been streamlined to be more powerful and less errorprone than in any other language now available.

Iteration

Iteration, one of the most powerful forms of programming flow control, means repeating, and repeating in a programming language means some form of loop construct. C# provides several different forms of loop constructs, including one new one, the **foreach** statement. Let's take a look at each form of loop construct, examining the reasons for its existence and the possible limitations of using it.

The first loop construct is the **for** loop. The **for** loop in C# is closely related to **for** loops in C++ and Java; they permit you to initialize, test, and increment a variable within a single block. **For** loops were invented because the designers of the C programming language noticed a common theme among programmers. When the designers of C# came along, they recognized the utility of the **for** loop and continued its existence in a way that was virtually unchanged from its C++ or Java cousins.

The basic form of the **for** loop is:

```
for ( initial-value statement; test statement; increment statement )
    Statement or block;
```

The major difference between **for** loops in C++ and those in C# is in scope. In the original version of C++ (and the one that Visual C++ still adheres to), the scope of the variable defined in a **for** loop went until it hit the end of the block that contained the **for** loop; in other words:

```
for ( int I=0; I<10; ++I)
    Console.WriteLine("I = {0}", I )
// I is still valid here.
```

In C#, however, the **for** loop index counter would go out of scope immediately following the end of the **for** loop so that when the **for** loop terminated by hitting one of its termination values, the variable would no longer be valid.

Another interesting thing about **for** loops is that they need not be integer values. You may have double values, for example, in a **for** loop. In addition, you may even use characters or strings in a loop. Consider this example:

```
using System;

class ForTest
{
    public static int i;

    static string NextString()
    {
        switch ( i )
        {
            case 0:
                i++;
                return "Two";
            case 1:
                i++;
                return "Three";
        }
        return "";
    }
```

```
public static void Main()
{
   i = 0;
   for ( char c='a'; c<'z'; ++c )
   {
      Console.WriteLine("c = {0}", c );
   }

   for ( String s = "One"; s != "Three"; s = NextString() )
   {
      Console.WriteLine("S = {0}", s );
   }
}
}
```

Besides **for** loops, C# offers **while** loops and **do-while** loops. They are really the same thing—a loop that iterates until a given condition becomes false. The difference occurs when the test is made. In a **while** loop, the test is made at the top of the loop, which means that the loop executes zero or more times. In a **do-while** loop, the test is made at the bottom of the loop, which means that the loop is always executed at least once. The two loops look like this

```
while ( condition )
{
}
```

and this:

```
do
{
} while ( condition );
```

The only criterion for C# loops that is different from C++ or Java is that the condition statement must be a Boolean value. In C++, for example, you could write something like this:

```
int i = 10;
while ( i )
{
   Console.WriteLine("I = {0}", i );
   i--;
}
```

But this example is not valid in C#. You must explicitly check for a Boolean condition, such as **while (i > 0)**. Otherwise, the compiler generate an error.

In all C# loops, you can use the "break" statement to get out of a loop. For example, you could check the return value of a function in an "infinite" loop and leave it when a given condition became true, as in:

```
public static Boolean CheckValue ( int i )
{
    if ( i == 5 )
        return true;
    return false;
}

public static void Main()
{
    int i = 10;
    while ( true )
    {
        Console.WriteLine("I = {0}", i );
        i--;
        if ( CheckValue( i ) )
            break;
    }
}
```

The final loop type in C# is the **foreach** loop construct. Borrowed from Visual Basic, the **foreach** loop allows you to iterate over a collection or array (any class that implements the **GetEnumerator** method can use a **foreach** loop). The standard form of the **foreach** loop is:

```
foreach ( value var in collection-var )
{
}
```

As an example, if you have an array of integers and want to iterate over each of them, you might do something like this:

```
int[] array = {1,2,3,4,5};
Foreach ( int I in array )
{
    Console.WriteLine("Element {0}", I )
}
```

This statement would allow you to print in order each of the elements in the array. However, you can create your own classes that allow the use of a **foreach** loop. All you are required to do is to implement an enumerator class within your own class and return an instance of that enumerator class to the caller via the **GetEnumerator** method. Here's a simple example:

```
using System;
public class ACollection {
    int[] items;
    public MyArray() {
        items = new int[5] {1, 2, 3, 4, 5};
    }
    public CollEnumerator GetEnumerator() {
        return new CollEnumerator(this);
    }
    public class CollEnumerator {
        int current;
        MyArray array;
        public CollEnumerator(MyArray a) {
            array = a;
            current= -1;
        }
        public bool MoveNext() {
            current++;
            return(current < array.items.GetLength(0));
        }
        public int Current {
            get {
                return(array.items[current]);
            }
        }
    }
}
```

This simple class now allows you to use the **foreach** loop to get each element of the array. Although you obviously wouldn't bother to do this for a static array, you could implement something like this to maintain a collection of database records, or cache buffers. The **foreach** loop is a powerful iterative construct in C#.

Conditionals

One of the most necessary aspects of the programming world is the ability to choose among different options in source code. The way this choice is usually accomplished is via an **if** statement. An **if** statement permits you to compare, contrast, or otherwise differentiate between two different choices. After the comparison has been made, the **if** statement allows you to take the path that makes the most sense to you, given the values of certain variables.

C# allows you to use two different forms of the **if** statement. First, it permits any variation of the standard **if-then-else** logic block. Second, it implements the C++ conditional (also called the ternary) operator. Both these constructs allow you to make choices based on variable types. As with the loop constructs, C# requires that the content of an **if** statement be only a Boolean type. In other words, you can do this

```
If ( I != 0 )
{
}
```

but not this:

```
if ( I )
{
}
```

With this notable exception, C# **if** statements are exactly like any other language. They are always of this form:

```
If ( condition )
    [ statements ]
[ else
    statements ]
```

You may or may not have an **else** clause. You may have a single statement following the **if** (or **else**) or a block of statements.

The other form of the **if** statement is the conditional (ternary)operator construct. In C#, it takes this form:

```
condition ? <if true> : <if false>
```

The conditional operator, as you can see, is simple shorthand for the **if** statement; rather than write

```
if ( x == 1 )
    Console.WriteLine("X = 1");
else
    Console.WriteLine("X <> 1");
```

you can do this in a single line, saving some space in your application, by rewriting it as:

```
Console.WriteLine( x == 1 ? "X = 1" : "X <> 1");
```

In the "Immediate Solutions" example shown in the section "Using an **if** Statement," later in this chapter, you can see examples of saving space in this way. Why would you want to do this? That's a good question. Conditional operators certainly have their place, often helping to take the place of several nested **if** statements. If you were not to use them, however, you would end up with much more readable code that was considerably easier to maintain. Honestly, I would say that the conditional operator should be restricted to cases in which high performance is a requirement. The conditional operator can be turned into optimized code much more easily than a standard **if** statement can. The reason is simple: The conditional operator can be turned into direct assembly code, and an **if** statement must be optimized using compiler constructs.

Namespaces

The concept of namespaces is not new to C#. C++ has them, and Java uses the same concept. A namespace is a "wrapper" around one or more structural elements that gives them uniqueness. For example, you can do something like this in C#:

```
namespace XYZCorporation
{
    public class Corp1
    {
    }
    enum CorpEnum
    {
    }
}
```

This namespace could be implemented to wrap around all the classes defined for a given corporation. If the company then bought a bunch of third-party software from another vendor that implemented the same class names, the namespace wrapper would protect the developer by allowing her to still refer to the proper class by using complete naming conventions. Suppose that you have two namespaces, **Name1** and **Name2**. They both contain a class named **List**. In some languages, this class would be a showstopper because you could not find a way to make the whole thing compile and link without changing names. If you owned one of the bodies of source code, you could, of course, change your own stuff. The problem occurs when both offending bodies of code are third-party software.

With the exception of fixing the problem of name collisions, namespaces are no more than syntactic sugar. They don't add anything to the system, nor are they required. All the code you write lives within an "implied" namespace that exists for the current context of your code.

The only other thing worth mentioning about namespaces is that they replace the C++ **#include** notation (and are the equivalent of the **import** statement in Java). That is, with the use of the using keyword, you tell the compiler which namespaces and libraries of code you want to use in the system. The most common use of the **using** keyword is in including the **System** namespace so that you can use most of the common functionality of the System group. You can write the following:

```
Using System;
// Call the console class in the System namespace
Console.WriteLine("Hello world");
```

If you didn't want to use the **using** statement, you could alternatively write:

```
System.Console.WriteLine("Hello world");
```

C# understands that both these statements are equivalent and in either case calls the same method (**WriteLine**) of the class **Console**. The **using** keyword simply makes things easier to understand by eliminating the hierarchy of namespaces that would otherwise be required.

Another issue with namespaces and the **using** keyword is that you can use it to create aliases for namespaces. This feature is especially useful when you have two namespaces that have a common method or when a long list of nested namespaces amount to a really long name. Suppose that your corporation insists on having three levels of namespaces wrapped around each class you create:

```
namespace Corporation
{
    namespace Dept
    {
        namespace Project
        {
            class InternalClass
            {
            }
        }
    }
}
```

Normally, to refer to this class, you would have to type a line like this:

```
Corporation.Dept.Project.InternalClass
```

Typing this line obviously would give you writer's cramp in a few hours. C# has an answer to this nightmare, however. You could write

```
using DCN=Corporation.Dept.Project;
```

and then write

```
DCN.InternalClass
```

where DCN stands for, obviously, Dumb Corporate Name. This technique would certainly cut down on your typing. Namespaces provide convenience. Don't turn them into a nightmare in your code.

Unsafe Code

Perhaps this heading should be in a warning block. Don't use unsafe code—it's unsafe. In C#, however, the unsafe code label is applied whenever you want to use elements the new language does not allow, but that you need to use in order to get your job done. For example, if you want to call out to a Windows API function from C#, you might need to use a pointer to iterate through a returned block of structures. The problem is, of course, that C# doesn't have pointers. Only C++ has them. Yet, you need the ability to call that function to get your job done. This area is where C# really shines. It helps you get your job done, as long as you understand the risk you are taking.

The purpose of unsafe code is to accomplish something that is, by its nature, an unsafe thing to do. One good example is in using pointers. Another is in using memory that cannot be safely collected by the garbage-collection mechanism in the C# runtime environment. Something worth noting is that even in an unsafe environment, C# doesn't allow you to violate type safety (with one notable exception: void pointers). Thus, you can write:

```
unsafe
{
    Int[] x = new int int[10];
    Int *px = &x;
}
```

In this case, you've defined an unsafe block that allows you to assign a pointer to an array so that you can step through it in typical array fashion, by incrementing the pointer. However, you still cannot do the following:

```
unsafe
{
    int *x = new int[10];
}
```

An integer pointer is not an array; therefore, you cannot assign an array to it. You cannot delete the array under any circumstances. You must allow it to be garbage-collected.

Sometimes, you need to be able to create a pointer to call an external function. The problem, of course, is that the pointer is pointing at a block of memory that can be garbage-collected or moved in memory without your knowing about it. In cases like these, C# provides for the **fixed** statement, which allows you to pin a pointer in memory until you are done with it. Here's how you use it:

```
unsafe
{
    int[] x = new int[10];
    fixed(int xp = &x)
    {
        CallAFunctionWthAPointer(xp);
    }
}
```

As you can see in this example, the **fixed** keyword pins the pointer in memory until you are done with it, which happens to be the closing brace of the **fixed** statement. You cannot fix a pointer in memory forever. Fixing a pointer is a temporary step: The lock stays in place only for the duration of the block, which is surrounded by the **fixed** keyword.

Extending the Language

No language is perfect. No language is so well designed that it never encounters something it needs to be used for that it doesn't do well. In cases like these, the language must be extended in some way to allow it to accomplish the tasks that need to be done in the real world. C# provides two different methods, managed C++ and COM components, for doing tasks the language doesn't intrinsically do.

Managed C++

First, a word of explanation—managed C++ is not really C#. It happens to be a compiler that ships with C# and allows C++ developers to use many of the same techniques and library components as they did in C#. However, managed C++ is a different compiler and is really C++ in the .NET environment rather than a C# extension. The reason I cover it in this book is that managed C++ is a natural extension to the use of C# programming concepts in the .NET environment.

What is managed C++? Simply, managed C++ is the way in which you can run C++ programs in a managed environment, as C# does. Managed C++ gives you access to many C# extensions, such as garbage collection, the CLR, and exception handling from the ground up. Managed C++ does follow standard C++ rules, in that you can use the new operator to create objects. However, classes marked as being available for garbage collection may not use the **delete** operator to delete those objects. C++ classes in a managed environment can also contain properties and use the managed components of the C# library, such as the **String** class.

To utilize the managed C++ environment, you must be using the newest version of the C++ compiler, which ships with Visual Studio.NET and the NWGS (the .NET SDK framework on its own) SDK versions of the compiler. You must further use the COM+ enhancements to the C++ language by using the **/com+** compiler directive. Rather than go into great detail about managed C++ because it is not really a part of the C# system, I suggest that you look instead at the "Immediate Solutions" example in the section "Using Managed C++ Code," later in this chapter.

COM Components

The Common Object Model (COM) and Windows is a topic that evokes great emotion from developers. In general, people either love the idea or hate it, but no middle ground seems to exist. The issue is moot, however, because COM is here to stay, whether you like it or not. Because COM is here to stay, you should leverage the capabilities it offers you whenever you can take advantage of them in your own development work. C# is built around a core of COM and exposes that functionality wherever it can. Interfaces, binary components, and versioning are all obvious facets of the COM-like nature of C#.

C# makes creating COM components easy. It also makes utilizing existing COM components in new applications easy. This ease of use is important because many companies have a vested stake in their legacy COM components. Using a COM component in C# is a simple matter of converting it into a type library that the C# runtime environment and compiler understand and then linking the resulting metadata into your application. From there, you simply use the COM library as if it were just another C# namespace.

First, you need to convert the COM component into something the C# compiler understands. To do this, you use the TLBIMP utility. This utility, named for a *type library import* facility, allows you to convert a standard COM DLL or EXE file into a loadable metadata assembly for use in C#. Assume that a COM component is implemented as a DLL that you created for your project at work some time ago. This component, found in the COMPANY.DLL file, implements a library named **Company**. Within this library are two COM classes, named **Class1** and **Class2**.

Here are the simple steps you would take to use the **Class1** and **Class2** COM components in your new C# application:

1. Locate the DLL file that contains your COM components. In this case, assume that it is in a directory named **ComComponents** and is named COMPANY.DLL.

2. Run the TLBIMP program on the DLL file to create a new DLL file you can import into your application:

```
TLBIMP ComComponents\COMPANY.DLL
```

This line creates a new COMPANYLIB.DLL file in your application directory. You can now use this component in your C# application by simply referencing it in the application, like this:

```
using System;
using CompanyLib;
```

3. Create an instance of the class you want to use in your application. In this case, use the **Class1** COM component, as in:

```
Public static void Main()
{
    Class1 c1 = new Class1();
}
```

4. You can call methods on a COM component either directly or indirectly. To use them directly, simply call the proper method from the IDL file of the COM component:

```
c1.CallAMethod();
```

5. Alternatively, you can call any method of a class by using the **Invoke-Method** method to call whatever method you want. You simply call the method with the dispatch ID of the method you want to call. You can retrieve this information from the IDL file for that COM component. This following simple example calls the first method (**dispatch id = 1**) in the COM object:

```
c1.InvokeMethod( "[dispid=1]", BindingFlags.InvokeMethod, null, c1, null )
```

One last note about COM objects: When the object is loaded into the C# environment, some types are automatically converted from their C++ or COM equivalents into C# data types. Table 4.1 shows a list of the COM types and what they are mapped to in C#.

Table 4.1   Conversion types between COM and C#.

COM Type from Type Library	C# Type
char, Boolean, small	sbyte
wchar_t, short	short
long, int	int
hyer	long
unsigned char, byte	byte
unsigned short	ushort
unsigned long, unsigned int	uint
unsigned hyper	ulong
single	float
double	double
HRESULT, SCODE	uint
HRESULT *, SCODE *	ushort
BSTR	string

To get a better feeling for how COM and C# interface, check out the "Immediate Solutions" example in the section "Invoking COM Components from C#," later in this chapter. The example should make clear the ease with which COM objects can be used in C#.

I hope that by now you have a pretty fair understanding of the constructs and concepts of using C#. At this point, you can move on to the examples in the "Immediate Solutions" section of this chapter to get quick and easy solutions, with code, to many of your programming problems.

4. Programming Concepts

Immediate Solutions

Using a **switch** Statement

The most basic selection element in C# is the **if** statement. The **switch** statement is the next logical step after simple **if** statements. As you will see, **switch** statements in C# are much more powerful than their C++ or Java counterparts. For example, you can base a **switch** statement on any type of data. Therefore, you can use a **switch** statement with a character string, which makes decision trees vastly easier.

In the first example, look at the various ways in which **switch** statements can be used, including the idea of jumping between switch labels. Listing 4.1 shows most of the possible uses for a **switch** statement.

Listing 4.1   Using a switch statement.

```
using System;

class CH4_1
{
    public static void MakeADecision( string s )
    {
        switch ( s )
        {
            case "Hello":
                System.Console.WriteLine("Hello yourself!");
                break;
            case "Goodbye":
                System.Console.WriteLine("Goodbye!!");
                break;
            default:
                System.Console.WriteLine("Huh?");
                break;
        }
    }
    public static void MakeANumericDecision( string s )
    {
        int nVar = 0;

        if ( s == "Hello" )
            nVar = 1;
```

```
    if ( s == "Goodbye" )
        nVar = 2;
    if ( s[0] == '#' )
    {
        string temp = "";
        for ( int i=1; i<s.Length; ++i )
            temp += s[i];
        nVar = temp.ToInt16();
    }

    switch ( nVar )
    {
        case 0:
            goto default;
        case 1:
            case 2:
            MakeADecision( s );
            break;
        default:
            System.Console.WriteLine("Number {0}", nVar);
            break;
    }

}

public static void Main(string[] args)
{
    if ( args.Length > 0 )
        MakeADecision( args[0] );
    MakeANumericDecision("#0");
    MakeANumericDecision("#1");
    MakeANumericDecision("#2");
    MakeANumericDecision("#3");
}
}
```

As you can see from the highlighted line, **switch** statements allow you to jump around to different labels within the switch. These statements also can have multiple labels that handle a single case. One interesting difference between C++ and C# is that you cannot do the following:

```
switch ( x )
{
    case 0:
        System.Console.WriteLine("Case 0");
```

```
case 1:
        System.Console.WriteLine("Case 1");
}
```

No **break** statement appears between the statement in the first case and the second case line. In C++, this statement would simply drop through and execute the second print statement. In C#, you get an error at compile time for allowing the code to drop through a statement, which looks like the following:

```
error CS0163: Control cannot fall through from one case label ('case :"Case
    0"') to another
```

This is just another example of how C# protects you from known silly mistakes made in the past by other developers. You can still go to another label, but you must use the **goto** construct to do so.

Using a for Loop

The **for** loop exists in most modern programming languages in one form or another. The **for** loop allows you, the programmer, to create a loop that initializes, increments, and validates a loop counter. **For** loops can be used for simple indices or for more complicated loops involving arrays and elements. C# has several variants of the **for** loop, which I illustrate in this example.

Listing 4.2 shows several ways in which a **for** loop can be used in C#. First, you see an example of a simple **for** loop with all its components. Next, you see an example of two sets of **for** loops that show how initialization can be skipped. Finally, the sample code shows a **for** loop that works with a non-integer value and shows how to skip the increment phase.

Listing 4.2   Using a for loop.

```
using System;

class CH4_2
{
    public static void Main()
    {
        // Illustrate a simple for loop that counts from 1 to 5
        for ( int i=0; i<5; ++i )
            System.Console.WriteLine( "I = {0}", i );
```

```
// Illustrate two loops to first find a letter in a string
// and then to print it out until a space is encountered.
// This shows you how to skip initialization in the second
// loop
int nPos = 0;
string s = "this is a test of the emergency broadcast system";

for ( nPos = 0; nPos < s.Length; ++nPos )
   if ( s[nPos] == 'b' )
      break;
for ( ; nPos < s.Length; ++nPos )
{
   if ( s[nPos] == ' ' )
      break;
   System.Console.Write(s[nPos]);

}
System.Console.WriteLine("\n");

// Finally, illustrate how to use the for loop for something
// other than an integer and how to change the increment
int state = 0;
for ( double d = 0.0; d < 5.0; )
{
   System.Console.WriteLine( "D = {0}", d );
   switch ( state )
   {
      case 0:
         d += 0.1;
         break;
      case 1:
         d += 0.2;
         break;
      case 2:
         d += 0.5;
         break;
   }
   state ++;
   if ( state > 2 )
      state = 0;
}
}
}
```

If you look at the output from this program, you see some interesting results:

```
I = 0
I = 1
I = 2
I = 3
I = 4
broadcast

D = 0
D = 0.1
D = 0.30000000000000004
D = 0.8
D = 0.9
D = 1.1
D = 1.6
D = 1.7000000000000002
D = 1.9000000000000001
D = 2.4000000000000004
D = 2.5000000000000004
D = 2.7000000000000006
D = 3.2000000000000006
D = 3.3000000000000007
D = 3.5000000000000009
D = 4.0000000000000009
D = 4.1000000000000005
D = 4.3000000000000007
D = 4.8000000000000007
D = 4.9
```

As you can see, the incrementing of a floating-point number is a tad strange in C#, which is something to be aware of in working with floats. You can never be quite sure how the compiler will generate instructions to add fractional numbers. The printing of the word *broadcast* shows how you can easily parse a string in C#. Of course, the first block illustrates the most basic use of a **for** loop.

Using a **foreach** Loop

The **foreach** loop allows programmers to quickly and easily work their way through arrays in order to process each element in the array. Although the **foreach** statement is new to C++ and Java programmers, it is quite familiar to VBScript programmers. This statement, a simple shorthand technique for the **for** loop, automatically uses the **GetEnumerator** interface to step through a given array or collection.

In Listing 4.3, you can see several different examples of using the **foreach** statement in your code. This listing contains an example of iterating over an array of integers as well as over an array of strings. Finally, the listing contains an example of iterating over one of the C# CLR collections, the **Dictionary** class.

Listing 4.3   Using a **foreach** loop.

```
using System;
using System.Collections;

class CH4_3
{
   public static void Main()
   {
     // First, an array of integers
     int[] arrayOfInt = { 1, 2,3, 4, 5 };
     foreach ( int i in arrayOfInt )
     {
        Console.WriteLine("Int {0}", i );
     }

     // Now, how about an array of strings?
     string[] arrayOfStr = { "Hello", "Goodbye", "Why me?" };
     foreach ( string s in arrayOfStr )
     {
        Console.WriteLine("String {0}", s );
     }

     // Finally, let's look at a dictionary collection
     Dictionary d = new Dictionary(10);

     d.Add( 100, "Science");
     d.Add( 200, "Math");
     d.Add( 300, "English");
     d.Add( 400, "History");
     d.Add( 500, "Gym");

     foreach ( DictionaryEntry de in d )
     {
        Console.WriteLine( "Entry Key {0} Value {1}", de.Key, de.Value );
     }
   }
}
```

As you can see, the **foreach** statement is quite powerful. Because it is scripting shorthand for using the C# enumeration facilities, it allows you to create your own classes that support a **foreach** statement. All you need to do is to implement the **GetEnumerator** method in your class and provide the appropriate type of enumerator to retrieve data. Then, you can use **foreach** as if your class were built into the language.

Using a **while** Loop

The **for** loop in C# does initialization, validation, and incrementing all in one place. For many programming problems, however, doing all that work is unnecessary. Sometimes, you simply want to repeat a process until a given condition becomes true or false. For times when you want only to check a given condition, you should use the **while** loop. It checks to see, at the top of each loop increment, whether the loop should continue. If the condition is false coming into the loop, the loop is never executed. For this reason, you say that a **while** loop executes zero or more times.

In Listing 4.4, you can see several different examples of a **while** loop. In each case, the **while** loop executes over a given type of expression. In the first example, the **while** loop is used simply to emulate a **for** loop. In the second example, the **while** loop operates with a Boolean value that is set in response to the value of a variable. In the final example, the **while** loop is not executed because the condition is met before the first iteration.

Listing 4.4   Using a while loop.

```
using System;
class CH4_4
{
    public static void Main()
    {
        // An example of a simple while loop
        Console.WriteLine("Loop 1:");
        int i = 0;
        while ( i < 5 )
        {
            Console.WriteLine("I = {0}", i );
            i++;
        }

        // A while loop with a boolean
        Boolean flag = false;
```

```
i = 0;
Console.WriteLine("\nLoop 2:");
while ( !flag )
{
    if ( i > 5 )
    flag = true;
    Console.WriteLine("I = {0}", i );
    i++;
}

// A loop that will never execute
Console.WriteLine("\nLoop 3: ");
while ( i < 5 )
{
    Console.WriteLine("I = {0}", i );
    i++;
}
}
}
```

The last example is probably most frustrating to beginning programmers. The loop looks like it should work, but does not ever execute. The reason is that, unlike a **for** loop, the **while** loop does not initialize the index counter (the *i* variable, in this case) to 0 before starting the loop. As a result, the variable retains its previous value and is already greater than 5 when the loop is encountered. To understand why this happens, look at the output from the program:

```
Loop 1:
I = 0
I = 1
I = 2
I = 3
I = 4

Loop 2:
I = 0
I = 1
I = 2
I = 3
I = 4
I = 5
I = 6

Loop 3:
```

As you can see, the index value is already 6 when the third loop comes into play. As a result, the loop is never executed. You will find that **while** loops are especially useful when you want to be sure that a given set of code is executed several times only if a condition has not already been met. You can think of a **while** loop as an **if** statement and a **goto** statement, as in this example:

```
Label: If (condition) then
      Statements
Goto Label
```

Using a do Loop

The **do** loop is quite similar to both the **for** loop and **while** loop. Unlike the **for** loop, however, it does not initialize anything, nor is it automatically incremented. Unlike the **while** loop, the **do** loop checks its state at the bottom of the loop rather than at the top. As a result, the **do** loop is always executed at least once. If you recall, the **while** loop could execute zero or more times. The **do** loop, therefore, executes one or more times, no matter what the initial conditions of the system.

In this example, I explore some variations of the **do** loop. For example, you can have a **do** loop that increments a value. Another example contains a **do** loop that checks a Boolean flag. The final example shows the contrast of the **do** loop to the **while** loop, by having a condition that is false initially.

Listing 4.5 shows three examples of how **do** loops are used in C# applications. Note that the test is in the **while** portion of the loop at the bottom of each loop block. As you can see, the results are different than for the **while** loop cases.

Listing 4.5   Using a do loop.

```
using System;
class CH4_5
{
    public static void Main()
    {
        // First, a simple do loop that
        // increments a counter
        int i = 0;
        Console.WriteLine("Loop 1:");
        do
        {
            Console.WriteLine("I = {0}", i );
            i ++;
        } while ( i < 5 );
```

```
    // Next, the same case, but using a
    // boolean rather than an index

    i = 0;
    Boolean done = false;
    Console.WriteLine("\nLoop 2:");
    do
    {
       Console.WriteLine("I = {0}", i );
       i ++;
       if ( i > 5 )
          done = true;
    } while ( !done );

    // Finally, a conditional that is true before
    // You get into the loop
    do
    {
       Console.WriteLine("Into Loop 3");
    } while ( !done );

  }
}
```

The output from this program is:

```
I = 0
I = 1
I = 2
I = 3
I = 4

Loop 2:
I = 0
I = 1
I = 2
I = 3
I = 4
I = 5
Into Loop 3
```

The **do-while** loop (unlike the **while** loop) always executes at least once, as you can see with the third loop. The **done** flag is already set before the program gets to the beginning of the loop, but the program goes through the loop once anyway.

Using an if Statement

The **if** statement is by far the most common conditional statement in computer programming. Programmers usually talk about things in terms of the **if-then-else** logic that applies to any given condition in a system. C# offers a rich variety for the **if** statement and allows many different variants of it. As mentioned in the "In Depth" section, earlier in this chapter, C# has two different kinds of **if** statements. First, the normal **if-then-else** statement contains at least the **if** portion of the statement and may contain an addition **else** portion. The second kind of **if** statement is called the *conditional* (or *ternary*) operator statement. This example shows both these kinds of **if** statements so that you can better understand how to use this powerful programming concept.

Listing 4.6 shows three different forms of the **if** statement. First, a typical **if** statement uses a Boolean value to check a setting and prints a status-information line if the value is true. Note that with a Boolean expression, you do not need to compare the value to a true or false value, just as with C++ or Java. The expression itself evaluates into a true or false value. The second example, an **if-else** block, illustrates that you can compare Boolean values to true or false—you just don't have to. In this case, the statement is false, so the **else** statement is executed. Finally, the third example shows the use of the conditional operator to do some checking of a value in-line and make an appropriate decision on which string to output to the user.

Listing 4.6   Using an if statement.

```
using System;

class CH4_6
{
    public static void Main()
    {
        Boolean bValue = true;

        // Test a simple boolean, print  a result
        if ( bValue )
        {
            Console.WriteLine("bValue is TRUE");
        }

        // Test a boolean, print a result if true, otherwise
        // a different result.
        bValue = false;
        if ( bValue == true )
        {
```

```
        Console.WriteLine("bValue is TRUE");
    }
    else
    {
        Console.WriteLine("bValue is FALSE");
    }

    // A ternary if statement
    Console.WriteLine("bValue is {0}", bValue ? "TRUE" : "FALSE" );

  }
}
```

The output from this program is:

```
bValue is TRUE
bValue is FALSE
bValue is FALSE
```

Note how the shaded line is used in this program. This is the conditional, or ternary, operator. It takes this form:

```
expression ? (what to do if true) : (what to do if false)
```

You may find that the ternary operator is confusing. If so, don't use it. The optimization gained by this small change is not worth the possible confusion to anyone having to read the program. As you can see when I talk about nested **if** statements and nested ternary operators, this situation can quickly get ugly.

Using Nested **if** Statements

Although **if** statements are powerful and convenient ways to test a given value and execute a given block of code, sometimes they are not enough by themselves. If you have a set of possible cases, you have two choices. You can use a **switch** statement to evaluate the possibilities, or you can use a set of nested **if** statements that evaluate the problem. The decision is usually a matter of how the comparisons are structured. For example, if you are simply going to perform a given task based on the value of a variable, the **switch** statement is ideally suited for your task. On the other hand, if you have several possibilities, all of which are mutually exclusive, you probably want some form of nested **if** or nested **if-then-else** statements.

In this example, I explore some possibilities of nested **if** statements of various sorts. The nested **if** world has three real possibilities. First, you see the simple case of an **if** statement within the context of another **if** statement. Next, you see the case of an **if** statement within the context of an **if-else** block. Finally, you see the ugly case of a nested ternary operator statement. Listing 4.7 shows examples of how to do all these things.

Listing 4.7   Using nested if statements.

```
using System;

class CH4_7
{
    public static int PrintTwo( String[] args )
    {
        Console.WriteLine("Argument 1 {0} Argument 2 {1}", args[0], args[1] );
        return 2;
    }
    public static int PrintOne( String[] args )
    {
        Console.WriteLine("Argument 1 {0}", args[0]);
        return 1;
    }
    public static int PrintNone()
    {
        Console.WriteLine("You didn't supply the right number of arguments!");
        return 0;
    }

    public static void Main(String[] args)
    {
        // Check for arguments. Use a nested if to handle
        // two special cases.
        if ( args.Length == 2 )
        {
         Console.WriteLine("Argument 1 {0} Argument 2 {1}", args[0], args[1] );
            if ( args[0] == "Hello" )
                Console.WriteLine("Well, hello yourself!");
        }

        // Alternatively, you could have a nested if-else statement
        if ( args.Length == 2 )
        {
         Console.WriteLine("Argument 1 {0} Argument 2 {1}", args[0], args[1] );
        }
        else
```

```
        if ( args.Length == 1 )
            Console.WriteLine("Argument 1 {0}", args[0] );
        else
            Console.WriteLine(
                "You didn't supply the right number of arguments!");

    // You can do the same thing with a ternary operator.
    // Warning: Its ugly!
    Console.WriteLine("Printing... {0}", args.Length == 2 ? PrintTwo(args) :
                        args.Length == 1 ? PrintOne(args) :
            PrintNone() );
    }
}
```

First, take a look at the output from the program, when run with no arguments:

```
You didn't supply the right number of arguments!
You didn't supply the right number of arguments!
Printing... 0
```

Now, take a look at what happens when you run the program with two arguments:

```
Argument 1 Hello Argument 2 world
Well, hello yourself!
Argument 1 Hello Argument 2 world
Argument 1 Hello Argument 2 world
Printing... 2
```

As you can see, all three forms of the **if** statements work the same way. One other thing worth mentioning about this nested **if** example is the block highlighted at the end of the listing. This code sample is far and away the ugliest one you are ever likely to run into in your programming career. (At least I certainly hope so.) Don't write code like this in real world production applications.

Dropping through a **switch** Statement

One of the common problems in implementing conditional logic through a **switch** statement is that you often need to handle the same problem for different cases. For example, you might have to do some initialization work in one case, but not in another, and yet after that always do the same thing. In these cases, using a language like C++, you would implement this kind of initialization problem by having a **case** statement handle the special initialization work and then "drop through" to the next **case** statement to handle the other work. C# does not permit you to drop through a **switch** statement because the designers of the language have found that it is an error-filled proposition; for example:

```
switch ( x )
{
    case 0:
      // Do some stuff
    case 1:
      // Do some other stuff
      break;
    case 2:
      // Yet more stuff
}
```

The question is whether the developer really meant to drop through from **case 0** to **case 1** without stopping. Or did an inadvertent mistake lead that person to leave out the **break** statement following the **case 0** code? The compiler cannot tell the intentions of the developer in this case.

The C# designers understood the need to share code among **switch** statements. They therefore allowed for the possibility of "dropping through" **switch** statements, but chose to implement the process in a way that made clear your intention in writing the code. In Listing 4.8, you see an example of how to drop through a **switch** statement by going to a specified case in the **switch** statement. The neat thing about this example is that it shows how even labels are object-like in C#. You can go to a string label in this example.

Listing 4.8   Dropping through a **switch** statement.

```
using System;

class CH4_8
{
    public static void Main(String[] args)
    {
        // Handle the input
        if ( args.Length == 0 )
        {
            Console.WriteLine("No arguments supplied!");
            return;
        }

        Boolean done = false;
        for ( int i=0; i<args.Length && done == false; ++i )
        {
            switch ( args[i] )
```

```
        {
            case "Hello":
                Console.WriteLine("Hello there!");
                break;
            case "Goodbye":
                Console.WriteLine("Oh, ok, guess you gotta go!");
                goto case "Finished";
            case "Welcome":
                Console.WriteLine("Well, thank you!");
                break;
            case "Finished":
                Console.WriteLine("All Done!");
                done = true;
                break;
        }
    }
  }
}
```

Note the shaded line in the code listing. That is how you tell the compiler and runtime environment that you want to transfer control from the current case to that particular case in the **switch** statement. If you run this program, you get this output:

```
C:\>ch4_8 Hello Goodbye Welcome
Hello there!
Oh, ok, guess you gotta go!
All Done!
```

Notice how the program terminates when the **Goodbye** element is processed. This example shows another way to end a **for** loop.

Breaking Out of a Loop

One of the problems with loops that have defined beginnings and endings is that sometimes you need to get out of the loop without finishing tasks. In one simple example, you discover an exceptional case in the data you are processing and cannot continue. In another case, you might read in 20 different commands, but find in the middle a command that the user used to terminate the run. This situation happens often in the parser business. C# was designed from the ground up to be an industrial-strength language. As a result, the designers of the language considered issues such as getting out of loops and presented developers with several options for doing so.

You have three general ways to get out of a loop:

- Terminate the loop normally by processing the required number of elements or changing the status of a variable.

- Use the **break** statement to terminate the loop by ending the processing immediately.

- Have a secondary condition that terminates the loop, such as a **for** loop that allows for a condition ending that loop without going through all its iterations.

Listing 4.9 shows examples of how you can use these various techniques to break out of a loop without completing it in the normal way. You can see the various possibilities and how they work in the real world.

Listing 4.9   Breaking out of a loop.

```
using System;
class CH4_9
{
    public static void Main(String[] args)
    {
        // How to break out of a for loop, two ways.
        Console.WriteLine("Loop 1:");
        for ( int i=0; i<5; ++i )
        {
            if ( i == 3 )
                break;
            Console.WriteLine("I = {0}", i );
        }

        Boolean done = false;
        Console.WriteLine("Loop 2:");
        for ( int i=0; i<5 && done == false; ++i )
        {
            if ( i == 2 )
                done = true;
            Console.WriteLine("I = {0}", i );
        }

        // Another method using a goto
        done = false;
        int counter = 0;
        Console.WriteLine("Loop 3:");
        do
        {
            if ( counter == 5 )
                goto handle_done;
            Console.WriteLine( "Counter: {0}", counter );
```

```
        counter ++;
        goto not_done;

handle_done:
        done = true;
not_done:
        Console.WriteLine("End of Loop 3");

    } while ( !done );

    Console.WriteLine("Loop 4:");
    for ( int i=0; i<5; ++i )
    {
        if ( i == 2 )
            i = 5;
        Console.WriteLine("I = {0}", i );
    }
  }
}
```

Two elements—the **goto** statements in the third loop and the index modification in the fourth loop—show you techniques that work in C#, but probably should be avoided. **Goto** statements create ugly code, and modifying an index in a **for** loop is generally frowned on because of the difficulties of debugging the code. Just because things can be done doesn't mean that they *should* be done.

Creating a Namespace

C# introduces the notion of namespaces, which solve several problems in the programming world. For one thing, namespaces avoid the problem of name collision. This problem occurs when you use several third-party libraries, all of which use classes or objects of the same name. For example, you might have a windowing library, a serial communications library, and a utility library, all of which implement a linked list class named **List**. How would the compiler or linker know which **List** class you mean if you write something like this:

```
List obj = new List();
```

On the other hand, if you were to be able to tell the compiler that you want to use the windowing library version of the **List** class, by writing something like the following, the compiler would have little problem understanding what you mean:

```
Windowing.List = new Windowing.List();
```

The ability to create namespaces is quite powerful, and the process is easy in C#. In Listing 4.10, you can see how to create a namespace in a program and then use it, fully qualified, within another class.

Listing 4.10   Creating a namespace.

```
using System;

namespace MyNamespace
{
    public class Foo
    {
        int _Value;
        public Foo()
        {
            _Value = 0;
        }
        public int getValue()
        {
            return _Value;
        }
    }
}

class CH4_10
{
    public static void Main()
    {
        MyNamespace.Foo foo = new MyNamespace.Foo();
        Console.WriteLine("Foo.Value = {0}", foo.getValue());
    }
}
```

The C# convention is to have a single namespace in a file, although, as you can see, there is no particular reason for it. This convention simply makes life easier if you keep namespace files separate from other files so that you can quickly and easily find the right file in which to make modifications. Note that when you use a class from a namespace, you must be sure to use the whole name of a class, which is of the form *<namespace>.<class>*.

Note that you can have anything within a namespace. Classes, enumerations, and structures can all be created within a namespace. For that matter, you may have nested namespaces. Consider the simple enhancement to Listing 4.10 that I show in Listing 4.11.

Listing 4.11   Nested namespaces.

```
using System;

namespace MyNamespace
{
    namespace Nested
    {
        public class Foo
        {
            int _Value;
            public Foo()
            {
                _Value = 0;
            }
            public int getValue()
            {
                return _Value;
            }
        }
    }
}

class CH4_10
{
    public static void Main()
    {
        MyNamespace.Nested.Foo foo = new MyNamespace.Nested.Foo();
        Console.WriteLine("Foo.Value = {0}", foo.getValue());
    }
}
```

In this example, you can see that one namespace is embedded inside another. This embedding is perfectly okay, and it lets you put all your corporate code, for example, under a single namespace that is the name of the corporation. Note, however, that when you use the nested namespace, you must fully qualify both namespace names.

Incorporating a Namespace into Your Application

If you have created a namespace or have a namespace you were given to work with, the next issue is figuring out how best to incorporate that namespace into your application so that you can use it most easily and efficiently. For this purpose, the C# language provides the **using** statement. It allows you to shortcut the long naming conventions of namespaces and to make life easier for developers to understand what is going on. You've seen uses of the **using** statement in earlier examples in this book. However, I have never used it for discriminating between the internal and external versions of namespaces.

In Listing 4.12, I show you how to create your own namespace and then call a method within that namespace as well as one from outside that namespace. In this way, you can see how the **using** statement shortcuts the long naming convention needed in most cases. You can also always qualify a namespace call if the compiler is unsure of what you mean.

Listing 4.12 Incorporating a namespace into your application.

```
using System;

namespace MyNamespace
{
    class CH4_11
    {
      public static void WriteLine( String s )
      {
          Console.WriteLine(" Calling Internal WriteLine");
          Console.WriteLine( s );
      }


      public static void Main()
      {
         WriteLine("This is a test");
         Console.WriteLine("This is another test");
      }
    }
}
```

As you can see from the shaded block, you can call a method from within a method of the same name, as long as the compiler is sure of which namespace version you are trying to call. If these were nonstatic methods, of course, the compiler would be able to know what you meant by the class of the object you used to call the method. For static methods (functions, more accurately), you have to tell it which one you mean if multiple methods have the same name. In the **Main** function of the application, you can see the usage of two methods of the same name. One is local to this namespace and does not need to be qualified. The other is interpreted as a local call unless you fully qualify it. In each case, however, you do not need to write out the full name (**System.Console.WriteLine**) because of the using statement that brings in the full **System** namespace.

The output from this little application is, not surprisingly:

```
Calling Internal WriteLine
This is a test
This is another test
```

Creating an Alias

Imagine that you work in a big corporation that has adopted C# as its standard development environment. (This situation isn't too farfetched if you are reading this book.) In this case, the likely scenario is that you are creating multiple namespaces that all fall within the corporate umbrella namespace. Furthermore, the individual namespaces often contain nested namespaces, which can cause something like the following to occur when you're trying to refer to the class you want in an application:

```
CorporationXYZ.DepartmentABC.WindowingProject.MyClasses.Foo foo = new
CorporationXYZ.DepartmentABC.WindowingProject.MyClasses.Foo();
```

Obviously, within a short period, writing things like this over and over will drive a programmer insane, not to mention encourage a serious case of carpal tunnel syndrome. A better way of doing things has to exist. As it turns out, the C# designers felt the same way. To get around the problem of typing and retyping namespace names, the designers allowed for the concept of an alias. An *alias* is simply a replacement string for a longer string that allows you to use one in place of the other. In Listing 4.13, you see an example of a bad set of nested namespaces along with an alias that makes the names more manageable. In addition, you can see how that namespace is used to differentiate between a global class and a local one.

Listing 4.13   Creating an alias.

```
using System;
using FooClasses=MyNamespace.Nested.MyFooClasses;

namespace MyNamespace
{
   namespace Nested
   {
      namespace MyFooClasses
      {
         public class Foo
         {
```

```
        int _Value;
        public Foo()
        {
            _Value = 0;
        }
        public int getValue()
        {
            return _Value;
        }
      }
    }
  }
}


class ch4_12
{
    public static void Main()
    {
        FooClasses.Foo myFoo = new FooClasses.Foo();
        Console.WriteLine("Value {0}", myFoo.getValue());
    }
}
```

As you can see, the alias line is shown in the shaded text, which reduces the ugly namespace name collection of **MyNamespace.Nested.MyFooClasses** all the way down to **FooClasses**. (This technique should save you from lots of trips to the doctor.)

Related solution:	Found on page:
Creating a Derived Class	57

Using the unsafe Keyword

A rather annoying issue about moving to a new language that is a derivative of a language you are already using is your inability to use the constructs you are accustomed to because someone has deemed them improper in the "new regime." The C# architects were well aware of the resistance to a new language that could replace C++. For this reason, they elected to create a language that permitted C++ programmers to continue to do what they had done in the past, as long as they were made aware that it was not the world's greatest idea. In many ways, this decision may have been a mistake because the majority of problems with C++ can be traced to its roots and its compatibility with C. However, because the designers gave you this ability, you should understand how to take advantage of it.

The **unsafe** keyword in C# allows you to write (almost) standard C++ code within the context of a C# application. This rule has numerous exceptions because you still cannot do anything that would cause a fundamental language problem. For example, although you can use pointers, as you are used to doing in C++, you cannot allocate blocks of memory the way you used to. For example, you cannot write

```
char *s = new char[10];
```

within the context of a C# application because you have no way to convert from a character pointer to a character array directly. You still must allocate an array of characters the "new-fashioned" way:

```
char[] s = new char[10];
```

This technique isn't really a hardship, however, because you are quite capable of using that character array as a pointer. You just have to know the secret to doing it. In this example, I explore the case of a C++ programmer having an overwhelming desire to use pointers in a C# application and showing how to accomplish this task. Listing 4.14 shows an application that uses pointers in a C# application.

Listing 4.14   Using the unsafe keyword.

```
using System;

class CH4_13
{
    public static unsafe String UnsafeCodeExample( String s )
    {
        int   len = s.Length;
        char[] str = new char[len+1];
        string stemp = "";
        int nPos = 0;

        fixed(char* sptr = str)
        {
            // Copy the string in backward
            for ( int i=len-1; i>=0; --i )
            {
                sptr[nPos++] = s[i];
                sptr[nPos] = (char)0;
            }
        }
```

```
            // Now, copy it back
            for ( int i=0; i<len; ++i )
                stemp += sptr[i];
        }
        return stemp;
    }
    public static void Main()
    {
        String s = UnsafeCodeExample("This is a test");
        Console.WriteLine( "Reversed: {0}", s );
    }
}
```

Here's the output from this program so that you can see that it really works:

```
Reversed: tset a si sihT
```

Two important parts of this application are worth studying. The first is the first shaded line in the listing, which illustrates the use of the unsafe keyword in C#. The unsafe keyword indicates to the compiler that you are using techniques and programming capabilities that are frowned on in C#. These capabilities includes pointers because they are considered bad news in the new programming world.

The second important concept to take away from this illustration is in the use of the fixed block to retrieve a pointer to a character array and use it as a C++ pointer. The fixed statement permits you to "fix" a pointer to an array and pin it in memory without allowing it to be garbage-collected for the scope of the statement. In this case, the scope is the entire shaded block because it is the beginning and end of the fixed block.

Of course, after you have a pointer to a character string, you can do whatever you want to it, just as you could in C++, including running off the end of the array, which would cause the usual garbage, rather than valid data, to be used. Arrays of characters allocated by C++ do not contain any sort of length information; C# has no such capability when you're using C++ pointers. For example, take a look at this block:

```
string s = "Another test";
char[] str = new char[s.Length+1];
for ( int i=0; i<s.Length; ++i )
{
    str[i] = s[i];
    str[i+1] = (char)0;
}
```

4. Programming Concepts

```
fixed(char* sptr = str)
{
    for ( int I=0; I<20; ++I )
        Console.WriteLine("S[{0}] = {1}", I, sptr[I] );
}
```

In this little code snippet, you can see that I am walking all over the end of an array of characters. If you were to put something like this in a real application, its output would contain the first set of characters from the real string followed by whatever junk happened to be in memory following that block. No exceptions would be thrown for an invalid array index, no errors would be caught, and you would have no way to recover from any catastrophic failure that resulted. This scenario is the downside of using unsafe code.

Calling Out to a Win32 Function

An annoying feature of Java is that it makes writing Windows applications difficult. Of course, a large part of the problem is that Java was built from the ground up to be platform independent. That's understandable, but the majority of programmers are still Windows programmers. Programmers love Java for its power and flexibility and portability. (A contradiction is in there someplace, but you can ignore it.) Programmers also hate Java, though, because they can't do what they used to do in Visual C++. The designers of C# understood this conundrum. They gave you the capability to call out to the Windows API in order to call on the functionality and prebuilt code that is in the API, without having to wait for them to encapsulate that power in a C# component.

The designers of C# were smarter than previous people (such as the designers of C). Rather than give programmers headers that contained all the functionality of the Win32 API wrapped up in C#-appropriate types so that they could use the functionality, the designers improved the process. The C# language contains built-in marshalling code that allows you to call any sort of a function defined externally in a dynamic link library (DLL). You can then not only use the functionality of the Win32 API but also call a function that exists in one of your own prebuilt DLLs that have been around for some time. The only issue, then, is how you go about accomplishing this task.

In this example, you see a simple way to use the Win32 API. For obvious reasons of space, this example is not complicated. It only calls out to a single API function and prints some of the resulting information. However, in this simple example, you see how to use a Windows API structure, pass a pointer back and forth between the Windows API and C#, extract data from the returned pointer, and deal with errors that might occur.

Listing 4.15 shows the complete functionality of the application, from defining the interface to the Win32 API function to making the call, casting the result to a proper type, and printing the returned data. Take a look at the listing, short as it is, and then you can look at the components of that listing.

Listing 4.15   Calling out to a Win32 function.

```
using System;
using System.Runtime.InteropServices;


class CH4_14
{
    [System.Runtime.InteropServices.StructLayoutAttribute
            (LayoutKind.Sequential, CharSet=CharSet.Auto)]
    public struct _SYSTEM_INFO
    {
        public int dwOemID;
        public int dwPageSize;
        public int lpMinimumApplicationAddress;
        public int lpMaximumApplicationAddress;
        public int dwActiveProcessorMask;
        public int dwNumberOfProcessors;
        public int dwProcessorType;
        public int dwAllocationGranularity;
        public short wProcessorLevel;
        public short wProcessorRevision;
    }

    [sysimport(dll="Kernel32.dll")]
        unsafe private static extern void
            GetSystemInfo([marshal(UnmanagedType.LPVoid)]uint* bufptr);

    public static unsafe void Main()
    {
        try
        {
            _SYSTEM_INFO si = new _SYSTEM_INFO();
            GetSystemInfo( (uint *)&si );
            Console.WriteLine("Processor Type = {0}", si.dwProcessorType );
            Console.WriteLine("Number of Processors = {0}",
                    si.dwNumberOfProcessors );
            Console.WriteLine("Processor Level = {0}", si.wProcessorLevel );
            Console.WriteLine("Processor Revision = {0}",
                    si.wProcessorRevision );
        }
```

```
      catch ( Exception e )
      {
         Console.WriteLine("Exception Caught! {0}", e );
      }
   }
}
```

The interesting points in this example are shown in the shaded blocks. For one thing, you first need to define the structure, **_SYSTEM_INFO**, that is used by the API function. This structure is what the API function is expecting. Translating a structure from the Windows API version to the C# version can sometimes be a challenge. In this case, the structure contains several **DWORD** values. Notice that these values simply translate into an **int** in C#, which makes life easier. Other values are **WORD** values in the C structure, which become short values in the C# version.

The next interesting part is the declaration of the actual API function. As you can see, C# took a page from the Visual Basic handbook and allows you to define not only the prototype for the function, but also the location of the function in the system dynamic link library (DLL)—in this case, **"kernel32.dll"**. The runtime environment knows how to find system libraries; other ones must be in a valid path or have a hard-coded path for them. Finally, you instruct the COM interface in C# how to marshal the data between the C API function and the C# interface. In this case, you simply call the structure pointer to be a void pointer, and it is cast to the appropriate type later in the program.

Working with the Win32 API functions in C# is sometimes a difficult task, simply because of the need to convert between pointers and types that do not directly exist in C#. In these cases, as shown earlier in this chapter, you need to use the unsafe keyword and go back to "standard" C and C++ to get at the data you want. Fortunately, the language gives you the power and flexibility to do what you need to do to get the job done.

Using Managed C++ Code

One of the nicest things about the .NET environment is that you can use many of the same classes, no matter what language you are working in. Although this book is about C#, the concept of managed C++ code comes into play because you can create in this "new" version of C++ some reusable components that contain many of the same elements as C#. For example, you can create garbage-collected objects in the new C++ as well as create properties and use the entire CLR library. To accomplish this task, of course, extensions were added to the language syntax by the Visual C++ team.

4. Programming Concepts

In this example, I explore some things you can do with the new C++ compiler that ships with Visual Studio.NET. Creating these types of applications is easy using the integrated development environment (IDE), but in this simple example, I explore how to do it the hard way, using the command-line interface. Listing 4.16 shows a simple managed C++ application that shows the kinds of things you can do in managed C++. To compile this application, you need to make sure that you are using the new C++ compiler that ships with Visual Studio.NET and not the one that came with Visual Studio (or Visual C++) version 6.0. To compile a managed C++ application, you need to use the **/com+** option on the compile line. In this case, the compile line looks like this:

```
C:\>cl13 /com+ ch4_15.cpp
```

Notice that this file has, rather than a .cs extension, the standard C++ .cpp extension. Managed C++ is just that—C++. It is not a C# application, although, as you can see in Listing 4.16, it uses many of the same techniques and library calls.

Listing 4.16   A managed C++ application.

```cpp
#include <stdlib.h>
#include <stdio.h>

#using <mscorlib.dll>

using namespace System;

__gc class CH4_15
{
    String *s;
    int     mAge;
public:
    CH4_15()
    {
        s = new String("This is a test");
        mAge = 21;
    }
    ~CH4_15()
    {
    }
    void Print()
    {
        Console::WriteLine("String is {0}", s );
    }
    __property int get_Age()
```

```
    {
        return mAge;
    }
    __property void set_Age(int age)
    {
        mAge = age;
    }
};

int main(void)
{
    CH4_15 *app = new CH4_15();
    app->Age = 25;
    app->Print();
    printf("Age = %d", app->Age);
}
```

As you can see from the listing, substantial differences exist between working in C# and working in managed C++. For one thing, you are back to the notion of having a **main** function in the program. For another, you are using the -> notation rather than the . (period) notation for accessing methods. However, quite a few similarities exist between the managed C++ and C# code. You implement the **using** statement to import the **System** classes, although you are required to do it the C++ way, using a namespace with the **using namespace** statement. The **__gc** keyword is new too. It indicates to the compiler that this managed class will be garbage-collected when it goes out of scope. You no longer use the **delete** command to get rid of managed C++ classes.

One of the more interesting extensions in managed C++ is that you can now use properties in C++ as you would in C#. Note the **__property** keyword in front of the **get** and **set** functions for **Age**. This keyword indicates to the compiler that you are defining a property called **Age** that is both readable and writeable. Just like in C#, you can define properties that either read-only or write-only or any combination of the two. Note how I use the **Age** property in the main function at the bottom of the listing.

The last interesting thing is that you can still use the **WriteLine** method of the **Console** class in **System** in managed C++, although the syntax is a bit different. Note that rather than have the . operator used to get the scope of the class static method **WriteLine**, you use the C++ scoping operator (**::**). Other than that, the managed C++ application could easily be mistaken for a regular C++ one—or for a C# application, for that matter.

Invoking COM Components from C#

Certainly the most powerful aspect of the C# language and environment is that you can easily extend it using the flexibility and power of the Component Object Model (COM) system. COM permits you to write binary portable objects, which can be used in a number of different environments, such as C++, Visual Basic, VBScript, and ASP. COM also happens to form the core of the .NET environment. As a result, C# (not surprisingly) makes using COM components in your applications easy. Besides using system COM components, such as the ADO library or the components that make up Microsoft Excel or Microsoft Word, you can also use your own components in C#. This is a boon for companies that have lots of money invested in legacy COM objects.

In this example, I show you how to create a COM object, using a standard Visual C++ ATL COM project. I add a single method to that COM component and then create an instance of the COM component in a simple C# application. All the source code for the C++ COM component is on the accompanying CD-ROM as well as the project to build it. In this example, I simply show you the one method I add in the IDL and C++ files.

First, create the COM component in your Visual Studio (or Visual C++) 6.0 or 7.0 environment. Add to the COM component a single method named **ReturnAnInt**. This method should have a single argument, an **[out]** parameter called **pInt** of type int pointer. The IDL for this method looks like this:

```
interface ICSharpComTest : IDispatch
{
    [id(1), helpstring("method ReturnAnInt")] HRESULT
                ReturnAnInt([out]int *pInt);
};
```

Note that the class is called **CSharpComTest** and that the interface for the class is called **ICSharpComTest**. The implementation for the method is shown in the next code snippet:

```
STDMETHODIMP CCSharpComTest::ReturnAnInt(int *pInt)
{
    *pInt = 10;

    return S_OK;
}
```

The only other thing you need from the IDL file is the GUID for the class, which is found in a block of code that looks like this:

```
library COMTESTLib
{
    importlib("stdole32.tlb");
    importlib("stdole2.tlb");

    [
        uuid(3951140F-555A-4E4D-8EC9-8315AF089FBD),
        helpstring("CSharpComTest Class")
    ]
    coclass CSharpComTest
    {
        [default] interface ICSharpComTest;
    };
};
```

Copy the selected line; you will need it when you create the C# application. Now, compile the new COM component and register it (the IDE does this for you automatically when you compile and link the component). The only thing left to do is to create the actual C# application to use this COM component:

```
using System;
using COMTESTLib;

class MainClass
{
    public static void Main()
    {
        CSharpComTest com = new CSharpComTest();
        ICSharpComTest intf = (ICSharpComTest)com;
        int i=0;
        intf.ReturnAnInt(ref i);
        Console.WriteLine("Integer: {0}", i);
    }
}
```

It all looks pretty simple, doesn't it? You just use the library for the class from the COM component DLL and then create the object as a class. Retrieve the interface you want by simply casting the object to the correct interface name, and you can call the methods as if the interface were a standard C# class.

The only problem, of course, is that if you want to compile and run this application, you get an error. The compiler has no idea where to find the **COMTESTLib** class or what it means. To get around this minor problem, I turn to another utility in the C# development environment, called Tlbimp (for *type library import*), which can convert a COM component (or other DLL) into an assembly that the C# compiler can use to import information about what classes it can find in the DLL and how to call them. You use this utility as follows:

```
Ctlbimp COMTest\debug\comtest.dll
TlbImp - TypeLib to COM+ Assembly Converter Version 2000.14.1812.10
Copyright (C) Microsoft Corp. 2000.  All rights reserved.

Typelib imported successfully to COMTESTLib.dll
```

Note that the argument to this utility is the DLL file constructed by the VC compiler when you originally built the COM component. In this case, I have the DLL file in a subdirectory under the current directory, and the DLL file is in the Debug directory of that directory (COMTest). The COMTESTLib.dll file is created in the local directory; it is the one with the C# program in it.

Finally, you need to bind in this type library information when you compile the C# program. To do this, you need to modify the compile options you use when compiling the C# program. Use these command-line compile options:

```
C:\ csc /reference:COMTestLib.dll ch4_16.cs
Microsoft (R) C# Compiler Version 7.00.8905 [NGWS runtime 2000.14.1812.10]
Copyright (C) Microsoft Corp 2000. All rights reserved.
```

As you can see, the instruction tells the compiler to "reference" the type library to get the information it needs in order to construct the class and its interfaces. Finally, you can simply run the resulting executable file in the runtime environment. You see this output:

```
Integer: 10
```

Success! The COM component was created and called properly and the result marshaled over into the C# environment. All that from a few lines of simple code. That is impressive, isn't it?

Related solution:	*Found on page:*
Creating a New Form	280

Chapter 5

Delegates and Events

In Depth

The most powerful and exciting new constructs in C# are tied up in the delegate- and event-handling systems. These systems permit you to write infinitely expandable and flexible systems that take away much of the grunt work of allowing developers to write more generic code and implement specific solutions in more specific classes. This concept, the core of object-oriented programming, allows you to worry more about the flow of the system at the lowest level, without worrying about how the specifics of individual tasks will be handled.

In this chapter, I examine two specific concepts that are extremely important in understanding how C# works and how best to use it to accomplish what you need to get done in your daily workday. When you look at the Common Language Runtime (CLR) graphical user interface (GUI) elements in Chapter 9, you need to have the concepts in this chapter down cold. If you don't, you will quickly get lost in the event-handling process.

Delegates

In the United States, we elect delegates to represent us in our legislature. These delegates, often called Congresspeople (or sometimes Congress-critters, depending on who is doing the talking) stand in for us to vote on issues that we do not have time to consider. Likewise, in the United Nations, one or two delegates discuss matters of national importance in a forum that would be impossible if entire populations were present to represent countries. What do Congress and the United Nations have in common? Each has a stand-in that represents a placeholder for a larger body. C# has delegates as well. These delegates are placeholders for functionality that exists outside the realm of the class or method using the delegate. In short, a delegate can be thought of as the equivalent of a function pointer in C++ or C.

What is the purpose of a delegate? C# contains two kinds of objects: those that create change and those that respond to change. A *delegate* acts as the conduit between the two kinds of objects, funneling information from one side to the other. C# delegates are class methods and can be either static or class instance methods. Your delegate can therefore keep track of its own state, by maintaining information in the object to which it belongs.

I could easily continue talking about delegates, but you probably don't have the time to read about the nitty-gritty details when you are trying to get things to work. As a result, take a look at a simple delegate and see what is going on under the covers.

The first thing you need to use to create a delegate is the new **delegate** keyword. This keyword is used in the same way you would use the **typedef** keyword in C++:

```
public delegate void ADelegate();
```

What is going on here? What you have defined in this statement is a simple delegate type. This is not a method or a function of any sort. In fact, it comes closer to being a definition of a function pointer. You can't directly use a delegate—you need to associate a function with one. This process has two steps. First, you need to have a delegate in a class that acts as the conduit pointer for use by the delegate source. Next, you need to associate a real, live method (in this class or another one) that acts as the concrete functionality that is called when the delegate is invoked.

Let's look at each part of the problem. First, create a simple class that uses a delegate to accomplish some internal task from an external source:

```
class DelegateUser
{
    public ADelegate del;  // (1)
    public DelegateUser() // The constructor
    {
        del = new ADelegate(); // (2)
    }
    public void CallADelegate()
    {
        if ( del )
            del(); // (3)
    }
}
```

Notice the three lines marked with comment numbers. Each of these lines represents one piece of what is necessary in your own code to implement and use a delegate. The first line, marked with (1), shows how to define the delegate variable in your class. In this case, you are making the delegate member variable public. The reason becomes clear when you examine the other side of the equation, the implementation of the delegate method. Like nearly all objects in C#, a delegate is a pointer, which means that simply declaring it is not enough. You must then allocate a new object for the pointer to point at. Otherwise, the pointer is null and you cannot use it. The allocation process takes place in the line marked with (2). As you can see, a delegate is simply a pointer to an object.

In fact, the **delegate** keyword simply creates a new class derived from the **System.Delegate** class. When you write the line

```
public delegate void ADelegate();
```

you are really creating a new class named **ADelegate**, which is derived from **System.Delegate**:

```
public class ADelegate : System.Delegate
{
    public void Invoke();
}
```

Fortunately, all of these methods are automatically generated behind the scenes. All you, the developer, need to think of is that the delegate is a function pointer. To use the function pointer, therefore, you just invoke it as shown in the code listing with the line marked (3). From the perspective of the delegate user, this step is all that is involved in creating and using a delegate.

The Other Side of the Mirror

The implementation of the functionality of a delegate takes place outside the class that uses the delegate. You can change the functionality for a given delegate function without the original class knowing anything about what is going on. All the source class knows is that it has a function pointer that it is supposed to invoke and that an object out there will need to be notified when that pointer is invoked. What about that other side, however? How do you create a delegate method and associate it with the delegate pointer? That's what I show you next.

Assume that you are implementing a class and want to be notified when a given change takes place. Assume also that the change takes place in the method **CallADelegate** in the class that is receiving the notification. You do not want to have the **delegate** class know about your class because you want the flexibility to change how the change is handled when it occurs. Fortunately, the designer of the original class set up this wonderful delegate that is invoked when the change occurs. The question is "How do you associate your method with the delegate?" Take a look:

```
class MyDelegateHandler()
{
    public static void Handler()
    {
        // Do something when the change happens
    }
}
```

This class simply implements a single static method (a function, in C and C++ parlance) that you want to use when the change occurs. This method doesn't have to be associated with an object because it is static. As a result, you can do anything you want in the method, as long as you don't need any state information kept.

At this point, you have both sides of the problem covered: A delegate is defined and invoked when a change occurs in a given class, and another class is the target of the delegate when the change occurs. The problem, of course, is how to get from one to the other. How do you associate the **delegate** function pointer with the function you have created? That's the final step in the process:

```
public class OurClass
{
    public static void Main()
    {
      // Step 1: Create the source
      DelegateUser du = new DelegateUser();
      // Step 2: Create the delegate handler
      DelegateUser.ADelegate del = new
          DelegateUser.ADelegate(MyDelegateHandler.Handler());
      // Step 3: Associate one with the other
      // Delegates are "chained" by "adding" them to the delegate list.
      du.del += del;
}
```

As you can see, after you have defined both sides of the problem, you need to take three steps to make all the pieces work. Step 1 creates the source object, the class that contains the delegate. Remember that in your constructor for the class, you create the delegate pointer and allocate memory for it. Step 2 creates the delegate handler. This association is the one I have talked about between the function pointer type (**ADelegate**) and the method you will use (**MyDelegateHandler.Handler**) when the delegate is invoked. The final step is the odd-looking statement that sets the delegate pointer in the class to the delegate handler you have created in Step 2.

Why do you need to use the **+=** statement to associate a handler with a delegate pointer? Wouldn't it make more sense to have the **=** statement simply assign the delegate handler to the pointer? The answer is yes, it would, but good reasons exist for doing it this way. For one thing, as you soon see, you can create multiple handlers for a given delegate and associate them all so that they are called in sequence when the delegate is called. Try doing that with a simple function pointer! You take a look at this concept in a few pages, when I discuss multicast delegates, and in the "Immediate Solutions" example in the "Chaining Events" section, later in this chapter.

An Example

Take a look at a complete but simple example of why you might use a delegate. In this case, you create a delegate pointer, associate it with a method, and then pass that delegate to another class in order to have a "callback function" when something important happens:

```
public delegate SwapItems( ref string s1, ref string s2 );
public class Sort
{
    public Sort()
    {
    }
    public SortItems( string[] array, SwapItems func )
    {
        // Swap the first and last elements
        func( ref array[0], ref array[array.Length-1]);
    }
}
public class MyApp
{
    public static void Swap( ref string s1, ref string s2)
    {
        string temp = s1;
        s1 = s2;
        s2 = temp;
    }
    public static void Main()
    {
        string[] strings = {"One", "Two", "Three"};
        SwapItems si = new SwapItems( Swap );
        Sort sort = new Sort();
        Sort.SortItems( strings, si );
    }
}
```

You look at more complex and full examples in the "Immediate Solutions" section, later in this chapter, so feel free to leap ahead and look at those.

As you can see in this simple example, you can use a delegate directly without having to create an instance of the delegate within a class. A delegate can also be thought of as a function pointer that can be passed around. In this example, you have a simple swap function that exists independently of the sort routine in which it is being used. This is the simplest example of a delegate—using it as a true function pointer that points to one static method in a class. At this point, you know all the basic information needed to implement and use delegates. Now it is time to get into the power of them.

You may have noticed that C# uses two different kinds of delegate: single and multicast. Let's take a look at each type and see what the difference between them is and how you can use each one to your best advantage.

Single Delegates

A single delegate, which is a simple function pointer, can be used as a placeholder for a function or method from a class to another class. Until now, you have looked only at delegates that are static methods. There is no reason, however, that a delegate can't be a method of an instantiated class that is nonstatic. To show you an example, consider the delegate shown in the following code snippet:

```
public delegate Boolean CheckValue( int nValue );
```

Suppose that you have a simple class that implements a method that conforms to this function signature:

```
class Foo
{
    public Foo() {}
    public Boolean Check( int nValue )
    {
            return true;
    }
}
```

You can still use this method as a delegate function, despite the fact that it requires an object in order to use the method. Let's see how to do that:

```
Foo foo = new Foo();
CheckValue cvd = new CheckValue( foo.Check );
```

At this point, you can use the **cvd** variable anywhere that a **CheckValue** delegate can be used. This is the major difference between delegates and C or C++ function pointers: You have no way to associate a nonstatic method of a class with a function pointer. You can have method pointers in C++, but they suffer from the problem that you cannot assign simple functions to them. It's an either-or proposition. C# avoids that problem by allowing either a static or nonstatic method to be used interchangeably. If you use a nonstatic method, of course, you have access to the full data stored in the object for which the method is being called. The object calling the delegate, however, has no idea whether an object is attached to the delegate pointer it is using.

Multicast Delegates

If all delegates did was act as a conduit between one class and another, they would be valuable enough. However, C# goes this task one better by allowing for the concept of multicast delegates. A *multicast* delegate permits you to chain together several delegate handlers and have them called in sequence when you want to have a notification message sent. You can do this in C++ or Java, of course, but you would need to know how many handlers to call or have to have each handler call the next one in the chain. In C#, this process is done for you behind the scenes.

As you may recall, when you assign an event handler to a delegate pointer, you do so using the **+=** operator. At the time I brought up this subject, it didn't seem to make sense. Why "add" a handler to a pointer? With the notion of multicast delegates, however, the use of this operator makes considerably more sense. You add in order each handler you want to have invoked, and the delegate-handling system deals with making sure that the process takes place as you intended. Let's look at a simple example. First, look at the standard class to handle delegate calls:

```
class DelegateUser
{
    public ADelegate del;
    public DelegateUser()
    {
        del = new ADelegate();
    }
    public void CallADelegate()
    {
        if ( del )
            del();
    }
}
```

Next, you have a class to implement the handlers. Before, you always had a single method to use the delegates. In this case, you have two:

```
class MyDelegateHandler()
{
    public static void Handler1() { Console.WriteLine("Handler1"); };
    public static void Handler2() { Console.WriteLine("Handler2"); };
}
```

Finally, you have to make the association, which is where the **+=** operator comes into play most importantly:

```
public class OurClass
{
    public static void Main()
    {
        DelegateUser du = new DelegateUser();
        DelegateUser.ADelegate del1 = new
            DelegateUser.ADelegate(MyDelegateHandler.Handler1();
        DelegateUser.ADelegate del2 = new
            DelegateUser.ADelegate(MyDelegateHandler.Handler2();
        du.del += del1;
        du.del += del2;
}
```

Notice in the example that you are still calling the delegate in the **CallADelegate** method. How can this be? After all, the delegate simply calls the first method assigned to the delegate (or perhaps the last—you can never be sure), doesn't it? The answer is no, it doesn't. In fact, if you were to run this little application (or run the "Immediate Solutions" example in the section "Creating Multiple Delegates," later in this chapter), you would see the following output:

```
Handler1
Handler2
```

One important note about multicast delegates: They are required not to return a value and must use the **void** return type. The reason soon becomes apparent as I discuss delegates and event handlers.

This example shows the power of delegates. They can do an amazing amount of work for you. Delegates are good elements to know about. Where the real power of delegates comes into play, however, is in the C# event-handling system, the next topic of discussion.

Events

An *event* is the outcome of something happening. Events are a way of letting the world know that something going on is worth mentioning to other people. The development world doesn't really involve many other people, of course—you generally have only a single user. Events consist of two parts: an object that performs an action that wants to let any object interested know that the action is being performed and one or more objects that want to know when that particular action is performed.

In a given application, many objects are doing many tasks. How can any individual object know which of these many objects might be interested in knowing of a change in that particular object's state? For C#, the answer lies in the twin constructs of event sources and event handlers.

Event Sources

An *event source* is an object that notifies other objects or tasks that something has changed. The event source determines when the notification takes place or, in fact, whether the notification even takes place. Event notification in C# takes the form of callbacks. In other systems, event handling is more in the form of *publish-and-subscribe*: The event source sends out a general message when it wants to notify other objects of a change, and then anyone interested in the message reads it and interprets it. Although this mechanism is powerful and quite useful, it is not the most efficient way of doing things. Publish-and-subscribe requires that you have a generalized broadcast mechanism and that all objects receive all messages.

In C#, each event source maintains one or more events that it publishes. These events are noted in the source code and documentation for the object, although the specifics of when the events are fired is not necessarily known. Events in C# are considered to be asynchronous from the perspective of the caller. A callback does not occur when the caller wants it to, but rather when the event-firing object decides that something of note has happened.

Event Handlers

Event handlers receive event notifications. When an event source decides that something has happened that merits notification, all the event handlers that have registered for notification of that event are told about the occurrence. An event handler may be either a static or nonstatic method of a class. In the case of a static method, event handlers simply respond to a given event source and take a course of action based on the information passed to the handler. For nonstatic event handlers, the entire state of the object can be considered when working with the event, allowing an object to make intelligent decisions for a given event.

As a simple example, consider an event handler that deals with account underflows. This event occurs when the owner of an account posts a debit (withdrawal) from the account that would make the account negative. When this situation happens, you might want to send the user an email message to notify her that unless the account is brought to balance that day, she will be charged a fee. To do this, of course, the event handler would need to be notified of the fact that a debit had driven the balance negative. Imagine, however, that the writer of the accounting component had not considered the need to track an event, such as the account going negative. Instead, the writer simply dealt with the more general case of firing an event for the object whenever the balance of the account changed, through either a credit or a debit.

If you had created an additional object to "monitor" accounts and keep track of the balance yourself, you could maintain an internal state of the balance of the account. That would allow your monitoring application to track what the balance is as each credit or debit is posted to the account. This way, you could quickly and easily watch for changes that will drive the account to have a negative balance. In this way, event handling is a powerful way to extend classes without using any form of inheritance.

Events and Delegates

You might be asking yourself what the relationship between events and delegates is. The answer is quite simple: The entire event mechanism in C# is based around delegates. A delegate acts as the conduit between the event source and the event-handler methods. The delegate carries the information about the event to the event handler and allows it to carry information back to the event handler. In C#, unlike in some other languages, events can be a two-way street, as you see in the "Immediate Solutions" example in the section "Firing an Event," later in this chapter.

Events are simple to implement. To show you the process you need to use, look at a simple example of an event, firing the event, and receiving notification that an event has occurred. In this example, a simple class contains an event that can be fired. The first two elements you need are the event itself and a delegate that is called when the event is fired. Here are the definitions that are needed in the code to handle these two items:

```
// This is the event itself
public event ValueChangedEventHandler Changed;

// Allow a handler for the event
public delegate void ValueChangedEventHandler();
```

The next piece of the puzzle is the event-firing method. This method is used to make the connection between the object event source and the method that might be assigned to handle the event on the other side of the process:

```
// This method is used to fire the event
protected virtual void OnChanged()
{
   if (Changed != null)
     Changed();
   else
      Console.WriteLine("Event fired. No handler!");
}
```

As you can see, the event-firing mechanism is simple: It looks exactly like a function call. Like a function or method call, the event handler can accept arguments. You look at an example in the "Immediate Solutions" example in the section "Creating Multiple Delegates," later in this chapter. For this example, imagine that the class that is the event source contains a value named **nValue**, which is what you want to monitor. Whenever a user changes the value or the value is changed by some internal mechanism, you want to inform any listeners that a change has taken place. To do this, you fire the event that could represent the method used to modify the internal value, as shown in the following snippet:

```
public void SetValue( int nV )
{
    if ( nValue != nV )
    {
        nValue = nV;
        // Fire the event
        OnChanged();
    }
}
```

The event mechanism is by no means automatic. If a method in this test class modifies the internal member variable directly, without calling the **setValue** method, it therefore does not fire the event. Events are handled by the developer, not by the system. In other words, if you wrote a method like this

```
public void BadMethod()
{
    nValue ++;
}
```

no event is fired.

In this case, the event denoting that the variable has changed is not fired because the system does not recognize that the event is tied to the value of the member variable. Be careful when working with events that check these types of values, to be sure that you are always calling the event-firing mechanism when appropriate. The best way to do that is to embed in the accessor the firing of the event for the variable you are modifying.

On the other side of the wall that is event handling, you want to be able to define an event handler in another class to watch for the change in the member variable of the test case. Look at a simple example:

```
public static void HandleChange()
{
    Console.WriteLine("Handler Called");
}

public static void Main()
{
    TestClass tc = new TestClass(3);

    // Create a handler for this class
    tc.Changed += new
            EventTestClass.ValueChangedEventHandler(
                HandleChange);
```

In this case, you can see that a static method was chosen to use as the event handler. The event handler method signature must match the signature of the event itself. In this case, the delegate method signature specifies a method that contains no arguments and returns no value (a void return). Notice that the event handler method contains the same signature. If you try to use a method that accepts any arguments or returns any sort of value for this event handler, the compiler flags it as an error. Suppose, however, that you want to pass in the current value of the variable and have the event handler let you know whether this value is acceptable. In this case, you might modify the delegate to read:

```
public delegate Boolean ValueChangedEventHandler(int nValue);
```

If you were to make this change, you would also modify the event-firing mechanism in the **OnChanged** method of the event source to read:

```
protected virtual void OnChanged()
{
    if (Changed != null)
        if ( Changed(nValue) );
        // Commit the change
}
```

Meanwhile, in the event handler object, the code then needs to be modified to validate the input. You might have something like this validation in a class, which acts like a derived class to screen out unwanted values:

```
public static Boolean HandleChange(int nValue)
{
    if ( nValue <= 0 || nValue >= 10 )
        return false;
    return true;
}
```

As you can see, this method then forces the member variable in the event source class to be between the values of 1 and 9. Any other value triggers the return of a false condition, which prevents the event source from setting the value in the member variable. Returning to the example of a class that monitors for negative balances, you can see that you could use event handlers to reject a transaction that would cause the balance to "go negative." You see an excellent example of how to do this task in the "Immediate Solutions" example in the "Working with an Event Source" section, later in this chapter.

Multiple Event Handlers

One interesting event-handling feature is the programmer's ability to add multiple event handlers to a single event. You may have noticed that, in the preceding example, when setting the event handler in place for a given event in a given event source object, you used the **+=** operator to add the event handler. The reason for using this operator—and not the **=** or another operator—is that additional handlers can be defined for the event from either the same event-handling object or multiple ones.

Why would you want to handle an event a multiple number of times? The answer is quite simple: The system is often already "trapping" an event, such as a button push or a click in a list box, where you want to allow the default processing to take place while adding processing of your own. This concept is the object-oriented paradigm of extending a solution while keeping the initial functionality in place.

Probably the most useful thing about the event-handling system in C# is that all this functionality is performed for you without your having to know anything about it. As you probably noticed in the preceding section, the event source called the delegate for the event handler only once. The event source was not concerned that multiple handlers might have been available, nor did it worry that any one of the handlers might have called other handlers. After all, if a given event handler was in an object that fired an event, another object could easily have defined an event handler for that event. This situation leads to a bubbling effect, where an event ripples across the system. However, in no case did you have to worry about whether the event was one of a series of events.

You might wonder what would happen if you do something like this:

```
using System;

public class EventTestClass
{
    // Allow a handler for the event
    public delegate Boolean ValueChangedEventHandler(int nValue);
```

```
        // This is the event itself
        public event ValueChangedEventHandler Changed;

        // This method is used to fire the event
        protected virtual Boolean OnChanged(int nV)
        {
            if (Changed != null)
                return Changed(nV);
            else
                Console.WriteLine("Event fired. No handler!");
            return true;


        }
    }


public class EvtTest
{
    public Boolean HandleChange1(int nv)
    {
        if ( nv <= 0 || nv >= 10 )
            return false;
        return true;
    }
    public Boolean HandleChange2(int nv)
    {
        if ( (nv & 1) == 1 )
            return false;
        return true;
    }
    public static void Main()
    {
        EventTestClass etc = new EventTestClass(3);
        EvtTest app = new EvtTest();

        // Create a handler for this class
        etc.Changed += new
                EventTestClass.ValueChangedEventHandler(
                    app.HandleChange1);
        etc.Changed += new
                EventTestClass.ValueChangedEventHandler(
                    app.HandleChange2);

        etc.SetValue(5);
        etc.SetValue(6);
        etc.SetValue(3);
    }
}
```

In this example, you are adding two different event handlers that return a Boolean value to indicate whether a given value is okay. How does the system know whether to use the value and chain to the next delegate? The answer is that C# is smarter than you might imagine. It knows that a multicast delegate, which is the only sort that can be used to chain event handlers, cannot return a value. Therefore, you get a runtime error when you try to run this little program, producing this useful error message:

```
Exception occurred: System.MulticastNotSupportedException: Combine may not
    be preformed on non-MulticastDelegate delegates.
```

First, I suspect that the last line is supposed to say that the operation could not be *per*formed rather than *pre*formed. Ignoring that little typo, you see that the real error is that two methods are being combined that do not conform to a multicast delegate specification, which requires that the method return no value.

That's the last of the information you need to get up and running with delegates and events. You must understand the event-handling mechanism and, by extension, the delegate mechanism in C#. Without a good understanding of these mechanisms, you will have serious problems when trying to work with the CLR (see Chapter 8) or visual element (see Chapter 9) portions of this book and in writing applications with C#. Now, move on to the examples portion of this chapter so that you can get the immediate solutions to the problems that might be confronting you in your own work.

Immediate Solutions

Creating a Delegate

A *delegate* is nothing more or less than a function pointer that can be applied to the method of a class. Creating a delegate requires that you use the special **delegate** keyword and that you know both the name of the method to which you want to create a pointer and what you want to do with that pointer. One of the best uses for delegates is as another form of object derivation. Rather than have to derive an entirely new class from a base class to override the process of a single method, you can simply pass in a delegate that knows a different way to process data.

Delegates are often spoken of in conjunction with events. However, as you see in the example in this section, delegates are considerably more powerful than that. You can use them to change the behavior of a program at runtime rather than have to rewrite and recompile the application. In Listing 5.1, you look at a simple example of creating a delegate that maintains account balances in an accounting system. The delegate does that work of handling credits and debits to an account, and the account database simply decides which delegate to call based on whether an amount posted to an account is positive or negative. This listing also provides some interesting insights into how to use arrays of objects in the C# system—something that is explored in more depth in Chapter 2.

Listing 5.1   Creating a delegate.

```
using System;

public class Account
{
    private string Name;
    private string Address;
    private double Balance;

    public Account( string n, string a )
    {
        Name = n;
        Address = a;
        Balance = 0.0;
    }
```

```
        public void AddToBalance( double amount )
        {
            Balance += amount;
        }
        public void RemoveFromBalance( double amount )
        {
            Balance -= amount;
        }
        public string getName()
        {
            return Name;
        }
        public string getAddress()
        {
            return Address;
        }
        public double getBalance()
        {
            return Balance;
        }
    }

public class AccountHandler
{
    public AccountHandler()
    {
    }
    public Boolean AccountInc( Account a, double amt )
    {
        a.AddToBalance( amt );
        return true;
    }
    public Boolean AccountDec( Account a, double amt )
    {
        a.RemoveFromBalance( amt );
        return true;
    }
}


public class AccountDB
{
    Account[]  accounts;
    int        nNumAccounts;
```

```
    // Declare delegates
    public delegate Boolean IncrementAccountDelegate( Account a,
            double d );
    public delegate Boolean DecrementAccountDelegate( Account a,
            double d );

    public AccountDB()
    {
        accounts = new Account[10];
        nNumAccounts = 0;
    }


    // A method to create a new account
    public void AddAccount( string n, string a )
    {
        accounts[nNumAccounts++] = new Account(n,a);
    }
    public void PostToAccount( int nAcct, double d,
            IncrementAccountDelegate inc,
            DecrementAccountDelegate dec )
    {
        if ( d < 0 )
            dec( accounts[nAcct], -d );
        else
            inc( accounts[nAcct], d );
    }
    public void PrintAccountStatus()
    {
        for ( int i=0; i<nNumAccounts; ++i )
        {
            Console.WriteLine( "Name {0} Address {1} Balance {2}",
            accounts[i].getName(), accounts[i].getAddress(),
            accounts[i].getBalance() );
        }
    }
}

class CH5_1
{
    public static void Main()
    {
        AccountHandler ah = new AccountHandler();
        AccountDB adb = new AccountDB();
```

```
// Add two accounts
adb.AddAccount("Fred Jones", "1000 Main St" );
adb.AddAccount("Ralph Smith", "1234 Pine St" );

// Create the delegates
AccountDB.IncrementAccountDelegate iad =
    new AccountDB.IncrementAccountDelegate( ah.AccountInc );
AccountDB.DecrementAccountDelegate dad =
    new AccountDB.DecrementAccountDelegate( ah.AccountDec );

// Okay, add some stuff and decrement it
adb.PostToAccount( 0, 100.00, iad, dad );
adb.PostToAccount( 0, 200.00, iad, dad );
adb.PostToAccount( 0, -50.00, iad, dad );

adb.PostToAccount( 1, 500.00, iad, dad );
adb.PostToAccount( 1, 300.00, iad, dad );
adb.PostToAccount( 1, -150.00, iad, dad );

// Print out the totals
adb.PrintAccountStatus();

    }
}
```

The relevant parts of this program are shown in the highlighted sections. For example, the first shaded area shows how you define a delegate in the class that uses it. The second shaded area shows how the delegates are passed into a class method and used. The third shaded area shows how you can create new delegates of the appropriate types and connect them to real methods that do the processing. You can think of delegates as simple placeholders for real functionality.

Using a Delegate in a Method

You know what a delegate is—a fancy function pointer. You know how to create one, by simply adding the **delegate** keyword to a public method of a class. However, if you are simply given a delegate and told to use it, how do you go about it? In this example, I explore the hows and whens of using delegates in your own methods.

One big difference between delegates and function pointers in C++ is that delegates can point to either static or nonstatic methods. In the example in the preceding section, you explored the use of a delegate as a member function of a class. In the example in this section, you do the opposite—explore the use of a delegate as a pointer to a static method of a class, which C++ programmers can think of as a function.

In Listing 5.2, you explore the idea of having a delegate that is not a part of any given class so that it can be used in any class you like. In addition, you explore the use of a static method (or true function) as the target of a delegate. Finally, you see how you can check for the kind of object you receive in a delegate (or other) method by using the **is** keyword.

Listing 5.2   Using a delegate in a method.

```
using System;

public delegate void PrintAnObjectDelegate( object o );

class A
{
    public A()
    {
    }
    public void Print()
    {
        Console.WriteLine("I'm an A!");
    }
}

class B
{
    public B()
    {
    }
    public void Print()
    {
        Console.WriteLine("I'm a B!");
    }
}

class C
{
    public C()
    {
    }
    public void Print()
    {
```

```
            Console.WriteLine("I'm a C!");
        }
    }


class Printer
{

    public PrintAnObjectDelegate dele;

    public Printer()
    {
        dele = null;
    }
    public void DoPrint( object o )
    {
        if ( dele != null )
            dele( o );

    }
}

class CH5_2
{
    public static void ObjPrint( object o )
    {
        if ( o is A )
        {
            ((A)o).Print();
        }
    }
    public static void Main()
    {
        Printer p = new Printer();
        PrintAnObjectDelegate pao = new
            PrintAnObjectDelegate(ObjPrint);

        p.dele = pao;
        A anA = new A();
        B aB = new B();
        C aC = new C();

        p.DoPrint( anA );
        p.DoPrint( aB );
        p.DoPrint( aC );
    }
}
```

As you can see in this example, a delegate is really just a type. Because it is a type, it does not need to exist within the scope of a class or structure. Instead, creating a "generic" delegate type that can handle certain types of operations is perfectly reasonable. Notice that within the delegate handler, you then check for the specific type of object being passed to you to see whether it is something you want to work with. You then use a C-style cast to make the object into what you want it to be so that you can invoke the proper methods for that class of object.

The cast could be written in a more C#-style fashion by using the **as** operator:

```
if ( o is A )
{
   (o as A).Print();
}
```

Now you should understand how to use delegates as function pointers in your C# application. Delegates are a valuable tool in deciding how to implement a given algorithm and should be considered at the design stage of application development.

Creating a New Event

An *event* is the outcome of an action. In C#, you use events to keep objects notified of the current state of another object or condition, in a way that can be done asynchronously. For example, a monitor object might care about the state of a specific variable— the number of rows in a database, for example. When the Database Manager object adds, deletes, or even potentially modifies a row, it could directly notify this monitor object that the database has been changed. This process is costly, however, because the database manager then needs to know all about the internals of the monitor object. If the monitor is changed, or additional monitor objects added, the program needs major modifications.

Events solve the problem of object notifications, without requiring a great deal of knowledge about external objects within the event-generating system. In C#, you have two classes of event objects, event sources, and event handlers. Event sources, as you saw in the "In Depth" section, earlier in this chapter, generate the events and call the delegates assigned to those event handlers. Event handlers, on the other hand, maintain a more passive role and are simply told when an event occurs. What they do then is up to them. As you see in later examples, events can be even more powerful and can deny a given change to the event source.

In Listing 5.3, you show a simple event source object. This object contains a given internal member variable that can be set using a member function. Each time this member variable is changed, the event source fires an event to notify any listeners that changes are pending. If no event handlers are defined, the event source tells you about that too.

Listing 5.3   Creating a new event.

```
using System;

public class EventTestClass
{
    // The value to track
    private int nValue;

    // Allow a handler for the event
    public delegate void ValueChangedEventHandler();

    // This is the event itself
    public event ValueChangedEventHandler Changed;

    // This method is used to fire the event
    protected virtual void OnChanged()
    {
        if (Changed != null)
            Changed();
        else
            Console.WriteLine("Event fired. No handler!");

    }

    public EventTestClass(int nValue)
    {
        SetValue( nValue );
    }
    public void SetValue( int nV )
    {
        if ( nValue != nV )
        {
            nValue = nV;
            // Fire the event
            OnChanged();
        }
    }
}
```

```
public class CH5_3
{
   public static void Main()
   {
      EventTestClass etc = new EventTestClass(3);
      etc.SetValue(5);
      etc.SetValue(5);
      etc.SetValue(3);
   }
}
```

The output from this program is:

```
Event fired. No handler!
Event fired. No handler!
Event fired. No handler!
```

As you can see, the event handler is called three times. One time, it did not fire because the value had not changed.

Related solution:	Found on page:
Creating an Event for a Component	570

Chaining Events

Event handling is a fairly common occurrence in many programming languages. Visual Basic, for example, permits you to define an event handler for each event that a button or other GUI element fires off. The problem, however, is that most of the time you can define only a single event handler for each event. What if you want to have two (or three) handlers for the button being clicked? That might not seem like a rational thing to do, until you want to implement logging for your application and quickly and easily keep track of everything a user does. Then, suddenly, you modify your event handlers for each and every event to add the logging capability. Wouldn't it be easier if you could find a better way?

C# provides a solution to the problem of multiple event handlers for a given event. C# does this by allowing you to add as many handlers as you like and have the underlying system deal with calling them all when the event-firing mechanism triggers. In Listing 5.4, you see an example of having multiple event handlers for a single event. Notice specifically that the event-firing code does not know or care about the added handlers.

Listing 5.4   Chaining events.

```csharp
using System;

public class EventTestClass
{
    // The value to track
    private int nValue;

    // Allow a handler for the event
    public delegate void ValueChangedEventHandler();

    // This is the event itself
    public event ValueChangedEventHandler Changed;

    // This method is used to fire the event
    protected virtual void OnChanged()
    {
        if (Changed != null)
            Changed();
        else
            Console.WriteLine("Event fired. No handler!");
    }

    public EventTestClass(int nValue)
    {
        SetValue( nValue );
    }
    public void SetValue( int nV )
    {
        if ( nValue != nV )
        {
            nValue = nV;
            // Fire the event
            OnChanged();
        }
    }
}

public class CH5_4
{
    public void HandleChange1()
    {
        Console.WriteLine("Handler 1 Called");
    }
```

```
public void HandleChange2()
{
    Console.WriteLine("Handler 2 Called");
}
public CH5_4()
{
}

public static void Main()
{
    EventTestClass etc = new EventTestClass(3);
    CH5_4 app = new CH5_4();

    // Create a handler for this class
    etc.Changed += new
            EventTestClass.ValueChangedEventHandler(
                    app.HandleChange1);
    etc.Changed += new
            EventTestClass.ValueChangedEventHandler(
                    app.HandleChange2);

    etc.SetValue(5);
    etc.SetValue(5);
    etc.SetValue(3);
}
}
```

The most interesting part of this example is in the **OnChanged** event, which is in the highlighted section. Notice that this event source does not appear to know about how many event handlers are defined for this particular event. The event source simply calls the delegate function. However, when you run the program, you see that both event handlers are called by the application. This process happens by the internal logic of the delegate mechanism, which "chains" together the event handlers behind the scenes. You don't have to worry about who else might be watching this event. As the event firer, you don't have to worry about how many people are watching the event. Everything just happens automatically for you.

Working with an Event Source

When you talk about events, the equation always has two sides. First, an event source pays attention to firing events and detecting when an event should be fired. Next, the event handler deals with receiving the information an event has fired and verifying that information about that event is present. In C#, some event sources are capable of firing events with virtually any information. To fit into the .NET framework, however, an event should provide certain basic information in the form of event arguments that allows it to work with other languages in the environment, such as Visual Basic.NET.

In Listing 5.5, you find a prototypical event system. This class fires an event with a set of arguments and the source of the events as the object passed to the event handler. This model is the one you should use for your own event-handling and -firing system.

Listing 5.5   Working with an event source.

```
using System;
public class MyEventArgs : EventArgs
{
    private readonly Boolean IsDebit;
    private readonly Boolean IsCredit;
    private readonly double  Amount;
    public MyEventArgs( Boolean IsD, double Amt )
    {
        if ( IsD )
        {
            IsDebit = true;
            IsCredit = false;
        }
        else
        {
            IsDebit = false;
            IsCredit = true;
        }
        Amount = Amt;
    }
    public Boolean IsADebit()
    {
        return IsDebit;
    }
    public Boolean IsACredit()
    {
        return IsCredit;
    }
    public double AmountOfDebitOrCredit()
    {
        return Amount;
    }
}
```

```
public delegate Boolean AccountEventHandler(object sender, MyEventArgs e);
public class Account
{
    private double Total;
    private AccountEventHandler ah = null;
    public Account()
    {
        Total = 0;
    }
    public double getTotal()
    {
        return Total;
    }
    // Method to add a new OnPost handler
    public void AddOnPost(AccountEventHandler handler)
    {
        ah = (AccountEventHandler)Delegate.Combine(ah, handler);
    }
    // Method to remove an OnPost handler
    public void RemoveOnPost(AccountEventHandler handler)
    {
        ah = (AccountEventHandler)Delegate.Remove(ah, handler);
    }
    // Handle the debit case
    public void PostDebit(double amt)
    {
        // First, create an argument list
        MyEventArgs ev = new MyEventArgs( true, amt );
        // Fire the event, checking to see if the return is ok
        Boolean okToSubtract = true;
        if ( ah != null )
            okToSubtract = ah(this, ev);
        if ( okToSubtract )
        {
            Console.WriteLine("Debit ok!");
            Total -= amt;
        }
        else
        {
            Console.WriteLine("Debit NOT ok! Not posting");
        }
    }
    public void PostCredit(double amt)
    {
        // First, create an argument list
        MyEventArgs ev = new MyEventArgs( false, amt );
```

```
                // Fire the event, checking to see if the return is ok
            Boolean okToAdd = true;
            if ( ah != null )
                okToAdd = ah(this, ev);
            if ( okToAdd )
                Total += amt;
        }
}
public class CH5_5
{
    public static Boolean CheckPost( object o, MyEventArgs arg )
    {
        if ( arg.IsADebit() )
        {
            // See if it went negative
            Account a = (Account)o;
            if ( arg.AmountOfDebitOrCredit() > a.getTotal() )
              return false;
        }
        return true;
    }

    public static void Main()
    {
        Account a = new Account();
        AccountEventHandler evh = new
            AccountEventHandler( CheckPost );
        a.AddOnPost( evh );

        a.PostDebit( 100.00 );
        a.PostCredit( 200.00 );
        a.PostDebit( 100.00 );
    }
}
```

The output from this little program is as follows:

```
Debit NOT ok! Not posting
Debit ok!
```

What can you learn from this simple example? For one thing, you can use event handling for much more than notification. You can use event handling to do verification as well. Imagine how useful this technique would be for a specialized edit control that needs to screen out certain characters! Another important concept to take from this example is that event handlers should be passed a standard interface, the object being manipulated, and a series of arguments defining what kind of manipulation is taking place. To do this, your event arguments should be derived from the **EventArgs** system class. This class allows reflection (see Chapter 6) for other languages to determine what type and name of event arguments are available.

As you can see in the example in this section, you add a handler to a simple class that does accounting, to allow for different business rules to be applied. One interesting thing about this example is that it follows more of an object-oriented approach to the design and implementation by not allowing users direct access to the event handlers for the class. Instead, you provide public methods to add and remove handlers for this event type. This technique is good to use because you never know when you might want to limit the number of handlers for performance considerations. As you may notice, it is necessary to type-cast the return from the **Delegate.Combine** method to be the proper type. The reason is that the **Combine** method is in the base class and does not know what sort of delegate you are returning. Because you know that it is of a higher class, you do the conversion.

Event handling is one of the most powerful built-in technologies in the .NET environment. Besides garbage collection, it is probably the single biggest reason that programmers are so excited about the new languages. For this reason, you must consider event handling at the time you design your classes so that you don't need to go back and add it after the fact. Building-in event handling, as you can see, is easy. Adding it later is difficult. Always strive to take the easy approach, and your programming life will be much smoother.

Creating a Simple Delegate in Managed C++

Until this point, I have discussed delegates only in terms of their applicability to C#. Like everything else in the .NET environment, however, anything that can be done in C# can be done in the managed version of C++. For C++ programmers trying to make the transition to the .NET environment, having an example of using the delegate mechanism in managed C++ is helpful.

Listing 5.6 shows the mechanics of using a delegate in managed C++. In this example, a simple calendar entry keeps track of a given month and day in the year. For this class, a single method determines whether the date is a holiday. For simplicity's sake, you have considered only New Year's Day to be a holiday. (Of course, if you work in today's nonstop software development world, that might be the only holiday you get! Let's hope not, and hope instead that this is only a simple example.)

Listing 5.6   Creating a simple delegate in managed C++.

```cpp
#using <mscorlib.dll>
using namespace System;
#include <stdio.h>
#include <string.h>
#include <stdlib.h>


__delegate Boolean IsHolidayDelegate();

__gc class HolidayCalendar
{
private:
   int m_nMonth;
   int m_nDay;
public:
   HolidayCalendar()
   {
      // Default to January 1st
      m_nMonth = 1;
      m_nDay   = 1;
   }
   HolidayCalendar(int nMonth, int nDay)
   {
      m_nMonth = nMonth;
      m_nDay   = nDay;
   }
   void setDate(int nMonth, int nDay )
   {
      m_nMonth = nMonth;
      m_nDay   = nDay;
   }

   Boolean IsHoliday()
   {
      if ( m_nMonth == 1 && m_nDay == 1 )
         return true;
      return false;
   }
};

void main ()
{
   IsHolidayDelegate * pHD = NULL;  // declare delegate type
```

```
// Create an instance of the class
HolidayCalendar * pcal = new HolidayCalendar();

// Create the delegate
pHD = new IsHolidayDelegate(pcal, &HolidayCalendar::IsHoliday);

Boolean bFlag = pHD->Invoke();
printf("Case 1\n");
if ( bFlag )
    printf("The calendar IS a holday\n");
else
    printf("The calendar is NOT a holday\n");

pcal->setDate( 3,3 );
printf("Case 2\n");
bFlag = pHD->Invoke();
if ( bFlag )
    printf("The calendar IS a holday\n");
else
    printf("The calendar is NOT a holday\n");

}
```

To compile this application, simply use the **/com+** flag to the C++ compiler:

```
Cl /com+ CH5_6.cpp
```

The output from this application is as follows:

```
Case 1
The calendar IS a holday
Case 2
The calendar is NOT a holday
```

This output, of course, is exactly what you would expect from this simple example. Initially, the default constructor creates an object with a date of 1/1, which is a holiday according to your internal logic. You then change the date to 3/3, which is not a holiday. The results are printed to the console.

Notice the use of the **Invoke** method to call the delegate. This technique shows how close the C# and managed C++ delegate mechanism is to the underlying COM functionality that implements it.

5. Delegates and Events

Creating Multiple Delegates

C# provides two kinds of delegates. First, the single delegates have a one-to-one relationship with the events, or reasons they are being called. Second, and more importantly for event handling, multicast delegates allow you to combine several delegate handlers for a given event source into a single linked list that can be called either directly, under program control, or indirectly, by triggering the event mechanism.

One nice thing about calling delegate linked lists under program control is that you can modify the input to those delegates. For example, if you want to keep track of the chain of events going to a given delegate, you could increment a counter and pass it to the delegate handler as an input argument. Alternatively, you could simply bypass certain handlers, if you knew what they were. This would allow you to do specialized logging, for example.

The core of the multicast delegate system is the **Combine** method. This method allows you to create the chained link list of delegates to be called when the event is fired. If you were using the first beta (Beta 1) of the C# compiler, notice that the delegate (multicast) syntax was necessary to indicate that you were using a multicast delegate for your handler. This syntax is no longer necessary.

In Listing 5.7, a complete application shows an example of creating a multicast delegate handler and calling it both directly and indirectly. Note the use of the **Combine** method to create a linked list of handlers. Note also the use of the **GetInvocationList** method to be able to retrieve the individual handlers in a simple array to call individually.

Listing 5.7   Creating multiple delegates.

```
using System;

public class EventHandler1Class
{
    public static void HandleEvent1(string s)
    {
        Console.WriteLine("EventHandler1::HandleEvent1 called [{0}]", s);
    }
}

public class EventHandler2Class
{
    public static void HandleEvent1(string s)
    {
        Console.WriteLine("EventHandler2::HandleEvent1 called [{0}]", s);
    }
}
```

```
public class EventClass
{
    public delegate void OnEventFired( string s );

    private string fS;
    public OnEventFired evf = null;

    public EventClass( string s )
    {
        fS = s;
        OnFireEvent();
    }
    public void setString(string s)
    {
        fS = s;
        OnFireEvent();
    }

    private void OnFireEvent()
    {
        // Just fire the event
        if ( evf != null )
            evf( fS );
    }

    public void CallAllEventHandlers( string s )
    {
        if ( evf == null )
            return;

        Delegate[] list = evf.GetInvocationList();
        for ( int i=0; i<list.Length; ++i )
        {
            OnEventFired oef = (OnEventFired)list[i];
            oef( s );
        }
    }
}

public class CH5_7
{
    public static void Main()
    {
        // Create the event handlers
        EventClass.OnEventFired ev1 = new
            EventClass.OnEventFired( EventHandler1Class.HandleEvent1 );
```

```
EventClass.OnEventFired ev2 = new
    EventClass.OnEventFired( EventHandler2Class.HandleEvent1 );

// Now, create an instance of the class
EventClass e = new EventClass("Hello world");

// Set up the handler
e.evf = (EventClass.OnEventFired)Delegate.Combine( ev1, ev2 );

// Change something so that it is called
e.setString("Hello!");

// Now, call all the handlers
e.CallAllEventHandlers("Goodbye!");

    }
}
```

As you can see from this code listing, using the functionality of multicast delegates to your advantage is not difficult. The output from this program shows that you can either choose to know about all the available delegates for the handlers in the class or allow the multicast delegate-handling functionality do all the work for you. Here is what the program outputs:

```
EventHandler1::HandleEvent1 called [Hello!]
EventHandler2::HandleEvent1 called [Hello!]
EventHandler1::HandleEvent1 called [Goodbye!]
EventHandler2::HandleEvent1 called [Goodbye!]
```

Notice that the output from both strings is the same, whether the change was caused by the indirect modification of the internal data (via the **setString** method call) or by the physical invocation of each handler in the linked list for the event handler.

Firing an Event

Sometimes, being able to fire an event manually is convenient. For example, you might have functionality that is called in another object when a button is clicked. Rather than have to find the other object, invoke the method on it, and deal with the result when you need that same functionality, it would be useful if you could simply simulate a user clicking on the button. Another good example is being able to select an item in a list and call a method for that item as well as being able to double-click that item. Both actions invoke the same functionality, but you have no reason to duplicate all the code to do both. You can see throughout the Windows operating system many examples of these two ways of selecting items and executing methods for them. In many dialog boxes, for example, double-clicking a list entry selects that item and closes the dialog box. Wouldn't you rather simply select the item on the double-click and then "tell" the dialog box that the user clicked the OK button? Of course, you would.

In this example, you see how you can go about doing similar tasks in your own objects. The example makes a few assumptions, such as the fact that your event-firing mechanism must be public. In addition, the example assumes that calling an event-firing method makes sense for your application. In most cases, however, both assumptions are true.

This same technique works in managed C++. However, in managed C++, the **Invoke** method of the delegate for the event handler is available to the caller (as shown in the "Creating a Simple Delegate in Managed C++" example, earlier in this section), so you need not go through all this worrying about public-versus-private event handlers. As you can see in Listing 5.8, firing an event is quite easy.

Listing 5.8   Firing an event.

```
using System;

public delegate Boolean AccountEventHandler(object sender, double amt);

public class Account
{
    private double Total;
    public AccountEventHandler ah = null;

    public Account()
    {
        Total = 0;
    }
    public double getTotal()
    {
        return Total;
    }
    public void AddOnPost(AccountEventHandler handler)
    {
        ah = (AccountEventHandler)Delegate.Combine(ah, handler);
    }
    public void RemoveOnPost(AccountEventHandler handler)
    {
        ah = (AccountEventHandler)Delegate.Remove(ah, handler);
    }
```

```
    public Boolean OnPost( double amt )
    {
        if ( ah != null )
            return ah(this, amt );
        return true;
    }

    public void PostDebit(double amt)
    {
        // Fire the event, checking to see if the return is ok
        Boolean okToSubtract = OnPost(amt);
        if ( okToSubtract )
        {
            Console.WriteLine("Debit ok!");
            Total -= amt;
        }
        else
        {
            Console.WriteLine("Debit NOT ok! Not posting");
        }
    }
    public void PostCredit( double amt )
    {
        Total += amt;
    }
}

public class CH5_5
{
    public static Boolean CheckPost( object o, double d )
    {
        // See if it went negative
        Account a = (Account)o;
        if ( d > a.getTotal() )
            return false;
        return true;
    }

    public static void Main()
    {
        Account a = new Account();
        AccountEventHandler evh = new
            AccountEventHandler( CheckPost );
        a.AddOnPost( evh );
```

```
        // Can we debit 100?
        if ( a.OnPost( 100.00 ) )
            a.PostDebit( 100.00 );
        else
            Console.WriteLine("Cannot debit 100.0");
    }
}
```

As you can see from the shaded portion of this code, you have exposed most of the functionality of the event-handling system for this class, without making the event handler delegate public. This action permits you to expose the **OnPost** method, which fires the event, to the caller.

Using a Delegate to Choose the Right Function to Call

Once upon a time, writing a program that called different functions based on different values was a chore. You ended up writing either something that was hard-coded, as in this example

```
switch ( value )
{
    case 0:
            CallFunc0();
            Break;
    case 1:
            CallFunc1();
            Break;
}
```

or a series of function pointers passed into a function:

```
typedef void (*funcptr)(char *s);
void HandleValue(  funcptr arrayoffuncptrs[10], int value )
{
    arrayoffuncptrs[value]( "Hello" );
}
```

Both these methods have serious problems. For one thing, no easy mapping exists between the input values and the functions that are called. If something changes, you need to modify the code in all places to be sure that you associated the right function or function pointer with the right value.

C# gives you a way to get around this situation in a simple and elegant way, using delegates. In this example, you see a simple way to use a hashtable of delegates to decide which function to call when a given input comes in from a user. Furthermore, you see how to handle error conditions, such as unexpected input values. This system is flexible, infinitely expandable, and quite trivial to understand. As a result, systems written in this manner are less errorprone and are easier to maintain than anything you have used in the past. Listing 5.9 shows how to implement this type of hashtable delegate system.

Listing 5.9   Using a delegate to choose the right function to call.

```
using System;
using System.Collections;

public delegate bool HandleKeyword( string key );

public class Parser
{
   Hashtable parseTable;

   public Parser()
   {
      parseTable = new Hashtable();
   }

   public void AddKeywordHandler( string key, HandleKeyword handler )
   {
      parseTable.Add( key, handler );
   }

   public bool ParseKeyword( string key )
   {
      HandleKeyword func = (HandleKeyword)parseTable[ key ];
      if ( func == null )
         return false;

      return func( key );
   }
}

public class HandleHello
{
   public static bool HandleIt( string s )
   {
```

```
         Console.WriteLine( "HandleHello::HandleIt {0}", s );
         return true;
      }
   }

public class HandleGoodbye
{
   public static bool HandleIt( string s )
   {
      Console.WriteLine( "HandleGoodbye::HandleIt {0}", s );
      return true;
   }
}

public class HandleWhy
{
   public static bool HandleIt( string s )
   {
      Console.WriteLine( "HandleWhy::HandleIt {0}", s );
      return true;
   }
}

class CH5_6
{
   public static void Main(string[] args)
   {
    // Create the objects
    Parser p = new Parser();

    // Add the handlers
    p.AddKeywordHandler( "hello", new HandleKeyword(HandleHello.HandleIt) );
    p.AddKeywordHandler( "goodbye", new
        HandleKeyword(HandleGoodbye.HandleIt) );
    p.AddKeywordHandler( "why", new HandleKeyword(HandleWhy.HandleIt) );

    // Do the parsing
    for ( int i=0; i<args.Length; ++i )
       if ( p.ParseKeyword( args[i] ) == false )
          Console.WriteLine("Unknown keyword {0}", args[i] );
   }
}
```

5. Delegates
and Events

When you run this program with the following data, you get this output:

```
C:\ >ch5_6 hello there why goodbye
HandleHello::HandleIt hello
Unknown keyword there
HandleWhy::HandleIt why
HandleGooebye::HandleIt goodbye
```

As you can see, not only are the values you understood properly handled, but invalid values are also easily screened out. Furthermore, you can see that extending this system to handle new input is as simple as adding a new handler method and adding it to the **Parser** object.

Chapter 6

Reflection

In Depth

When the philosophers of olden days sat back and pondered what it was that made up their world, they were said to be "reflecting on things." *Webster's Dictionary, Tenth Edition*, defines *reflection* this way:

> **re·flec·tion** (ri-'flek-shən) *n.* The act of reflecting or the state of being reflected. Something, such as light, radiant heat, sound, or an image, that is reflected. Mental concentration; careful consideration. A thought or an opinion resulting from such consideration. An indirect expression of censure or discredit: *a reflection on his integrity*. A manifestation or result: *Her achievements are a reflection of her courage*. Anatomy. The folding of a membrane from the wall of a cavity over an organ and back to the wall. The folds so made.

You might think that reflection in C# would fit none of these definitions, but the fact is that it fits virtually all of them. Okay, reflection in C# has little to do with anatomical membrane folding; C# has few membranes in it, and none of them gets folded. However, C# reflection has everything to do with the anatomy of your applications.

Reflection in C# is the process whereby the runtime environment can discover information about the classes and other types that are defined within assemblies in an application. I haven't discussed assemblies much until now because they have everything to do with the runtime environment and little to do with the compile-time environment.

An *assembly*, which is the core part of the application runtime executable, is the collection of all information needed by the interpreted runtime environment to load and execute your application for users. Information in an assembly is broken down into two discrete components: the code component, which is made up of the executable code you write for your programs, the metadata. *Metadata*, which is the description of what the program is all about, describes the classes, enumerations, structures, and other types that build an application. Without metadata, you would be unable to load an application safely in C#. Security would be impossible with the metadata that explains to the runtime executable file how an assembly is working and what data values it requires. Reflection is made possible by the metadata in C#; that metadata and its retrieval are the focus of this chapter.

What Is Reflection?

Reflection is the process of finding out about the internals of an application without having access to the source code. You can use reflection to find all classes in an assembly and all the methods, properties, and events that might be supported by each of those classes. Reflection allows you to look at all kinds of information about a class, from the base class it is derived from to the interfaces it supports.

Reflection allows a C# program to inspect and manipulate itself from the outside looking in. You can inspect all the information about a class and also use reflection techniques to dynamically invoke methods of the class at runtime. You can dynamically create code on the fly so that the generated code can be executed directly in the application at runtime. This technique is rather dangerous, however, and not one that is recommended for production code.

Reflection allows you to view the information in the metadata segment of your assemblies at runtime. In a nutshell, you get to see the data the way the compiler sees it when it is building your application into an executable. You then have the flexibility to create applications that can be extended at runtime by taking advantage of other functionality on a user's system. You could use reflection, for example, to investigate whether certain classes exist in your home directory and, if so, to load them into your own application and use them. You can think of reflection as the aspect of Dynamic Link Libraries (DLLs) that never existed but was required in order to be able to know what was in them at run-time..

Without reflection, DLLs required you to know which classes, functions, and types existed in them before you started using them. DLLs could be loaded dynamically (hence their name), but not used that way. You could not, for example, search through a set of DLLs for a function of a given name. Even if you could find it and load the function, you had no way to "ask" the system what parameters to pass to it. C# reflection gives you that capability.

Why Do You Need Reflection?

The compiler and runtime system need the reflection capabilities of C#, whether or not you ever want them or use them. Reflection is necessary in any interpreted language because the runtime system needs to be able to find out what it is loading and how the methods of the classes that are loaded will be called. Because C# was designed from the start to be extensible by the developer (through inheritance) and by the language implementers, the power of reflection is available to you as an end developer.

Reflection is necessary for adequate versioning, for dynamic loading of classes, and for proper security handling. Without reflection, the runtime environment cannot perform security handling properly because it cannot determine whether a given block of code should be loaded until after it is already in memory. If you are accustomed to working with COM type libraries, you have already begun to understand the power of reflection and the need for it in the .NET world.

Reflection is likely to become more and more frequently used in the C# programming world. If you do not take the time to understand this concept now, you will get lost later on when it forms the core of new development. Now is the time to move out of the static programming world and into one where users take control. That is the purpose of the .NET initiative, and reflection forms the core of that work. Give users the power to create their own applications from your framework and components, and extend those applications using other people's components; then you can change the way the software development world works.

How Is Reflection Used?

To understand reflection, you first need to understand the core components of the C# internal system. First, you need to understand two major concepts: assemblies and manifests.

An *assembly* is the basic unit of deployment in a .NET application. An assembly contains the code, the metadata, and the "rules" (versioning and security) for implementing and running an application within the runtime environment. An *assembly file* is a self-describing file that contains the Intermediate Language (IL) code loaded by the runtime environment when the application is loaded into memory. The IL code contains information that describes the types and methods in that assembly, which can be used in much the same way as you might use the Query Interface functionality of classic COM.

A manifest contains information about the assembly as a whole. *Manifests* contain naming and version information that can be used by the runtime environment to ensure that you are loading the proper version of a file when you want it in your application. In addition, because the manifest contains references to other assemblies, the entire package can be loaded into memory at one time, and the runtime can verify that all pieces of the application are present before it starts up the program. This technique avoids the "missing DLL" problem so prevalent in previous versions of Windows programming.

Manifests also contain security information, detailing the boundaries the application is permitted to access during its run. This concept is incredibly important because of the varied types of applications you can create in C#. For example, you certainly don't want a system service having the same level of access as a Web-based application, which must have intense security to avoid people hacking into your system. A system service, on the other hand, needs the freedom to do what it needs to do without people getting involved in running it.

The final component of the manifest is the list of all the types found in the assembly. Types are important not only because they are the fundamental building blocks of the application, but also because, without them, you cannot use the functionality installed in an assembly. Reflection deals primarily with manifest information in the C# runtime environment.

How might you use reflection in your own applications? Three major components require the technology inherent in C# reflection: scripting, property sheets, and dynamic extensibility. Each of these areas could be its own complete application or a piece of a larger system.

Scripting is important to users in modern programming environments. The ability to customize the behavior of the system via a script is one of the ways in which truly great applications separate themselves from the rest of the pack. With C#, you can expose the entire functionality of your application objects to a script writer. Using reflection, you can even allow the objects to add their own functionality to enhance and extend the functionality of your own application. Imagine being able to run a script that loads a third-party database into your own database structure. You could do this if you had access to the third-party database software, of course. If you don't provide that functionality, what is a user to do? Assuming that the third-party database vendor provides a COM interface to its application, a user could load that COM object into a C#-based script and import data by using the two systems concurrently. Wouldn't that be a wonderful concept for the user community?

Property sheets are an important invention that once were used only for programmers and have now moved out into the user world. Word and Excel and other modern applications have property sheets. The Windows operating system is filled with property sheets for everything from configuring printers to adding users to accessing lists. If you have user-accessible objects within your system, you need to be able to set properties in them, and C# reflection lets you do that. Furthermore, C# reflection allows you to view all the events of the objects in the system, as you see in the examples in this chapter. Imagine that an object in your system defines an alarm clock. You might be using this object to do scheduled downloads from the Web or to do scheduled backups. Why wouldn't you want users to be allowed to set up their own scheduled events and remind them of those events? By allowing them to create "callbacks" for the scheduled event firing, you could easily run a script when such an event fired. This would be a new win for users in today's world.

Dynamic extensibility is all about adding functionality to an application at runtime. You can accomplish this via COM or scripting extensions and also by upgrades. Imagine that your application supports a word processing component. You could interrogate that object each time the application is loaded to see whether any new functionality is available to users. Perhaps you have added a spell-checking or grammar-checking capability within your component. That is the simplest form of dynamic extensibility. A more complicated example is adding new objects to the system and allowing them to "play" with the existing functionality. You can download only new components for your application without having to get the whole thing at one time. Wouldn't that cut down on upgrade time and size? Of course, it would.

All these functions require reflection. Most of these functions require the ability to dynamically load an assembly at runtime. What does dynamically loading assemblies mean, and how do you accomplish it? That is the next topic of discussion.

What Is Dynamic Loading?

Let's look at the simplest form of reflection: loading an assembly at runtime and investigating what information you can find out about that assembly. To do this, you need to make use of the **Reflection** namespace. You can get to all this functionality in your application by using the following import:

```
using System.Reflection;
```

After you have loaded the reflection library functionality into your application, you can then load individual assemblies from the outside world. To do this, you use the **Assembly** class from the **Reflection** library. Loading an assembly is a simple matter of using the **LoadFrom** static method of the **Assembly** class. Assuming that you have the name of the assembly you want to load in a variable named *assemblyName*, you would write:

```
Assembly assembly = Assembly.LoadFrom (assemblyName);
```

After you have access to the assembly object, you can interrogate it. The easiest way to do that is via the **GetTypes** method. This method returns an array of Type objects that contain information about the various kinds of types defined in this assembly. You can find out the class names, namespaces, access levels, and much more from the **Type** object for a given type:

```
Type[] types = assembly.GetTypes()
```

After you have the list of available types in an assembly, what kinds of information can you find from them? The first group of functions available in the **Type** class determines what kind of a type you are dealing with. Table 6.1 shows the possible types available to you as a developer using a **Type** object.

Using these four simple properties, you can determine what *any* sort of type is and deal with it appropriately. After you have the type of the type, so to speak, you can then determine whether it is publicly available to use in an application.

Table 6.1 **Available Type information types.**

Property	Purpose
IsClass	If this property is true, the type is a class.
IsEnum	If this property is true, the type is an enumeration.
IsInterface	If this property is true, the type is an interface.
IsValueType	If this property is true, the type is a value type (a struct).

Two properties are available for determining the access scope of a type: The **IsPublic** property indicates whether a method is declared public, and its complementary property, **IsNotPublic**, tells you whether the method is not declared public. Note that you have no simple way to determine whether a nonpublic method is protected or private. For example, to show all the public types in an assembly, you could write code like this:

```
Type[] types = assembly.GetTypes();
foreach ( Type t in types )
{
    if ( t.IsPublic )
        Console.WriteLine("Class {0} is public!", t.FullName );
}
```

I describe more about classes in "Obtaining Class and Type Information from an Assembly" in the "Immediate Solutions" section later in this chapter.

An obvious question about reflection comes up immediately. Because you can "look into" a class and see what is implemented and what sorts of parameters its class methods accept, can you also get a "dump" of the code of the method? If the answer is yes, it would be easy to steal algorithms and code from a C# assembly for sale by unscrupulous individuals. For this reason, the answer is no, you cannot retrieve the code.

The set of methods that allow you to get information about the types defined in the class all have a common motif. (It was tempting to call them a reflecting pool, but that would be a bit gauche.) Table 6.2 lists the most common methods used to retrieve information about types in general as well as the information stored within those types.

To use these methods, you first retrieve the types from the assembly itself, using the **GetTypes** method. This method returns an array of types for the assembly. This array consists of classes, structures, enumerations, and events. If you check for the appropriate type of the **Type** object (which sounds horrible) and verify that it is a class or structure, you can then apply the other methods (**GetMethods** and **GetConstructors**, for example) to retrieve the information you are interested in.

Table 6.2   Type retrieval methods in C# reflection.

Method Name	Purpose
GetTypes	Retrieves all types for a given assembly
GetMethods	Retrieves all methods for a given class
GetConstructors	Retrieves all constructors for a given class
GetProperties	Retrieves all properties for a given class
GetEvents	Retrieves all events for a given class
GetInterfaces	Retrieves all interfaces supported by a given class

For more information on this process, check the "Immediate Solutions" example in the "Dumping the Methods and Their Parameters for a Class" section, later in this chapter.

Despite the incredible power offered by the construct, reflection is a simple thing to use. You should seriously consider adding reflective techniques to your production releases wherever possible.

Immediate Solutions

Obtaining Class and Type Information from an Assembly

The purpose of reflection is to be able to find out information about classes and other types in C# without having to look at the source code manually. With reflection, you could easily build a complete picture of a class, interface, enumeration, or other type without having the source code. The big picture is an important maintenance functionality because it allows you to see what is going on at the highest level of an application without having to dig through the source code to find out all the information.

Of course, reflection is also a great tool for documentation. Imagine that you are looking for a class that implements certain methods. You could use reflection to write a tool that allows you to see all the classes in all the assemblies you know about in your company and to examine each of them for the class names and other type information available in them. In this simple example, you examine an assembly and see what classes, interfaces, and events are present within that assembly. Listing 6.1 shows the code you can use to inspect an assembly for simple information about the classes and their contents. To properly utilize the various type information methods in the reflection section, you need to fully understand the array type in C# and the looping constructs.

Listing 6.1   Obtaining class and type information from an assembly.

```
using System;
using System.Reflection;

class CH6_1
{
    public static void ShowInterfaces( Type t )
    {
        Type[] interfaces = t.GetInterfaces();
        Console.WriteLine("Implemented Interfaces");
        foreach (Type in interfaces)
        {
            Console.WriteLine ("Interface : {0}", type.FullName);
            if ( type.IsPublic )
                Console.WriteLine("Scope: Public" );
```

```
                else
                    Console.WriteLine("Scope: Private" );
            }
        }
    public static void ShowEvents ( Type t )
    {
        EventInfo[] events = t.GetEvents();
        Console.WriteLine("Implemented Events");
        foreach (EventInfo e in events)
        {
            Console.WriteLine("Event name: {0}", e.Name );
            Console.WriteLine("Multicast: {0}", e.IsMulticast ? "Yes" : "No"
);
            Console.WriteLine("Member Type {0}", e.MemberType.ToString() );
        }
    }

    public static void ShowTypes( string name, Assembly assembly )
    {
        Type[] typeArray = assembly.GetTypes ();

        Console.WriteLine ("Assembly Name: {0}", name);
        foreach (Type in typeArray)
        {
            if ( type.IsClass )
            {
                Console.WriteLine ("\nNamespace : {0}", type.Namespace);
                Console.WriteLine ("Class : {0}", type.FullName);
                if ( type.BaseType != null )
                    Console.WriteLine ("Base Class : {0}",
                        type.BaseType.FullName);
                else
                    Console.WriteLine ("Class not derived from anything");

                // Check if abstract
                if ( type.IsAbstract )
                    Console.WriteLine("Abstract base class");
                else
                    Console.WriteLine("Instantiable class");
                if ( type.IsPublic )
                    Console.WriteLine("Scope: Public" );
                else
                    Console.WriteLine("Scope: Private" );
                ShowInterfaces( type );
                ShowEvents( type );
            }
```

```
            else
               if ( type.IsInterface )
               {
                  Console.WriteLine ("\nNamespace : {0}", type.Namespace);
                  Console.WriteLine ("Interface : {0}", type.FullName);
                  if ( type.IsPublic )
                     Console.WriteLine("Scope: Public" );
                  else
                     Console.WriteLine("Scope: Private" );
               }
               else
                  if ( type.IsEnum )
                  {
                     Console.WriteLine("\nEnumeration: {0}", type.FullName );
                  }
                  else
                     Console.WriteLine("\nType: {0}", type.FullName );
      }
   }
   public static void Main (string[] args)
   {
      for ( int i=0; i<args.Length; ++i )
      {
         // Get the assemble object (from System.Reflection)
         Assembly assembly = Assembly.LoadFrom (args[0]);

         ShowTypes( args[0], assembly );
      }
   }
}
```

As you can see, the work is straightforward. To load information from an assembly, you simply perform a call to **Assembly.LoadFrom** and the name of the DLL or EXE file that contains the assembly information generated by the C# or other .NET compiler. For a normal console application, for example, that information would be in the executable file name, such as CH6_1.exe.

To test this scenario, you need an example of the various types of elements that make up the C# system. Here's the sample program you use to test the program:

```
using System;

public enum DayOfTheWeek
{
```

```
        Monday,
        Tuesday,
        Wednesday,
        Thursday,
        Friday,
        Saturday,
        Sunday
    };

    public struct _SYSTEM_INFO
    {
        public int dwOemID;
        public int dwPageSize;
        public int lpMinimumApplicationAddress;
        public int lpMaximumApplicationAddress;
        public int dwActiveProcessorMask;
        public int dwNumberOfProcessors;
        public int dwProcessorType;
        public int dwAllocationGranularity;
        public short wProcessorLevel;
        public short wProcessorRevision;
    }


    public class EventTestClass
    {
        // The value to track
        private int nValue;

        // Allow a handler for the event
        public delegate Boolean ValueChangedEventHandler(int nValue);

        // This is the event itself
        public event ValueChangedEventHandler Changed;

        // This method is used to fire the event
        protected virtual Boolean OnChanged(int nV)
        {
            return true;
        }
        public EventTestClass(int nValue)
        {
            SetValue( nValue );
        }
```

```
        public void SetValue( int nV )
        {
            if ( nValue != nV )
            {
                if ( OnChanged(nV) )
                    nValue = nV;
                // Fire the event
            }
        }
        public static void Main()
        {
        }
    }


public interface Channel
{
    void Next();
    void Previous();
}


public class TestIntf : Channel
{
    void Next()
    {
        Console.WriteLine("Channel Next");
    }
    public void Previous()
    {
        Console.WriteLine("Previous");
    }
}
```

This code does a good job of exercising the complete spectrum of possible types in the C# system. You can see enumerations, interfaces, structures, and classes. From this example, you can take a close look at the power of reflection in the C# system. If you compile these two applications (an assembly must be compiled in order to use reflection on it) and then run the inspection program on the resulting assembly from the test, you get the following output:

```
Assembly Name: ch6_1test.exe

Enumeration: DayOfTheWeek

Type: _SYSTEM_INFO
```

```
Namespace :
Interface : Channel
Scope: Public

Namespace :
Class : TestIntf
Base Class : System.Object
Instantiable class
Scope: Public
Implemented Interfaces
Interface : Channel
Scope: Public
Implemented Events

Namespace :
Class : EventTestClass
Base Class : System.Object
Instantiable class
Scope: Public
Implemented Interfaces
Implemented Events
Event name: Changed
Multicast: No
Member Type 2

Namespace :
Class : EventTestClass$ValueChangedEventHandler
Base Class : System.Delegate
Instantiable class
Scope: Private
Implemented Interfaces
Interface : System.ICloneable
Scope: Public
Interface : System.Runtime.Serialization.ISerializable
Scope: Public
Implemented Events
```

Obtaining Member Information from a Class

If you have access to an assembly that contains one or more classes, you might be interested in finding out the methods and properties the class contains. This information is useful, for example, if you have a Dynamic Link Library (DLL) that contains classes you know you want to use, but you are unsure how to use them. Perhaps you have the ambition to write a brilliant editor for C# that permits you to automatically call the right methods with the right parameters when a user is typing code that uses an assembly. With C#, this task would not be particularly hard to accomplish.

Using reflection techniques and methods, you can examine each class in an assembly and show whatever information you need to know about that class. Virtually the only thing you cannot do is to retrieve the original comments the software developer created in writing the class. Of course, you could write something to disassemble the byte code back into real instructions, but you would still lose the comments and variable names. This situation is reasonable, of course, only because otherwise no code security would exist.

Listing 6.2 shows a simple little program that uses reflection to inspect the methods and properties of a class. As you can see, C# is consistent in how it implements reflection. You simply call the *Get<x>* routine, where **<x>** is the portion of the reflection information you are interested in, whether it's methods, properties, parameters, or whatever. This routine returns an array of **<x>Info** objects, which contain further information about each one of the individual elements in that type. Note that all returned information can be accessed with a **foreach** loop, which you learned about in Chapter 3.

Listing 6.2   Obtaining member information from a class.

```
using System;
using System.Reflection;

class CH6_2
{
    public static void Main( string[] args)
    {
      if ( args.Length > 0 )
         ShowClasses( args[0] );
    }
    public static void ShowMethods( Type t )
    {
       MethodInfo[] methods = t.GetMethods();
```

6. Reflection

235

```
        foreach( MethodInfo m in methods )
        {
            Console.WriteLine("\nMethod Name: {0}", m.Name );
            Console.WriteLine("Return Type: {0}", m.ReturnType );
        }
    }
    public static void ShowProperties( Type t )
    {
        PropertyInfo[] props = t.GetProperties();
        foreach( PropertyInfo p in props )
        {
            Console.WriteLine("\nProperty Name: {0}", p.Name );
            Console.WriteLine("Type: {0}", p.MemberType );
        }
    }

    public static void ShowClasses( string name )
    {
        Assembly assembly = Assembly.LoadFrom( name );
        if ( assembly != null )
        {
            // Get the classes from the assembly
            Type[] typeArray = assembly.GetTypes ();

            Console.WriteLine ("Assembly Name: {0}", name);
            foreach (Type in typeArray)
            {
                if ( type.IsClass )
                {
                    Console.WriteLine("Class: {0}", type.FullName );
                    ShowMethods( type );
                    ShowProperties( type );
                }
            }
        }
    }
}
```

In this listing, you can see some elements you can obtain from a class using reflection.

Dynamically Invoking Methods from Classes in an Assembly

If you are creating a new scripting language or other form of interpreter, it is helpful to be able to create the objects for which you can find information. In addition, it would be convenient, of course, to be able to call the methods and properties of those objects after you have them. Fortunately, C# offers this capability in its reflection library. You can not only find out about different objects in the system, but also invoke methods on them dynamically, if you know the name of the method you want to call and the arguments you want to pass to that method.

In addition to transferring information into a method, C# allows you to return information from a method to the calling function. This way, if the method you want to call returns a value, you can get that information back from the method into your calling application. In Listing 6.3, you take a look at a simple set of classes. First, a class that implements a specific interface is presented so that you can identify the class you want to call. Next, you call some of those methods directly, to show the output of the functions. Finally, you dynamically invoke some of those methods to show how that particular process takes place.

Listing 6.3 Dynamically invoking methods from classes in an assembly.

```
using System;
using System.Reflection;

interface IMyInterface
{
    void PrintAString( string s );
    void PrintAnInteger( int i );
    void PrintSomeNumbers( string desc, int i, double d);
    int  GetANumber( string s );
}

public class DoMyInterface : IMyInterface
{
    public DoMyInterface()
    {
    }
    public void PrintAString( string s )
    {
        Console.WriteLine( "PrintAString: {0}", s );
    }
    public void PrintAnInteger( int i )
    {
        Console.WriteLine( "PrintAnInteger: {0}", i );
    }
```

```
public void PrintSomeNumbers( string desc, int i, double d)
{
    Console.WriteLine("PrintSomeNumbers:");
    Console.WriteLine( "String: {0}", desc );
    Console.WriteLine( "Integer: {0}", i );
    Console.WriteLine("Double: {0}", d );
}
public int GetANumber( string s )
{
    Console.WriteLine("GetANumber: {0}", s );
    return 34;
}
public int DoItAll(string s, int i, double d )
{
    IMyInterface mi = (IMyInterface)this;
    mi.PrintSomeNumbers( s, i, d );
    return mi.GetANumber( s );
}
}

public class CH6_3
{
    public static void DoDynamicInvocation( string assembly )
    {
        Assembly a = Assembly.LoadFrom( assembly );
        foreach( Type t in a.GetTypes() )
        {
            if ( t.IsClass == false )
                continue;
            if ( t.GetInterface("IMyInterface") == null )
                continue;
            Console.WriteLine("Creating instance of class {0}", t.FullName );
            object obj = Activator.CreateInstance(t);
            object[] args = {"Dynamic", 1, 98.6};
            object result;
            Console.WriteLine("Invoking method DoItAll dynamically");
            try
            {
                result = t.InvokeMember("DoItAll",
                    BindingFlags.Default |
                    BindingFlags.InvokeMethod,
                    null,
                    obj,
                    args );
                Console.WriteLine("Result of dynamic call: {0}", result );
```

```
            // Call an interface method
            object[] args2 = {12345};
            t.InvokeMember("PrintAnInteger",
                    BindingFlags.Default | BindingFlags.InvokeMethod,
                    null,
                    obj,
                    args2 );

        }
        catch ( Exception e )
        {
            Console.WriteLine("Exception: {0}", e );
        }
    }
}
public static void Main(string[] args)
{
    DoMyInterface dmi = new DoMyInterface();
    dmi.PrintSomeNumbers("PrintEm", 1, 12.45 );
    int i = dmi.GetANumber("GiveMeOne");
    Console.WriteLine("I = {0}", i );

    DoDynamicInvocation(args[0]);
}
}
```

Before you get into the specifics of how all this works, take a quick look at the output from this little application, when it is run on itself. Compiling the application as ch6_3.exe, you then run it on itself by using the command-line entry:

```
ch6_3 ch6_3.exe
```

The output from this command is as follows:

```
PrintSomeNumbers:
String: PrintEm
Integer: 1
Double: 12.45
GetANumber: GiveMeOne
I = 34
Creating instance of class DoMyInterface
Invoking method DoItAll dynamically
PrintSomeNumbers:
String: Dynamic
Integer: 1
Double: 98.6
```

```
GetANumber: Dynamic
Result of dynamic call: 34
PrintAnInteger: 12345
```

As you can see, the application works as advertised. The initial group of functions is called from the main method of the class in a direct way. Following that, the assembly for the class itself is loaded dynamically, and the methods are invoked the indirect C# way.

Note the use of the Binding flags attribute to specify that you are calling a method in the default manner. You must do that to make the method load properly.

Verifying That a Class Contains a Method

If you're writing a scripting language that allows the use of C# objects, you might want to verify that a given class contains a method before you allow the script writer to create a script using that method. After all, if the method doesn't exist, it doesn't make a great deal of sense to call it, does it? Of course not. You need to be as proactive as possible in verifying that the script is valid up front rather than wait until runtime to see whether it is valid.

Using the reflection capabilities of C#, you can easily determine whether a given class contains a method by a given name. In fact, you could go further and check to see whether the number and type of arguments the script passes to the method are correct. What is more interesting, however, is checking for which classes can contain the method in question. Suppose that the script writer creates a script containing an undefined variable that calls a method named **Foo**. You could mark that variable as undefined when your script parser encountered it because you have not found a declaration of a variable of that name at the point in the script where it is used. However, it's more useful and valuable to users if you show them the possible values of the variable. If only a single class is in all the available assemblies for the application which contains that particular method, you can reasonably assume that it is the one the user wants. Issuing a warning and continuing is considerably more polite than simply terminating with an error, such as **Unknown Variable <x>**.

In this example, you explore the capabilities of C# reflection by creating an application that can search a given assembly for a given method name. Any class that contains a method of that name is printed to the console for users to view. This application is a much more convenient way to do searching than, for example, full-text searching within the source code for the assembly. In many cases, after all, you do not have access to the source code for the assembly. The CLR is a good example of an assembly in which you have only binary access. Listing 6.4 shows the application source code.

Listing 6.4   Finding the class that contains a method in an assembly.

```
using System;
using System.Reflection;
using System.Collections;

class CH6_4
{
   public static void Main(string[] args)
   {
      // If they gave us at least two arguments,
      // check the assembly (arg 1) for a class
      // that contains a method (arg 2)
      if ( args.Length >= 2 )
         SearchForMethod( args[0], args[1] );
   }
   public static void SearchForMethod(
       string AssemblyName,
       string MethodName )
   {
      // Step 1: Open the assembly
      Assembly assembly = Assembly.LoadFrom(
               AssemblyName );
      if ( assembly == null )
      {
         Console.WriteLine("Unable to open {0}",
         AssemblyName );
         return;
      }

      // Step 2: Loop through all classes in
      //         the assembly

      foreach ( Type t in assembly.GetTypes() )
      {
         // Is this a class?
         if ( t.IsClass == false )
            continue; // No. Skip it

         // Get all of the methods in the class
         foreach ( MethodInfo m in t.GetMethods() )
         {
            if ( m.Name == MethodName )
            {
```

```
                    Console.WriteLine("Class {0} contains method",
                        t.FullName );
                }
            }
        }
    }
}
```

To show how this particular little application works, you can run it on itself. Let's search for the method **Main** across the assembly. Given the preceding source code, the application should find the CH6_4 class and print it. Cross your fingers and give it a try. Here is the result of running this application:

```
C:\ >ch6_4 ch6_4.exe Main
Class CH6_4 contains method
```

As you can see, the application works properly. The question is, of course, how is it doing what it is doing? The answer lies in the nested loops on the **SearchForMethod** method. First, you are getting each type in the assembly that represents a class in the source code. After you have verified that it is a class, you are retrieving each and every method in the class and checking to see whether the name of the method is the same as the method passed into the application on the command line. As you can see, the process works quite well.

Reflection in C# is a powerful technique—one that can be used as much for proactive verification as for information processing. For example, you might check to see whether a given class contains a given method name to see whether that class is the same one you expect it to be. The process of proactive verification gives your application more pizzazz and more defense against unexpected conditions that might occur in the real world. C# was designed from the ground up to protect you from making silly mistakes. Help the language help you by watching for mistakes that can happen in a language that is interpreted rather than truly compiled.

Determining Whether a Class Is Derived from Another Class

Would you ever need to know what the base class of another class is? The answer is "Yes, more times than you might think possible." If you are working on a system using a binary component that does not have a good set of documentation, you might need to know which classes in the component that are derived from some common base are available to you. Knowing this information would help you to understand the use of these classes. Another good example is trying to determine who in your company is making use of your classes. If you are paying bonuses based on the reuse of base classes, this information would certainly be important to the writers of the class. If this type of activity could be automated, you could easily pay the bonuses each month.

In this example, you explore how to search through a set of classes in an assembly for the ones derived from a common base class or interface. After all, if you can determine from reflection what the base class is, you certainly should be able to determine which interfaces it supports. Interface checking is probably as useful, if not more so, than base class checking because knowing that something implements a given interface tells you a great deal about the functionality of that class.

Listing 6.5 shows the small application you use to examine each of the base classes for a given class as well as the interfaces it supports. In addition the application will check all these base classes and interfaces against arguments passed into the program by users. Remember that a base class can be anywhere in the tree of classes supported by a given class. That is, if A is derived from B, and B is derived from C, and C is derived from D, then A is derived, in linear fashion, from D. If you are searching for all classes derived from D, you should see A, B, and C listed.

Listing 6.5   Determining the base classes and interfaces for a class.

```
using System;
using System.Reflection;
using System.Collections;

class CH6_5
{
    public static void Main(string[] args)
    {
        // If they gave us at least two arguments,
        // check the assembly (arg 1) for a class
        // that is derived from another class (arg 2)
        if ( args.Length >= 2 )
            CheckBaseClass( args[0], args[1] );
    }
    public static void CheckBaseClass(
        string AssemblyName,
        string ClassName )
    {
        // Step 1: Open the assembly
        Assembly assembly = Assembly.LoadFrom(
                AssemblyName );
```

```
            if ( assembly == null )
            {
                Console.WriteLine("Unable to open {0}",
                    AssemblyName );
                return;
            }


            // Step 2: Loop through all classes in
            //          the assembly

            foreach ( Type t in assembly.GetTypes() )
            {
                // Is this a class?
                if ( t.IsClass == false )
                    continue; // No. Skip it

                // Check all of the base classes for this class, as well as
                // their base classes
                Type baseType = t.BaseType;
                while (baseType != null)
                {
                    if ( baseType.FullName.EndsWith(ClassName) )
                    {
                        Console.WriteLine("Class {0} is derived from {1}",
                            t.FullName, ClassName );
                    }
                    baseType = baseType.BaseType;
                }

                // Check if one of the types' interfaces is the type
                // we're looking for
                Type[] intfc = t.GetInterfaces();
                foreach (Type itf in intfc)
                {
                    if ( itf.FullName.EndsWith(ClassName) )
                    {
                        Console.WriteLine("Class {0} is derived from intf {1}",
                            t.FullName, ClassName );
                    }
                }
            }
        }
    }
```

Dumping the Methods and Their Parameters for a Class

Until now, this chapter has considered only the various elements of an assembly, such as the classes, derivations, and enumerations within that assembly. Considerably more common, however, is the need to know information about a single class. If you want to write a documentation tool, for example, you need to output all the information about a class. You have already looked at pieces of this task in some of the other examples in the "Immediate Solutions" section, but you have yet to look at the individual elements of a class and their methods and parameters. In this example, you explore the nuts and bolts of the class architecture, the methods of a class, and the parameters that make up those methods.

Listing 6.6 shows a simple application you can run on an assembly to dump the contents of a class. This application finds the class you indicate on the command line and then dumps each method of that class, including the constructors for the class and their parameters. Notice that constructors are a separate type of method in C# and are not lumped in with "normal" methods.

Listing 6.6   Dumping the methods and their parameters for a class.

```
using System;
using System.Reflection;
using System.Reflection.Emit;
using System.Collections;

class CH6_6
{
    public static void DumpParameters( ParameterInfo[] pars )
    {
        // Dump them out
        foreach ( ParameterInfo pi in pars )
        {
            Console.WriteLine("\n   Parameter Name: {0}",
                    pi.Name );
        Console.WriteLine("   Parameter Type: {0}",
            pi.ParameterType );
        Console.WriteLine("   Is In? {0}",
            pi.IsIn );
        Console.WriteLine("   Is Out? {0}",
            pi.IsOut );
        }
    }
```

```
public static void DumpType ( Type t )
{
    // Dump the constructors
    ConstructorInfo[] cons = t.GetConstructors();
    foreach (ConstructorInfo ci in cons )
    {
        // Get all the parameters
        ParameterInfo[] pars = ci.GetParameters();
        Console.WriteLine("\nConstructor: {0}", ci.Name);
        DumpParameters( pars );
    }

    // Dump each method
    MethodInfo[] methods = t.GetMethods();
    foreach ( MethodInfo m in methods )
    {
        Console.WriteLine("\nMethod: {0}", m.Name );
    Console.WriteLine("Return Type: {0}", m.ReturnType );
        // Get all the parameters
        ParameterInfo[] pars = m.GetParameters();
    // Dump the parameters
    DumpParameters( pars );
    }
}
public static void ShowType( string assemblyName,
                             string className )
{
    Assembly assembly = Assembly.LoadFrom( assemblyName );
    if ( assembly == null )
        return;

    Type[] types = assembly.GetTypes();
    foreach ( Type t in types )
    {
        // Only classes
        if ( t.IsClass == false )
      continue;
    // Only the one we want
    string Name = (string)t.FullName;
    if ( Name != className )
        continue;
    // Okay, this is it, dump it
    DumpType( t );
    }
}
```

6. Reflection

```
   public static void Main(string[] args)
   {
      if ( args.Length >= 2 )
         ShowType( args[0], args[1] );
   }
}
```

If you run this little application on itself, using the only class in the assembly as the class name to dump, you get the following output:

```
C:\ >ch6_6 ch6_6.exe CH6_6
Constructor: .ctor

Method: GetHashCode
Return Type: Int32

Method: Equals
Return Type: Boolean

   Parameter Name: obj
   Parameter Type: System.Object
   Is In? False
   Is Out? False

Method: ToString
Return Type: System.String

Method: DumpParameters
Return Type: System.Void

   Parameter Name: pars
   Parameter Type: System.Reflection.Para
   Is In? False
   Is Out? False

Method: DumpType
Return Type: System.Void

   Parameter Name: t
   Parameter Type: System.Type
   Is In? False
   Is Out? False

Method: ShowType
Return Type: System.Void
```

```
        Parameter Name: assemblyName
        Parameter Type: System.String
        Is In? False
        Is Out? False

        Parameter Name: className
        Parameter Type: System.String
        Is In? False
        Is Out? False

Method: Main
Return Type: System.Void

        Parameter Name: args
        Parameter Type: System.String[]
        Is In? False
        Is Out? False

Method: GetType
Return Type: System.Type
```

Note in this output the presence of several methods you didn't directly implement for the class. The compiler, with no need to do any extra work, automatically implements the **GetType**, **GetHashCode**, **Equals**, and **ToString** methods for you. This is just base class code you get for "free."

Chapter 7

Writing Applications

In Depth

If you are like most programmers, you don't need much handholding to get started with a new language or programming environment. Instead, you prefer to dive right in and see what the language has to offer and then go back and learn how to do things in a more efficient manner. This approach is the one taken in this book, allowing you to first delve into the nitty-gritty details of how the language works and how to take advantage of what it has to offer to you, before coming back to focus on the issues of creating software using Visual Studio.NET.

This book is not an introductory text. You don't walk through the steps of creating an application using the Integrated Development Environment (IDE). Instead, you see what kinds of applications the IDE can generate for you and see some issues involved in working with those types of applications. You also learn in this chapter about some issues involved in running and deploying various forms of applications in the .NET runtime environment.

To start out the conversation, take a look at the simplest form of application that can be generated by the Visual Studio.NET environment: the console application. You don't really need to use the IDE to create a console application, but if you do, you can use the integrated environment to debug, compile, and deploy your application more easily.

Console Applications

What exactly is a console application? In their simplest form, all applications can be run from a console window. However, the generally accepted definition of a console application for .NET is that a console application has no graphical user interface and communicates to users only through the console window. All input and output, with the exception of files, are therefore performed via the console window. In the olden days, console applications were called command-line utilities. You can still use console applications as command-line utilities, but they are capable of much more using C#.

Why should you use a console application? A graphical user interface is often simply overkill for the kinds of tasks you are trying to perform. For example, if you are writing an application that duplicates the Copy command, it makes little sense to have a GUI do it. You give the command two values: the old name and the new name. Why make someone bring up a form, enter some values into it, click around the thing, and then click an OK button just to perform a simple action?

7. Writing Applications

Having the program run from either the command line or the Run menu in Windows makes much more sense.

When you talk about console applications, you are generally talking about an application that accepts command-line arguments. In C#, command-line argument processing is done via the **Main** method of the application class in a given assembly. For example, if you have a program named Copy and the arguments to the function are two file names, you might have a console application skeleton that looks like this:

```
class Copy
{
    public static void Main( String[] args )
    {
        if ( args.Length < 2 )
        {
            Console.WriteLine(
              "Not enough arguments. Usage: copy input output");
            return;
        }

        CopyInputToOutput( args[0], args[1] );
}
```

If you have worked in C or C++, most of the command-line argument processing should look familiar. Rather than **argc** and **argv** variables that are mysteriously passed into the application, C# uses a simple string array. The array represents each of the arguments passed on the command line. Notice that unlike in C++ or C, the 0th element of the array is not the name of the program; the arguments all start from the program name onward and are zero based.

To understand how command-line processing works, look at a simple example. Suppose that a program named **Count** counts the number of command-line arguments to it. Run that console application with the following input:

```
count a b c "this is a test" 123 he lp
```

This program has seven arguments. They print as:

```
a
b
c
This is a test
he
lp
```

Note that **"this is a test"** is a single argument to a program because it is enclosed in quotation marks. You can use either single or double quotes to enclose a string to a console application.

You can debug a console application in one of two ways. If you are working in the IDE, you can use the built-in debugger to single-step through the program, looking at all the variables or states of the application. If you are working from the command-line compiler, you can use the **Console.WriteLine** method to output debugging information at each stage of the application process, to see where the problem is occurring. One tip you might find useful is to remove exception-handling blocks in the code when something strange is happening. You find that the C# debugger pops up when an exception occurs, allowing you to more easily and quickly track down the problem.

Remember that console applications are not limited in the way old MS-DOS programs were under Windows. You can do anything you want in a console application. You can display a form, although that would be a **WinForms** application. You can interface to databases, the Registry, files, and other elements without doing anything different than you would in any form of application in C#. All C# applications are console applications at their core.

The most important reason to work with console applications is the ease with which you can create, debug, and deploy them. You can write a console application in any programming editor, compile it using the command-line compiler, and run it from the command line. You can debug a console application without having to load the entire IDE debugger, by using write statements. You can even redirect output in a console application (as you see in the "Immediate Solutions" section, later in this chapter) to a file when you want to study it more closely. Console applications are powerful tools that form the core for other application types, such as Windows forms.

Windows Form Applications

If the console application is the MS-DOS lookalike program of the .NET world, the Windows Form application (called WinForms) is the standard Windows application version. A Windows form looks just like a standard window in a "normal" Windows application. Unlike "standard" Windows applications, however, a WinForm is more like a dialog box. Microsoft has moved away from the idea of Multiple Document Interface (MDI) and Single Document Interface (SDI) applications and toward the idea of simple forms. Users more intuitively grasp a single form application, and the learning curve for working with them is vastly decreased.

You must grasp the concept of WinForms applications. Because it forms the core of future versions of Windows, it is the future of Windows programming. WinForms are reusable, compact applications that not only expose the full power and functionality of the Windows operating system components, but also allow you to use COM components, .NET components, and your own custom components. WinForms can accept command-line arguments or read their information from users in input fields. Naturally, a WinForm application has access to the total functionality of the CLR in C# as well as to the basic components of the Windows operating system.

The classes available for WinForm components are an interesting blend of old and new functionality. As a simple example, consider the **ListView** component. It represents the Explorer-like functionality of the Windows operating system. Data can be presented in either iconic form (like file icons in Explorer) or in report detail form (like a directory listing). The ListView component has a property called **Columns**, which represents the column headers to use when displaying the component in report mode.

The **Columns** property is a C# collection of **ColumnHeader** information blocks. You can add a column header to the collection in several ways that closely resemble the methods you used in Win32 programming. Why follow this archaic form of adding information when you can do it in a simpler fashion? Because this is what programmers are used to. Some overloads are certainly simpler and easier to use, but they blend in with the more ornate ones.

After you get past the idea of the components being wrappers around the existing Windows components (list boxes and edit boxes, for example) and dealing with the difficult translation of those components to more simple uses, the next thing to consider is how you "talk" to components.

In Win32 programming, information is passed back and forth from components to a main processing loop in the form of messages. Messages have a number of problems, not the least of which is that you must coerce data types into oddball forms. Does it really make sense to cast a character string to a long value? Of course not. That technique makes for errorprone programs because you have no way to know whether the type you are coercing is correct. C# is designed to avoid errors like these, so the C# designers chose, not surprisingly, another model for the interface between the application code and the GUI elements.

The model chosen for the C# component interface is, not surprisingly, the delegate and event model. As you may recall from Chapter 5, delegates are a "conduit" between two objects. The event source side of the equation keeps track of when an event is to be fired and fires that event when the time is right. On the event receiver side of the equation, events are sent in an asynchronous fashion when the event is fired by the source. In many ways, this model is analogous to the Java "listener" interface. One or more objects register themselves to "listen" for a given event to occur. When it does occur, they each deal with the event as they see fit without worrying about what some other object else might be doing.

You can therefore have several objects in a system respond to a button click, for example, without having to manually chain them as you would in a standard Windows MFC application.

You see several examples of using event handlers in the "Immediate Solutions" section later in this chapter. The general form of the handler, however, looks like this:

```
protected void <object>_<Event> (object sender, System.EventArgs e)
```

The **<object>** tag is the visual element or component that is sending the notification to the listener. The **<Event>** tag is the event that might be taking place. Unlike standard MFC applications, or Windows applications, where all the messages are sent to a single place and then "cracked" into individual handlers, C# event handlers are specific to the kind of event they are dealing with. The two bits of information passed to the handler are the object that sent the message (such as a button, list box, or form) and the list of event arguments. The default event arguments simply tell you what happened with no other information. For most events, such as button clicks or key presses, the event arguments are more specific.

Events are one way in which reuse is accomplished in C#. The delegate mechanism allows you to reuse different handlers for different kinds of components, as long as they support the same event mechanism. As you see, reuse is an important facet of the C# system.

Form Reuse

One helpful benefit of separating out the event handlers from the GUI code is that forms can then be easily reused in the C# system. Because a form object is nothing more than a single source file, you can easily build forms into an application and then move them from place to place by simply importing them into the project. In Visual Studio.NET, you do this quite easily. When you have a project open in the IDE, right-click on the project name in the Solution Explorer window. Notice that the main menu in the application changes to add a Project menu item. From this menu, select the Add Existing Item menu item (or press Ctrl+Shift+A).

The other alternative for form reuse is to create a library of forms and reference them from your project. This is how the entire CLR is implemented, as a series of DLLs containing the classes that make up the CLR. Nothing stops you from creating a DLL containing your classes as well. To reference your classes within the IDE or your project, simply right-click the project name in the Solution Explorer window and select Add Reference. Navigate to the reference you want to add and select it. You now can use the **using** command to import the classes and methods of that assembly into your project as though it were part of the system.

The basic design of C# was for reuse and maximum efficiency by eliminating duplicate functionality. It therefore behooves you to take advantage of that architecture and extend it in your own applications.

Windows Services

The third class of application you can create within the IDE is the Windows Service class. A *Windows service* is an application that runs in the background, usually at system startup, whether or not a user is present. System services are usually monitoring or translating applications. C# makes creating a Windows service easy, by providing a wizard to do it, although a few "gotchas" are involved. You look at them in "Creating a Windows Service," in the "Immediate Solutions" section, later in this chapter.

The basic flow of a windows service is to have an object that is the service itself. This object is started and runs silently, doing whatever task it is supposed to perform. When the system is halted or a user kills the service, it shuts down. Windows services can do pretty much anything that any other sort of application can do, but they rarely have any true GUI element to them. The reason is simple: You have no guarantee that a user is present and logged in when the service is running, which makes having any input or a desktop display impossible.

One of the most important aspects of the Windows Service functionality is the ability to work with the Event Log and Registry elements of the Windows operating system. You look at the Event Log functionality in "Working with the Event Log," in the "Immediate Solutions" section, later in this chapter. *Event logs* are simply system-level circular files (to avoid running out of disk space) that maintain a list of events by all the various applications and services running on the system. You can add new events, delete events, or iterate through the events to look for one in particular.

The *Registry*, on the other hand, is the centralized database on which the Windows operating system works. Future versions of Windows will have individual registries for individual applications as well as a centralized registry for the system itself. If you are old enough to remember .INI files from Windows 3.1, you may find this statement oddly amusing. Everything in the computer world comes full circle every few years. In a decade or so, you will most likely discuss MFC with the same zeal as you approach C#.

Windows services are started and stopped through the Service Manager application. This manager uses, among other things, the Windows Registry to maintain a list of what it is supposed to run and at what times. You can get to the manager through the My Computer icon on your desktop, by selecting Manage. This application also allows you to view the Event Log.

No matter what sort of application you might build, from console application to full-blown windows service, you need to compile it, link it, and deploy it for users. The issue of deployment and compilation is tackled in the following section.

Application Building and Deployment

After you have design and implemented the system, it is time to build it. Building applications isn't difficult in C#, but you have to be aware of a few issues. First, you need to include all the referenced assemblies when you build your application. This inclusion is fine when you are working with the default assembly library (mscorlib.dll), but when you want to use individual C# components, such as the diagnostics library (in the namespace **System.Diagnostics**), you need to refer to it directly. Worse, you need to include its parent in the compilation instruction:

```
csc /r:System.DLL /r:System.Diagnostics.DLL myFile.cs
```

When you are working with a large number of imported libraries, it is often easier to allow the IDE to manage all this information. To do this, just add a new reference to the project you want to use. The Add Reference menu item is found on the Project main menu or within the Solution Explorer window by right-clicking on the References item.

The real advantage to using the IDE comes in managing projects in this way. Rather than have to create a new make file or remember all the required assemblies for a series of files, you can simply add them to the project solution space once and then move on without worrying about it. Naturally, you have to make sure that you back up another file (the new one you added) and keep the solutions file (*.sln) under source control, but that is just the application developer's way of life.

If you are using the Beta edition of the Visual Studio.NET and NGWS SDK systems, you find another problem. This problem comes up when you attempt to deploy an application to a new machine. In this case, you find that no runtime environment for the .NET system exists. For your application to run, it must have the full NGWS SDK installed on that machine. Although this is certain to be fixed before the final version of the system is released in late 2001 or early 2002, this anomaly makes using the system in a production environment difficult.

That concludes the tour of application development in the Visual Studio.NET environment using the NGWS SDK. I hope that you have begun to appreciate the power and flexibility that the new .NET system provides to you as a developer. Now, take a look at some immediate solutions to your common problems.

Immediate Solutions

Using the Console

The console is one of the easiest and most versatile pieces of the CLR system in C#. You can output data to the console, read in data from users, and dump status information to the console without worrying about whether someone is around to read it. Unlike with a file, you don't have to worry about the console's filling up with data when no more disk space is available. Unlike with a window, you don't have to have users there to view the information as it is displayed. The console allows you to write complex applications without worrying much about the display formatting or laying out forms.

In this example, you look at how you can utilize the power of the console in your applications. Listing 7.1 shows a typical console application, one that dumps a bunch of data to the console output and then asks users for some information. The listing shows how to use both the input and output functionality of the console.

Listing 7.1   Using the console.

```csharp
using System; // For the Console definition
using System.IO; // For TextWriter definition

class ATestClass
{
    private int x;
    private double y;
    private string s;

    public ATestClass()
    {
        x = 10;
        y = 23.45;
        s = "ATestClass Information";
    }
    public void Dump(TextWriter o)
    {
        o.WriteLine("X = {0}", x );
        o.WriteLine("Y = {0}", y );
        o.WriteLine("S = {0}", s );
    }
}
```

```
class CH7_1
{
    public static void Main()
    {
        // Output a few things to the console
        Console.WriteLine("This is a test");
        Console.WriteLine("This is an integer: {0}", 1 );

        ATestClass test = new ATestClass();
        Console.WriteLine("This is an object: {0}", test );
        Console.WriteLine("This is a dump of an object:");
        test.Dump( Console.Out );

        // Get input from the user until they say "End"
        Boolean done = false;
        while ( !done )
        {
            string s = Console.ReadLine();
            if ( s == "End" )
                break;
        }

        // Output things without a line break
        Console.Write("This");
        Console.Write(" ");
        Console.Write("is");
        Console.Write(" ");
        Console.Write("a");
        Console.Write(" ");
        Console.Write("test");
    }
}
```

Here is the output from this little console application:

```
This is a test
This is an integer: 1
This is an object: ATestClass
This is a dump of an object:
X = 10
Y = 23.45
S = ATestClass Information
End
This is a test
```

As you can see in this example, the console can read and write to the output device. You can get information from users using the **ReadLine** method and get output to users using either the **Write** or **WriteLine** method. The difference between these two methods is that the **Write** method does not output a carriage return and linefeed (advancing to the next line) when it is done writing the information you output. The **WriteLine** method does these things.

Another interesting facet of this example is the use of the **TextWriter** class that makes up the output object for the console. As you see in the following example, you can modify this value to redirect console output. This feature is quite valuable for applications that do a great deal of logging.

Changing the Console Standard Output to a File

Imagine that an application in your corporation dumps a great deal of logging information about the program state to the console. Debugging information, program state information, and other valuable data is being dumped to the console. Unfortunately, when the program terminates, normally or abnormally, the console window it was writing to is closed. All this useful debugging information is lost. This situation is obviously not the optimal solution. In fact, situations like these are the main reason that debuggers often go bald, from pulling their hair out over what might be causing an unseen problem.

If your program is a simple little console application, such as the one you have been developing in this book, modifying the output to use a file rather than the console would be no problem. Unfortunately, if you are worried about the amount of information being lost, you're likely to have a somewhat larger-scale application. In this case, changing all the **Console** output calls to a file write is a non-trivial exercise.

Wouldn't it be nice if someone had thought this process through and recognized that this kind of problem happens all the time? Isn't it amazing when someone else does think of these things for you and builds them in ahead of time? In the case of the **Console** component of the CLR, changing the output to go to another device, such as a file, is a simple matter after you know how to do it. In this example, you see exactly how to redirect the output of the console to another place.

In Listing 7.2, you find a simple application that first writes a bunch of data to the console and then changes the console to point to a file and writes out the same bunch of information. If you run the application, you find that the output goes first to the console device (the console window) and then to a file.

7. Writing Applications

Listing 7.2 Changing the console standard output to a file.

```
using System;
using System.IO;

class CH7_2
{
    FileStream fs;
    StreamWriter w;
    public void SetupConsoleToFile()
    {
        fs = new FileStream("log.txt", FileMode.OpenOrCreate,
                    FileAccess.Write);
        w = new StreamWriter(fs);
        Console.SetOut(w);
    }
    public void DoSomeConsoleOutput()
    {
        Console.WriteLine("This is a test");
        Console.WriteLine("This is another test");
        Console.WriteLine("An Integer: {0}", 123 );
        Console.WriteLine("A Floating Point Number: {0}", 123.456 );
    }
    public void Cleanup()
    {
        w.Close();
        fs.Close();
    }

    public static void Main(String[] args)
    {
        CH7_2 app = new CH7_2();

        app.DoSomeConsoleOutput();
        app.SetupConsoleToFile();
        app.DoSomeConsoleOutput();
        app.Cleanup();
    }
}
```

As you can see by the highlighted section of code, you simply create an output file you want to use for the console output. In the C# CLR, a file stream contains a stream writer, which can be accessed by using the **StreamWriter** constructor and passing it the newly created file stream. The **StreamWriter** class is derived from the abstract **TextWriter** class, which allows you to simply assign this **StreamWriter** object to the **Out** stream for the **Console** class. Internally, the

Console class simply relies on the interfaces supported by the **TextWriter** class to output its data.

Consider this valuable technique for your own application. By allowing users access to your internal components that are used for things like saving data, retrieving data, or displaying data, you can allow users to have the full functionality of your object with their own output devices.

Getting Input from Users

Although outputting data to users is the more exciting and interesting use of the console, you can also use it to read data from users. Data can be read in from the console only in the form of character information, whether it's single characters or strings. Unlike in C or C++ or even Java, you have no way to enter numeric data directly from users. You must enter a string and convert it to the type you want it to be.

In Listing 7.3, you can see several examples of using the console for input and formatting. The first example shows how to read in a string and then print it for users to see. The second example shows how to read a string and directly convert it to a number. The final example shows how to read single characters from the input stream. Note that when you run the little program, you have to enter a character and hit Return to read it into the program. You can enter several characters, and the first one is returned by the read. C# has no "immediate mode" entry, where you can detect a single key press by a user in the console window.

Listing 7.3   Getting input from a user.

```
using System;
using System.IO;

class CH7_3
{
    public static void Main()
    {
        Console.WriteLine("Enter a string: ");
        string s = Console.ReadLine();
        Console.WriteLine("You entered [{0}]", s );

        Console.WriteLine("Enter a number: ");
        int i = Console.ReadLine().ToInt16();
        Console.WriteLine("You entered [{0}]", i );
```

```
        double dollars = 1234.56;
        Console.WriteLine("Formatted Output: {0}",
            dollars.Format("C", null));

        // Read in a single character
        Console.Write("Enter a character: ");
        int c = Console.Read();
        Console.WriteLine("You entered: {0}", (char)c );
    }
}
```

The following sample run from the application shows what was entered and how
the program responded:

```
Enter a string:
Hello
You entered [Hello]
Enter a number:
123
You entered [123]
Formatted Output: $1,234.56
Enter a character: 123
You entered: 1
```

You might wonder what would happen if you enter something invalid for one of
the data types. Would the result be a default value, as it would be in C? Would
something awful happen in the application? The best way to find out something
like this is to try it, so give that one a shot:

```
Enter a string:
Bad Data
You entered [Bad Data]
Enter a number:
Hello

Exception occurred: System.FormatException:
    The input string was not in a correct format.
    at System.Number.ParseInt32(String s, NumberStyles style,
            NumberFormatInfo info)
    at System.Int16.Parse(String s,
            NumberStyles style,
            NumberFormatInfo info)
    at System.Int16.FromString(String s)
    at System.Convert.ToInt16(String value)
    at CH7_3.Main()
```

As you can see, C# protects you from invalid input by throwing an exception if the input is not in a valid form. You therefore don't have to worry about parsing and validating data. Simply check for an exception on conversion; you know that the data is incorrect, so you can ask the user for another try.

Accessing the Registry

The Registry is the single most important repository of information in the Windows operating system. The Registry (future versions of Windows will have multiple registries) contains information about the current system, settings for applications, program status information, and other data necessary for the system and its applications to run on a day-to-day basis. Working with the Registry is often a requirement of applications, so not surprisingly the C# CLR provides a rich set of functionality that gives you access to the Registry and its data.

The process for working with the Registry is quite simple. In this tree of keys, each key has a parent and potentially many children. To read the data you need from the Registry, you open a key at its highest level. You can use five potential keys to get "into" the system. These five keys have corresponding constant values in the Registry class in the CLR. This list describes the five keys:

- *HKEY_CLASSES_ROOT*—Represented by the **Registry.ClassesRoot** constant, this tree in the Registry is used for keeping track of all defined classes in the COM subsystem for the current machine. These classes are not specific to a given user or application, but rather span the entire realm of the operating system.

- *HKEY_CURRENT_USER*—Represented by the **Registry.CurrentUser** constant, this tree represents the settings for the current user in the system. For a machine that has multiple potential users, such as a business box running Windows 2000 with several users, this key points to the appropriate information for the user who is logged in.

- *HKEY_LOCAL_MACHINE*—Represented by the **Registry.LocalMachine** constant, this tree represents the settings for this machine, regardless of which user might be logged in. Information in this tree is independent of the current user, but contains the same kinds of data. The software installed for all users, the machine settings for networking, and similar elements are all found here.

- *HKEY_USERS*—Represented by the **Registry.Users** constant, this tree represents the sum of all users on the system. Depending on who is logged in to the machine, you find that one of these subkeys is the same as the current user (**Registry.CurrentUser**).

- *HKEY_CURRENT_CONFIG*—Represented by the **Registry.CurrentConfig** constant, this tree holds the current configuration settings for the system. This key holds a combination of the current security settings and the logged-in user.

Listing 7.4 shows how you work with the Registry in C#. As you can see from the listing, you must include the Registry information classes, which reside in the special namespace **Microsoft.Win32**. All the operating-system-specific functionality resides in this namespace. Using this namespace in your application guarantees that your application is not portable outside the Windows operating system family. As C# is ported to other operating systems, the importance of feature this becomes more obvious. For now, however, if you are writing Windows applications, you need not worry about it.

Listing 7.4 Accessing the Registry.

```csharp
using System;
using Microsoft.Win32;

class CH7_4
{
    public static void Main(String[] args)
    {
        // Let's read in something from the LocalMachine key
        RegistryKey rk = Registry.LocalMachine;
        RegistryKey subKey =
            rk.OpenSubKey(
                "HARDWARE\\DESCRIPTION\\System\\CentralProcessor\\0\\");
        object VendorID = subKey.GetValue("VendorIdentifier");
        Console.WriteLine("The Central Processor of this machine is: {0}",
            VendorID );

        // Now, open a key to a random spot
        RegistryKey randkey = Registry.CurrentUser;
        // Build the key out of the arguments
        string key = "";
        for ( int i=0; i<args.Length-1; ++i )
        {
            key += args[i];
            key += "\\";
        }
        RegistryKey subKey1 = randkey.OpenSubKey(key);
        object keyValue = subKey1.GetValue(args[args.Length-1]);
        Console.WriteLine("Key {0} Value {1} = {2}",
            key,
            args[args.Length-1],
            keyValue );
```

```
        // Let's create a new key for our company under LocalMachine
        RegistryKey companyKey = Registry.CurrentUser;
        RegistryKey subKey3 = companyKey.CreateSubKey("MyCompany");
        // Give the key some values
        subKey3.SetValue("Name", "MyCompany");
        subKey3.SetValue("RegistrationID", 1234567);
        subKey3.SetValue("Date", "01/01/2001");
        companyKey.Close();

        // Finally, read back in the company key to verify
        RegistryKey companyKeyRead = Registry.CurrentUser;
        RegistryKey subKey4 = companyKeyRead.OpenSubKey("MyCompany");

        object companyName = subKey4.GetValue("MyCompany");
        Console.WriteLine("Company Name: {0}", companyName );
        object regID = subKey4.GetValue("RegistrationID");
        Console.WriteLine("RegistrationID: {0}", regID );
        object theDate = subKey4.GetValue("Date");
        Console.WriteLine("Date: {0}", theDate );

    }
}
```

The listing shows two distinct pieces to working with the Registry: reading from it and writing to it. Reading from the Registry is a common event and is something you can do without concerning yourself with the ramifications of your actions. Writing to the Registry, on the other hand, can be a dangerous thing. Although writing your own data to the Registry is safe enough, modifying system values can destroy the operating system's ability to load itself. Carefully consider the effects of your actions before you undertake these tasks.

The output from this little application is as follows:

```
C:\ >ch7_4 software microsoft notepad 1fFaceName
The Central Processor of this machine is: GenuineIntel
Key software\microsoft\notepad\ Value 1fFaceName = Lucida Console
Company Name:
RegistrationID: 1234567
Date: 01/01/2001
```

As you can see, the application can read and write to the Registry. Although this application is quite simple, it does illustrate some things you can do with a Registry key in C#.

The Registry provides functionality for reading and writing as well as for deleting data. The **RegistryKey** class has methods for reading, writing, and deleting data, using the **GetValue**, **SetValue**, and **DeleteValue** methods.

Using Multiple Threads

Modern programming environments are, by their nature, multitasking. As the developer, you must be aware of other applications running at the same time as your own application. A related problem is the issue of multithreading. You often have in your application a number of different tasks that need to be running at the same time to get things accomplished in a reasonable amount of time. Multithreading is used whenever tasks need to be accomplished that do not require sequential tasks to be performed.

C# provides a considerable amount of support for multiple threads in an application. The entire **Threading** library in the **System** namespace allows you to create threads, run them, stop them, and monitor them. Threads receive unique identification numbers and can communicate with the outside world via member variables or delegates or by calling member methods of the class in which they reside. In this example, you look at a case where multiple threads help get something accomplished more quickly. You create a character-counting application that allows you to count multiple files at the same time. Because the only way to do things "at the same time" is with threading, that is the approach you use.

Listing 7.5 shows the application that utilizes multiple threads to count characters. Following the listing, you explore the ways in which it works.

Listing 7.5   Using multiple threads.

```
using System;
using System.IO;
using System.Threading;

public class CH7_5
{
    Thread[] threads;
    string[]   sFileNames;
    int[]      iThreadIDs;

    public void RunThread()
    {
        string sFile = "";
        int id = Thread.CurrentThread.GetHashCode();
        // Find it in the list
        for ( int i=0; i<iThreadIDs.Length; ++i )
            if ( id == iThreadIDs[i] )
                sFile = sFileNames[i];
```

```
        // If we found a filename for this thread, count the
        // letters in it
        StreamReader sr = File.OpenText(sFile);
        int nCount = 0;
        while (sr.Peek()!=-1)
        {
            int ch = sr.Read();
            nCount ++;
        }
        sr.Close();
        Console.WriteLine("There were {0} characters in file {1}",
            nCount, sFile );

    }


    public void StartThreads(String[] args)
    {
        threads =  new Thread[args.Length];
        sFileNames = new string[args.Length];
        iThreadIDs = new int[args.Length];

        for ( int i=0; i<args.Length; ++i )
        {
            sFileNames[i] = args[i];
            threads[i] = new Thread( new ThreadStart(RunThread) );
            iThreadIDs[i] = threads[i].GetHashCode();
            Console.WriteLine("Thread ID {0} is with file {1}",
                iThreadIDs[i],
            sFileNames[i] );

            threads[i].Start();
        }
    }

    public static void Main(String[] args)
    {
        CH7_5 app = new CH7_5();

        app.StartThreads(args);
    }
}
```

A number of interesting things happen in this example. First, notice how you create the threads in accordance with the number of files a user passes in on the command line. You have no reason to create too many threads to accomplish your task, nor do you have justification for creating fewer than you need. Also notice that the method **GetHashCode** is used to retrieve a unique identifier for each thread. This method gives you a way to associate a thread ID, which is nonsequential, with the information you want to give to that thread, which in this case is the file name to process.

After the thread is started, it kicks off the method used to process it, which in this example is the **RunThread** method. This method first determines which thread it is running in and then uses that thread ID to map itself to the file that needs to be processed by the thread. After it has finished, the method ends and the thread terminates itself.

When the application was run over several of the listings of code for this chapter, the results looked something like this:

```
C:\ >ch7_5 ch7_5.cs ch7_4.cs ch7_3.cs
Thread ID 9 is with file ch7_5.cs
Thread ID 12 is with file ch7_4.cs
Thread ID 13 is with file ch7_3.cs
There were 1427 characters in file ch7_5.cs
There were 1913 characters in file ch7_4.cs
There were 686 characters in file ch7_3.cs
```

The last point to notice in this example is that the **Console.WriteLine** method is threadsafe and is not interrupted in the middle of a line. Otherwise, because the threads finish at close to the same time, you would see a mix of characters on-screen.

Using the Date and Time Functions

Dates and times are important facets of application programming. Users want to know when something occurred, and they want to see the dates and times expressed in a way they can understand. Under the covers, so to speak, C# does dates and times the way most languages do, by keeping track of the number of seconds since some arbitrary date in the past. However, C# and the CLR also allow you to work with dates and times as though they were human-readable entities. You can format dates or times, create objects that represent a specific month/day/year combination, and even do math on date and time objects.

Several bits of functionality are supported by the C# **DateTime** structure. First, notice that the **DateTime** structure, although not a true "class" in the object-oriented sense, has methods, properties, and overloaded operators, just like any "real" class. C# blurs the distinction between classes and structures.

In Listing 7.6, you can see examples of using the **DateTime** structure. First, take a look at the listing and then the discussion of how the various components of the system work.

Listing 7.6   Using the **DateTime** functions.

```
using System;
using System.Globalization;

class CH7_6
{
    public static void Main()
    {
        // Create some date/time objects
        DateTime dt = new DateTime();
        DateTime dt1 = new DateTime( 2001,12,31 );
        DateTime dt2 = new DateTime( 2000,12,31,23,59,59);

        // Print them out as strings
        Console.WriteLine("DT as string: {0}", dt.ToString() );
        Console.WriteLine("DT1 as string: {0}", dt1.ToString() );
        Console.WriteLine("DT2 as string: {0}", dt2.ToString() );

        // Do some comparisons
        if ( dt2 < dt1 )
           Console.WriteLine("Dt2 < Dt1" );
        else
           if ( dt2 == dt1 )
         Console.WriteLine("Dt2 == Dt1");
     else
         Console.WriteLine("Dt2 > Dt1");

        // One year as a time span
        TimeSpan year = new TimeSpan( 365 * TimeSpan.TicksPerDay );

        // Add a few of these to the date/time object
        for ( int i=0; i<10; ++i )
           dt += year;

        Console.WriteLine("DT as string: {0}", dt.ToString() );

        // Look at the min and max date/time values
        Console.WriteLine("Min Date: {0}", DateTime.MinValue.ToString () );
        Console.WriteLine("Max Date: {0}", DateTime.MaxValue.ToString () );
```

```
// Current date and time
Console.WriteLine("Current Date and Time: {0}",
        DateTime.Now.ToString());
Console.WriteLine("Current Date Only: {0}",
        DateTime.Today.ToString());

// Do some leap year checks
int[] years = {1984, 2000, 1999, 2002 };
for ( int i=0; i<years.Length; ++i )
{
    if ( DateTime.IsLeapYear(years[i]) )
        Console.WriteLine("Year {0} is a leap year", years[i] );
    else
        Console.WriteLine("Year {0} is NOT a leap year", years[i] );
}

// Do some date time math
DateTime today = DateTime.Today;
today = today + new TimeSpan(TimeSpan.TicksPerDay);
Console.WriteLine("Tomorrow is: {0}", today.ToString() );
today = DateTime.Today - new TimeSpan(7*TimeSpan.TicksPerDay);
Console.WriteLine("Last Week on this day it was: {0}",
        today.ToString());

// Last thing to do: some pretty formatting
string[] format = {
    "d", "D",
    "f", "F",
    "g", "G",
    "m",
    "r",
    "s",
    "t", "T",
    "u", "U",
    "y",
    "dddd, MMMM dd yyyy",
    "ddd, MMM d \"'\"yy",
    "dddd, MMMM dd",
    "M/yy",
    "dd-MM-yy",
};
string date;
for (int i = 0; i < format.Length; i++)
{
```

```
        date = dt.Format(format[i], DateTimeFormatInfo.InvariantInfo);
        Console.WriteLine(String.Concat(format[i], " :" , date));
    }


    }
}
```

Many **DateTime** structure methods are clear and straightforward. Notice that C# has quite a few built-in constants for working with dates and times, such as the concept of **Now**, which represents the current date and time, and **Today**, which simply represents the current time.

Mathematical manipulation of the **DateTime** structure is done via the **TimeSpan** structure. A **TimeSpan** object represents a *delta* in time, which is the expression of a length of time rather than a specific time or date. You can see how the **TimeSpan** structure is used in the highlighted line in the code listing.

The final piece of the **DateTime** listing shows how to format dates and times in various ways. If you were to look at the output of this little application, you would see not only the default formatting, using the **ToString** method, but also all the individual formats. Here is what happens when you run this application on the console:

```
DT as string: 0001-01-01T00:00:00
DT1 as string: 2001-12-31T00:00:00
DT2 as string: 2000-12-31T23:59:59
Dt2 < Dt1
DT as string: 0010-12-30T00:00:00
Min Date: 0001-01-01T00:00:00
Max Date: 9999-12-31T23:59:59
Current Date and Time: 2001-06-01T07:47:46
Current Date Only: 2001-06-01T00:00:00
Year 1984 is a leap year'
Year 2000 is a leap year
Year 1999 is NOT a leap year
Year 2002 is NOT a leap year
Tomorrow is: 2001-06-02T00:00:00
Last Week on this day it was: 2001-05-25T00:00:00
d :12/30/0010
D :Thursday, December 30, 0010
f :Thursday, December 30, 0010 00:00
F :Thursday, December 30, 0010 00:00:00
g :12/30/0010 00:00
G :12/30/0010 00:00:00
m :December 30
r :Thu, 30 Dec 0010 07:00:00 GMT
```

```
s :0010-12-30T00:00:00
t :00:00
T :00:00:00
u :0010-12-30 07:00:00Z
U :Thursday, December 30, 0010 07:00:00
y :December, 0010
dddd, MMMM dd yyyy :Thursday, December 30 0010
ddd, MMM d "'"yy :Thu, Dec 30 '10
dddd, MMMM dd :Thursday, December 30
M/yy :12/10
dd-MM-yy :30-12-10
```

As you can see, C# provides a rich formatting capability for **DateTime** objects.

Listing All Servers Using the Windows API

C# is a brand-new language, with brand-new concepts and a strong leaning toward safe programming. The problem, however, is that it runs on the Windows operating system, which is neither new nor safe. Windows applications use the Windows API to do nearly all the things they need to get done. The Windows API is full of functions and macros that use unsafe elements, like pointers, void casts, and strange indirections. How can you expect to use C# then, without thinking that you need to reinvent the world?

The designers of C# recognized that it was important to give programmers the same access to the Windows API that they had when using their older programming languages. Without this access, the designers reasoned, the CLR writers would have had to have taken into account every single API call and wrapped each one of them in a type-safe manner. This process wasn't feasible, if the language was going to be released in a reasonable period and keep up with the changes in the API. Imagine trying to keep up with the Microsoft API-of-the-week while still trying to maintain the integrity of your runtime library. (My mind boggles at the prospect.)

To solve this problem, the C# designers chose to allow you to use the same old pointers and void casts that existed in languages older than .NET, but with one catch: You could do things that you knew were not safe, but you will have to prove to the compiler that you understand they were not safe. To accomplish this task, you use the **unsafe** keyword. To illustrate this usage, take a look at a common programming task in Windows, enumerating all the servers within a domain.

Listing 7.7 shows how to use the **unsafe** keyword in an application and how to make calls to a Windows API function that requires pointers.

Listing 7.7 Listing all servers using the Windows API.

```
using System;
using System.Runtime.InteropServices;

class CH7_7
{
    public enum ServerTypeEnum
    {
        steNone = 0,
        steWorkstation = 0x00000001,
        steAll = 0x00000002,
        steSQLServer = 0x00000004,
        steDomainController = 0x00000008
    }

    [sysimport(dll="netapi32.dll")]
    private static extern void
            NetApiBufferFree([marshal(UnmanagedType.U4)]uint bufptr);

    [sysimport(dll="netapi32.dll")]
    unsafe private static extern uint
            NetServerEnum([marshal(UnmanagedType.LPWStr)] string
ServerName,
        uint level,
        [marshal(UnmanagedType.LPVoid)]uint* bufptr,
        uint prefmaxlen,
        ref uint entriesread,
        ref uint totalentries,
        uint servertype,
        [marshal(UnmanagedType.LPWStr)] string domain,
        uint resume_handle);

    [System.Runtime.InteropServices.StructLayoutAttribute
            (LayoutKind.Sequential, CharSet=CharSet.Auto)]
    public struct SERVER_INFO_101
    {
        public int dwPlatformID;
        public int lpszServerName;
        public int dwVersionMajor;
        public int dwVersionMinor;
        public int dwType;
        public int lpszComment;
    }

    public static void ListServers(string domain)
    {
```

```
string servername = null;
uint level = 101, prefmaxlen = 0xFFFFFFFF,
            entriesread = 0, totalentries = 0,
        resume_handle = 0;
    ServerTypeEnum _ServerType = ServerTypeEnum.steAll;

unsafe
{
    // Get a pointer to the server info structure
    SERVER_INFO_101* si = null;
    SERVER_INFO_101* pTmp;
    uint nRes = NetServerEnum(servername, level,
      (uint *) &si, prefmaxlen, ref entriesread,
            ref totalentries,
      (uint)_ServerType, domain, resume_handle);

    if (nRes == 0)
    {
        if ((pTmp = si) != null)     //assign the temp pointer
        {
            for (int i = 0; i < entriesread; i++)
            {
                try
                {
                    Console.WriteLine(Marshal.PtrToStringAuto(
                        pTmp->lpszServerName));
                }
                catch (Exception e)
                {
                    Console.WriteLine(e.Message) ;
                }
                pTmp++;
            }
        }
    }
    NetApiBufferFree((uint)si);
}
}

    public static void Main(String[] args)
{
    if ( args.Length > 0 )
        ListServers( args[0] );
}
}
```

If you run this application, passing it the name of your server domain on the command line, you see it dump a list of the servers available to you. This list shows that the application is communicating with the Windows API functions and that the unsafe code works, well, safely.

Related solution:	Found on page:
Using the **unsafe** Keyword	168

Working with the Event Log

One of the joys of programming is tracking down what happened when something goes wrong in your application. Sometimes, the problem is that an application didn't load properly or failed to initialize. At other times, the problem occurs when an unhandled error in the application causes it to crash. In other cases, a combination of poor programming practices and unexpected data values causes a disaster to occur.

Whatever the source of the problem, tracking down the issue is usually a matter of trying to see what happened and then tracing that information back to the original source code to see why it happened. Only when you know what went wrong and why can you have any hope of fixing it so that it doesn't happen again. The question is how can you find out what went wrong after the fact?

If you have created some kind of application log, you can trace through and see where your application might have failed. Writing logging code and maintaining it so that you can read it back in or view it in another system is a tedious and errorprone task, however. Fortunately, the Windows operating system already contains such a device, called the Event Log subsystem.

In keeping with the C# concept of providing as much built-in functionality as possible, the CLR nicely wraps up the Event Log into an object you can use in C# style programming in your application. Using that functionality, however, can be a bit tricky because the **EventLog** class is part of a separate component of the system, called the Diagnostics subsystem. In this example, shown in Listing 7.8, you explore how you can use the Event Log in your application as well as how to get the compiler to load the entry information for an external dynamic link library (DLL).

Listing 7.8   Working with the Event Log.

```
using System;
using System.Diagnostics;

class CH7_8
{
    public static void WriteLog()
    {
        string source = "EventSource";
        string log    = "CH7_8.LOG";

        // Create a new Event Log
        EventLog el = new EventLog();

        // See if it exists
        if (!EventLog.SourceExists(source))
        {
            EventLog.CreateEventSource(source,log);
        }
        el.Source = source;

        String message =  "Starting Up";
        el.WriteEntry(message, EventLogEntryType.Information);
        message =  "Processing";
        el.WriteEntry(message, EventLogEntryType.Information);
        message =  "Shutting down";
        el.WriteEntry(message, EventLogEntryType.Information);
    }
    public static void ReadLog()
    {
        string source = "EventSource";

        // Create a new Event Log
        EventLog el = new EventLog();

        // See if it exists
        if (!EventLog.SourceExists(source))
        {
            Console.WriteLine("Event Log does not exist!");
            return;
        }
        el.Source = source;

        foreach (EventLogEntry entry in el.Entries) {
            Console.WriteLine("\tEntry: " + entry.Message);
```

```
        }
    }
    public static void DeleteLog()
    {
        string log    = "CH7_8.LOG";
        EventLog.Delete( log );
    }

    public static void Main()
    {
        WriteLog();
        ReadLog();
        DeleteLog();
    }
}
```

This listing shows off the three components of working with event logs. First, you create or open an event log and add some new entries to it. Next, you open that log and read back in the entries you added. Finally, you delete the log to show how you can clear out a custom event log in the system.

Here's the output from this application:

```
Entry: Starting Up
Entry: Processing
Entry: Shutting down
```

As you can see, the writing and reading parts work fine. But how do you verify that the deleting part of the log works? The answer is to run the application twice. If the log was not deleted, you would simply append to it and see the same set of messages twice. As you can verify, if you run the application a second time, you see the log entries only once, indicating that the log was deleted when the program ended.

Now, the tricky part. How do you get this program to compile and link with the compiler? If you simply run the standard compile command, **csc**, you find that you get a bunch of errors related to the fact that the **EventLog** class is not defined. These errors are caused by the fact that **System.Diagnostics** is not being loaded and read by the assembly interpreter. To make the diagnostics library work properly, you need to tell the compiler where to find the assembly that contains the class in question. Here's how you do it:

```
C:\ >csc CH7_8.cs /R:System.Dll /R:System.Diagnostics.Dll
Microsoft (R) Visual C# Compiler Version 7.00.9030
[CLR version 1.00.2204.21]
Copyright (C) Microsoft Corp 2000. All rights reserved.
```

As you can see, you have to give the compiler not only the **System.Diagnostics** file, but also the more general **System.DLL** file. The reason is that you get only one pass through the loading process and things have to be defined in the proper order to work.

Listing the Command-Line Arguments

If you are working with a console application, users commonly demand to be able to get information into the console application from the command line. This information can be initialization data or utility data to operate on. Whatever your use for the information, you need to be able to get it and interpret it.

In many command-line utilities in Windows, Unix, and other operating systems, the common way to use command-line arguments is via a command-and-argument metaphor. In this manner, the command you want to execute is prefaced with a hyphen (-), and all arguments to that command follow it on the command line. For example, you might have a command line that looks something like this:

```
runcmd -print file doc window -left 240 -right 300 -printtrailer
```

In this trivial example, you are executing four commands (**print**, **left**, **right**, and **printtrailer**) and passing arguments to three of them. For example, the **print** command on the command line receives the arguments **file**, **doc**, and **window**. The **left** command receives the argument **240**. The **printtrailer** command apparently requires no arguments.

In this example, you can see how to use the command-line arguments as well as how to determine which arguments are being passed to which commands on the command-line interface. Listing 7.9 shows an example of parsing and using the command-line arguments.

Listing 7.9   Listing the command-line arguments.

```
using System;

class CH7_9
{
    public static String Right( string s, int len )
    {
        // How many characters to skip?
        int nSkip = s.Length - len;
        // Copy
        string temp = "";
```

```
    for ( int i=nSkip; i<s.Length; ++i )
        temp += s[i];
    return temp;
}
public static int GetArgsToCommand( int nPos,
        String[] array )
{
    // Starting at nPos, work our way through
    // the array looking for something that
    // does NOT start with a hyphen
    int nEnd = nPos;
    for ( int i=nPos; i<array.Length; ++i )
    {
        if ( array[i][0] == '-' )
            break;
        Console.WriteLine("Command Argument: {0}",
            array[i] );
        nEnd = i;
    }
    return nEnd;
}


public static void Main(String[] args)
{
    // First, just print them out
    for ( int i=0; i<args.Length; ++i )
    {
        Console.WriteLine("Argument {0} = {1}",
            i, args [i] );
    }

    // Parse simply for instructions
    for ( int i=0; i<args.Length; ++i )
    {
        if( args[i][0] == '-' )
        {
            string cmd = Right(args[i], args[i].Length-1);
            Console.WriteLine("Command {0}", cmd );
            i = GetArgsToCommand( i+1, args );
        }
    }

}
}
```

Notice the utility function, **Right**, that is shown in the listing. This simple example implements a Visual Basic-like string-handling function in C#. Another thing to notice in this example is that you can modify a loop counter in a **for** loop from within. The shaded line of the listing shows how to do this, in order to skip over the command arguments within the string.

Running this application produces the following output:

```
C:\ >ch7_9 -print file doc window -left 240 -right 300 -open
Argument 0 = -print
Argument 1 = file
Argument 2 = doc
Argument 3 = window
Argument 4 = -left
Argument 5 = 240
Argument 6 = -right
Argument 7 = 300
Argument 8 = -open
Command print
Command Argument: file
Command Argument: doc
Command Argument: window
Command left
Command Argument: 240
Command right
Command Argument: 300
Command open
```

Creating a New Form

Until this point in the book, you have been creating exclusively console applications. Of course, C# is hardly only about console programs: It can also create all sorts of other applications. In addition, you have been simply entering the code from scratch in a code editor and running the command-line compiler to create the executables from the C# source code. This situation is about to change, however, as you begin to examine the C# compiler built into Visual Studio.NET and Visual C++ 7.0.

When you create a new application in Visual Studio, you see a display much like the one shown in Figure 7.1, with the code listing generated by the development environment. In this case, a Windows application project was selected.

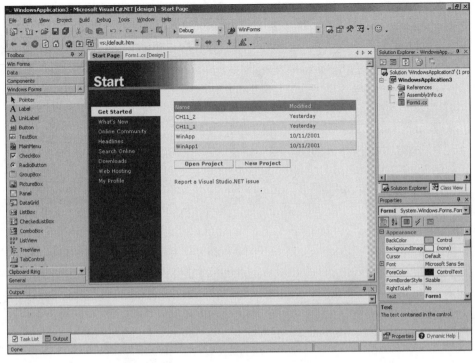

Figure 7.1   Visual Studio.NET with a new project.

Because this example is the first one for a Visual Studio application in this chapter, I walk you through it step by step. From now on, and in all other chapters, refer to this example in this chapter to review the steps involved.

First, you add a button to the form shown in the environment, by selecting the Toolbox while the form is displayed. This step shows you the elements you can click on to drop on the form. Select the WinForms entry and find the Button component. Click on the button component and drop it on the form. Your form should now look like the one shown in Figure 7.2.

The second step in the process is to modify the display of the button so that it contains the text *Close*. To close the form in a simple manner, a user selects this button. Select the button and right-click it to display the properties sheet in your Visual Studio.NET environment. Find the **Text** property in the list, and modify it to read *Close*.

The third and final step of this example is to add the code to close the form whenever a user clicks the Close button. If you switch to source code view (in this case, the source code file is named Form1.cs), you see the following code. The

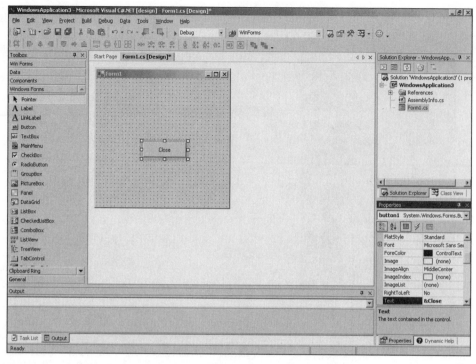

Figure 7.2   Visual Studio.NET environment with a new form and button.

highlighted lines are the ones added to close the form. To add the callback, simply double-click the button to bring up its default event, **Click**. Then add the **Close** method call:

```
namespace CH7_10
{
    using System;
    using System.Drawing;
    using System.Collections;
    using System.ComponentModel;
    using System.WinForms;
    using System.Data;

    /// <summary>
    ///     Summary description for Form1.
    /// </summary>
    public class Form1 : System.WinForms.Form
    {
        /// <summary>
        ///     Required designer variable.
```

```
/// </summary>
private System.ComponentModel.Container components;
private System.WinForms.Button button1;

public Form1()
{
    //
    // Required for Windows Form Designer support
    //
    InitializeComponent();

    //
    // TODO: Add any constructor code after InitializeComponent call
    //
}

/// <summary>
///     Clean up any resources being used.
/// </summary>
public override void Dispose()
{
    base.Dispose();
    components.Dispose();
}

/// <summary>
///     Required method for Designer support - do not modify
///     the contents of this method with the code editor.
/// </summary>
private void InitializeComponent()
{
    this.components = new System.ComponentModel.Container ();
    this.button1 = new System.WinForms.Button ();
    //@this.TrayHeight = 0;
    //@this.TrayLargeIcon = false;
    //@this.TrayAutoArrange = true;
    button1.Location = new System.Drawing.Point (112, 208);
    button1.Size = new System.Drawing.Size (75, 23);
    button1.TabIndex = 0;
    button1.Text = "Close";
    button1.Click += new System.EventHandler
                    (this.button1_Click);
    this.Text = "Form1";
    this.AutoScaleBaseSize = new System.Drawing.Size (5, 13);
    this.Controls.Add (this.button1);
}
```

```
    protected void button1_Click (object sender, System.EventArgs e)
    {
        Close();
    }


    /// <summary>
    /// The main entry point for the application.
    /// </summary>
    public static void Main(string[] args)
    {
        Application.Run(new Form1());
    }
  }
}
```

When you run the application within the environment, you see a display similar to the one shown in Figure 7.3.

Of course, a great deal of other code is generated for this simple form. The important methods for you to consider, are **InitializeComponent**, **button1_Click**, and **Main**. The rest of the code is primarily a bunch of accounting done for the Visual Studio.NET and WinForms subsystems.

The **Main** method, as you can see, simply creates an instance of the form you have created and then uses the **Application** class to run the program with that form as the main entry point.

The **InitializeComponent** method, called in the constructor for the form, creates all the visual elements for the form. In this method, you should do any one-time startup functionality, such as creating any other elements you need to run with, connecting to a database, or performing other initialization functions.

Finally, the **button1_Click** method is called in response to a user clicking the button on the form. Notice how a delegate is used in the **InitializeComponent**

Figure 7.3   The Close form running.

method to attach the handler (**button1_Click**) to the event **button1.Click**. After all the associations are complete, the program runs. When a user clicks the button, the form closes. That's all there is to it!

Related solution:	Found on page:
Creating a New Event	201

Using Events with Form Objects

The most important part of the C# WinForms subsystem is the event-handling subsystem. Fortunately, the Visual Studio.Net Integrated Development Environment (IDE) makes it easy to work with the events and event handlers that are needed to process most work in an application. When you select an item in the IDE, you may then select the Properties window in the IDE. One option in the Properties window is the **Events** supported by that particular visual or nonvisual element. Double-clicking the name of the event handler permits you to create a new handler in your application for that event.

How does the IDE know what events and properties are supported by a given component? The IDE uses the same reflection API you can use to view information about a class or event. By reading the reflection information from the assembly that contains a given component, the IDE can then dynamically create a property list that contains all the available public properties and events you can modify in the environment.

In this example, you create the form shown in Figure 7.4. This form, as you can see, contains a label, a text box, two buttons, and a list box. The purpose of this application is to allow users to do three things. First, they should be able to enter a name in the text box and click the Add button to add that name to the list box. Second, they should be able to select a name in the list box by double-clicking that entry and seeing the index displayed in a Message box. Finally, clicking the Close button should close the application

Listing 7.10 shows the code used to support all three of these functions. The code has been stripped down to just the important sections to save space. Anything not shown is automatically generated by the IDE when creating and maintaining the form.

7. Writing Applications

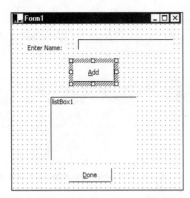

Figure 7.4   A form that supports various events.

Listing 7.10   Using events with form objects.

```
private void InitializeComponent()
{
    this.components = new System.ComponentModel.Container ();
    this.textBox1 = new System.WinForms.TextBox ();
    this.button1 = new System.WinForms.Button ();
    this.label1 = new System.WinForms.Label ();
    this.listBox1 = new System.WinForms.ListBox ();
    this.button2 = new System.WinForms.Button ();
    //@this.TrayHeight = 0;
    //@this.TrayLargeIcon = false;
    //@this.TrayAutoArrange = true;
    textBox1.Location = new System.Drawing.Point (112, 24);
    textBox1.TabIndex = 1;
    textBox1.Size = new System.Drawing.Size (168, 20);
    button1.Location = new System.Drawing.Point (104, 72);
    button1.Size = new System.Drawing.Size (72, 32);
    button1.TabIndex = 2;
    button1.Text = "&Add";
    button1.Click += new System.EventHandler (this.button1_Click);
    label1.Location = new System.Drawing.Point (24, 32);
    label1.Text = "Enter Name:";
    label1.Size = new System.Drawing.Size (72, 16);
    label1.TabIndex = 0;
    listBox1.Location = new System.Drawing.Point (64, 120);
    listBox1.Size = new System.Drawing.Size (152, 108);
    listBox1.TabIndex = 3;
    listBox1.DoubleClick += new System.EventHandler
            (this.listBox1_DoubleClick);
    button2.Location = new System.Drawing.Point (96, 240);
    button2.Size = new System.Drawing.Size (75, 23);
```

```
        button2.TabIndex = 4;
         button2.Text = "&Done";
        button2.Click += new System.EventHandler (this.button2_Click);
        this.Text = "Form1";
        this.AutoScaleBaseSize = new System.Drawing.Size (5, 13);
        this.Controls.Add (this.button2);
        this.Controls.Add (this.listBox1);
        this.Controls.Add (this.button1);
        this.Controls.Add (this.textBox1);
        this.Controls.Add (this.label1);
    }

protected void listBox1_DoubleClick (object sender, System.EventArgs e)
{
        // Which item did they double click on?
        int nIndex = this.listBox1.SelectedIndex;
        MessageBox.Show("You selected " + nIndex, "Selection",
            MessageBox.IconExclamation | MessageBox.OK);
    }

protected void button1_Click (object sender, System.EventArgs e)
{
    if ( this.textBox1.Text.Length != 0)
    {
        this.listBox1.Items.Add(
            this.textBox1.Text );
            this.textBox1.Text = "";
            this.textBox1.Focus();
    }
}

protected void button2_Click (object sender, System.EventArgs e)
{
        Close();
}
```

As you can see, when a user clicks the Close button, you simply invoke the **Close** method of the **Form** object, which closes the window and, because that form is the main object of the application, closes the application.

When a user clicks on the Add button, several things happen. First, you verify that something is in the text box to add to the list. Then, you get the text from the text box via the **Text** property and add it to the **List.Items** collection. This collection represents each of the strings in the list box. This technique is much easier than the way things used to be in Windows programming, when you would have to keep track of all the items yourself and use arcane API calls to add or remove elements from a list. After the item is added, you clear out the text in the text box and reset the input focus to be the text box. You can then make life easier for users, who can simply click on the Add button and have the program do its job and prepare itself for the next entry.

The only other thing this application does is to handle the double-click event in the list box. To do this, the program takes advantage of the fact that a double-click first selects the item (the standard click event) and then calls the double-click handler. For this reason, the program can simply test the **SelectedIndex** property to see which item was selected and then display that information for users.

As you can see, working with events in the WinForms subsystem is a breeze when you are working in the Integrated Development Environment (IDE). The IDE makes this process simple by giving you the opportunity to view all the events available for a given component and then to add your own handlers simply and easily.

Related solution:	Found on page:
Dynamically Invoking Methods from Classes in an Assembly	237

Using List Views

List view is one of the most versatile Windows visual components. List views allow you to show users elements in a variety of ways, including with icons or with details. The C# CLR makes working with **ListView** objects easy, as you see in the example in this section.

The **ListView** object has several different states of display, called *views*. The standard Explorer window in the Windows operating system shows off these views. You can have a view in either Report mode, which shows a series of column headers with data beneath them, or in LargeIcon mode, which displays icons next to the items arranged in columns horizontally. In this example, I explore both these view modes.

Figure 7.5 shows the project design mode for the form you create in this example. Note the addition of an **ImageList** object at the bottom of the form. You add an image list by selecting ImageList from the WinForms components in the toolbox. To add new images to the image list, select the object (the small, yellow square)

Figure 7.5   The **ListView** sample form.

and then select Properties from the right-click drop-down menu. In the Properties window, you find an Images property and a button. Click the button and select a few images. In this example, the images were culled from the default images found in the Common7 directory under the Visual Studio.NET main directory.

Listing 7.11 shows the code you need to add to the default CH7_12 project generated by Visual Studio to make this process happen. Look at the code first, and then explore how it all works.

Listing 7.11   The **ListView** sample code.

```
protected void radioButton2_CheckedChanged (object sender,
      System.EventArgs e)
{
    this.listView1.View = View.LargeIcon;
}


protected void radioButton1_CheckedChanged (object sender,
      System.EventArgs e)
{
    this.listView1.View = View.Report;
}


protected void button2_Click (object sender, System.EventArgs e)
{
    this.listView1.ListItems.Remove(0);
}


protected void button1_Click (object sender, System.EventArgs e)
{
    string[] subitems1 =
    {
      "Sub1.1",
      "Sub1.2",
      "Sub1.3"
    };
```

```
string[] subitems2 =
{
    "Sub2.1",
    "Sub2.2",
    "Sub2.3"
};
string[] subitems3 =
{
    "Sub3.1",
    "Sub3.2",
    "Sub3.3"
};
string[] subitems4 =
{
    "Sub4.1",
    "Sub4.2",
    "Sub4.3"
};

    this.listView1.ListItems.Add("Item 1", 0, subitems1 );
    this.listView1.ListItems.Add("Item 2", 1, subitems2 );
    this.listView1.ListItems.Add("Item 3", 2, subitems3 );
    this.listView1.ListItems.Add("Item 4", 3, subitems4 );

this.listView1.LargeImageList = this.imageList1;

// Add the column headers
this.listView1.Columns.Add("Title", 150,
    HorizontalAlignment.Center );
this.listView1.Columns.Add("Sub 1", 75,
    HorizontalAlignment.Center );
this.listView1.Columns.Add("Sub 2", 75,
    HorizontalAlignment.Center );
this.listView1.Columns.Add("Sub 3", 50,
    HorizontalAlignment.Center );
}
```

Some things that happen in the code are simple. For example, clicking one of the two radio buttons on the form changes the value of the View property in the **ListView** object. Figure 7.6 shows the form running in Report mode, and Figure 7.7 shows the form running in LargeIcon mode.

As you can see from the code listings, most of the work is done in the method, **button1_Click**, to add new data to the list view. This method does three things: adds new listing information to the **ListView** object, adds an image list to the list

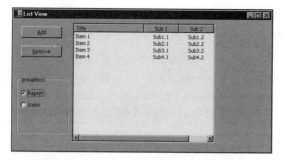

Figure 7.6   A ListView sample in Report mode.

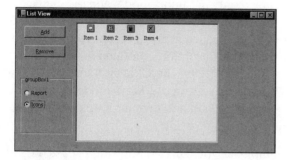

Figure 7.7   A ListView sample in LargeIcon mode.

view, and adds the column heading information needed to display the data in Report view.

When a list view is in Report view, it displays columns only as you have defined them. If you do not define any columns, the list view appears to be blank. Switching over to Icon view shows the default text for the first column. If you see a blank list view with a gray line at the top, you can be assured that you forgot to define the column headings. The column headings are attached by the **Add** method of the **Columns** property of the **ListView** object.

The **Column Add** method has this general form:

```
Add( string Title, int Width, HorizontalAlignment align);
```

You need to add a column header for each column you want displayed in the **ListView** when it is in Report mode.

After the column header information is displayed, you need to attach the image list to the **ListView** object so that it knows where to find the information to show for icons in one of the icon modes. C# has two icon modes, **LargeIcon** and **SmallIcon**, and it has two corresponding image lists, **LargeImageList** and

SmallImageList. In this example, you are using only the large icons, so all you set is the **LargeImageList** property to point to your own image list.

Finally, the data needs to be added to the ListView object so that something is displayed for users to see. (A list view with no data is like coffee without creamer: Some people find it appealing, but the rest of us find it dull and boring.) The information in a list view is added via the **ListItems Add** method. The general form of this method is:

```
Add( string MainEntry, int ImageIndex, string[] subitems );
```

The subitems information is displayed only in Report mode, and the image index information is used in only one of the icon modes (**LargeIcon** or **SmallIcon**). The image index corresponds to the zero-based array of icons or bitmaps stored in the **ImageList** property. After all this information is defined for a list view, the rest of the processing is done automatically by the CLR system. Changing the appearance of a list view is as simple as setting the **View** mode property. The system does all the work of arranging the data and keeping track of what a user changes (such as widening a column).

Removing items from the list is simple, as you can see. You simply pass the index of the item you want to remove to the Remove method of the **Items** property of the **ListView** object. The display is updated and the item removed.

Displaying a Message Box for a Form

If a single component is found in every known Windows application, it's the message box. Message boxes are used to keep users informed of what is going on or to display information or error status. You can display a message box with various buttons, icons, and textual information. Finding a message box in an application is so commonplace that users feel lost when they don't get the feedback that a message box provides for them.

If the preceding paragraph sounds a bit snide, that's my intention. Message boxes are generally overused in Windows applications, displaying information that users already know about and then forcing them to click OK to continue. Message boxes do have their uses, however, in informing people of exceptional events or statuses they have been waiting for. For example, you could use a message box to display something useless: "The file has been deleted. OK?" You simply have no reason to waste a user's time with that kind of message. On the other hand, you could display a useful message box: "Warning: This file is in use. Open ReadOnly? OK/Cancel."

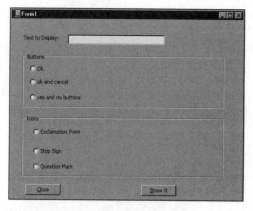

Figure 7.8   The Message Box form.

Figure 7.8 shows the form you use to explore the message box system.

Listing 7.12 shows a simple little form that allows you to check out the various options in using a message box by setting parameters in the form.

Listing 7.12   Displaying a message box for a form.

```
protected void button1_Click (object sender, System.EventArgs e)
{
    Close();
}


protected void button2_Click (object sender, System.EventArgs e)
{
    int nOptions = 0;
    if ( this.questionMark.Checked )
    {
        nOptions = MessageBox.IconQuestion;
    }
    if ( this.stopSign.Checked )
    {
        nOptions = MessageBox.IconHand;
    }
    if ( this.exclamationPoint.Checked )
    {
        nOptions = MessageBox.IconExclamation;
    }
    int nButtons = 0;
    // Now, check the button options
    if ( this.yesnobuttons.Checked )
    {
        nButtons = MessageBox.YesNo;
    }
```

```
if ( this.okcancelbutton.Checked )
{
    nButtons = MessageBox.OKCancel;
}
if ( this.okbutton.Checked )
{
    nButtons = MessageBox.OK;
}
MessageBox.Show( this, this.textBox1.Text,
    "MessageBox",
    nOptions | nButtons );
}
```

As usual, the listing has snipped out the code generated by Visual Studio.NET to save space. You can see the two methods used by the application to respond to events: **button1_Click** and **button2_Click**. The first one simply closes the form when a user clicks the Close button, and the second one uses the selected items to create a message box.

Getting Initial Arguments to a Form

One thing you get used to in working with utility programs is the ability to launch them from the command line with a series of arguments. For example, something as simple as the **copy** command has initial arguments:

```
copy fromFile toFile
```

When Windows applications came along, getting the arguments to the form was another matter. Because Windows programs aren't generally launched from the command line, if you wanted to add command-line arguments, you had to modify the launching icon or menu item for the application. This task was inconvenient and made it difficult to go back to the utility style usage to which people had grown accustomed.

C#, however, brings back this ability because a C# application is run just as easily from the command line as from a menu item. You can pass in arguments from the command line and have them quickly and easily loaded into the WinForms subsystem as the Console subsystem. You have no excuse for not allowing your users to pass in arguments for anything that might make sense.

In this example, you look at how you can pass in command-line arguments to your application and then use them within the program at startup time. The order

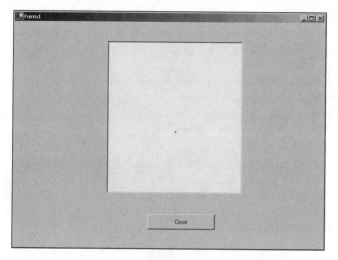

Figure 7.9   A form that displays initial arguments.

of doing things in an application is important, especially when it comes to working with visual elements. Figure 7.9 shows the form used for this example. It contains a list box that displays the arguments you pass into the form and a button that allows you to close the form.

Listing 7.13 shows the code used for this example. As you can see, the constructor and **InitializeComponent** methods of the form class have been modified to accept an array of strings that contain the initial arguments. These arguments are passed into the **Main** method of the class, just as they would be in any normal console application. No difference exists, fundamentally, between a Console application and a WinForms application, when it comes to programming them. This feature is another one that is often overlooked in C# programming.

Listing 7.13   Getting initial arguments to a form.

```
namespace CH7_14
{
    using System;
    using System.Drawing;
    using System.Collections;
    using System.ComponentModel;
    using System.WinForms;
    using System.Data;

    /// <summary>
    ///     Summary description for Form1.
    /// </summary>
    public class Form1 : System.WinForms.Form
```

```
{
    /// <summary>
    ///    Required designer variable.
    /// </summary>
    private System.ComponentModel.Container components;
    private System.WinForms.Button button1;
    private System.WinForms.ListBox listBox1;

    public Form1(String[] args)
    {
        //
        // Required for Windows Form Designer support
        //
        InitializeComponent(args);

    }


    /// <summary>
    ///    Clean up any resources being used.
    /// </summary>
    public override void Dispose()
    {
        base.Dispose();
        components.Dispose();
    }


    /// <summary>
    ///    Required method for Designer support - do not modify
    ///    the contents of this method with the code editor.
    /// </summary>
    private void InitializeComponent(String[] args)
    {
        this.components = new System.ComponentModel.Container ();
        this.button1 = new System.WinForms.Button ();
        this.listBox1 = new System.WinForms.ListBox ();
        //@this.TrayHeight = 0;
        //@this.TrayLargeIcon = false;
        //@this.TrayAutoArrange = true;
        button1.Location = new System.Drawing.Point (288, 400);
        button1.Size = new System.Drawing.Size (144, 32);
        button1.TabIndex = 1;
        button1.Text = "&Close";
        button1.Click += new System.EventHandler (this.button1_Click);
        listBox1.Location = new System.Drawing.Point (200, 40);
        listBox1.Size = new System.Drawing.Size (288, 316);
```

7. Writing
Applications

```
        listBox1.TabIndex = 0;
        this.Text = "Form1";
        this.AutoScaleBaseSize = new System.Drawing.Size (5, 13);
        this.ClientSize = new System.Drawing.Size (664, 469);
        this.Controls.Add (this.button1);
        this.Controls.Add (this.listBox1);

        for(int i=0; i<args.Length; ++i)
        {
            this.listBox1.Items.Add( args[i] );
        }
    }

    protected void button1_Click (object sender, System.EventArgs e)
    {
        Close();
    }

    /// <summary>
    /// The main entry point for the application.
    /// </summary>
    public static void Main(string[] args)
    {
        Application.Run(new Form1(args));
    }
  }
}
```

As you can see, adding the ability to get initial arguments to a form isn't much work, after you understand how the whole package works. The **Main** method is passed the data from the command line or launch window (if you launch the program from within the Windows Explorer system). This data is then passed along and put into the list box after it has been constructed and added to the form.

Adding a Menu to a Form

Menus are, from a user's perspective, the lifeblood of a Windows application. When an application first starts up, the main menu of the application is the first and most important thing users see. Responding to menu selections is what a program spends the majority of its time doing, so a developer would, not surprisingly, want to know exactly how to work with them.

In the example in this section, you add a new main menu to a form and allow users to view controls on the form based on which menu selection is chosen. To do this, create a new WinForms project in Visual Studio.NET and add three rows of controls. Row 1 should be a set of four radio buttons. Row 2 should be a set of four checkboxes. Row 3 should be a set of four buttons. Add a main menu component to the form with two main-level entries: File and Show. Under File, add a Close option. Under Show, add options for **Radio Buttons**, **Checkboxes**, and **Buttons**. Listing 7.14 shows the code that should end up being generated, along with the code needed to hide and show the components in response to menu item selections.

Listing 7.14   Adding a menu to a form.

```
protected void menuItem6_Click (object sender,
        System.EventArgs e)
{
    HideRadioButtons();
    HideCheckboxes();
    this.button1.Visible = true;
    this.button2.Visible = true;
    this.button3.Visible = true;
    this.button4.Visible = true;
}


protected void HideCheckboxes()
{
    this.checkBox1.Visible = false;
    this.checkBox2.Visible = false;
    this.checkBox3.Visible = false;
    this.checkBox4.Visible = false;
}


protected void menuItem5_Click (object sender,
        System.EventArgs e)
{
    HideRadioButtons();
    HideButtons();
    this.checkBox1.Visible = true;
    this.checkBox2.Visible = true;
    this.checkBox3.Visible = true;
    this.checkBox4.Visible = true;
}


protected void HideRadioButtons()
{
    this.radioButton1.Visible = false;
    this.radioButton2.Visible = false;
```

```
      this.radioButton3.Visible = false;
      this.radioButton4.Visible = false;
   }
   protected void HideButtons()
   {
      this.button1.Visible = false;
      this.button2.Visible = false;
      this.button3.Visible = false;
      this.button4.Visible = false;
   }

   protected void menuItem4_Click (object sender,
           System.EventArgs e)
   {
      HideCheckboxes();
      HideButtons();
      this.radioButton1.Visible = true;
      this.radioButton2.Visible = true;
      this.radioButton3.Visible = true;
      this.radioButton4.Visible = true;
   }
```

As you can see, the issue of responding to a menu event is exactly like any other event in WinForms. If you were to look at the code in the **InitializeComponent** method of the form, you would see events tied to menu selections, such as:

```
menuItem5.Click += new System.EventHandler (this.menuItem5_Click);
```

This line assigns an event handler to a user selecting a menu item. It is built, of course, like every other event handler in C#, which makes it easy to remember. No more ugly resource files, specialized menu callbacks, or other different coding techniques are needed to work with menus in .NET. Just point, click, drag, and drop your way to a whole new application.

Creating a Windows Service

A *system service* runs in the background of the operating system, doing things for users while they are doing whatever it is they want to be doing with applications. System services are not generally user interactive. They tend to be background tasks that monitor what is going on and log events as they find them.

C# appears to make creating a system service easy, although a few steps might not be intuitive to you. Take a look at an example of a system service, including how to create it, how to install it, and how to start and stop it. First, create a simple Windows service project in Visual Studio.NET. The code generator creates the skeleton for you; the coding is up to you. Listing 7.15 shows the basic skeleton of the service, along with shaded code that shows what the service does. In this case, the service simply logs itself to the Event Log of the Windows operating system when it starts or stops.

Listing 7.15   Creating a windows service.

```
namespace CH7_16
{
    using System;
    using System.Collections;
    using System.Core;
    using System.ComponentModel;
    using System.Configuration;
    using System.Data;
    using System.Web.Services;
    using System.Diagnostics;
    using System.ServiceProcess;

    public class WinService1 : System.ServiceProcess.ServiceBase
    {
        /// <summary>
        ///     Required designer variable.
        /// </summary>
        private System.ComponentModel.Container components;
        private EventLog eventLog;

        public WinService1()
        {
            InitializeComponent();
            string source = "Ch7_16";
            eventLog = new EventLog();
            eventLog.Source = source;
        }
        static void Main()
        {
            System.ServiceProcess.ServiceBase[] ServicesToRun;
            ServicesToRun = new System.ServiceProcess.ServiceBase[]
                { new WinService1() };
            System.ServiceProcess.ServiceBase.Run(ServicesToRun);
        }
        private void InitializeComponent()
        {
            components = new System.ComponentModel.Container();
            this.ServiceName = "WinService1";
```

```
        }
        protected override void OnStart(string[] args)
        {
          eventLog.WriteEntry("Ch7_16 starting up!");
        }
        protected override void OnStop()
        {
          eventLog.WriteEntry("Ch7_16 shutting down!");
        }
    }
}
```

As you can see, there isn't much to the service. When the service starts, the **OnStart** method is called. When the service is shut down, the **OnStop** method is called. The majority of the work involved with services is getting them installed and getting them started. If you follow the instructions that come with the system, you find that you are supposed to run an application named **installutil**:

```
installutil <servicename>
```

Unfortunately, this application doesn't work. You get a bunch of error messages telling you that no installer class is defined in this assembly. You need to add an installer to make it all work. Create a new file in your project and add the following code to it:

```
namespace CH7_16
{
    using System;
    using System.Collections;
    using System.Core;
    using System.ComponentModel;
    using System.Configuration.Install;

    [RunInstaller(true)]
    public class ProjectInstaller : System.Configuration.Install.Installer
    {
        private System.ComponentModel.Container components;
        private System.ServiceProcess.ServiceInstaller serviceInstaller1;
        private System.ServiceProcess.ServiceProcessInstaller
                        serviceProcessInstaller1;

        public ProjectInstaller()
        {
            InitializeComponent();
        }
```

```
private void InitializeComponent()
{
    this.components = new System.ComponentModel.Container ();
    this.serviceInstaller1 = new
        System.ServiceProcess.ServiceInstaller();
    this.serviceProcessInstaller1 = new
            System.ServiceProcess.ServiceProcessInstaller ();
    serviceInstaller1.ServiceName = "CH7_16";
    serviceProcessInstaller1.Password = null;
    serviceProcessInstaller1.Username = null;
    this.Installers.Add (this.serviceProcessInstaller1);
    this.Installers.Add (this.serviceInstaller1);
}
}
}
```

After you have added this file to the project and compiled it into the assembly, the install will complete properly. The next step is to start and stop the service in the operating system. You do this via the System Service Manager, which you can get to by right-clicking the My Computer icon on the desktop and selecting Manage.

You should see a screen like the one shown in Figure 7.10. Selecting the service you have created and right-clicking allows you to start or stop this service. When you do, the Event Log should be updated with two entries indicating that the service was started and then stopped.

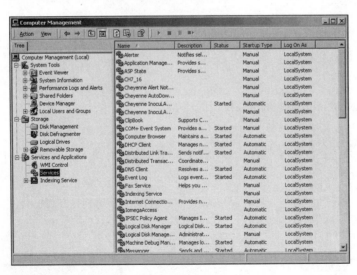

Figure 7.10   The Service Manager.

Working with a Database

The *database* is the central storage device of most applications in the business world. Databases are the core to keeping, finding, and mining information in the business development community. Without databases, you would still be working from paper worksheets and notepads. The Internet would be a distant fantasy because you wouldn't be able to search for anything in search engines or information repositories. Of course, most of us would also be without our current jobs and many fewer computer books would be written. This situation would be bad for those of us who make our living writing these books, so let's keep the databases!

Given the importance of databases, you shouldn't be surprised to know that C# provides excellent tools for working with them. If you have worked with the ADO libraries in C++ or Visual Basic or have worked with JDBC in Java, you are already accustomed to most of the functionality and processes in the CLR ADO database library.

In the example in this section, you work with a simple database, implemented in Microsoft Access 2000. This database contains a single table, named Contacts, that keeps track of information about a person (the person's name, address, and city, for example). You can find this database on the enclosed CD-ROM in this book. Working with the database is a three-step process: You connect to the database using the name of the Access file, execute whatever command you want to run against the database, and close the database connection. That's all there is to it.

Listing 7.16 shows the simple console application you use to access the database (excuse the pun) and exercise the ADO functionality.

Listing 7.16   Working with a database.

```
namespace CH7_17
{
    using System;
    using System.Data.ADO;

    public class Class1
    {
        private ADOConnection fConnection;
        private const string fConnString =
            "Provider=Microsoft.Jet.OLEDB.4.0;Data Source=CH7_17.MDB";
        public Class1()
        {
            fConnection = new ADOConnection(fConnString);
            fConnection.Open();
```

```
        }
        public void CloseDown()
        {
            fConnection.Close();
        }
        public void AddEntry()
        {
            try
            {
                string cmd =
                "INSERT INTO CONTACTS (Name, Address, City, State, ZipCode,
                        Age)";
                cmd +=
                " VALUES ('Herman Munster','1313 Mockingbird Lane','Golden',
                        'CO',
                            '80401', 39);";
                ADOCommand adocmd = new ADOCommand( cmd, fConnection );
                int nAdded = adocmd.ExecuteNonQuery();
                Console.WriteLine("# Added: {0}", nAdded );


            }
            catch ( Exception e )
            {
                Console.WriteLine("Exception in Add: {0}", e );
            }
        }
        public void ListEntries()
        {
            Console.WriteLine("Listing...\n");
            try
            {
                ADODataReader rdr;
                ADOCommand cmd = new ADOCommand(
                        "Select * from Contacts", fConnection );
                cmd.Execute( out rdr );

                while( rdr.Read() )
                {
                    Console.WriteLine( "\nName: {0}", rdr["Name"] );
                    Console.WriteLine("Address: {0}", rdr["Address"] );
                }
                rdr.Close();
            }
            catch ( Exception e )
```

```
        {
            Console.WriteLine("Exception in List: {0}", e );
        }
    }

    public static int Main(string[] args)
    {
        Class1 app = new Class1();
        app.AddEntry();
        app.ListEntries();
        app.CloseDown();
        return 0;
    }
}
}
```

Chapter 8

The Common Language Runtime Libraries

In Depth

The real power of an environment is not in the speed with which it works or the way in which it stores information efficiently. Instead, the real power of an environment is in the set of services it offers you as a developer and user. The .NET environment is rich with functionality that you can harness in your own applications quickly and easily. This functionality allows you to get up to speed with the system quickly and still allows you to write applications consistent with the environment itself. As most Windows programmers and users know, the most frustrating thing about Windows applications is that they all choose to do similar things differently. The core of that "sameness" for .NET programming is the Common Language Runtime (CLR) library system.

In this chapter, you explore some core elements of the CLR—the elements that make up the interior of your program. In Chapter 9, you explore the visual elements of the CLR, focusing on how you can use them to maximize your graphical user interface (GUI) experience.

Files and Directories

The core of any operating system is its file-and-directory structure. Although the CLR and .NET add no new functionality to the file system Windows uses, the classes of the CLR make working with files and directories vastly easier than they ever have been. For the first time, dealing with files and directories is no longer a chore, but rather a simple task. Using the CLR, you no longer have an excuse for not following the proper procedures with files.

The classes you deal with primarily when working with the file system in C# are **FileStream**, **StreamWriter**, **StreamReader**, **File**, and **Directory**. Take a quick look at each one in each section to see what you can use them for in your own applications.

The **FileStream** class is used to open files for reading, writing, or appending. You don't use the **FileStream** object to do the reading and writing—it couples with the **StreamReader** and **StreamWriter** classes to allow you to do that work independently of the file type. The **FileStream** class represents a stream of bytes that represent an open file. Information about the length of the file, the current write position in the file, and the locking status of the file is available in the class. In addition, you use the **FileStream** class to do asynchronous reads and writes, which block access to the file until you have finished. Using asynchronous reads and writes is one of the more advanced features of the CLR—using the **BeginRead/EndRead** and **BeginWrite/EndWrite** methods. For example, sometimes you want to simply buffer a bunch of data and then write it to a file, making sure that no other program or thread is operating on the file at the time. In this case, you issue a **BeginWrite** command with the data you want written and then immediately issue an **EndWrite** command with the handle you get back from **BeginWrite** to ensure that the operation is blocked on that file.

The **StreamWriter** and **StreamReader** classes are used to produce file output and input in either text or binary mode. These classes have several variants, including the **StreamWriter**, **BinaryWriter**, and **StringWriter** classes and their equivalent reader classes. For the most part, you use these classes exactly as if you were writing to the console window, using the **Write** and **WriteLine** methods to output data to the file and the **Read** and **ReadLine** methods to get information back from the file.

The **File** and **Directory** classes allow you to retrieve information about files without having to open them. C# differentiates between files and directories, which is something that Windows does not do by itself. You can get information back about the directories within a given directory tree as well as the files within each of those directories. See "Enumerating Files in a Directory" in the "Immediate Solutions" section later in this chapter for more information about working with files and directories.

Working with files and directories and with the information in each one requires that you deal with C# collections. You look at the collections classes next on this tour. The file classes contain logic for working with all the basic primitives in C# and for working with various encoding schemes, such as binary, ASCII, or Unicode.

Collections

A *collection* is the fundamental multiple object container in C#. A *container* allows you to keep track of a large number of objects without worrying about how many you might have. Containers also permit you to iterate over the objects and process each one easily and efficiently. C# has quite a few different kinds of collection classes, depending on what kind of information you want to store. See Chapter 1 for a complete rundown of the collection classes.

Because most of the underlying functionality of the CLR is based around collections, you should learn how to manipulate them. In general, every section of the CLR that works with collections (such as files and directories, the Clipboard, sockets, security, and other functionality) returns a collection or array of items. By using the **foreach** statement to inspect these items, you can work your way through them. As a simple example, imagine processing all the files in a given directory. In C#, using the CLR, the code looks like this:

```
Directory dir = new Directory( dirName );
File[] files = dir.GetFiles();
foreach( File f in files )
{
    ProcessFile( f.FullName );
}
```

This code gets a list of files from a directory object and then processes each one by its name. Other areas of the code are similar in structure. You can, for example, get all the services installed on a given machine and do something with them with the following code snippet:

```
ServiceController[] services = ServiceController.GetServices();
foreach ( ServiceController svc in services)
{
    ProcessService( svc.DisplayName );
}
```

You must understand, therefore, how to work with collections when you are dealing with the CLR. Please refer to Chapter 1 if you have any more questions about working with collections and arrays.

Dates and Times

Programming for users generally involves working with dates, times, and time spans. For this reason, the CLR provides a rich set of class libraries that works with these critical items. Between getting the current system date and time or determining the number of days between two dates, the CLR provides methods to do it all. More interestingly, the CLR also provides a complete scheduler system that can schedule events in a specific time pattern and notify the program when the event should be fired.

The basic class for date and time manipulation in C# is called, logically enough, **DateTime**. You might think that C# would have separate date and time classes, but it doesn't. The reason for this decision isn't clear, except that you can extract only the pieces you want from the **DateTime** class to get the data for both, so why not combine them? (Who understands the rationale of the architect of system libraries?)

Working with dates and times generally breaks down into three categories: initialization, processing, and formatting. The CLR **DateTime** class supports all three of these categories. For example, to initialize a **DateTime** object, you can use one of these methods:

```
DateTime now = DateTime.now;
DateTime today = DateTime.today;
DateTime date = new DateTime( year, month, day );
DateTime date = new DateTime( year, month, day, hour, minute, second );
```

Finally, the date-and-time package supports globalization through the use of the **Calendar** class. This class supports such elements as the Julian (standard U.S.) calendar as well as the old-style Gregorian calendar. You are unlikely ever to use the Gregorian calendar, unless you are working with a group of monks, but it is comforting to know that you can choose it.

Of course, you can also make copies of date objects by assigning them to another date-and-time object:

```
DateTime date1 = date2;
```

One important note about dates and times: If you create a default date object by using the void constructor

```
DateTime d = new DateTime( );
```

then the date in the variable **d** is initialized to all zeroes, not to the current date, as you might expect. Of course, it would be easy to create your own class, derived from **DateTime**, that initializes itself to today.

After you have initialized a date object, the next step is to work with it. For this purpose, the **DateTime** class supports a variety of different ways to add or subtract days, months, or years from an instance of the class. The methods to accomplish date addition and subtraction are shown in Table 8.1.

Table 8.1 **Date and time manipulation methods.**

Method	Purpose
AddDays	Adds a given number of days to a **DateTime** object
AddMonths	Adds a given number of months to a **DateTime** object
AddYears	Adds a given number of years to a **DateTime** object
AddSeconds	Adds a given number of seconds to a **DateTime** object
AddMinutes	Adds a given number of minutes to a **DateTime** objects
AddHours	Adds a given number of hours to a **DateTime** object

Of course, by substituting a negative number for the number of units to add, you can implement subtraction for the **DateTime** class. For example, if you want to find the day before today, you could write:

```
DateTime dt = DateTime.Today;
dt.AddDays( -1 );
```

The final step to working with dates and times is to be able to format them properly for output. You looked at the complete set of formatting objects in Chapter 7. In general, the process for formatting a date or time is to use the **Format** method of the **DateTime** class. For example, the following simple snippet of code formats the date and time according to a small subset of the available formatting options:

```
string[] format = {
    "dddd, MMMM dd yyyy",
    "ddd, MMM d \"'\"yy",
    "dddd, MMMM dd",
    "M/yy",
    "dd-MM-yy",
};
string date;
for (int i = 0; i < format.Length; i++)
{
  date = dt.Format(format[i], DateTimeFormatInfo.InvariantInfo);
  Console.WriteLine(String.Concat(format[i], " :" , date));
}
```

As you can see, manipulating dates and times and then outputting them in a format you want users to view is fairly easy. C# was designed from the ground up to be extensible and flexible for different user types.

Cryptography

If you store data in a system, sooner or later someone who isn't supposed to look at the data wants to anyway. This problem has been faced by the computer world for many years and will remain for a long time. Until the underlying operating system can protect against various users coming along and dumping the contents of a file, developers will have this problem. One of the most common ways to defend against this invasion is to store the data on the disk in an encrypted form.

Although the Windows operating system contains the basic functionality for encryption and decryption, using that functionality is a nightmare of specialized COM objects or Dynamic Link Libraries (DLLs) and calling various strange and esoteric functions in a prescribed order. Failure to do anything right would result in the process failing in an odd manner and leaving the file unprotected. Obviously, this was a less-than-optimal solution to a problem that affected users directly. For this reason, the CLR was built with industrial-strength encryption built-in.

The CLR contains classes to deal with the Data Encryption Standard (DES) algorithm. This algorithm, considered by many people to be the most secure data encryption process in the world, uses a large number of bits to encrypt a block of text using a given password. Using the algorithm is complex, however, so the CLR designers wrapped it up in a standard set of classes in its own namespace (**System.Security.Cryptography**) that gives you full access to the functionality of the encryption and decryption process without forcing you to understand how it all works.

For a simple example of how to encrypt a data stream and write it to a persistent storage device, please see "Encrypting Data" and "Decrypting Data" in the "Immediate Solutions" section later in this chapter. A discussion of the inner workings of the algorithm is well beyond the scope of this book.

Security

Windows NT, Windows 2000, and Windows XP are all about security issues. Preventing the wrong people from accessing the right information is the basic tenet of security in the programming world. This problem is complex enough on a standalone system, where your program can be accessed only by people who have logged in to the computer; when you are working with system services and the Internet, security takes on a whole new level of perversity.

The C# programming language has security features built into the runtime environment and the compiler itself. You can specify, for example, that a unit be allowed (or not allowed) to use unsafe code via the security mechanism. Any attempt to use a feature that has been turned off in the code results in an exception being thrown in the application and the termination of the program. For example, consider the case of calling out to native API functionality. By using the security flags, you can turn this functionality on or off in the application.

In the following little code snippet, the security flag is turned off for unmanaged (*native*) code in the system. Running this function results in a security violation and an exception being thrown and caught:

```
[SecurityPermission(SecurityAction.Deny, Flags =
    SecurityPermissionFlag.UnmanagedCode)]
private static void CallWithoutPermission()
{
```

```
try
{
    Console.WriteLine("Calling unmanaged code badly.");
    NativeMethods.MessageBox(0, "Native Code", "", 0);
    Console.WriteLine("Success!");
}
catch (SecurityException)
{
    Console.WriteLine("Security Exception!");
}
}
```

The alternative is to allow the use of unmanaged (native) code in the application. Here's a small code snippet that does just that; in this case, the call works fine and the message box is displayed properly with no exception thrown:

```
[SecurityPermission(SecurityAction.Assert, Flags =
        SecurityPermissionFlag.UnmanagedCode)]
private static void CallWithPermission()
{
    try
    {
        Console.WriteLine("Calling unmanaged code Ok.");
        NativeMethods.MessageBox(0, "Native Code", "", 0);
        Console.WriteLine("Success!");
    }
    catch (SecurityException)
    {
        Console.WriteLine("Security Exception!");
    }
}
```

Why are these flags important in your code? Consider the Internet and scripting. If you somehow allow outside users to corrupt or modify your code so that it makes calls to the underlying operating system, those users get unlimited access to your files and directories—not to mention internal data. By setting the proper security flags, as shown in these listings, you can prevent this situation from happening.

Sockets

Sockets are a method for talking between two programs or two machines, without having to worry about the underlying protocols or error handling needed to send information back and forth. If you have worked with Internet programming or database servers, you have likely worked with sockets, whether you knew it or not. The C# CLR provides a useful set of class libraries for working with sockets, including TCP/IP protocols and HTTP handling.

In general, the process for working with a socket in any of its myriad forms is to open a connection to another system, send a request, wait for a response, and then close the connection. This process applies whether you are communicating with a database server, an internal application, or a Web server. The kind of information you are working with makes no difference to the underlying protocol handler—only to the system you are talking to.

You perform the first step, connecting to the other system, by creating a **Socket** object and calling its connect method. This code looks something like this:

```
Socket s = new Socket(AddressFamily.AfINet, SocketType.SockStream,
    ProtocolType.ProtTCP );

if (s.Connect(EPhost) != 0)
{
    // Error!
}
```

In this case, you have created an Internet socket, using streams and the TCP/IP protocol to talk to the host. The host IP address is stored in the **EPhost** variable, which can be found by using the DNS class **Resolve** method:

```
IPAddress hostadd = DNS.Resolve(server);
```

After the connection is established, the second step in the process is to "talk" to the remote server. This give-and-take process involves sending a command to the server and waiting for a response. See "Writing a Socket Client in C#" in the "Immediate Solutions" section later in this chapter for the complete rundown.

Finally, you need to disconnect from the remote server. Failure to do this step is likely to result in leaks on the server side because the server is forced to handle more and more connections without closing the ones it has. Although a socket times out after a given period, you should explicitly close the connection using the **Close** method of the socket.

Remote Access

In the distributed world of computing, many machines are often involved in a given system. For example, one computer might act as a Web server, and a second as a database server. A third computer might act as a content provider for the information to display. Often, the problem is that you need to make sure that given services and applications are running on all these systems. Consider, for example, the case of a standard Web site. Sitting at a remote location is the operations staff, which needs to make sure that all the machines are running properly. Sometimes, the services on a given machine need to be stopped and then later restarted, perhaps for a backup. In the old world (before personal computers were invented), you would have walked down to the computer room, logged in to the machine, and then stopped and started the services. This process doesn't work quite as well if the machine in question is in California and the operations people are in New York!

The answer to these problems, of course, is remote application access. By running a service or program from another machine regardless of where you happen to be physically, you can make sure that everything is the way it should be. The C# CLR helps you out, of course, by providing the **ServiceControl** class in the **ServiceProcess** namespace. By using this class, you can work with services on either your local machine or a remote one. For an example, see "Activating a Program Remotely" in the "Immediate Solutions" section later in this chapter.

The other mechanism for activating a program on another machine is the **IActivator** interface. This interface, which is similar to the DCOM remote access methods, works something like this:

```
IActivator activator = (IActivator)Activator.GetObject(
        typeof(Activator),
        "http://www.JoeMachine.com/JoeApp/RemoteActivationService.rem");
```

After you have an activator object, you can then run the application using the methods of the interface. The specific method you want to use is **Activate**. After the instance of the object is retrieved via this method, you can use it as though it were any other object in your application, ignoring the fact that it is not running on your machine.

Clipboard

The final topic I discuss in this section of the chapter is the Windows *Clipboard*. It is used to transfer data from one application to another, such as to copy text from a money-management application to a Web page to provide a credit card number. The Clipboard can be used for many tasks, such as copying text, graphics, objects, or formatted information. The limitation, however, is that the Clipboard can handle only a single item at a time. Each succeeding item copied to the Clipboard simply replaces the preceding one.

Working with the Clipboard involves three separate processes:

- Find out what kind of information is on the Clipboard at any given time.
- Place your own information on the Clipboard for other applications to be able to use.
- Retrieve information in a given format from the Clipboard and use it in your own application.

The C# CLR Clipboard class contains methods to do all these tasks.

To work with the Clipboard, you first retrieve an **IDataObject** interface from the system **Clipboard** class:

```
IDataObject iData = Clipboard.GetDataObject();
```

After you have the object, you can inquire of it for a given format of data you are interested in. For example, if you want to work with text, you write something like this:

```
Boolean hasText = iData.GetDataPresent(DataFormats.Text);
```

If the data in that format (text) is present, the returned Boolean value is true. In this case, you want to retrieve the information:

```
string s = (String)iData.GetData(DataFormats.Text);
```

Alternatively, you might want to put data from your own application on the system Clipboard. In this case, suppose that you want to put a string in your program on the Clipboard so that the string is available for other applications to use. You do the following:

```
Clipboard.SetDataObject(myText);
```

That's all there is to working with the Clipboard.

As you can see, the CLR is a powerful and extremely flexible library of classes and functionality that can be used to perform amazingly complex tasks in the Windows operating system. Rather than reinvent the wheel each time you begin a new project, look through the CLR class library first. That way, you not only save yourself time and energy in creating the foundation for your application, but also ensure that your program is consistent with other Windows applications.

Immediate Solutions

Creating a New File

The most basic element of the operating system is probably the file. Files come in two different "flavors." *Text* files are human-readable files that can be printed, typed, or edited directly by users. *Binary* files, on the other hand, are computer readable and generally require the use of a specialized program to read or write them. I show you, later in this chapter, a program that can read and show you the contents of a binary file; for now, concentrate on an example of simply creating a file. In this example, you create both a binary file and a text file, using names retrieved from users. In addition, you see how to write data to those files after they are created.

Listing 8.1 shows a program that creates both binary and text files and outputs some data to each one. Because of the opening "mode" of the file, each file is truncated each time the program is run. If you want to change this behavior to append to the file, you can use **FileMode.CreateOrOpen** rather than using **FileMode.Create**.

Listing 8.1   Creating a new file.

```
using System;
using System.IO;

class CH8_1
{
    public static void CreateTextFile( string name )
    {
        try
        {
            FileStream fs = new
                FileStream(name, FileMode.Create, FileAccess.Write);
            StreamWriter sw = new StreamWriter(fs);
        sw.WriteLine("Test1");
            sw.Write("This is");
            sw.Write(" ");
            sw.Write("a test\n");
            sw.Close();
        }
```

```
        catch ( Exception e )
        {
            Console.WriteLine("Exception in CreateTextFile: {0}", e );
        }
    }

    public static void CreateBinaryFile( string name )
    {
        try
        {
            FileStream fs = new
                FileStream(name, FileMode.Create, FileAccess.Write);
            BinaryWriter bw = new BinaryWriter(fs);

            int x = 10;
            double y = 20.45;
            string s = "This is a test";

            bw.Write(x);
            bw.Write(y);
            bw.Write(s);

            bw.Close();
        }
        catch ( Exception e )
        {
            Console.WriteLine("Exception in CreateBinaryFile: {0}", e );
        }
    }

    public static void Main( string[] args )
    {
        if ( args.Length < 2 )
        {
            Console.WriteLine("Usage CH8_1 text-file-name binary-file-name");
            return;
        }

        CreateTextFile( args[0] );
        CreateBinaryFile( args[1] );
    }
}
```

Notice in this example that you create the file in the same way, whether it is a binary or text file. Only the choice of the writer classes for the file determines how it is used, which is interesting because it means that you can "mix and match" text and binary data in a file by simply opening different writers for that file. Note also the two forms of the output command for text files: **Write** and **WriteLine**. **WriteLine** does the same thing as **Write**, but adds a carriage return/linefeed combination to the end of the output.

Related solution:	*Found on page:*
Creating a Literal	31

Reading from a Text File

Reading a text file is often necessary, especially when writing text parsers or file viewers. In C#, reading from a text file is particularly easy, given the capabilities of the **FileStream** and **StreamReader** classes. These two classes provide all the functionality you need in order to read a text file and parse the resulting input.

In the example in this section, you create a simple application that dumps out a text file, along with line numbers for each line. This application would be useful, for example, in creating listing files for source code, with line numbers indicating the lines you want to discuss or comment on. As you see in Listing 8.2, the work is done almost exclusively by the CLR classes, with only error checking done by the program itself.

Listing 8.2   Reading from a text file.

```
using System;
using System.IO;

class CH8_2
{
    public static void ShowFile( string name )
    {
        try
        {
            FileStream fs = new FileStream( name, FileMode.Open );
            StreamReader sr = new StreamReader( fs );

            string line = "";

            int lineNo = 0;
```

```
    do
    {
       line = sr.ReadLine();
       if ( line != null )
       {
               Console.WriteLine("{0}: {1}", lineNo, line );
               lineNo ++;
       }
          } while ( line != null );
    }
    catch ( Exception e )
    {
       Console.WriteLine("Exception in ShowFile: {0}", e );
    }
  }

  public static void Main(string[] args)
  {
     if ( args.Length < 1 )
     {
        Console.WriteLine("Usage: Ch8_2 text-file-name");
    return;
     }

     Console.WriteLine("Dumping file {0}:", args[0] );
     ShowFile( args[0] );
  }
}
```

If you were to run this program on itself, you would see the following output (snipped for size constraints in this book):

```
Dumping file ch8_2.cs:
0: using System;
1: using System.IO;
2:
3: class CH8_2
4: {
5:    public static void ShowFile( string name )
6:    {
7:        try
8:        {
9:           FileStream fs = new FileStream( name, FileMode.Open );
10:           StreamReader sr = new StreamReader( fs );
11:
12:           string line = "";
```

```
13:
14:            int lineNo = 0;
15:      do
16:      {
17:        line = sr.ReadLine();
18:        if ( line != null )
```

The program displays, of course, the entire program source listing. However, it's enough to give you an idea of what is going on. As you can see, the program accurately reads each line of the file into a string buffer and then displays that line for users, along with an incrementing line counter. This simple 40-line program takes the place of much more complicated and longer C or C++ programs that have been around for years. (C# is earning its keep already!)

Reading from a Binary File

When I was a young lad, just starting out in the programming world, the most useful program in the world was a hex dump utility. You could look into the arcane world of the binary file without having to have a specialized application to interpret the data. This program was particularly useful for figuring out how to "crack" the data files for various applications and games. (Not that anyone would do that sort of thing, of course—it was a purely intellectual exercise.) Whatever the reason, the need for hex dump utilities hasn't changed. Even when you have applications that can view and interpret data in a file, in some cases they don't work. Determining, for example, why a given file is crashing your program when you load it can be a chore when you can't look at the file in a standard way.

In this example, you resurrect the hex dump program and bring it back up to speed in C#. You can see how to read binary files, format the binary information, and ensure that your program doesn't crash when you read something invalid. Listing 8.3 shows the hex dump utility, in all its glory.

Listing 8.3   Reading from a binary file.

```
using System;
using System.IO;

class CH8_3
{
    public static void ShowFile( string name )
    {
        try
        {
```

```
      FileStream fs = new FileStream( name, FileMode.Open );
      BinaryReader sr = new BinaryReader( fs );

int nPos = 0;
Boolean bHeader = false;
int nChar = -1;
int[] nLine = new int[16];
int nLinePos = 0;

do
{
   nChar = sr.Read();
   if ( nChar != -1 )
   {
      // See if we are at a line break.
      if ( bHeader == false )
      {
         // If we have any characters, dump them in ascii if possible
     if ( nLinePos > 0 )
     {
       for ( int i=0; i<16; ++i )
          if ( nLine[i] >= ' ' && nLine[i] < 'z' )
         Console.Write("{0}", nLine[i].ToChar());
      else
         Console.Write(".");
     }
         Console.Write("\n{0}: ", nPos.Format("X5", null) );
     bHeader = true;
     nLinePos = 0;
      }

          Console.Write("{0} ", nChar.Format("X2", null) );
      nLine[nLinePos] = nChar;
      nPos ++;
      nLinePos ++;
      // See if the next position is a line break
      if ( nPos % 15 == 0 )
         bHeader = false;
   }
   } while ( nChar != -1 );

   // Fill in the line
for ( int i=nPos; i%15 != 0; ++i )
   Console.Write("   ");
```

```
            // If we have any characters, dump them in ascii if possible
            if ( nLinePos > 0 )
            {
               for ( int i=0; i<nPos%15; ++i )
                  if ( nLine[i] >= ' ' && nLine[i] < 'z' )
                  Console.Write("{0}", nLine[i].ToChar());
             else
                     Console.Write(".");
   }


      }
      catch ( Exception e )
      {
         Console.WriteLine("Exception in ShowFile: {0}", e );
      }
   }

   public static void Main(string[] args)
   {
      if ( args.Length < 1 )
      {
         Console.WriteLine("Usage: Ch8_2 text-file-name");
      return;
      }

      Console.WriteLine("Dumping file {0}:", args[0] );
      ShowFile( args[0] );
   }
}
```

Reading a binary file really isn't any different from reading a text file, as you can see. Note in this example the method of formatting the data. If you run this program over a simple binary file, such as the one you created earlier in this chapter, in the section "Creating a New File," you see output like this:

```
00000: 54 65 73 74 31 0D 0A 54 68 69 73 20 69 73 20 Test1..This is .
0000F: 61 20 74 65 73 74 0A                          a test.
```

Related solution:	Found on page:
Creating a Simple Array	19

Enumerating Files in a Directory

When you are working in the Windows operating system, the file system is often an important part of your project work. Fortunately, C# works well with the file system because it was written to replace most existing class library structures. As a result, the C# CLR contains excellent file-manipulation and directory-browsing functionality you can use in your own application.

In the good old days of MFC programming (back in the early 1990s), enumerating the files in a single directory was a painstaking process of opening a directory and then recursively processing each entry in the directory to see if it was a directory; if it wasn't, you dealt with the file information. As you see in this example, doing the same thing in C# is somewhat easier. For example, if you want just to retrieve all the C# source (.cs) files, you call this program with the following line, where . is the current directory:

```
ch8_4 . *.cs
```

Listing 8.4 shows the code needed to browse the files that reside in a given directory and search those files by a given mask.

Listing 8.4 Enumerating files in a directory.

```
using System;
using System.IO;

class CH8_4
{
   public static void ListFiles( string dirName )
   {
      Directory dir = new Directory( dirName );
      File[] files = dir.GetFiles();
      foreach( File f in files )
      {
         Console.WriteLine("{0}", f.FullName );
      }
   }
   public static void ListFilesMasked( string dirName, string mask )
   {
      Directory dir = new Directory( dirName );
      File[] files = dir.GetFiles(mask);
      foreach( File f in files )
      {
         Console.WriteLine("{0}", f.FullName );
      }
   }
```

```
public static void Main(string[] args)
{
    if ( args.Length < 1 )
    {
        Console.WriteLine("Usage: ch8_4 directory-name [file-mask]");
    return;
    }
    if ( args.Length > 1 )
        ListFilesMasked( args[0], args[1] );
    else
        ListFiles( args[0] );
}
}
```

As you can see, working with files isn't difficult in C#. Working with files in C# is based around collections of objects—in this case, the **File** object. This object contains descriptive information about a given file, including its name, size, attributes, and modification dates. With virtually no work, you could create a directory browser in C#!

Deleting a File

If you create files in the file system, sooner or later you have to get rid of some of them. Cleaning up after yourself is the sign of a good programmer. You have no reason, for example, to leave temporary files lying around when you are done with them. Keeping lots of intermediate files that your application created but never again used is a sign that your application is not quite ready for prime time. For this reason, you need to be able to delete a file from the file system from your program.

Fortunately, as you see in this example, deleting a file in C# is easy. Although you might think that you would use the directory class to delete files from the directory itself, that is not the case. Instead, you use the directory class to navigate to an instance of the file you are interested in and then use that file object to delete itself. This concept is not the most intuitive for people used to working with Windows; to anyone else, however, it makes perfect sense. Why would you delete a file from a directory? You ask the file to remove itself from the file system, of course.

Listing 8.5 shows how to find a given file when you know its name, whether or not that name is the same case as the "real" name in the directory structure. The program in the listing then calls the delete method on that file object to have it remove itself from the file system.

Listing 8.5   Deleting a file.

```
using System;
using System.IO;

class CH8_5
{
    public static void DeleteFile( string dirName, string fileName )
    {
        try
        {
            Directory dir = new Directory( dirName );
            File[] files = dir.GetFiles();
            foreach( File f in files )
            {
                if ( String.Compare(fileName, f.Name, true) == 0 )
                {
                    f.Delete();
                    Console.WriteLine("File {0} deleted", f.Name);
                }
            }
        }
        catch ( Exception e )
        {
            Console.WriteLine("Exception in DeleteFile: {0}", e );
        }
    }


    public static void Main(string[] args)
    {
        if ( args.Length < 2 )
        {
            Console.WriteLine("Usage: ch8_5 directory-name file-to-delete");
            return;
        }
        DeleteFile( args[0], args[1] );
    }
}
```

Notice the use of the **Compare** function in the shaded line in the code listing. This function can be used like the standard C library function **strcmpi** (compare strings, case insensitive) to see whether two strings are really the same. This function is necessary in this case because the **==** operator compares the two strings as equal only if all the characters match in letter and in case.

Getting the Current System Time

A display of the current date and time for users in your application is a helpful feature. After all, users can then politely look up and see how many days (or, more hopefully, hours) they had spent working on their data with your system. Come to think of it, maybe that isn't such a good idea. Users might decide to track you down and make you pay for all that time. In spite of that possibility, being able to get the current system date and time is helpful.

In this example, the program prints the date and time as a single string and then the date and the time as individual strings. You can see how to get the various components and how to format a date so that it looks the way you want. Listing 8.6 shows the code for displaying the various date and time components.

Listing 8.6   Getting the current system time.

```
using System;
using System.Globalization;


class CH8_6
{
    public static void Main()
    {
        // What is today?
        DateTime now = DateTime.Now;

        // Display it for the user
        Console.WriteLine("It is now: {0}", now );

        // Just the date
        DateTime today = DateTime.Today;

        // Display it for the user
        Console.WriteLine("It is now: {0}", today );

        // Hm. They don't want to see the time for today.
        Console.WriteLine("Today's Date: {0}",
            today.Format("dddd, MMMM dd yyyy",DateTimeFormatInfo.InvariantInfo)
        );
    }
}
```

The output from this program (on the day I ran it) is:

```
It is now: 6/7/2001 8:24 AM
It is now: 6/7/2001 12:00 AM
Today's Date: Thursday, June 07 2001
```

As you can see, even the current date is displayed with a time value in its default format. The reason is that it is a **DateTime** object, and the default format for a **DateTime** object is the full date and time of the contained information. The formatted information, on the other hand, can be displayed in any format you want.

Related solution:	Found on page:
Using the Date and Time Functions	268

Finding the Span between Two Dates and Times

Sometimes, just knowing what dates you are working with is not enough. You have to be able to do math on the dates, such as add a week or subtract a few hours. Lots of scheduling programs need to know the last time something ran or the next time it will be run. Picture an appointment book that needs to schedule weekly or monthly appointments. What if you could just add a month or a week to the current date and know when the next one is? With C#, it is that easy.

Listing 8.7 shows how to do various kinds of date manipulation to add to a date. It also shows how to figure out how far apart two dates might be, showing the span of those dates.

Listing 8.7 Finding the span between two dates and times.

```csharp
using System;

class CH8_7
{
    public static void AddDay( ref DateTime dt )
    {
        TimeSpan ts = new TimeSpan(TimeSpan.TicksPerDay);
        dt = dt + ts;
    }
    public static void AddWeek( ref DateTime dt )
    {
        TimeSpan ts = new TimeSpan(TimeSpan.TicksPerDay);
        for ( int i=0; i<7; ++i )
            dt += ts;
    }
```

```
        public static void AddMonth( ref DateTime dt )
        {
           DateTime dt1 = dt.AddMonths( 1 );
           dt = dt1;
        }
        public static void AddYear( ref DateTime dt )
        {
           DateTime dt1 = dt.AddYears( 1 );
           dt = dt1;
        }

        public static void Main()
        {
           DateTime dt1 = DateTime.FromString("01/01/2001");
           DateTime dto = dt1;

           Console.WriteLine("Starting out: {0}", dt1 );

           AddDay ( ref dt1 );
           Console.WriteLine("Add a day: {0}", dt1 );

           TimeSpan ts = dt1 - dto;
           Console.WriteLine("Time Span: {0}", ts );
           dto = dt1;

           AddWeek( ref dt1 );
           Console.WriteLine("Add a week: {0}", dt1 );
           ts = dt1 - dto;
           Console.WriteLine("Time Span: {0}", ts );
           dto = dt1;

           AddMonth( ref dt1 );
           Console.WriteLine("Add a month: {0}", dt1 );
           ts = dt1 - dto;
           Console.WriteLine("Time Span: {0}", ts );
           dto = dt1;

           AddYear( ref dt1 );
           Console.WriteLine("Add a year: {0}", dt1 );
           ts = dt1 - dto;
           Console.WriteLine("Time Span: {0}", ts );
        }
    }
```

The output from this little console application is:

```
Starting out: 1/1/2001 12:00 AM
Add a day: 1/2/2001 12:00 AM
Time Span: 1.00:00:00
Add a week: 1/9/2001 12:00 AM
Time Span: 7.00:00:00
Add a month: 2/9/2001 12:00 AM
Time Span: 31.00:00:00
Add a year: 2/9/2002 12:00 AM
Time Span: 365.00:00:00
```

As you can see, working with date and time spans in C# is really as easy as advertised.

Scheduling an Event at a Given Time

One of the most convenient features of the C# Common Language Runtime (CLR) is the ability to automatically schedule events based on your own criteria. This functionality, which doesn't really exist in Windows outside of application programs like the Scheduler (the NT **at** command), is useful for such tasks as performing automated backups, checking email, and tracking other events that happen regularly in an application.

The methodology for working with the scheduler is simple. You use the **Schedule** object to do all the work and apply patterns to it to tell it when it should perform tasks. You can specify start and stop times, start and stop days, and even the days of the month on which you want events to occur. All this is done via the various pattern classes, such as **DailyPattern**, **WeeklyPattern**, and **MonthlyPattern**. Listing 8.8 shows a simple program that prints a counter to the console window every 30 seconds, beginning at 8:00 in the morning and continuing until noon.

Listing 8.8   Scheduling an event at a given time.

```csharp
using System;
using System.Timers;
using System.Diagnostics;

public class Scheduler
{
    public static int Counter;

    public static void Main(string[] args)
    {
```

```
// Create the schedule and add the handler.
Schedule s = new Schedule();
s.EventOccurred+=new OccurredEventHandler(HandleEvent);

// Run the pattern every day
DailyPattern days = new DailyPattern(1);

// Start at 8:00 a.m.
days.StartTime = new TimeSpan(8,0,0);

// End at noon
days.EndTime = new TimeSpan(12,0,0);

// Do it once every half-minute
days.Interval = new TimeSpan(0,0,30);

// Add the pattern to the scheduler
s.RecurrencePatterns.Add(days);

// Initialize counter
Counter = 0;

// Enable it
s.Enabled = true;

// Wait for user to quit program.
Console.WriteLine("Press \'q\' to quit the sample");
while(Console.Read()!='q');
}

// Define the event handler.
public static void HandleEvent(object source, OccurredEventArgs e)
{
    Counter ++;
    Console.WriteLine("Counter: {0}", Counter );

}
}
```

If you were to run this program starting at 8:00, you would see something like this displayed to the console:

```
Press 'q' to quit the sample
Counter: 1
Counter: 2
Counter: 3
```

```
Counter: 4
Counter: 5
Counter: 6
```

As you can see, the program is called regularly. If you time it with a stopwatch, you find that the console output occurs approximately every 30 seconds. I say *approximately* because you cannot guarantee that events will happen exactly on 30-second boundaries. You should never use scheduling routines for a task that absolutely has to be done at a given time. Slack is built into the system for more critical events. If timing is that big of an issue, write your own thread handler and check the time yourself.

Encrypting Data

Encryption is an important part of data security. If you can't encrypt something so that someone else is unable to read it, you sacrifice a great deal of integrity in your system. People will mistrust your data because it can be modified by anyone at any time. The solution to this problem is to encrypt the data so that it can't be read by anyone else. Fortunately, the CLR provides a fairly simple mechanism for this task: C# has built-in classes in the CLR to encrypt data in various ways. In this example, you use the DES (Data Encryption Standard) algorithm to encrypt an input file using a password.

Listing 8.9 shows the entire program. For the most part, it is one of those "steal it and use it" applications. After the listing, I briefly describe how the objects work together; a discussion of the nuts and bolts of data encryption is a subject well beyond the scope of this book, however.

Listing 8.9   Encrypting data.

```
using System;
using System.IO ;
using System.Security;
using System.Security.Cryptography;

public class StoreCryptoStream : ICryptoStream
{
    static byte[] tag1 = {(byte)'[',(byte)'S',(byte)'a',(byte)'u' ,
            (byte)'d' ,(byte)'e',(byte)'s' ,(byte)']'};
    static byte[] tag2= {(byte)'[',(byte)'S',(byte)'a',(byte)'u' ,
            (byte)'r' ,(byte)'c',(byte)'2' ,(byte)']'};

    FileStream fs;
```

```
            public StoreCryptoStream(FileStream fout)
            {
                fs=fout ;
            }
            public virtual void CloseStream() {fs.Close();}
            public virtual void CloseStream(Object obj) {fs.Close();}
            public virtual void SetSink(ICryptoStream pstm) {}
            public virtual void  SetSource(CryptographicObject co) {}
            public virtual ICryptoStream  GetSink () {return null;}

            public virtual void Write(byte[] bin)
            {
                int len = bin.GetLength(0);
                Write(bin, 0, len);
            }

            public virtual void Write(byte[] bin, int start, int len )
            {
                fs.Write(bin,start,len);
            }
        }
        public class CH8_9
        {
            private byte[] symKey ;
            private byte[] symIV ;

            private bool GenerateKey(string password)
            {
                try
            {
                    int i;
                    int len;
                    char[] cp = password.ToCharArray();
                    len = cp.GetLength(0) ;
                    byte[] bt = new byte[len];

                    for(i=0 ; i<len ;i++)
                    {
                        bt[i] =(byte) cp[i];
                    }

                    symKey=new byte[8] ;
                    symIV = new byte[8] ;

                    SHA1_CSP sha = new SHA1_CSP() ;
                    sha.Write(bt) ;
                    sha.CloseStream() ;
```

```
        for(i=0 ; i<8 ; i++)
        {
            symKey[i] = sha.Hash[i] ;
        }
        for(i=8 ; i<16 ; i++)
        {
            symIV[i-8]= sha.Hash[i] ;
        }

        return true;
    }


    catch(Exception e)
    {
        Console.WriteLine("An Exception Occurred in Generating Keys:"
                +e.ToString()) ;
        return false ;
    }
}


private void EncryptData(string infile, string outfile)
{
    try
{
        // Input and output files
        FileStream fin = new FileStream
                (infile,FileMode.Open,FileAccess.Read) ;
        FileStream fout = new FileStream
                (outfile , FileMode.OpenOrCreate , FileAccess.Write);
        fout.SetLength(0) ;

        // Work space
        byte[] bin = new byte[4096] ;

        long totlen = fin.Length ;
        long rdlen=0;
        int len ;

        // Set up the various encryption option objects
        SymmetricAlgorithm des = new DES_CSP();
        StoreCryptoStream scs = new StoreCryptoStream(fout);
        SymmetricStreamEncryptor sse =
                des.CreateEncryptor(symKey, symIV);

        // Use Crypto-IP
        SHA1_CSP sha = new SHA1_CSP();
```

```
            sse.SetSink(sha);
            sha.SetSource(sse);
            sha.SetSink(scs);
            scs.SetSource(sha);

            // Loop through, reading in each block and encrypting it
            // to the output file
            while (rdlen < totlen)
        {
                len = fin.Read(bin,0,4096);
                sse.Write(bin,0,len);
                rdlen = rdlen + len;
        }

            // Free up the resources
            sse.CloseStream();
            fin.Close();
            fout.Close() ;
        }
        catch(Exception e)
        {
            Console.WriteLine("An exception occurred while encrypting :"
                    +e.ToString()) ;
        }
    }

    public static void Main(string[] args)
    {
        CH8_9 app = new CH8_9();
        app.GenerateKey(args[0]);
        app.EncryptData( args[1], args[2] );
    }
}
```

The general usage of the cryptography classes is to create the options you want and then pass them to the cryptographic objects and use them to encrypt or decrypt the data. Note that you first create keys for use by the objects and then just use the built-in functionality of those objects to make it all work.

One of the best things about the "plug and play" nature of the cryptography section of the CLR is that you can replace one algorithm with another in your application. For example, you can quickly and easily replace the DES algorithm with another one of your choice, as long as it follows the interface definition for cryptography.

Decrypting Data

In the preceding example, you looked at how to encrypt a file using the DES standard. Being able to decrypt a file also using that same standard would obviously be helpful. After all, an encrypted file isn't of much use to anyone. You have to put it back into its original format before you can use it. In this example, you see how to do just that. To use this example, you need a file that has been encrypted using the preceding example. You can use the CH8_10 file on this book's accompanying CD-ROM in the directory for this example.

Listing 8.10 shows the code needed to decrypt a file using the DES standard and a user-selected password.

Listing 8.10   Decrypting data.

```
using System;
using System.IO ;
using System.Security;
using System.Security.Cryptography;

public class StoreCryptoStream : ICryptoStream
{
    static byte[] tag1 = {(byte)'[',(byte)'S',(byte)'a',(byte)'u' ,
                (byte)'d' ,(byte)'e',(byte)'s' ,(byte)']'};
    static byte[] tag2= {(byte)'[',(byte)'S',(byte)'a',(byte)'u' ,
                (byte)'r' ,(byte)'c',(byte)'2' ,(byte)']'};

    FileStream fs;

    public StoreCryptoStream(FileStream fout)
    {
       fs=fout ;
    }

    public virtual void CloseStream() {fs.Close();}
    public virtual void CloseStream(Object obj) {fs.Close();}
    public virtual void SetSink(ICryptoStream pstm) {}
    public virtual void  SetSource(CryptographicObject co) {}
    public virtual ICryptoStream  GetSink () {return null;}

    public virtual void Write(byte[] bin)
    {
        int len = bin.GetLength(0);
        Write(bin, 0, len);
    }
```

```
        public virtual void Write(byte[] bin, int start, int len )
        {
            fs.Write(bin,start,len);
        }


    }

public class CH8_10
{
    private byte[] symKey ;
    private byte[] symIV ;

    private bool GenerateKey(string password)
    {
        try
    {
            int i;
            int len;
            char[] cp = password.ToCharArray();
            len = cp.GetLength(0) ;
            byte[] bt = new byte[len];

            for(i=0 ; i<len ;i++)
            {
                bt[i] =(byte) cp[i];
            }
            symKey=new byte[8] ;
            symIV = new byte[8] ;
            SHA1_CSP sha = new SHA1_CSP() ;
            sha.Write(bt) ;
            sha.CloseStream() ;
            for(i=0 ; i<8 ; i++)
            {
                symKey[i] = sha.Hash[i] ;
            }
            for(i=8 ; i<16 ; i++)
            {
                symIV[i-8]= sha.Hash[i] ;
            }

            return true;
        }

    catch(Exception e)
    {
        Console.WriteLine("An Exception Occurred in Generating Keys:"
            +e.ToString()) ;
```

```
                return false ;
        }
}

private void DecryptData(string infile, string outfile)
{
    try
    {
            FileStream fin = new FileStream
                    (infile,FileMode.Open,FileAccess.Read);
            FileStream fout = new FileStream
                    (outfile,FileMode.OpenOrCreate,FileAccess.Write);
            fout.SetLength(0) ;

            byte[] bin = new byte[4096] ;
            long totlen = fin.Length ;
            long rdlen=8;
            int len ;

            // Create the basic objects
            SymmetricAlgorithm des = new DES_CSP() ;

            // Create the stream.
            StoreCryptoStream scs = new StoreCryptoStream(fout);
            SymmetricStreamDecryptor ssd =
                des.CreateDecryptor(symKey, symIV);

            ssd.SetSink(scs);
            scs.SetSource(ssd);

            while (rdlen < totlen)
            {
                    len = fin.Read(bin,0,4096);
                    ssd.Write(bin,0,len);
                    rdlen = rdlen + len;
            }

            // Free up the resources
            ssd.CloseStream();
            fin.Close();
            fout.Close();
    }

    catch(Exception e)
    {
            Console.WriteLine("An exception occurred while decrypting:"
                    +e.ToString());
```

```
        }
    }

    public static void Main(string[] args)
    {
        CH8_10 app = new CH8_10();
        app.GenerateKey(args[0]);
        app.DecryptData( args[1], args[2] );
    }
}
```

No real difference exists between encrypting a file and decrypting it, which is how things should be. All you need to know is the name of the input and output files and the password used to encrypt them. The black-box DES algorithm does the rest.

Checking for Security Access

Getting and setting security access is an important task for administrators of a system. For programmers, however, it is more important that you know whether you are allowed to do something. In general, you shouldn't worry about granting yourself permission to do things because the system is in charge of those rights in the long run. However, before you try to do something, you should check to see whether you are entitled to do it. Otherwise, you can end up allowing users to try to do something that you could have verified they were not permitted to do within your application.

The permission classes of the CLR are all under the security umbrella of the system. The **System.Security.Permissions** namespace contains dozens of different kinds of permissions, from the right to change the Registry to the right to write to the console window. In this example, you look at a few of these permission classes, to see what kind of access you are entitled to within your application. Listing 8.11 shows you how to look at the various permissions for your running application.

Listing 8.11   Checking for security access.

```
using System;
using System.Security.Permissions;

class ch8_11
{
```

```
public static void Main()
{
    // Check for permission to read the registry key
    RegistryPermission f = new RegistryPermission(
        RegistryPermissionAccess.Read,
        "HARDWARE\\DESCRIPTION\\System\\CentralProcessor\\0"
    );

    if ( f.IsUnrestricted() )
    Console.WriteLine("Unrestricted Access allowed");
else
    Console.WriteLine("Unrestricted Access DENIED");

    // Check for local file access
    FileIOPermission fileIO = new
        FileIOPermission(PermissionState.None);
Console.WriteLine("All Local files read access: {0}",
            FileIOPermissionAccess.Read);
Console.WriteLine("All Local files write access: {0}",
            FileIOPermissionAccess.Write);

    // How about clipboard/window access?
UIPermission ui = new UIPermission(UIPermissionWindow.AllWindows,
    UIPermissionClipboard.AllClipboard );
if ( ui.IsUnrestricted() )
    Console.WriteLine("UI Unrestricted Access allowed");
else
    Console.WriteLine("UI Unrestricted Access DENIED");

}
}
```

The output from this particular program is as follows (for my system):

```
Unrestricted Access DENIED
All Local files read access: Read
All Local files write access: Write
UI Unrestricted Access allowed
```

As you can see, for my system, I can read or write files as well as display items to the console or Clipboard. I do not have the right to change the hardware description key in the Registry because that is a system-controlled key.

Writing a Socket Server in C#

If you have ever considered writing a server of any sort in any language, the chances are that you have written it using the standard socket library. *Sockets* are a phone line of sorts between two applications that use various protocols to send and receive messages from one place to another. Being able to allow the underlying protocol and socket layer gives a programmer the freedom to worry about the content of the message and its response rather than the technical details of how to implement the communication. The C# CLR provides an excellent socket library as well as a TCP/IP protocol layer that takes care of the nitty-gritty details of sending information from one side to another.

In this solution, you explore how you go about writing a simple server in C# that waits for a request from a client application, returns an answer, and then exits. The fundamentals of this system provide enough for you to write more complicated servers as well as multithreaded ones. A Web server is nothing more than a complicated socket server, so you could easily extend this example to support a full-blown Web server or file server for your network. All that from a few lines of code—*that* is impressive. Listing 8.12 shows an example of how easily you can create a socket server in C#.

Listing 8.12   Writing a socket server in C#.

```
using System;
using System.IO;
using System.Net;
using System.Net.Sockets;
using System.Text;

class CH8_12
{
    public static void Main(String[] args)
    {
        Encoding ASCII = Encoding.ASCII;

        // Create a listener on port 8227
        TCPListener myListener = new TCPListener(8227);

        // Start the listener
        myListener.Start();
        Console.WriteLine("Waiting for request");

        // Program blocks on Accept() until a client connects
        Socket mySocket = myListener.Accept();
        Console.WriteLine("Got a request");
```

```
Byte[] RecvBytes = new Byte[256];

// Receive the page, loop until all bytes are received
Int32 bytes = mySocket.Receive(RecvBytes, RecvBytes.Length, 0);
string s = ASCII.GetString(RecvBytes, 0, bytes);

if ( s == "GetDate" )
{
    // Get current date and time
    DateTime now = DateTime.Now;
    String strDateLine = now.ToShortDateString() + " " +
                now.ToLongTimeString();

    // Convert to byte array and send
    Byte[] byteDateLine =
            System.Text.Encoding.ASCII.GetBytes(
                    strDateLine.ToCharArray() );
    mySocket.Send(byteDateLine,byteDateLine.Length,0);
}
else
{
    Console.WriteLine("Unknown command: {0}", s );
}

myListener.Stop ();
    }
}
```

The procedure for creating a socket server is quite simple. Just follow these steps:

1. Create a new instance of a **TCPListener** class using the port number you agree on with the client.

2. Wait for a request to come in by "blocking" (waiting on) the socket using the **Accept** method of the listener object.

3. Receive the request using the **Receive** method.

4. Process the request and send back the information using the **Send** method of the socket class.

5. When you have finished processing requests, use the **Stop** method to shut down the listener.

That's all there is to writing a socket server. You can use servers such as this one for intermachine communication on either a network or the Internet. In addition, you can use socket server intramachine communication for services that supply data to other applications, such as a database server.

Writing a Socket Client in C#

If you need to get information from another process on another machine, or even on the same machine your application is running on, you probably should consider a socket client/server arrangement. In the preceding example, you looked at how to write a socket server. In this example, you look at how to connect to a given socket server with a socket client. You explore also how to send messages to a socket server and receive information back in the client.

In Listing 8.13, you find the complete code for a socket client. To run the code, you need to pass it the server name (for a stand-alone machine, use **localhost**), the port (8227), and the command you want to send to the server (**GetDate**). The program then connects to the server if it is running and sends it a command, printing to the console window the result it receives.

Listing 8.13   Writing a socket client in C#.

```
using System;
using System.IO;
using System.Net;
using System.Net.Sockets;
using System.Text;

public class CH8_13
{
    public static void SendRequest( string server, int port, string cmd )
    {
        Encoding ASCII = Encoding.ASCII;
        Byte[] ByteGet = ASCII.GetBytes(cmd);
        Byte[] RecvBytes = new Byte[256];

        IPAddress hostadd = DNS.Resolve(server);
        IPEndPoint EPhost = new IPEndPoint(hostadd, port);

        // Create an Internet socket to stream data.
        Socket s = new Socket(AddressFamily.AfINet, SocketType.SockStream,
            ProtocolType.ProtTCP );

        // Connect to host using IPEndPoint
        if (s.Connect(EPhost) != 0)
        {
        Console.WriteLine("Unable to connect to host!");
            return;
        }
```

```
        // Sent the command to the host
        s.Send(ByteGet, ByteGet.Length, 0);

        // Receive the response
        Int32 bytes = s.Receive(RecvBytes, RecvBytes.Length, 0);
        // Convert the input bytes to a C# string
        string strRetPage = ASCII.GetString(RecvBytes, 0,
                    bytes);

        while (bytes > 0)
        {
            bytes = s.Receive(RecvBytes, RecvBytes.Length, 0);
        if ( bytes > 0 )
                strRetPage = strRetPage + ASCII.GetString(
                    RecvBytes, 0, bytes);
        }
    Console.WriteLine("Received: {0}", strRetPage );

    }

    public static void Main(string[] args)
    {
        if ( args.Length < 3 )
    {
       Console.WriteLine("Usage: ch8_13 server port cmd");
       return;
    }

        // Get the server name from the arguments
    string server = args[0];

        // Get the port id from the arguments
     int port = args[1].ToInt16();

        SendRequest( server, port, args[2] );

    }
}
```

When the program is run with the server running, the following message is displayed in the console window:

```
C:\>ch8_13 localhost 8227 GetDate
Received: 06/11/2001 14:04:27
```

As you can see, socket communication is quick and easy using C# and the CLR.

Performing an HTTP **get** Command

The http **get** command is used to retrieve Web pages and other information from a Web server. Sometimes, the concept of "Web scraping" can be useful in your own applications. For example, you might connect to a specific auction Web site to get information about the auctions a person is bidding on. Rather than force that person to use a browser and constantly hit the Refresh button, you could write a simple program to retrieve the page, parse it, and regularly display the results.

The syntax of the HTTP **get** command is fairly arcane and definitely no fun to mess around with. A series of carriage returns and linefeeds need to be in the right place, along with version numbers and other information. Writing a **get** command used to be a constant struggle against changing standards. With the C# CLR, however, all this is no longer needed. In this example, you look at just how simple it is to use the Web support classes in the CLR to accomplish your tasks.

Listing 8.14 shows a simple little program that goes out and retrieves an HTML page from a specified site using the HTTP protocol. This program can be run against any URL and displays in the console window the HTML page for that particular site.

Listing 8.14   Performing an HTTP get request.

```
using System;
using System.IO;
using System.Net;
using System.Net.Sockets;
using System.Text;

class CH8_14
{
    public static void Main(String[] args)
    {
        Encoding ASCII = Encoding.ASCII;

        // See if they gave us a URL to retrieve
        if ( args.Length < 1 )
        {
            Console.WriteLine("Usage: ch8_14 url");
        return;
        }

        // Create the web request
        HttpWebRequest req =
            (HttpWebRequest)WebRequestFactory.Create
            (args[0]);
```

```
HttpWebResponse resp =
    (HttpWebResponse)req.GetResponse();

StreamReader str = new StreamReader(
    resp.GetResponseStream(), Encoding.ASCII);

string sLine;
do
{
    sLine = str.ReadLine();
Console.WriteLine("{0}", sLine);
}
while (sLine != null);
str.Close();
}
}
```

Running this little program against a Web page you know about should display the HTML source code for you to view.

Performing an HTTP **post** Command

The HTTP **post** command is used to send information to a Web server in a nonvisible manner. Unlike the standard method of sending information to a Web server, using the **get** command with arguments to the server on the command line, the **post** command "hides" the data it is sending within a series of values and cookies in the command string. Normally, constructing a **post** command is a tedious affair of putting the right lines in the right place with the right number of carriage returns and linefeeds in the right regions of the request and then making sure that the values you are sending are formatted correctly.

When you use the C# CLR, however, issuing a **post** command is a breeze. You just set the right properties and then tell the system to make your request to the remote server. Listing 8.15 shows a simple **post** command application that sends the request of your choice to the server of your choice.

Listing 8.15   Performing an HTTP **post** command.

```
using System;
using System.IO;
using System.Net;
using System.Net.Sockets;
using System.Text;
```

```
public class CH8_15
{

    string retrieveHTTP (WebRequest request)
    {
        WebResponse response = request.GetResponse();
        Stream responseStream = response.GetResponseStream();
        StreamReader reader = new StreamReader (responseStream);
        return reader.ReadToEnd ();
    }

    void writeHTTP(WebRequest request, string data)
    {

        byte [] bytes = System.Text.Encoding.ASCII.GetBytes (data);
        request.ContentLength = bytes.Length;
        Stream outputStream = request.GetRequestStream ();
        outputStream.Write (bytes, 0, bytes.Length);
        outputStream.Close ();
    }

    void postHTTP (string server, string data)
    {
        // Create the Web Request Object
        WebRequest request = WebRequestFactory.Create (server);

        // Setup a post request
        request.Method = "POST";
        request.ContentType = "application/x-www-form-urlencoded";

        // Write out the data to the Web server
        writeHTTP(request, data);

        // And get the response
        string page = retrieveHTTP(request);
        Console.WriteLine("Retrieved Page: {0}", page );

    }

    public static void Main(String[] args)
    {
        if ( args.Length < 2 )
        {
            Console.WriteLine("Usage: ch8_15 server values");
         return;
        }
```

```
        CH8_15 app = new CH8_15();

        app.postHTTP( args[0], args[1] );
    }
}
```

Again, you see how well organized and how well-thought-out the C# CLR system is for you to use. The most complex tasks of the past have become trivial to use and to extend in the future.

Activating a Program Remotely

Sometimes, you need to start or stop from your local machine a program or service running on a remote machine. Examples include the remote maintenance of Web servers or the remote monitoring and administration of database servers and the like. Completing this task used to involve going down to the computer room, finding the right machine that was running the service you want to stop, and then logging in and killing the service. With the advent of remote administration in Windows, however, this process is no longer necessary. You could use the service controller application to administer remote programs. The problem is that you had to use this interactive program. If your program needed to kill something during its run, it would have to wait until you were finished.

With the advent of C# and the CLR, however, these hassles are a memory of the past. You can simply and easily work with remote machines, remote applications, and remote services. You still need to have administrator rights on the machine you want to manipulate, but that is an underlying requirement of the Windows security system, not of the CLR.

In Listing 8.16, you explore how you can start, stop, and list the services running on either the local machine or a remote machine. The same process is used for either machine, so if you are running this application at home on a stand-alone machine, you can see the results as well as if you were checking on a remote machine at the office.

Listing 8.16 Activating a program remotely.

```
using System;
using System.ServiceProcess;

class CH8_16
{
    public static void StartService( string server, string service )
    {
```

```
    try
{
        Console.WriteLine("About to start the {0} Service", service );
    ServiceController svcCtrl;

    if ( server.Length != 0 )
       svcCtrl = new ServiceController(server, service);
    else
       svcCtrl = new ServiceController(service);

        svcCtrl.Start();
}
    catch(Exception e)
{
        Console.WriteLine("Caught exception of : {0}", e.ToString());
    }
  }

  public static void StopService( string server, string service )
  {
     try
{
        Console.WriteLine("About to stop the {0} Service", service );
    ServiceController svcCtrl;

    if ( server.Length != 0 )
       svcCtrl = new ServiceController(server, service);
    else
       svcCtrl = new ServiceController(service);

        svcCtrl.Stop();
}
    catch(Exception e)
{
        Console.WriteLine("Cought exception of : {0}", e.ToString());
    }
  }

  public static void ShowServices( string server )
  {
     try
{
    ServiceController[] services;
    if ( server.Length != 0 )
          services = ServiceController.GetServices(server);
```

```
    else
      services = ServiceController.GetServices();

        foreach ( ServiceController svc in services)
    {
            Console.WriteLine("Found service : {0}", svc.DisplayName);
        }
}
    catch(Exception e)
{
        Console.WriteLine("Cought exception of : {0}", e.ToString());
    }
  }


    public static int Main(string[] args)
    {
        if(args.Length == 0)
        {
            Console.WriteLine(
                "Syntax: service <server> <command> [service_name]");
            return -1;
        }

        if ( args[1] == "Start" )
    {
      StartService( args[0], args[2] );
    }

        if ( args[1] == "Stop" )
    {
      StopService( args[0], args[2] );
    }

  if ( args[1] == "Show" )
  {
      ShowServices( args[0] );
  }

        return 0;
    }
}
```

Copying to the Clipboard

The Clipboard is one of the most helpful features of the Windows operating system—and one of the simplest to understand from a user's perspective. The Clipboard allows you to copy text, graphics, and even program objects from one program to another. You can, for example, copy the credit card number from your checkbook program into a browser to pay a bill on the Web. The handy Clipboard feature helps users to make their lives easier.

Fortunately, C# makes copying information to the Clipboard easy. In this example, you look at a simple way to copy text to the Clipboard. The process is the same for any other type of data, although text is the easiest to verify. You use the form shown in Figure 8.1, which contains a simple edit box in which a user enters some information before clicking the Copy button to put it on the system Clipboard. After the data is there, you can paste it into any other application.

Listing 8.17 shows the code needed to accomplish this task. As you can see by the highlighted sections, it's not hard to do. A few lines of code, and you can have any information you like on the Clipboard. Note that the automatically generated code has been removed from this listing to show you only the parts that apply.

Listing 8.17   Copying to the Clipboard.

```
namespace CH8_17
{
    using System;
    using System.Drawing;
    using System.Collections;
    using System.ComponentModel;
    using System.WinForms;
    using System.Data;

    public class Form1 : System.WinForms.Form
    {
        private System.ComponentModel.Container components;
      private System.WinForms.Button button2;
      private System.WinForms.Button button1;
      private System.WinForms.TextBox textBox1;
      private System.WinForms.Label label1;
```

Figure 8.1   The Clipboard copy form.

```
public Form1()
{
    InitializeComponent();
}

public override void Dispose()
{
    base.Dispose();
    components.Dispose();
}

private void InitializeComponent()
{
            // Generated code removed.
    button1.Click += new System.EventHandler
                        (this.button1_Click);
    button2.Click += new System.EventHandler
                        (this.button2_Click);
    this.Text = "Form1";
}

protected void button2_Click (object sender, System.EventArgs e)
{
        Close();
}

protected void button1_Click (object sender, System.EventArgs e)
{
        if ( textBox1.Text != "")
            Clipboard.SetDataObject(textBox1.Text);
    }

public static void Main(string[] args)
{
    Application.Run(new Form1());
}
    }
}
```

Copying from the Clipboard

If you have on the system Clipboard some data you want users to be able to "paste" into your application, you need to have the ability to find out what is there and to copy it into your application. Quite a number of different Clipboard data formats are available that a user might have copied to the Clipboard. Only one format is active at any time because the Clipboard replaces each previous selection with the current one.

Using the Clipboard and its formats from C# is easy, as you see in this example. To begin with, you need to create a form to display the formats you might want to see. The form, in Design mode, is shown in Figure 8.2.

Listing 8.18 shows the code that was added to the default project skeleton code to make this program work. All non-essential code is stripped out to save space in the book, but is available on the accompanying CD-ROM.

Listing 8.18   Copying from the Clipboard.

```
namespace Ch8_18
{
    public class Form1 : System.WinForms.Form
    {
        public Form1()
        {
        }

        public override void Dispose()
        {
            base.Dispose();
            components.Dispose();
        }
```

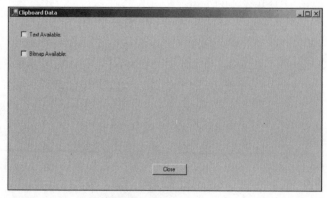

Figure 8.2   The Clipboard display form.

```
    private void InitializeComponent()
{
            // Extra code removed
    button1.Click += new System.EventHandler
                    (this.button1_Click);

            // Extra code removed.

    // See if there is data available on the Clipboard for our
    // formats.
        IDataObject iData = Clipboard.GetDataObject();

        if (iData.GetDataPresent(DataFormats.Text))
    {
        TextCheckbox.Checked = true;
            TextLabel.Text = (String)iData.GetData(DataFormats.Text);
    }
    if ( iData.GetDataPresent(DataFormats.Bitmap) )
    {
        BitmapCheckbox.Checked = true;
        pictureBox1.SizeMode = PictureBoxSizeMode.StretchImage ;
        pictureBox1.Image = (Bitmap)iData.GetData(DataFormats.Bitmap);

    }
    }

protected void button1_Click (object sender, System.EventArgs e)
{
        Close();
}

    public static void Main(string[] args)
    {
        Application.Run(new Form1());
    }
    }
}
```

If you run this application while selecting text in another program, you see a display similar to the one shown in Figure 8.3. On the other hand, if you bring up a Web page with an image on it in Internet Explorer and right-click to select the image, you might see a picture like the one shown in Figure 8.4.

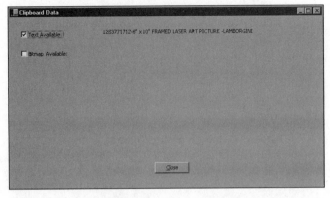

Figure 8.3   The Clipboard program showing copied text.

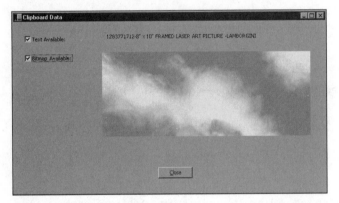

Figure 8.4   The Clipboard program showing a copied picture.

Chapter 9

Visual Elements

In Depth

The core of the .NET system is the Common Language Runtime (CLR). This core set of libraries and components makes up all the functionality shared across all development environments. In this chapter, you get more intimately involved in understanding what makes up the visual aspects of the CLR, for use in your own Windows and Internet applications.

As a developer, you generally think of the application as the set of objects that converse and work together to implement the functionality of the system. To users, however, the application is generally perceived as the GUI elements that allow them to interact with that functionality. Users are less impressed by the way in which data is stored on the persistent storage device as they are by the way in which the system allows them to find and sort that data. The way in which the data is presented is generally the way in which the program is thought about when it is used or reviewed. For this reason, you should strongly consider the GUI elements when you are writing applications. Too often, developers think more in terms of features and less in terms of how the pieces of an overall application flow together. By using the CLR visual (and other) elements properly, you won't have this problem in your own applications. For more information on writing applications, see Chapter 7; to find out more about nonvisual CLR elements, see Chapter 8.

When you talk about "visual" elements, you are generally talking about two specific concepts: Elements appear directly on Windows forms, and elements are visible to users. This combination is important because many elements in the CLR are available to you as a developer for use directly on a form without being directly visible to users. This chapter does not discuss these types of elements, most of which are in Chapter 8.

Elements in the CLR and its extensions break down into three general categories, which you look at in this chapter:

- *The general components that the CLR supports and that you can place directly on your forms*—This category, the largest by far, occupies most of this chapter.

- *The set of user-defined components*—The CLR and C# permit you to create your own components, visual and nonvisual, for use in your applications. You should understand how to complete this process. These components can be either visual elements written from scratch to perform a specific action or extensions to existing CLR components (such as owner-drawn components).

- *The "other" components in the visual spectrum*—Examples are standardized dialog boxes, tool tips, and printing support.

In the next section, you take a look at each of these groups, one at a time.

General Components

The general category of the CLR consists of the "standard" Windows controls, wrapped up nicely in C# components. This category contains buttons, checkboxes, radio buttons, list boxes, edit controls, and other simple controls that users are accustomed to working with in the Windows operating system.

NOTE: *The difference between the CLR and other frameworks, such as the Microsoft Foundation Classes (MFC) library, is that the CLR components were designed to wrap the controls without being dependent on the operating system. Therefore, when the CLR is ported to other operating systems, such as Linux, you can run your programs with little or no modification.*

Buttons

Buttons are a way to have users give specific instructions on what to do. Few things are more clear and obvious to users than buttons that say Exit or Print. Buttons are thought to be one-shot entities, intended to perform a single action and then return control to the application. A user can get easily annoyed when a button changes the state of the application. Picture a scenario in which a button in your application puts you into a new "mode" in the system. Your application has three states: entering data, processing data, and displaying data. Furthermore, when you click a button on the main form, it allows you to switch to the next state. The problem occurs when a user clicks the button. What should happen? The system should do something—that's the purpose of the button, after all. But it doesn't really *do* anything. Instead, the system switches modes. You shouldn't add events like these in your applications.

To reiterate, a button in C# is used to perform a single, specific action. To change modes, use a menu. To define specific states on a given form, use a radio button or checkbox. Don't use buttons to move between states. If a multiple-step process must be performed, use multiple forms and a Previous and Next button set to move between them. That way, users know exactly what will happen when the button is clicked. Buttons should always operate on the principle of "least astonishment," in which events happen the way users most expect them to and have as few side effects as possible.

What can you do with a button in the CLR? Buttons have quite a few properties, as shown in Table 9.1. You can set the text that appears on them and the colors used to display the text. You can set an image to be used for the background of

Table 9.1   Button properties.

Property	Purpose
Cursor	The cursor to be displayed when the mouse is over this button
Font	The font to use in displaying the button text
Image	The image to use for the background of this button
Text	The text to display for the button
TextAlign	How to align the text (right, left, or center) for the button
ForeColor	The foreground (text) color of the button
BackColor	The background color of the button

the button and define how the text on the button is aligned. All these properties are available at either design time or runtime for the button.

TIP: For a better effect, you can combine an image and text on a single button.

When working with buttons, you can directly define *accelerator keys*, which are keyboard shortcuts to work with when the button is shown on the screen. For example, you might have on your form a Close button that you want users to be able to select without having to move the mouse over and click on it. You do this via the shortcut key. To implement a shortcut key, just put an ampersand (&) before the letter you want to be the shortcut. Pressing the Alt key and then that letter automatically selects the action of that button. (If multiple shortcuts have the same letter, the system sets the focus to the first button.)

The important aspect of buttons, of course, is in the events for the button. Table 9.2 shows the available button events in C#. An *event* is what happens when a

Table 9.2   Button events.

Event	Meaning
Click	A user clicks the button.
MouseEnter	A user moves the mouse into the button area.
MouseLeave	A user moves the mouse out of the button area.
MouseHover	A user keeps the mouse cursor in the button area without moving it.
MouseMove	A user moves the mouse in the button.
MouseDown	A user holds the mouse button down while in the button area.
MouseUp	A user releases the mouse button while in the button area.
KeyDown	A user presses a key while the button has input focus.
KeyUp	A user releases a key while the button has input focus.
KeyPress	A user clicks a key while the button has input focus.

user does something with the button, such as move the mouse over it. If you have seen an application where the button seems to "shine" when the mouse is moved over it, for example, you have seen a system where that event is handled.

Of all the events on the list, you should be concerned about only the **Click** event. This event occurs when a user clicks the button to make something happen. For the aforementioned **MouseEnter** and **MouseLeave** events, here's a simple example of what you might do to reverse the colors of the button to make it "flash" when a user moves the mouse in and out of the button area:

```
protected void button1_MouseLeave (object sender, System.EventArgs e)
{
   // Change the foreground and background color when the mouse
   // leaves the button area
   this.button1.ForeColor = Color.White;
   this.button1.BackColor = Color.Blue;
}

protected void button1_MouseEnter (object sender, System.EventArgs e)
{
   // Change the foreground and background color when the mouse
   // enters the button area
   this.button1.ForeColor = Color.Blue;
   this.button1.BackColor = Color.White;
}
```

This code flashes the button blue and white as the mouse moves across and out of its region of the form. You can find all the code for this example in the CH9_Button project on this book's accompanying CD-ROM.

List Boxes

List boxes are the general selection mechanisms of the CLR library system. Along with their brother controls, combo boxes, list boxes are a way to display fixed lists of options and have users select one or more of them. A list box has two forms:

- The *simple* list box allows you to display just a list of items and permits users to click on them to select them. Extended selection permits you to select more than one item in the list by holding down either the Ctrl or Shift key on the keyboard and selecting items.

- The *checked* list box is similar to the standard list box, but it also allows you to select multiple items more simply by presenting, to the left of the items, a checkbox that can be checked or cleared.

Table 9.3   List box properties.

Property	Meaning
BackColor	The background color of the list box
ForeColor	The text color for the list box
Font	The font to use for displaying the text strings
Items	The list of strings displayed in the list box

The list box classes all share a given set of properties, as shown in Table 9.3. Of all the list box properties, the most important is the **Items** property, which contains the list of strings displayed in the list.

Unlike the "standard" Windows controls that are available in systems like MFC, the CLR components are designed from the ground up to be usable. That is why the foreground and background colors are available in either design or runtime modes. Given this approach, it is odd that you cannot directly set the foreground and background colors of individual items or set their fonts. However, as you will see when I talk about owner-drawn list boxes, those elements are easy to add.

The list box events are straightforward and easy to understand. Although numerous events apply to different kinds of list boxes, the standard ones are shown:

- **SelectedIndexChanged**—Fired when a user changes the selection list for a list box

- **DoubleClick**—Happens when a user clicks twice quickly on a given item

Like all other controls, the component supports mouse-entering, mouse-leaving, and mouse-moving events.

Why would you want a double-click event, anyway? One reason is to conform to the default Windows standard, which is to close a dialog box when a user double-clicks to select an item in a single list box. For example, in the CH9_Listbox project on the accompanying CD-ROM is a simple application that allows you to select an input source. If a user double-clicks on an item, the "dialog box" form processes that entry (shows you a message box with your selection number) and then closes itself. The code you use is simple:

```
protected void listBox1_DoubleClick (object sender, System.EventArgs e)
{
    // Process the user selection
    int sel = this.listBox1.SelectedIndex;
    MessageBox.Show( this, "You selected: " + sel );

    Close();
}
```

Text Boxes

Text boxes are the standard entry tools for data in Windows. If you need to know names, addresses, or monetary amounts, for example, you generally use text boxes to get them. For the most part, text boxes are simple to use. You put one on a form, wait until you need the information, and then get the text property of the box to use as your input. You might, however, want to use one of several ways to customize a text box in your own applications.

Two obvious tasks you can perform with text boxes are to filter out bad input and to auto-complete user input based on entries you have on hand. Filtering output is something you usually do by deriving a class from the base **TextBox** class to do the proper kind of filtering. Suppose that you want to use a text box that accepts only numeric entries. You could create a **TextBox** subclass named **NumericInput** that looks like this:

```
public class NumericInput : System.WinForms.TextBox
{
    protected override bool ProcessKeyEventArgs(ref Message m)
    {
        if ( m.msg == 0x0102 ) // WM_CHAR
        {
            char c = (char)m.wParam;
            if ( c < '0' || c > '9')
            {
                return true;
            }
        }
        return base.ProcessKeyEventArgs(ref m);
    }
}
```

Given that events are called when a user hits a key, you might think that you could trap one of them (**OnKeyPress**, for example) and handle the input there. Unfortunately, because the data has already gone to the control, you can't do it that way. Subclassing is the only way to accomplish this task.

NOTE: *When you are working with text boxes and you know that your input is valid, you can access the **Text** property at any time. This is a change from such systems as MFC, where you need to force the "component" to update itself internally from the external Windows control. In C#, the component can be thought of as the Windows control.*

Labels

The **Label** class allows you to put static text on your forms. You can modify the font, color, and size of the label. In addition, you can modify any or all of the properties at runtime or design time. Labels are generally used for such tasks as putting a prompt in front of an input field or putting display information (copyright information, for example) in front of users, where it belongs.

Checkboxes and Radio Buttons

The checkbox and radio button components are used when you want users to make a choice about something and the number of options is limited. The real difference between the two is that checkboxes are used when the options can be combined, whereas radio buttons are used when the options are mutually exclusive. Suppose that you are asking users to define their gender. Because people are (usually) only male or female, the right answer for the gender question is a radio button. On the other hand, a form entry might ask for your ethnic background. Asking someone who has a Hispanic parent and a Caucasian parent to just "pick one" is too simplistic. Instead, give users the choice of telling you that they are a little of each by supplying checkboxes, rather than radio buttons, for the answers.

Checkboxes and radio buttons have the usual array of properties, as shown in Table 9.4. The most important property for either one is **Checked**, which indicates whether the item is selected. As you see in the "Immediate Solutions" section later in this chapter, selecting a single radio button in a group always unselects all other entries in the group, whether it's done by users or programmatically. For a checkbox, any number of entries—whether they're in a group or not—can be selected or unselected.

Although you rarely have to worry about when a checkbox or radio button is selected or cleared, the controls support events for this action. For example, you might want to always enable or disable a set of components based on the setting of a given checkbox. See the CH9_Check example on this book's accompanying CD-ROM. You might have something like this in your code:

```
private void EnableSet3()
{
    this.textBox4.Enabled = this.checkBox3.Checked;
}
```

Table 9.4   Checkbox and radio button properties.

Property	Meaning
BackColor	Shows the background color of the component
ForeColor	Shows the foreground (text) color of the component
Checked	Indicates whether the component is selected
Font	Shows the font used to display the text in the component

```
protected void checkBox1_CheckedChanged (object sender,
      System.EventArgs e)
{
   EnableSet1();
   EnableSet2();
   EnableSet3();
}
```

As you can see, working with checkboxes and radio buttons is quite simple using the power of the CLR.

User-Defined Components

User-defined components are created by users from whole cloth or as extensions of existing components in the CLR. I looked a bit at the extension concept when I talked about the text box that supports only numeric input. I look some more at this concept when I discuss owner-drawn components in this section.

Custom Components

Custom components were invented to do a specific job that the CLR doesn't address directly. For example, no component displays an EKG trace (such as you might see in a hospital). If you want to create this type of component, you have to write your own from scratch. Fortunately, the CLR makes that step unnecessary. Instead, it offers you some tools and frameworks you can use to build your own components. This extensibility is one of the true hallmarks of C# programming— and one that makes your life considerably easier in the long run.

To create a custom component, you derive your new class from the **RichControl** base class. For example, in the "Immediate Solutions" section later in this chapter, you create a component named **Clock** that displays a digital time clock on the screen. This component can be created in your form, used in other applications, or even dropped on a Web page. To create it, you work from a skeleton that looks like this:

```
public class Clock : System.WinForms.RichControl
{
    public Clock()
    {
       // Initialization work
    }

    protected override void OnPaint(PaintEventArgs pe)
    {
       // Do the painting of the control here.
    }
}
```

As you can see, creating a component is mostly a matter of filling in the blanks to make the component do what you want it to do when it is shown and interacted with on a user form. The only required part of the component is the **OnPaint** method, which renders the control. If you want to receive input from the component, you override the proper handlers for the mouse or keyboard.

The properties that affect input are shown in Table 9.5. Working from these possible handlers, you can handle virtually any form of input your component might need.

TIP: *For more information, see the clock example in "Creating a Custom Control" in the "Immediate Solutions" section of this chapter.*

Table 9.5   Input properties for custom controls.

Property	Meaning
KeyDown	A user presses a key while the control has focus.
KeyPress	A user presses a key and releases it while the control has focus.
KeyUp	A user releases a key while the control has focus.
MouseDown	A user presses the mouse button while the pointer is over a control.
MouseEnter	A mouse pointer moves into the area of the control.
MouseHover	A mouse pointer is in the area of the control and has not moved.
MouseLeave	A mouse pointer has crossed the control boundaries.
MouseMove	A mouse pointer has moved within the control boundaries.

Immediate Solutions

Creating a Button on a Form

Although the integrated environment is wonderful for designing and building forms you can use in your application, sometimes that environment is not enough. Imagine that you want to create an application that is *dynamic*, changing in response to the input a user might select. You might need to dynamically create new components on the form and then use them in your application. If you are accustomed to working only with a form created by the Visual Designer, you probably have no idea how to create and use them. In this example, therefore, you look at how you can create your own components and place them on a form at runtime.

Figure 9.1 shows a form that contains two buttons and a label. The first button dynamically adds a button to the runtime form. The second button simply closes the form and shuts down the application.

Listing 9.1 shows the code that implements the dynamic button. Although the comments have been stripped out of the generated code to save space, the remainder of the application is complete, for a change, so that you can see exactly what you need to add by hand to the application to make it work. As you can see from the shaded portions of the code, which indicate necessary changes, not much is needed to make it work properly.

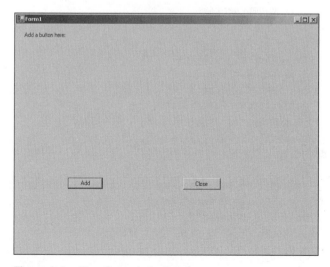

Figure 9.1   The dynamic button form.

9. Visual Elements

Listing 9.1   Creating a dynamic button.

```
namespace CH9_2
{
    using System;
    using System.Drawing;
    using System.Collections;
    using System.ComponentModel;
    using System.WinForms;
    using System.Data;

    public class Form1 : System.WinForms.Form
    {
        private System.ComponentModel.Container components;
        private System.WinForms.Button button2;
        private System.WinForms.Button button1;
        private System.WinForms.Label label1;
        private System.WinForms.Button myButton;

        public Form1()
        {
            InitializeComponent();
        }

        public override void Dispose()
        {
            base.Dispose();
            components.Dispose();
        }

        private void InitializeComponent()
        {
         this.components = new System.ComponentModel.Container ();
         this.button1 = new System.WinForms.Button ();
         this.label1 = new System.WinForms.Label ();
         this.myButton = new System.WinForms.Button ();
         this.button2 = new System.WinForms.Button ();
         button1.Location = new System.Drawing.Point (112, 320);
         button1.Size = new System.Drawing.Size (75, 23);
         button1.TabIndex = 1;
         button1.Text = "Add";
         button1.Click += new System.EventHandler (this.button1_Click);
         label1.Location = new System.Drawing.Point (16, 16);
         label1.Text = "Add a button here:";
         label1.Size = new System.Drawing.Size (100, 16);
         label1.TabIndex = 0;
```

```
        myButton.Size = new System.Drawing.Size (75, 23);
        myButton.TabIndex = 0;
        button2.Location = new System.Drawing.Point (360, 320);
        button2.Size = new System.Drawing.Size (80, 24);
        button2.TabIndex = 2;
        button2.Text = "&Close";
        button2.Click += new System.EventHandler (this.button2_Click);
        this.Text = "Form1";
        this.AutoScaleBaseSize = new System.Drawing.Size (5, 13);
        this.ClientSize = new System.Drawing.Size (648, 477);
        this.Controls.Add (this.button2);
        this.Controls.Add (this.button1);
        this.Controls.Add (this.label1);
    }

    protected void button1_Click (object sender, System.EventArgs e)
    {
        myButton.Location = new System.Drawing.Point (116, 16);
        myButton.Size = new System.Drawing.Size (75, 23);
        myButton.TabIndex = 1;
        myButton.Text = "New Button";
        myButton.Click += new System.EventHandler (this.myButton_Click);
        this.Controls.Add (this.myButton);
    }

    protected void button2_Click (object sender, System.EventArgs e)
    {
        Close();
    }

    protected void myButton_Click (object sender, System.EventArgs e)
    {
        MessageBox.Show( this, "You Clicked Me!");
    }
    public static void Main(string[] args)
    {
        Application.Run(new Form1());
    }
    }
}
```

The most interesting parts of this listing are how the button is placed on the form and how the events for the button are handled. As you can see, nothing is magical about the dynamic creation of buttons. They are done in exactly the same way as the system generates the code for them in the first place. Likewise, when you set up a delegate to handle the click event for the button, all you are doing is handling the code as though the system had written it for you.

One thing this application sample points out is that you can easily add new handlers to visual elements at runtime. This feature is important because the way in which you handle something may depend on information you don't have until runtime, such as the type of user you are working with.

To add a new visual element to a form, you must take several important steps:

1. Create the component, such as the button.

2. Assign the properties to the button to position it and place the text on it and to do whatever other tailoring you want to do for the component.

3. Finally, to make the component appear on the form, you need to add the component to the form list of controls, using this line:

```
this.Controls.Add (this.myButton);
```

If you do not add this line, you find that the button never appears on the form at runtime, even though it is being created properly.

Creating a List Box on a Form

The list box is one of the most versatile and powerful components in the C# CLR visual element collection. You can display things in a list box that are much bigger than the available screen real estate. You can detect when a user selects one or clicks on the box itself. At runtime, you can insert entries into a list box, delete entries from a list box, or modify existing entries in the list box. A list box is therefore more than a simple display component, such as a label or a tree. It is an interactive component—one that can be used to update status elements for the application or allow users to modify settings at runtime, for example.

In this example, you explore how to work with list boxes, from determining what is selected to modifying and adding to the strings displayed in the list. To do this, you need to understand two of the important properties of the list box component: the **SelectedIndex** property and the **Items** collection.

The **SelectedIndex** property tells you which item a user has selected in the list box. You can either set or read this property, allowing you to find out whether a user has made a selection and, if so, which one it is. By setting the selection, you can programmatically move the selection around in the list box.

The **Items** collection contains an entry for each item you add to the list box. As long as you add an object that can be converted to a string, you can work with the item's array of data. Normally, this collection is simply a list of strings you can modify, add to, delete from, or read from.

Figure 9.2 shows the form you work with in this example. The Add, Delete, and Modify buttons allow you to change the contents of the list box itself. The Add button places the contents of the edit box into the list. The Delete button removes the selected item from the list box. The Modify button replaces the selected item text with the text in the edit box. The two little buttons on top move the selected item up or down in the list box.

Listing 9.2 shows the code necessary to implement the preceding form. Note that much of the automatically generated code is removed from this listing. You can find it on the accompanying CD-ROM for this book or simply look at the code that is generated when you drag and drop visual elements onto your form if you are creating it from scratch.

Listing 9.2   Creating and modifying a list box on a form.

```
namespace Ch9_2
{
    public class Form1 : System.WinForms.Form
    {
        private int fSelIndex;

        public Form1()
        {
```

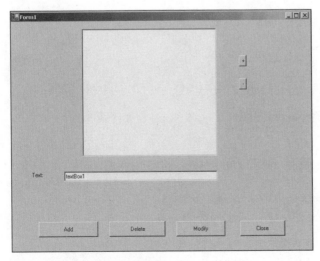

Figure 9.2   The list box form.

```
            InitializeComponent();
    }
    protected void button6_Click (object sender, System.EventArgs e)
    {
        if ( this.listBox1.SelectedIndex > 0 )
        {
            this.listBox1.SelectedIndex--;
        }
        else
            this.button6.Enabled = false;

        if ( this.listBox1.SelectedIndex < this.listBox1.Items.Count)
        {
            this.button5.Enabled = true;
        }


    }


    protected void button5_Click (object sender, System.EventArgs e)
    {
        if ( this.listBox1.SelectedIndex < this.listBox1.Items.Count-1)
        {
            this.listBox1.SelectedIndex++;
        }
        else
            this.button5.Enabled = false;

        if ( this.listBox1.SelectedIndex > 0 )
        {
            this.button6.Enabled = true;
        }
    }


    protected void button3_Click (object sender, System.EventArgs e)
    {
        this.listBox1.Items[fSelIndex] = this.textBox1.Text;
    }


    protected void button2_Click (object sender, System.EventArgs e)
    {
        fSelIndex = this.listBox1.SelectedIndex;
        this.listBox1.Items.Remove( fSelIndex );
    }


    protected void button1_Click (object sender, System.EventArgs e)
```

```
    {
        this.listBox1.Items.Add( this.textBox1.Text);
    }


    protected void listBox1_SelectedIndexChanged (object sender,
            System.EventArgs e)
    {
        // We need to keep track of the currently selected item
        // and place the text in the edit box
        fSelIndex = this.listBox1.SelectedIndex;
        string t = (string)this.listBox1.SelectedItem;
        this.textBox1.Text = t;
    }


    protected void button4_Click (object sender, System.EventArgs e)
    {
        Close();
    }

    public static void Main(string[] args)
    {
        Application.Run(new Form1 ());
    }
  }
}
```

Related solution:	Found on page:
Enumerating Files in a Directory	325

Populating a List Box

Imagine that you are trying to show users all the files that exist in a given directory, to allow them to pick the file they want. You could put a large number of checkboxes on a form and allow users to pick one. But how would you know ahead of time how many you would need? One alternative is to simply create them at runtime and allow users to click the one they want. However, if you have a large directory, with a large number of files in it, the list would become impossible to manage, even in a short period. How do you show something that makes up a list of items when you don't know how many items you will have? The answer is the standard Windows list box control.

The C# CLR visual elements contain a list box component that is a complete wrapper around the list box control. This component allows you to display multiple items in a small amount of space and to control how those elements are sorted and displayed. In this example, you see how to use the list box component to display all the files in a given directory for a user and allow him to browse through them quickly and easily.

Figure 9.3 shows the form used for this example. This form contains the text box that holds the name of the directory to browse as well as a button to start the listing process. The list box itself is prominent in the middle of the form and is followed by a button that allows you to close down the form and, therefore, the application.

The process of listing the items is simple enough: You use the **Directory** component to create an interface to the directory itself. Then the directory object is queried for an array of file objects to store in the list box. Finally, the array is iterated over, and each element is used to populate the list box. Listing 9.3 shows the complete code for the application, with the generated code from the wizard removed to save space.

Listing 9.3   Populating a list box.

```
namespace CH9_3
{
    public class Form1 : System.WinForms.Form
    {
        private System.ComponentModel.Container components;
        private System.WinForms.Button button2;
        private System.WinForms.Button button1;
        private System.WinForms.TextBox textBox1;
        private System.WinForms.Label label1;
        private System.WinForms.ListBox listBox1;

        public Form1()
        {
            InitializeComponent();
        }
```

Figure 9.3   The directory listing form.

```
public override void Dispose()
{
    base.Dispose();
    components.Dispose();
}

protected void button1_Click (object sender, System.EventArgs e)
{
    if ( this.textBox1.Text.Length != 0 )
    {
      // Load the list box
      Directory d = new Directory( this.textBox1.Text );
      File[] files = d.GetFiles();
      foreach( File f in files )
      {
          this.listBox1.Items.Add( f.FullName );
      }
    }
}

protected void button2_Click (object sender, System.EventArgs e)
{
    Close();
}

public static void Main(string[] args)
{
    Application.Run(new Form1());
}
    }
}
```

When you run this application, enter a directory name in the text box and click on the button. You see the list box filled with the names of all the files in that directory. Note that none of the subdirectories is shown. The C# **Directory** component differentiates between files and directories.

Adding a Border to a Form

Forms have many attributes that can be set at design time. For example, you can set the title and size of the form and determine whether the form contains a help button on the caption. In "classic" Windows applications, you could not change certain attributes without doing a great deal of work behind the scenes. One attribute that could not be easily changed was the border style of the form. If you want to change the form to have no border, for example, so that you can blend it with other windows on the screen, you would have to destroy the original form object and re-create it with the new style. This solution was, obviously, less than optimal.

With the new C# CLR system, you can modify virtually any attribute of any object at runtime without incurring any penalty. One easy thing to change is the form border style. In this example, you see exactly how to modify the form border at runtime to get things just the way you want them.

Figure 9.4 shows the form used for this example. The individual border styles are shown as radio buttons because the styles are mutually exclusive. You cannot, for example, have a form that has both a dialog-box-style border and no border. It just doesn't make sense to have multiple border styles.

Listing 9.4 shows the program you use to check out various form styles. As you can see, changing the style is as simple as picking the proper style enumeration from the **FormBorderStyle** type and assigning it to the **BorderStyle** property of the form.

Listing 9.4   Adding a border to a form.

```
namespace Ch9_4
{
    using System;
    using System.Drawing;
    using System.Collections;
    using System.ComponentModel;
    using System.WinForms;
    using System.Data;

    public class Form1 : System.WinForms.Form
    {
```

Figure 9.4   The border style form.

```csharp
public Form1()
{
    InitializeComponent();
}

public override void Dispose()
{
    base.Dispose();
    components.Dispose();
}

protected void button1_Click (object sender, System.EventArgs e)
{
        Close();
}
protected void radioButton7_CheckedChanged (object sender,
        System.EventArgs e)
{
        this.BorderStyle = FormBorderStyle.SizableToolWindow;
}

protected void radioButton6_CheckedChanged (object sender,
        System.EventArgs e)
{
        this.BorderStyle = FormBorderStyle.Sizable;
}

protected void radioButton5_CheckedChanged (object sender,
        System.EventArgs e)
{
        this.BorderStyle = FormBorderStyle.FixedToolWindow;
}

protected void radioButton4_CheckedChanged (object sender,
        System.EventArgs e)
{
        this.BorderStyle = FormBorderStyle.FixedSingle;
}

protected void radioButton3_CheckedChanged (object sender,
        System.EventArgs e)
{
        this.BorderStyle = FormBorderStyle.FixedDialog;
}
```

```
protected void radioButton2_CheckedChanged (object sender,
    System.EventArgs e)
{
    this.BorderStyle = FormBorderStyle.Fixed3D;
}

protected void radioButton1_CheckedChanged (object sender,
    System.EventArgs e)
{
    this.BorderStyle = FormBorderStyle.None;
}

    public static void Main(string[] args)
    {
        Application.Run(new Form1());
    }
}
}
```

Formatting a Rich Edit Control Text String

One of the best new features of the C# CLR library is its wonderful wrapper for the Windows rich edit control. This component allows you to format all the information in a rich edit control quickly and easily without much programming work. With the rich edit control, you can change the fonts, colors, and sizes of text within the display area. A rich edit control is perfect for displaying legal information and for working with electronic text displays, such as in the new electronic books, or e-books, which are displayed on computers or other dedicated reading devices (such as handheld computers). An e-book's text formatting and styling are built into its rich edit control.

For this example, you create a simple form (as shown in Figure 9.5) that contains a rich edit control and several checkboxes. The checkboxes control what aspects of the font attributes are used to display the text. By selecting different checkboxes, you can view the text with different attributes in the edit control. Simply enter a text string in the text box, select the attributes you want, and then select Add to put the text into the control with those attributes.

Listing 9.5 shows all the code needed to implement this form. As you can see, not much work is involved. Most of the calculations determine for which part of the text string in the component you need to apply the new formatting information.

Figure 9.5   The rich edit control form.

Listing 9.5   Formatting a rich edit control text string.

```
namespace ch9_5
{
    using System;
    using System.Drawing;
    using System.Collections;
    using System.ComponentModel;
    using System.WinForms;
    using System.Data;

    public class Form1 : System.WinForms.Form
    {

      public Form1()
      {
          InitializeComponent();
      }

      public override void Dispose()
      {
          base.Dispose();
          components.Dispose();
      }

      protected void AddText( string text )
      {
        FontStyle fs = new FontStyle();
        if ( this.checkBox1.Checked)
        {
            fs |= FontStyle.Bold;
        }
        if ( this.checkBox2.Checked)
        {
```

```
                    fs |= FontStyle.Italic;
            }
            if ( this.checkBox3.Checked )
            {
                fs |= FontStyle.Underline;
            }

            Font f = new Font("Arial", 12, fs);
            int start = this.richTextBox1.Text.Length;
            this.richTextBox1.Text += text;
            this.richTextBox1.SelectionStart =
                start;
            this.richTextBox1.SelectionLength =
                text.Length;
            this.richTextBox1.SelectionFont = f;

        }

        protected void button1_Click (object sender, System.EventArgs e)
        {
            if ( this.textBox1.Text.Length != 0 )
            {
                AddText( this.textBox1.Text );
                this.textBox1.Text = "";
            }
        }

        public static void Main(string[] args)
        {
            Application.Run(new Form1());
        }
    }
}
```

The preceding code clears the previous selection criteria. If you want to apply formatting to the text and keep it across the selections, you need to use the formatting objects within the rich edit control.

Checking and Clearing Checked List Box Entries

One of the most annoying problems about working with Windows involves selecting a component that allows you to pick multiple entries. The obvious choice for a component to make selections from a long list is the list box. The problem with list boxes is that selecting multiple entries is just a pain in the neck. Various custom components make the job slightly easier, but usually it is a matter of holding down the Ctrl or Shift key and then selecting the entries you want. Determining *whether* you want one selected is another annoying matter. During many years of Windows programming, users complained about this situation, but nobody seemed to have a good solution. Finally, the checked list box was invented.

The checked list box allows you to select entries the "normal" way for a list box—by simply clicking on them and highlighting them. This technique permits you to perform single selection or get information about an item in the list. The addition of the checkbox, however, gives users an easy way to determine whether an item was "selected" for whatever process you want to apply to the selections. In addition, because the selection process is more natural, the checked list box became immediately popular with users in the Windows world.

The problem with the original checked list box was that it was difficult to program for. You communicated with the list box control via a series of complicated, and not well-documented, messages. Fortunately, with the advent of the CLR, this situation changed. Working with a checked list box, as you see in this example, is easy and straightforward.

Figure 9.6 shows the form you create in this example to explore the capabilities and concepts involved with the checked list box. The various buttons allow you to see what is checked or to clear or check all the elements in the list.

The code to work with the checked list box is mostly straightforward. To retrieve information for a given item, you use the **Items** property of the **CheckedListBox** object. To work with a given item, such as for checking or clearing the checkbox, you use the object itself and work through one of the methods provided. Checking an item is done with the **SetItemChecked** method, whereas you use the **GetItemChecked** method to see if an item is checked . Clearing an item is just a matter of passing a different flag (false) to the **SetItemChecked** method. Listing 9.6 shows the application that works with the form.

Figure 9.6   The checked list box form.

Listing 9.6   Checking and clearing checked list box entries.

```
namespace Ch9_6
{
    using System;
    using System.Drawing;
    using System.Collections;
    using System.ComponentModel;
    using System.WinForms;
    using System.Data;

    public class Form1 : System.WinForms.Form
    {
        private System.ComponentModel.Container components;
        private System.WinForms.Button button4;
        private System.WinForms.Button button3;
        private System.WinForms.Button button2;
        private System.WinForms.Button button1;
        private System.WinForms.CheckedListBox checkedListBox1;

        public Form1()
        {
            InitializeComponent();
        }

        public override void Dispose()
        {
            base.Dispose();
            components.Dispose();
        }

        private void InitializeComponent()
        {
            // Add the items.
            this.checkedListBox1.Items.Add("Red");
            this.checkedListBox1.Items.Add("Green");
            this.checkedListBox1.Items.Add("Blue");
            this.checkedListBox1.Items.Add("Yellow");
            this.checkedListBox1.Items.Add("Orange");
        }

        protected void button1_Click (object sender, System.EventArgs e)
        {
```

```
        for ( int i=0; i<this.checkedListBox1.Items.Count; ++i)
        {
          if ( this.checkedListBox1.GetItemChecked(i) )
          {
             MessageBox.Show(this, "Item " + i + " is checked");
          }
        }

    }


    protected void button4_Click (object sender, System.EventArgs e)
    {
        // Set all the list box items to be unchecked.
        for ( int i=0; i<this.checkedListBox1.Items.Count; ++i)
        {
          this.checkedListBox1.SetItemChecked( i, false );
        }
    }

    protected void button3_Click (object sender, System.EventArgs e)
    {
        // Set all the list items to be checked
        for ( int i=0; i<this.checkedListBox1.Items.Count; ++i)
        {
          this.checkedListBox1.SetItemChecked( i, true );
        }
    }

    protected void button2_Click (object sender, System.EventArgs e)
    {
        Close();
    }

    public static void Main(string[] args)
    {
        Application.Run(new Form1 ());
    }
  }
}
```

Working with the checked list box is easy after you know what you are doing. As you can see from this example, you need to understand only a few different methods to utilize the full power of the checked list box.

Creating a Custom Control

One useful element of C# is that it comes with so many prebuilt components to do nearly everything you can think of doing in an application. Unfortunately, the thrill of accessing that huge CLR library goes away when you can't find a component to do a task for you that you've been doing yourself. Having a huge class library of visual components is certainly a good idea, but it is of no use if it doesn't have the component you want. Fortunately, C# comes with an answer to that problem: the custom control.

Custom controls can be written quickly and easily in C# to accommodate virtually any need. Furthermore, by taking advantage of the huge amount of basic functionality addressed by the underlying CLR, you can easily make complex components with a minimum of fuss or coding. In the example in this section, you create a simple custom control to display a clock that updates itself every second on the display.

The form you end up with looks like the one shown in Figure 9.7. As you can see, the clock is a simple component. It just displays the time in hours, minutes, and seconds and updates itself every second. Take a look at the code that implements this custom control, which is shown in Listing 9.7.

Listing 9.7   The clock custom-component source code.

```
namespace Ch9_7
{
    using System;
    using System.Collections;
```

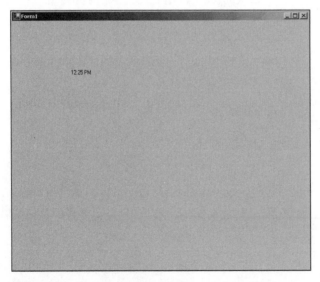

Figure 9.7   The clock component.

```
using System.Core;
using System.ComponentModel;
using System.Drawing;
using System.Data;
using System.WinForms;
using System.Globalization;
using System.Timers;

public class Clock : System.WinForms.RichControl
{
    private System.Timers.Timer aTimer;
    private void InitializeComponent ()
    {
    }

    public Clock()
    {
        aTimer = new System.Timers.Timer();
        aTimer.Tick+=new EventHandler(OnTimedEvent);
        // Set the interval to 1 second.
        aTimer.Interval=100;
        aTimer.Enabled=true;

    }

    public void OnTimedEvent(object source, EventArgs e)
    {
        Invalidate();
    }

    protected override void OnPaint(PaintEventArgs pe)
    {
        // Get the current time
        DateTime dt = DateTime.Now;

        // Format it as a string
        string t = dt.Format("HH:mm:ss",
        DateTimeFormatInfo.InvariantInfo );

        // And display it
        StringFormat style = new StringFormat();
        style.Alignment = StringAlignment.Center;
        pe.Graphics.DrawString(t, Font, new SolidBrush (ForeColor),
            ClientRectangle, style);
    }
}
}
```

9. Visual Elements

To use this control in your form, you add it just as you would add a "normal" component. Here's a sample program (you can find it under the CH9_7 directory source code on the enclosed CD-ROM) that uses the component to show you how it is done:

```
namespace Ch9_7
{
    using System;
    using System.Drawing;
    using System.Collections;
    using System.ComponentModel;
    using System.WinForms;
    using System.Data;

    public class Form1 : System.WinForms.Form
    {
        private System.ComponentModel.Container components;
        private Clock clk;

        public Form1()
        {
            InitializeComponent();
        }
        public override void Dispose()
        {
            base.Dispose();
            components.Dispose();
        }

        private void InitializeComponent()
        {
            this.components = new System.ComponentModel.Container ();
            this.clk = new Ch9_7.Clock ();
            clk.Location = new System.Drawing.Point (100, 100);
            clk.TabIndex = 0;
            clk.Size = new System.Drawing.Size (100, 50);
            this.Text = "Form1";
            this.AutoScaleBaseSize = new System.Drawing.Size (5, 13);
            this.ClientSize = new System.Drawing.Size (640, 517);
            this.Click += new System.EventHandler (this.Form1_Click);
            this.Controls.Add (this.clk);
        }

        protected void Form1_Click (object sender, System.EventArgs e)
        {
```

```
    }
    public static void Main(string[] args)
    {
        Application.Run(new Form1());
    }
  }
}
```

To get the initial control into the form, I simply wrote the highlighted lines when I was creating the form class. The system then imported the component, and it showed up in the Visual Form Designer. This interesting example shows how C# is a two-way interactive environment.

Adding a Label

Labels are common elements in most forms. They can be used as descriptors to tell users what sort of information they are supposed to enter or select. In addition, labels can be used for displaying other general information, such as who wrote an application or what its version number is. In standard Windows applications, labels are straightforward and boring. You can change the text they are displaying, and in most cases you can change the alignment of the text so that it is centered or left- or right-justified. Beyond these simple changes, the label class in Windows is quite limited.

In the C# CLR library, however, the label class was given much more power in response to the many ways in which users want labels to be displayed. For example, in the CLR label class, you can change the text and text alignment as usual, and you can also change the foreground and background colors and the font in which the label is displayed. In the example in this section, you explore how you go about doing that at runtime.

Figure 9.8 shows the form you use to play with label settings. As you can see, the form contains methods for changing the font, color, text, and alignment of the label at the top. As you see from the code, the changes to make it all work together are quite simple to make.

Listing 9.8 shows the label form code, including all the methods used to change the settings of the label on the form. Compile and run the application, and play with it a bit, changing various settings. You see the changes immediately reflected in the label at the top of the form.

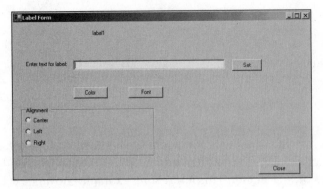

Figure 9.8   The label form.

Listing 9.8   Adding a label to a form.

```
namespace Ch9_8
{
    using System;
    using System.Drawing;
    using System.Collections;
    using System.ComponentModel;
    using System.WinForms;
    using System.Data;

    public class Form1 : System.WinForms.Form
    {
        private System.ComponentModel.Container components;
        private System.WinForms.ColorDialog colorDialog1;
        private System.WinForms.Button button4;
        private System.WinForms.Button button3;
        private System.WinForms.RadioButton radioButton4;
        private System.WinForms.RadioButton radioButton3;
        private System.WinForms.RadioButton radioButton2;
        private System.WinForms.GroupBox groupBox1;
        private System.WinForms.RadioButton radioButton1;
        private System.WinForms.Button button2;
        private System.WinForms.Button button1;
        private System.WinForms.TextBox textBox1;
        private System.WinForms.Label label2;
        private System.WinForms.Label label1;

        public Form1()
        {
            InitializeComponent();
        }
```

```
public override void Dispose()
{
    base.Dispose();
    components.Dispose();
}


protected void button2_Click (object sender, System.EventArgs e)
{
    FontDialog MyDialog = new FontDialog();
    MyDialog.ShowHelp = true ;
    if ( MyDialog.ShowDialog() == System.WinForms.DialogResult.OK)
    {
        this.label1.Font =  MyDialog.Font;
    }

}


protected void button1_Click (object sender, System.EventArgs e)
{
    ColorDialog MyDialog = new ColorDialog();
    MyDialog.ShowHelp = true ;
    if ( MyDialog.ShowDialog() == System.WinForms.DialogResult.OK)
    {
        this.label1.ForeColor =  MyDialog.Color;
    }
}


protected void button4_Click (object sender, System.EventArgs e)
{
    if ( this.textBox1.Text.Length != 0 )
    {
        this.label1.Text = this.textBox1.Text;
    }
}


protected void radioButton4_CheckedChanged (object sender,
     System.EventArgs e)
{
    this.label1.TextAlign = HorizontalAlignment.Right;
}


protected void radioButton3_CheckedChanged (object sender,
     System.EventArgs e)
{
    this.label1.TextAlign = HorizontalAlignment.Left;
}
```

```
        protected void radioButton2_CheckedChanged (object sender,
            System.EventArgs e)
        {
            this.label1.TextAlign = HorizontalAlignment.Center;
        }

        protected void button3_Click (object sender, System.EventArgs e)
        {
            Close();
        }

        public static void Main(string[] args)
        {
            Application.Run(new Form1());
        }
    }
}
```

Modifying a Label Caption

Labels appear to be static items that you put on a form to tell someone what to do or to indicate what information to enter in a field. Nothing could be further from the truth, however. You can modify a label at runtime to make it do whatever you want. For example, you might have to combine a few fields on a form into a single field to display for users. Depending on what users might enter into certain fields, you might need to update the display at runtime. The label class allows you to do this easily and with a minimum of fuss.

In this example, you take a simple look at how to change a label based on other information from the form. The form itself is shown in Figure 9.9. The code for implementing the functionality is shown in Listing 9.9. As you can see, there really isn't much to working with labels. Labels are so simple that they should be trivial to work with.

Figure 9.9   The label caption form.

Listing 9.9   Modifying a label caption.

```
namespace Ch9_9
{
    using System;
    using System.Drawing;
    using System.Collections;
    using System.ComponentModel;
    using System.WinForms;
    using System.Data;

    public class Form1 : System.WinForms.Form
    {
        private System.ComponentModel.Container components;
        private System.WinForms.Button button1;
        private System.WinForms.Label label3;
        private System.WinForms.Label label2;
        private System.WinForms.TextBox textBox2;
        private System.WinForms.TextBox textBox1;
        private System.WinForms.Label label1;

        public Form1()
        {
            InitializeComponent();
        }

        public override void Dispose()
        {
            base.Dispose();
            components.Dispose();
        }

        protected void button1_Click (object sender, System.EventArgs e)
        {
            string s = this.textBox1.Text;
            s += " ";
            s += this.textBox2.Text;
            this.label1.Text = s;
        }

        public static void Main(string[] args)
        {
            Application.Run(new Form1());
        }
    }
}
```

Seeing if a Checkbox Is Checked

Working with the various selection boxes in C# can be an interesting experience. The checkbox, radio button, and group box all form a chain of controls that work together in various fashions with various rules. For example, you can have as many checkboxes as you want in a group box, and all of them work absolutely independently. As you see in this example, however, the same statement is not true for radio buttons. The checkbox is intended for use where users can either select an option or clear it. Checkboxes apply to a single option; radio buttons apply in a series of mutually exclusive options. In standard Windows applications, this difference is not always enforced. As you see in the CLR version of these controls, these rules are enforced by the underlying library functionality.

For this example, you work with the form shown in Figure 9.10. As you can see, the example uses three separate sets of controls as well as a checkbox "living out on its own" (it's an independent checkbox). The groupings of controls are not accidental. When you run the program, you see that the CLR enforces the groupings in ways that might not be obvious but that make perfect sense when you think about them.

If you select the button to set all the checkboxes, you observe that each and every checkbox on the form is checked. Likewise, if you clear all the checkboxes, you see that they are all cleared, regardless of whether they are on their own or in a group box. The radio buttons, however, have a different story. Setting all the radio buttons results in only two radio buttons being set. This situation happens because radio buttons apply in groups. Within the group box, the three radio buttons (Option 1, Option 2, and Option 3) are considered to be a single group. This arrangement makes sense because it is the purpose of the group box. However, radio buttons in a group are mutually exclusive, so when you set each one, you watch it get set and then cleared as the next one is selected. This process happens to even the ones outside the group box because they are considered to be in a single group of their own. It makes no difference if a control is between them (as the checkbox on the right is) because they are still in one group.

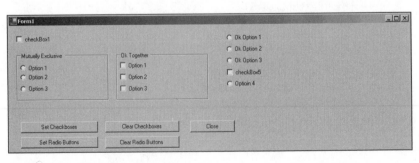

Figure 9.10   The option box form.

Listing 9.10 shows all the code needed to implement this form. Note that checking and clearing a radio button or a checkbox is exactly the same process. The **Checked** property controls the setting, and the control defines the behavior for the property.

Listing 9.10 The checkbox form.

```
namespace Ch9_10
{
    using System;
    using System.Drawing;
    using System.Collections;
    using System.ComponentModel;
    using System.WinForms;
    using System.Data;

    public class Form1 : System.WinForms.Form
    {
        private System.ComponentModel.Container components;
        private System.WinForms.RadioButton radioButton7;
        private System.WinForms.CheckBox checkBox5;
        private System.WinForms.RadioButton radioButton6;
        private System.WinForms.RadioButton radioButton5;
        private System.WinForms.RadioButton radioButton4;
        private System.WinForms.Button button5;
        private System.WinForms.Button button4;
        private System.WinForms.Button button3;
        private System.WinForms.Button button2;
        private System.WinForms.Button button1;
        private System.WinForms.CheckBox checkBox4;
        private System.WinForms.CheckBox checkBox3;
        private System.WinForms.CheckBox checkBox2;
        private System.WinForms.GroupBox groupBox2;
        private System.WinForms.RadioButton radioButton3;
        private System.WinForms.RadioButton radioButton2;
        private System.WinForms.RadioButton radioButton1;
        private System.WinForms.GroupBox groupBox1;
        private System.WinForms.CheckBox checkBox1;

        public Form1()
        {
            InitializeComponent();
        }

        public override void Dispose()
        {
```

```
            base.Dispose();
            components.Dispose();
    }


    protected void button5_Click (object sender, System.EventArgs e)
    {
            this.radioButton1.Checked = false;
            this.radioButton2.Checked = false;
            this.radioButton3.Checked = false;

            this.radioButton4.Checked = false;
            this.radioButton5.Checked = false;
            this.radioButton6.Checked = false;
            this.radioButton7.Checked = false;
    }


    protected void button4_Click (object sender, System.EventArgs e)
    {
            this.radioButton1.Checked = true;
            this.radioButton2.Checked = true;
            this.radioButton3.Checked = true;

            this.radioButton4.Checked = true;
            this.radioButton5.Checked = true;
            this.radioButton6.Checked = true;
            this.radioButton7.Checked = true;
    }


    protected void button3_Click (object sender, System.EventArgs e)
    {
            Close();
    }


    protected void button2_Click (object sender, System.EventArgs e)
    {
            this.checkBox1.Checked = false;
            this.checkBox2.Checked = false;
            this.checkBox3.Checked = false;
            this.checkBox4.Checked = false;
    }


    protected void button1_Click (object sender, System.EventArgs e)
    {
            this.checkBox1.Checked = true;
            this.checkBox2.Checked = true;
```

```
        this.checkBox3.Checked = true;
        this.checkBox4.Checked = true;
    }
    public static void Main(string[] args)
    {
        Application.Run(new Form1());
    }
  }
}
```

Selecting a File

When you are working with users, the chances are that you have to work with files they have saved or want to save. To do this, you need to be able to allow users to give you a file name that you can either load data from or save data to. In the bad old days, you did this by allowing users to type a file name, including the full path, which was then used to save the file. This process was errorprone because it relied on users' typing skills, which were rarely as good as those of the programmers. Users never seem to get the hang of using the backslash and forward slash or know where the colon goes or understand why a file name can't contain weird characters. As a result of these problems, programmers created file dialog boxes that allow users to navigate to a file and then to select it.

The problem with file dialog boxes is that so many of them exist. Each application has a file dialog box type associated with it. Sometimes, the dialog boxes showed previews of the files. At other times, the file dialog boxes contained information about the file. The display of the dialog boxes and their usage were not consistent throughout the Windows system. Programmers often used the same dialog box to open an existing file and to create a new one, a practice that is hardly a good idea. The C# CLR changes that situation by offering standardized file dialog boxes that work the same way as the Windows operating system itself. Users can then use a single method for opening files as well as one for finding and creating files. (Consistency may be the hobgoblin of small minds, but it is also a joy for software users.)

In this example, you create a small form that allows users to select a file and get the name into the application. The form permits you to validate whether the file exists and allows a selection only if the file does exist. The form you create looks like the one shown in Figure 9.11.

The process of getting a file name into the application is simple enough. Simply put up an instance of the **OpenFileDialog** class (the **SaveFileDialog** class has a

Figure 9.11   The select file form.

corresponding version) and wait for users to either select something and press OK or cancel the operation. The code for this task is shown in the sample application in Listing 9.11.

Listing 9.11   Selecting a file.

```
namespace Ch9_11
{
    using System;
    using System.IO;
    using System.Drawing;
    using System.Collections;
    using System.ComponentModel;
    using System.WinForms;
    using System.Data;

    public class Form1 : System.WinForms.Form
    {
        private System.ComponentModel.Container components;
        private System.WinForms.Button button3;
        private System.WinForms.Button button2;
        private System.WinForms.Button button1;
        private System.WinForms.Label label1;
        private System.WinForms.TextBox textBox1;

        public Form1()
        {
            InitializeComponent();
        }
```

```
public override void Dispose()
{
    base.Dispose();
    components.Dispose();
}


protected void button3_Click (object sender, System.EventArgs e)
{
    Close();
}


protected void button2_Click (object sender, System.EventArgs e)
{
    // See if they entered something
    if ( textBox1.Text.Length != 0 )
    {
        if ( File.FileExists( this.textBox1.Text ) )
        {
            MessageBox.Show(this, "Valid File!");
            Close();
        }
        else
            MessageBox.Show(this, "Invalid File Name!!");

    }
}


protected void button1_Click (object sender, System.EventArgs e)
{
    FileDialog fd = new OpenFileDialog();
    if ( fd.ShowDialog() == System.WinForms.DialogResult.OK )
    {
        textBox1.Text = fd.FileName;
    }
}


public static void Main(string[] args)
{
    Application.Run(new Form1());
}
}
}
```

Creating an Owner-Drawn List Box

For all the power afforded you as a programmer by the list box component of the CLR, sometimes it just isn't enough to let you do what you want in your application. For example, although you can put items in any order and change the way in which users work with the list box, you might need to display list box entries in a different color or font. In times like these, you need the power of an owner-drawn list box. *Owner-drawn* list boxes permit you to display the strings in a list in any way you see fit. You can change the way highlighted (selected) entries are shown, change the fonts used to display entries, or even change the colors of the normal entries.

The art to creating owner-drawn list boxes lies in setting a single property, **DrawingMode**, for the list box. If you were to set this property to be either **OwnerDrawnFixed** or **OwnerDrawnVariable**, you would receive draw-message events. These events can be caught and overridden in your code, as you see in this example. After the event is captured, you can do whatever you want when it occurs. Of course, as always, you have to consider a few things. First, you need to make sure that you clear out the area used for displaying a given item. This area is defined in the **Bounds** property of the graphics object passed into your handler. Next, you need to do something when the item is selected because users are accustomed to seeing selected items differently from nonselected ones. In this case, you capitalize the selected item, just to be different.

For this example, you use the form shown in Figure 9.12. As you can see, this example uses a standard list box as well as two radio buttons that control how

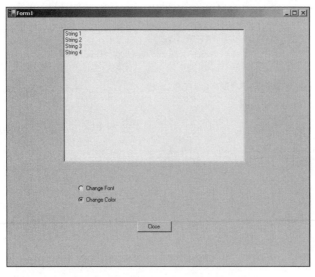

Figure 9.12   The owner-drawn list box form.

the list box is displayed. If a user selects the color change, the list box entries are shown in blue. If a user selects the font change, the list box entries are shown in a larger font than usual. Otherwise, they look "normal."

Drawing the items is done with the **Graphics** object that comes in as the **DrawItemEventArgs** argument to the event handler. This object contains a number of methods for working with the display, including drawing text on the screen. Listing 9.12 shows the complete code for displaying the owner-drawn list box and responding to various events.

Listing 9.12   Creating an owner-drawn list box.

```
namespace ch9_12
{
    using System;
    using System.Drawing;
    using System.Collections;
    using System.ComponentModel;
    using System.WinForms;
    using System.Data;
    public class Form1 : System.WinForms.Form
    {
        public Form1()
        {
            InitializeComponent();

            this.listBox1.Items.Add("String 1");
            this.listBox1.Items.Add("String 2");
            this.listBox1.Items.Add("String 3");
            this.listBox1.Items.Add("String 4");

        }
        public override void Dispose()
        {
            base.Dispose();
            components.Dispose();
        }
        protected void listBox1_SelectedIndexChanged (object sender,
                    System.EventArgs e)
        {
            this.listBox1.Refresh();
        }
        protected void button1_Click (object sender, System.EventArgs e)
        {
            Close();
        }
```

```
            protected void radioButton2_CheckedChanged (object sender,
                        System.EventArgs e)
            {
                this.listBox1.Refresh();
            }
            protected void radioButton1_CheckedChanged (object sender,
                System.EventArgs e)
            {
                    this.listBox1.Refresh();
            }
            protected void listBox1_DrawItem (object sender,
                System.WinForms.DrawItemEventArgs e)
            {
                // Get the text
                string text = (string)this.listBox1.Items[e.Index];

                // If it is selected, make it capitalized
                if ( e.Index == this.listBox1.SelectedIndex )
                {
                    string temp = "";
                    for ( int i=0; i<text.Length; ++i)
                    {
                        temp += Char.ToUpper(text[i]);
                    }
                    text = temp;
                }

                // Clear the drawing region
                e.Graphics.FillRectangle( new SolidBrush(
                        System.Drawing.Color.White),
                        e.Bounds );

                // Determine if we are changing the font or the color
                if ( this.radioButton1.Checked )
                {
                    Font myFont = new Font("Arial", 14);
                    e.Graphics.DrawString( text, myFont, new SolidBrush(
                            System.Drawing.Color.Black), e.Bounds );
                }
                else
                    if ( this.radioButton2.Checked )
                    {
                        e.Graphics.DrawString( text, Font, new SolidBrush(
                                System.Drawing.Color.Blue), e.Bounds );
                    }
```

```
            else
            {
                e.Graphics.DrawString( text, Font, new SolidBrush(
                    System.Drawing.Color.Black), e.Bounds );
            }

        }

        public static void Main(string[] args)
        {
            Application.Run(new Form1 ());
        }
    }
}
```

Creating a File Viewer with Line Numbering

In this example, I describe some of the capabilities of the rich text component to show how you can use it to make a simple file viewer. The rich text component is capable of loading a file from disk directly, but it can't modify that file to show, for example, the line numbers of each line. This ability would be useful for programmers, for example, to see the program lines the way the compiler does and to quickly and easily find problems and specific issues.

Figure 9.13 shows the form you use to create the line-numbering file viewer. As you can see, there really isn't much to it. The form consists of just a rich text box to display the data and a set of controls that allow you to enter the file to display.

In a similar fashion, the code to load the file and display it in the rich text component is both simple and straightforward. The lines are read in from the file, one at a time, using a **StreamReader** component, and then loaded into the rich text component. To make it all work, the text is manipulated to add the line number and then the text. Finally, a carriage-return-and-linefeed combination is added to make it all look more readable to users. All this code is shown in Listing 9.13.

Listing 9.13   Creating a file viewer with line numbering.

```
namespace ch9_13
{
    using System;
    using System.IO;
    using System.Drawing;
    using System.Collections;
    using System.ComponentModel;
```

Figure 9.13   The file viewer form.

```
using System.WinForms;
using System.Data;
public class Form1 : System.WinForms.Form
{
    private System.ComponentModel.Container components;
    private System.WinForms.Button button1;
    private System.WinForms.TextBox textBox1;
    private System.WinForms.Label label1;
    private System.WinForms.RichTextBox richTextBox1;

    public Form1()
    {
        InitializeComponent();
    }
    public override void Dispose()
    {
        base.Dispose();
        components.Dispose();
    }

    protected void button1_Click (object sender, System.EventArgs e)
    {
        // Load the file
        string line = "";
        int    lineNo = 1;
```

```
        StreamReader sr = File.OpenText(this.textBox1.Text);
        while (sr.Peek()!=-1)
        {
            String input = sr.ReadLine();
            this.richTextBox1.Text += lineNo;
            this.richTextBox1.Text += " ";
            this.richTextBox1.Text += input;
            this.richTextBox1.Text += "\r\n";
            lineNo ++;
        }
        sr.Close();
    }

    public static void Main(string[] args)
    {
        Application.Run(new Form1());
    }
  }
}
```

There really isn't much to the code, as you can see. The power of the CLR does most of the work for you, which is the way it ought to be.

Adding a Form Icon

Sometimes, the little things in life make users happy, like an informative icon in the corner of a form. By default, the C# CLR provides an icon for forms created in the system, but that icon isn't particularly distinctive. Like the pyramid of blocks used by the MFC, the C# form icon is, well, boring. It would be useful to be able to load a more distinctive icon into place and use it when the program is running. It would be even nicer to be able to change that icon at runtime to indicate various program states. Fortunately, the CLR makes this process easy too.

Figure 9.14 shows a form you use to change the icon displayed in the upper-left corner of a form when it is loaded and run.

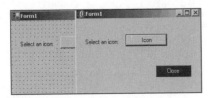

Figure 9.14   The form icon form.

9. Visual Elements

How hard is it to change the icon? The amount of code needed to change the icon for a form is exactly one line. The amount of code needed to load the icon from a dynamically selected file is a few more lines. As you can see from Listing 9.14, the complete program is composed of only a few lines of code within the wrapper of the C#-generated application framework code.

Listing 9.14   Adding a form icon.

```
namespace ch9_14
{
    using System;
    using System.Drawing;
    using System.Collections;
    using System.ComponentModel;
    using System.WinForms;
    using System.Data;

    public class Form1 : System.WinForms.Form
    {
        private System.ComponentModel.Container components;
        private System.WinForms.Button button2;
        private System.WinForms.Button button1;
        private System.WinForms.Label label1;

        public Form1()
        {
            InitializeComponent();
        }
        public override void Dispose()
        {
            base.Dispose();
            components.Dispose();
        }
        private void InitializeComponent()
        {
            this.components = new System.ComponentModel.Container ();
            this.button1 = new System.WinForms.Button ();
            this.label1 = new System.WinForms.Label ();
            this.button2 = new System.WinForms.Button ();
            button1.Location = new System.Drawing.Point (104, 32);
            button1.Size = new System.Drawing.Size (88, 24);
            button1.TabIndex = 1;
            button1.Text = "Icon";
            button1.Click += new System.EventHandler (this.button1_Click);
            label1.Location = new System.Drawing.Point (16, 40);
            label1.Text = "Select an icon:";
```

```
        label1.Size = new System.Drawing.Size (80, 24);
        label1.TabIndex = 0;
        button2.Location = new System.Drawing.Point (168, 96);
        button2.Size = new System.Drawing.Size (75, 23);
        button2.TabIndex = 2;
        button2.Text = "&Close";
        button2.Click += new System.EventHandler (this.button2_Click);
        this.Text = "Form1";
        this.AutoScaleBaseSize = new System.Drawing.Size (5, 13);
        this.ClientSize = new System.Drawing.Size (264, 149);
        this.Controls.Add (this.button2);
        this.Controls.Add (this.button1);
        this.Controls.Add (this.label1);
    }

    protected void button1_Click (object sender, System.EventArgs e)
    {
        OpenFileDialog fd = new OpenFileDialog();
        if ( fd.ShowDialog() == DialogResult.OK )
        {
        // Load the icon file
        System.Drawing.Icon icon = new
            System.Drawing.Icon(fd.FileName);
        // Now set the form to be that icon
        this.Icon = icon;
        }
    }

    protected void button2_Click (object sender, System.EventArgs e)
    {
        Close();
    }
      public static void Main(string[] args)
      {
        Application.Run(new Form1());
      }
    }
}
```

Chapter 10

Files and Databases

In Depth

When you are writing applications of any scope whatsoever, sooner or later you need to save data persistently for a different session. Whether you are saving data to a local file or a database stored on the Internet somewhere, the data still must be stored in a way in which you can retrieve it later when it is needed. In this chapter, you explore some of the ways in which you might save data persistently. From the simple file to the complex multiuser database, C# provides classes and methods to get the job done for your systems.

The simplest data-storage mechanism available to you in C# is the file. Files are accessed via the stream classes in the Common Language Runtime (CLR). First, take a look at streams, what they are, and how you use them. Then you can consider the relationship between the stream and the file in application development.

Streams

A *stream* is a series of bytes that can be read from some source of input. That source can be a socket, a file, a Web page, or a user's console input. The stream classes in C# require that you deal with two different entities: An actual source of data, such as a file object, and the kind of stream you want to work with for that data source. For example, you might want a stream that allows you to move around in a nonsequential manner for the data source. Using this type of stream makes perfect sense if you are working with a file. Other streams provide data in a sequential manner, which is more appropriate for sockets or user input devices, like keyboards.

The basic stream functionality is implemented in the **System.IO.Stream** abstract class. This class forms the basis for all other stream classes in the .NET system and gives a programmer access to the data in the stream in a wide variety of ways. The properties of the basic stream class are shown in Table 10.1.

If you open a stream for writing, you expect that the **CanWrite** property will be set to true, the **CanRead** property set to false, and the **CanSeek** property set to either, depending on the type of stream you have opened. Streams support either synchronous or asynchronous reading and writing for applications that have a need to perform these operations. You're unlikely to want asynchronous writes to a text file, but you might well want an asynchronous read from a socket. The

Table 10.1   The stream class properties.

Property	Meaning
CanRead	Indicates whether this stream supports input
CanSeek	Indicates whether this stream is sequential or random-access
CanWrite	Indicates whether you can send output to this stream
Length	Indicates the length, in bytes, of this stream
Position	Indicates the current position for reading or writing to the stream

type of stream you are working with usually defines the types of operations you want to perform.

The CLR has quite a few kinds of streams, depending on the type of information you want to pass to and from them. If you are working with a text file or text-based input device (such as a socket), you might want to use a **StreamReader** or **StreamWriter** class object. If, on the other hand, you are working with binary files, such as a proprietary file system or an external device that requires header blocks, you use the **BinaryStreamWriter** or **BinaryStreamReader** classes to work with the devices. Finally, if you need random access to the data, you need to treat the device as a file. The CLR provides the **FileStream** class for this purpose. Table 10.2 describes the stream classes in the C# CLR system.

As you can see, the stream classes in C# provide a rich set of functionality for dealing with input and output. How do you use a stream? Consider the following simple example of reading a file, one that is text based:

Table 10.2   The stream classes.

Class	Functionality
StreamReader	Provides wide character (multibyte) access to input devices
StreamWriter	Provides wide character (multibyte) access to output devices
StringReader	Allows the input of strings from a device, such as the console
StringWriter	Allows a programmer to send strings to a device, a file, or the console
BinaryReader	Allows you to read objects from a file
BinaryWriter	Allows you to write objects to a file
FileStream	Allows random access to a file or other device
MemoryStream	Allows a stream to be maintained in memory for performance
BufferedStream	Allows a stream to be buffered and written to or read from disk in chunks, to optimize speed
TextReader	The base, abstract class for all sequential output streams
TextWriter	The base, abstract class for all sequential input streams

10. Files and
Databases

```
using System;
using System.IO;

public class ReadFileText
{
    public static void Main(String[] args)
    {
        StreamReader sr = File.OpenText("Input.txt");
        while (sr.Peek()!=-1)
        {
            String input = sr.ReadLine();
            Console.WriteLine (input);
        }
        sr.Close();
    }
}
```

Note in this code snippet a few things that indicate the process you need to follow when working with streams. First, notice that you must include the **System.IO** namespace to have access to all the stream classes. This namespace contains all the basic stream classes listed in Table 10.2. In addition, you need to reference the System.IO.DLL import file through either the Add Reference menu option in Visual Studio or the **/r:System.IO.DLL** option on the command-line compiler.

Working with streams is simple enough, but how do streams attach themselves to files and other elements? That's the next topic of discussion.

Files

When you talk about a file in most languages, you're referring to both file *properties* (location, size, and name, for example) and file *content* (text or binary information). In C#, however, the file concept is *separated* into file properties and file content. The content, as I have already discussed, is set or retrieved via the stream mechanism. Properties, on the other hand, are accessed via the **File** object.

The C# CLR system consists of several classes involved with working with files. First, the **Directory** class represents a set of folders that may contain either files or other **Directory** objects. Within a directory, the **File** object represents a single file on the persistent storage device. The **File** object contains information about the individual properties of the container file itself. Information such as the size, name, and last access date and time are all contained within the **File** object.

Table 10.3 shows the properties of the **File** object, indicating what you can find out about a file when you have one. To get a file, use the **File.Open** method.

Table 10.3   File properties in .NET.

Property	Purpose
Attributes	Gets or sets the attributes of the current file
CreationTime	Gets the creation time of the current file
Directory	Creates an instance of the parent directory
DirectoryName	Returns the full path of a file
Exists	Determines whether a file exists
FullName	Retrieves the full path of the directory or file
IsDirectory	Indicates whether the object is a directory
IsFile	Indicates whether the object is a file
LastAccessTime	Returns the time the current file or directory was last accessed
LastWriteTime	Returns the time the current file was last written to
Length	Returns the size of the current file or directory
Name	Retrieves the name of the file

As you can see, the C# **File** object provides quite a bit of information about the file it represents on the persistent storage device. Note that many of these properties are applicable to either files or directories.

Directories

The **Directory** object in C# is similar to a file in that it represents a unit of storage on a persistent storage device. Unlike a file, which contains some amount of content, the directory object represents a folder that contains files and other directories, mirroring the way the Windows (and other) operating system works. The directory class properties are shown in Table 10.4.

In addition to the properties shown in Table 10.4, the directory class contains a variety of methods for working with directories. These methods allow you to do such things as create a new file or directory, delete an existing directory and its contents, or retrieve the list of files or subdirectories within a directory. The entire list of directory methods is described in Table 10.5.

Databases

When you discuss persistent storage in programming, the talk sooner or later turns to file systems that support complicated searching and access. In programming parlance, these file systems are known as databases. C# provides a rich set of classes that provide access to various databases in virtually any format, by using the ADO.NET access library package.

Table 10.4   The directory class properties.

Property	Purpose
Attributes	Retrieves or sets directory attributes, such as read-only and hidden
CreationTime	Retrieves the creation time of the current directory
Exists	Determines whether a directory exists
FullName	Retrieves the full path of the directory or file
IsDirectory	Indicates whether the object is a directory
IsFile	Indicates whether the object is a file
LastAccessTime	Retrieves the day the current directory was last accessed
LastWriteTime	Retrieves the time the current directory was last written to
Name	Gets the name of the current directory and is read-only
Parent	Retrieves the parent directory of a subdirectory
Root	Retrieves the root portion of a path

Table 10.5   Directory methods.

Method	Purpose
CreateFile	Creates a file in a specified path and opens it with read/write permission
CreateSubdirectories	Creates subdirectories on the specified path
CreateSubdirectory	Creates a subdirectory of the specified directory
Delete	Deletes a directory and its contents from a path
Equals	Determines whether the specified object is the same instance as the current object
GetDirectories	Returns an array of directories in the current directory
GetFiles	Returns a file list from the current directory
GetFileSystemEntries	Retrieves an array of strongly typed **FileSystemEntry** objects
GetHashCode	Serves as a hash function for a particular type and is suitable for use in hashing algorithms and data structures, like hash tables
GetType	Returns a **Type** object representing this class
MoveTo	Moves a directory and its contents to a new path
Refresh	Refreshes the state of the object
ToString	Returns the fully qualified path

A *database* is a collection of tables. Each table consists of rows and columns that make up the information about the data. A *row* represents a single record in the database, and a *column* represents a single field for that record. Not surprisingly, this sounds like a spreadsheet. In many ways, the database was built on the spreadsheet motif, or perhaps it was vice versa.

NOTE: *The ADO.NET system is perfectly capable of connecting to an Excel or other type of spreadsheet and treating it as a database.*

To work with a database in the ADO.NET system, you need to know a little bit about SQL. This language, usually pronounced "see-quel," allows you to query, update, and delete from database tables. Let's take a quick look at SQL, although the full scope of the language is well beyond the scope of this book.

SQL

The SQL language consists of three basic kinds of statements. First, selection statements retrieve data from the database. These statements allow you to filter the data you want to see while permitting you to get whatever information you want from the database. The basic form of the select statement is:

```
SELECT <fieldlist> FROM <tablelist>
[WHERE] <conditionlist> [ORDER BY] <orderlist>;
```

Let's take a look at the pieces of this statement to see how they all work. First, the field list is generally a list of the individual columns you want retrieved from the tables in the select statement. A select statement, by the way, is generally referred to by database people as a *query*. Suppose that a table has the following fields in it to represent a contact list:

Name	Text
Address	Text
City	Text
State	Text
ZIP Code	Text
Age	Numeric

To refer to the Name, City, State, and ZIP Code fields in a select query, you could write something like this:

```
Select name, state, zipcode from . . .
```

The second part of the statement, the table list, can consist of one or more tables from which you want to retrieve data. If more than one table is listed, you need to use the **Where** clause to identify how to link the tables. The table list can be a single table. For example, to retrieve all the names, cities, and ZIP codes from the Contact table, you would write:

```
Select name, state, zipcode, from Contact;
```

The third piece of the puzzle, the **Where** clause, is used for conditional results. Suppose that you want to retrieve only people who have a last name that begins with the letter *S*. You could use the select statement you just wrote to retrieve all the names in the database and then go through them one at a time until you have just the ones that begin with the letter *S*. However, a quicker and considerably more efficient technique uses the **Where** clause:

```
Select name, state, zipcode from Contact where name like 'S%';
```

Note that because the name field is a text field, you do not use the equality (**=**) operator to test for names beginning with *S*. Instead, you use the **Like** operator, which was intended for this purpose. The other interesting element of this example is the way wild cards are used in SQL. You can use the question mark (?) character to match a single character, and you can use the percent (%) sign to indicate that you want to match the remaining characters in a string.

If you want to select in the Contact table all people over the age of 35, you use a different form of the select statement:

```
Select name, state, zipcode from Contact where age > 35;
```

Note that you don't have to include in the select list the field you are screening with (**age**, in this case) when you are retrieving data from the database. Suppose, however, that in addition to wanting to select those over the age of 35, you want them sorted by their names. This request brings in the last of the entities described in this section: the **Order By** clause.

To use the **Order By** clause, you select the fields by which you want the database to sort the returned set of rows. For example, to sort the returned list of people over the age of 35 by their names, you would use the following SQL query:

```
Select name, state, zipcode from Contact where age > 35 order by Name;
```

One last note about SQL query statements (and all other SQL statements, for that matter): They are case insensitive. It does not matter whether you use upper- or lowercase or a mixture of the two. Only when you are comparing exact strings is the result case sensitive, such as when you use something like this:

```
Select zipCode from Contact where name = "Smith";
```

The second type of SQL statement, the **Update** statement, allows you to modify data in the database according to the rules you set. The general form of the update statement is:

```
Update <table> set <field> = <value> where <condition>;
```

The field listed here is the name of a column in the database, and the value shown is the value you want the field to be equal to when the statement finishes. The condition determines which of the rows in the database is affected when you run the statement against the database. For example, if you want to change the state to Louisiana for all people who have the ZIP code 77543, you could write a statement like this:

```
Update Contact set state = "LA" where ZipCode = "77543";
```

This statement makes the required changes and updates the required rows in the database. The **Update** statement is a combination of a selection query and a modify statement.

The third type of SQL statement, the **Insert** statement, allows you to place new data into a database, using the field names and table names that describe where you want the data to go in the spreadsheet-like environment that is the SQL database. The general form of the **Insert** statement is:

```
Insert into <table> (<columnlist>) values (<valuelist>);
```

Going back to the Contact table example, suppose that you want to add a new record to the database with the data that someone has given you. You might write this simple statement:

```
Insert into Contact (name, address, city, state, zipcode, age) values ("Matt
Telles", "1313 Mockingbird Lane", "New York", "NY", 11591, 40);
```

The database engine generally attempts to convert the data types as best it can, but if you have a text field, you need to insert textual data. Likewise, if you have a numeric field, such as age, you need to insert a numeric value. Depending on how the data is used, it results in the truncation of floating-point numbers into integers, although the data is always stored in the format you requested when you defined the database table in the first place.

The final type of SQL statement, the **Delete** statement, removes records from a database based on criteria you supply. The general form of a **Delete** statement is

```
Delete from table <tablename> where <condition>;
```

where **tablename** is the name of the table from which you want to delete. Advanced users may note that this may also be a view or other result that returns a row set. The **condition** is the condition under which you want the records deleted. Suppose that you are cleaning out your Contact table and want to get rid of everyone who lives in Colorado. Rather than flood the state (the deer would be upset), you could write something like this:

```
Delete from table Contact where state = "CO";
```

After this statement is run, the records that had a state field equal to CO (the Colorado postal code) would be gone. Of course, this begs the question "What if you make a mistake?" How can you undo your changes to the database? The answer lies in the concept of transactions.

Transactions

A *transaction* is a series of changes to the database that must all either happen or not happen. For example, if I were posting debits and credits to a bank account, I would not want money taken from one account to be put into another account, unless that money was definitely removed from the first account. The steps involved look something like this:

```
Start
Add money to account B
Remove money from account A
End
```

The **Start** and **End** markers in this example are the beginning and end of a transaction in the database. If everything goes right, you reach the **End** statement and all the changes are written correctly to the database. However, if something goes wrong and an error pops up, you want the database to revert to its former state with no changes made. Of course, you also want to log this event so that you can figure out what went wrong. Databases make all these things easy. You start a transaction, log whatever it is you are doing to the database, and then "commit" the transaction to the database to ensure that everything is written properly. If something goes wrong, you log the error and what you were doing at the time and then abort the transaction.

The C# system contains methods for implementing transactions in your code. You are not required to use them. If you do not use them, the entire session with the database—from the time you open the database to the time you close it—is considered to be a single transaction. If something goes wrong, you lose everything.

As you can see in "Using Database Transactions" in the "Immediate Solutions" section later in this chapter, you can easily set up, commit, and abort transactions using the ADO.NET library classes that come with the .NET framework.

XML

The last topic I discuss in this part of the chapter is XML. XML, or Extensible Markup Language, was created as an extension of HTML that would permit developers to store data as well as content in files. This data can be recovered at runtime and modified by the application or by the direct manipulation of files. Basically, *XML* is a hierarchical language in which "objects" are stored as nested series of fields and values. Look at a simple XML file to get an idea of what I discuss in this section:

```
<?xml version="1.0" standalone="yes" ?>
- <NewDataSet>
<xsd:schema id="NewDataSet" targetNamespace="" xmlns=""
    xmlns:xsd="http://www.w3.org/1999/XMLSchema"
xmlns:msdata="urn:schemas-microsoft-com:xml-msdata">
- <xsd:element name="Employees">
- <xsd:complexType content="elementOnly">
- <xsd:all>
  <xsd:element name="EmployeeID" minOccurs="0" type="xsd:int" />
  <xsd:element name="FirstName" minOccurs="0" type="xsd:string" />
  <xsd:element name="LastName" minOccurs="0" type="xsd:string" />
  <xsd:element name="Title" minOccurs="0" type="xsd:string" />
  </xsd:all>
  </xsd:complexType>
  </xsd:element>
- <xsd:element name="NewDataSet" msdata:IsDataSet="True">
- <xsd:complexType>
- <xsd:choice maxOccurs="unbounded">
  <xsd:element ref="Employees" />
  </xsd:choice>
  </xsd:complexType>
  </xsd:element>
  </xsd:schema>
- <Employees>
  <EmployeeID>5</EmployeeID>
```

```
<FirstName>Steven</FirstName>
<LastName>Buchanan</LastName>
<Title>Sales Manager</Title>
</Employees>
```

This file snippet shows a piece of a database dump of an XML table, which you look at in "Saving a Dataset As XML" in the "Immediate Solutions" section later in this chapter. As you can see, the file breaks down into three major components. First, the header information tells whatever is reading this file that this is an XML file, what version of XML it uses, and whether it requires linked files. Next, the transform information allows other programs to display and comprehend the data in the file. The transform information is all stored under the **xsd:** keys in the file. Finally, in the actual data, only a part of one record is shown, and it begins with **Employees**.

In XML, you write out a key/value pair by opening the key ***<key>***, writing out one or more values or subkeys, and then closing the key ***</key>***. The C# system comes with a built-in set of libraries for working with XML, so you need not know much about the actual storage format of XML in order to work with it. This is important because XML, the storage format of the future, forms the core of such important technologies as .NET and Simple Object Access Protocol (SOAP).

Immediate Solutions

Creating and Using a Stream in C#

Streams are the basic unit of input and output in C#. Using streams is the way in which you create files, write out data, and read in data from those files. In this example, you look at the notion of a basic configuration file for an application. Information is written out to note the version of the program, the time and date of the information, and the data stored in the program itself. In this way, you should be able to see how to use C# to create information repositories you can view in a simple text editor (or by typing them out to the console window).

The basic process to follow when working with a stream (in this case, a **FileStream**) is to open the stream with the permissions you want to use (read, write, and create, for example) and then to read or write from or to the stream. When you are done reading or writing, you flush out the contents of the stream to disk and then close the stream. Listing 10.1 shows a typical way in which a stream object is used to save configuration information for an application. Note how the hash table object is used to store the information in the program for configuration purposes.

Listing 10.1 Creating and using a stream in C#.

```
using System;
using System.IO;
using System.Collections;

class CH10_1
{
    public static void PrintHashTable( Hashtable ht, StreamWriter sw )
    {
        IDictionaryEnumerator myEnumerator = ht.GetEnumerator();
        while ( myEnumerator.MoveNext() )
            sw.WriteLine( "{0}: {1}", myEnumerator.Key, myEnumerator.Value );
    }
    public static void Main(String[] args)
    {
        Hashtable ht = new Hashtable();
        ht.Add( "Name", "matt telles");
        ht.Add( "Address", "1313 Mockingbird Lane" );
```

```
// Create a text file
FileStream fs = new FileStream(@"c:\ch10_1.txt" ,
        FileMode.OpenOrCreate,
        FileAccess.Write);
StreamWriter m_streamWriter = new StreamWriter(fs);

// Write to the file using StreamWriter class
m_streamWriter.BaseStream.Seek(0, SeekOrigin.End);

// Log some information to the file.
m_streamWriter.WriteLine("{0} {1}",
        DateTime.Now.ToLongTimeString(),
        DateTime.Now.ToLongDateString());

m_streamWriter.WriteLine("Version 1.0");

// Now, dump the hashtable
PrintHashTable( ht, m_streamWriter );

m_streamWriter.Flush();
    }

}
```

Note the use of the at (@) sign in front of the literal string. This character allows you to not have to embed multiple backslash (\) characters to get the single one you want to use in your directory string.

Connecting to an Access Database

If you are working on a small-scale system, you are likely to be using C# with some sort of database. For single-user or single-machine systems, that database is most likely to be Microsoft Access. This powerful SQL database allows you to do some amazing things, but isn't really scaled for large, corporate databases. Not that this situation stops people from trying to use Access on Web servers; however, you might seriously rethink your strategy if you are considering this route. For now, however, assume that you are using Access as it was meant to be used. The process you follow works with SQL Server databases too (or with any other database that ADO.NET can talk to), except that the data source connect string changes.

The process for "talking" to a database is simple: You simply specify a connection string and use the ADO.NET object **ADOConnection** to connect to the database.

After you are there, you can browse the contents of a table or database. In this example, you write a simple browser that allows you to view the *schema* (column information) for a given database table. You pass in the name of the Access database file and the name of the table you are interested in, and the database object does the rest. Listing 10.2 shows how.

Listing 10.2   Connecting to an Access database.

```
using System;
using System.Data;
using System.Data.ADO;

public class CH10_2
{

    public static void Main (String[] args)
    {
        // Set Access connection and select strings
        string strAccessConn =
                "Provider=Microsoft.Jet.OLEDB.4.0;Data Source="+args[0];
        string strAccessSelect = "SELECT * FROM " + args[1];

        // Create the dataset and add the Categories table to it
        DataSet myDataSet = new DataSet();
        myDataSet.Tables.Add(args[1]);

        // Create my Access objects
        ADOConnection myAccessConn = new ADOConnection(strAccessConn);
        ADODataSetCommand myAccessDataSetCmd = new ADODataSetCommand();
        myAccessDataSetCmd.SelectCommand = new
                ADOCommand(strAccessSelect,myAccessConn);

        myAccessConn.Open();
        try
        {
            myAccessDataSetCmd.FillDataSet(myDataSet,args[1]);
        }
        finally
        {
            myAccessConn.Close();
        }

        try
        {
            DataColumn[] drc = myDataSet.Tables[args[1]].Columns.All;
            int i = 0;
```

```
            foreach (DataColumn dc in drc)
            {
                Console.WriteLine(
                    "Column name[{0}] is {1}, of type {2}",i++ ,
                        dc.ColumnName, dc.DataType);
            }
        }
        catch (Exception e)
        {
            Console.WriteLine("Caught an exception:\n{0}", e.Message);
        }
    }
}
```

For sample output, I ran this program against the Northwind database that ships with Visual Studio and Visual Basic. I used the Employees database to dump. The program produced this output:

```
C:\ >ch10_2 NWIND.MDB Employees
Column name[0] is EmployeeID, of type Int32
Column name[1] is LastName, of type System.String
Column name[2] is FirstName, of type System.String
Column name[3] is Title, of type System.String
Column name[4] is TitleOfCourtesy, of type System.String
Column name[5] is BirthDate, of type System.DateTime
Column name[6] is HireDate, of type System.DateTime
Column name[7] is Address, of type System.String
Column name[8] is City, of type System.String
Column name[9] is Region, of type System.String
Column name[10] is PostalCode, of type System.String
Column name[11] is Country, of type System.String
Column name[12] is HomePhone, of type System.String
Column name[13] is Extension, of type System.String
Column name[14] is Photo, of type System.Byte[]
Column name[15] is Notes, of type System.String
Column name[16] is ReportsTo, of type Int32
```

As you can see, the database table is dumped as it is shown in the Access database program itself, which is a good way to learn about the structure of a table if you aren't aware of it in advance. Unfortunately, you have no easy way to dump the list of tables from the database, unless you have write access to the **MsysObjects** table. Unfortunately, the ADO.NET components of the CLR were not meant to be used for general-purpose database functionality. This means that they do not easily support browsing.

Retrieving Data from the Database

If you have a database in your application definition, the chances are that you have to get data back out of it at some point. A database isn't really useful unless you can load things from it. Other than that, it might as well be a pad of paper. You can therefore safely assume that you want to get data from the database in your application. Fortunately, by using the ADO.NET objects built into the .NET CLR, getting the data is quite easy in C#.

To retrieve information from a database, you need a certain amount of knowledge about the database. For example, you need to know the name of the table or tables from which you want to retrieve information. If multiple tables are in the database from which you want to get information, you need to know the relationship between those tables and how to join them. Suppose that you want to get all the columns back in a single table, without worrying about filtering the data. For a bit of excitement, you sort the resulting data set that is retrieved.

This example again uses the Northwind database from the Visual Studio examples. This database contains a table, named Employees, that has information about the people who work for the company that owns the database. In this example, you want to retrieve and print the last names of all the employees, sorted in alphabetical order by last name. To do this, you use the code shown in Listing 10.3.

Listing 10.3   Retrieving data from the database.

```
using System;
using System.Data;
using System.Data.ADO;

public class CH10_2
{
    public static void Main ()
    {
        // Define the connection string
        string strConn =
            "Provider=Microsoft.Jet.OLEDB.4.0;Data Source=NWIND.MDB";

        // Define our selection criteria
        string strRec = "SELECT * FROM Employees ORDER by LastName";

        // Create the connection object, using our connection string
        ADOConnection myConn = new ADOConnection(strConn);

        // Create the command object from our selection criteria string
        ADOCommand myCmd = new ADOCommand( strRec, myConn );
```

```
        // Try to execute the command
        ADODataReader outData = null;
        try
        {
            // This will make the connection to the database
            myConn.Open();

            // This will run our query and put the result in outData
            myCmd.Execute( out outData );


            // See if we got something back
            if ( outData != null )
            {
                while (outData.Read() )
                {
                    Console.WriteLine( "Last Name: {0}",
                        outData["LastName"]);
                }
            }

        }
        catch ( Exception e )
        {
            Console.WriteLine("Exception {0}", e );
        }
    }
}
```

The output from this program, when run over the NWIND.MDB database file supplied with Visual Studio, is:

```
C:\ >ch10_3
Last Name: Buchanan
Last Name: Callahan
Last Name: Davolio
Last Name: Dodsworth
Last Name: Fuller
Last Name: King
Last Name: Leverling
Last Name: Peacock
Last Name: Suyama
```

Note that the names are in alphabetical order, as you requested in the **Order By** clause of the **Select** statement. Not much work is involved in working with the data in a database to retrieve it. You need a certain amount of information up front and a fair amount of code to do what you want, but the rest is simple.

Adding Data to the Database

If you have a database in your application, it has one of two forms. First, it might hold some information you keep statically that you want to retrieve in a read-only fashion. This situation is unlikely, however. Usually, databases are used to store information a user provides and then to retrieve it for later work. To be able to retrieve the data later, you need to be able to add the data to the database now. Adding data to the database is done via the **INSERT** statement in SQL. In this example, you explore how you could get information from a user and enter it into the database using a SQL **INSERT** statement.

Listing 10.4 shows the simple console application you use to insert data into the application database. Although you later work with Windows forms to work with databases in a more aesthetically pleasing fashion, understanding what is going on with a simple console application is considerably easier than with a complicated form class. For this reason, this example sticks with the console. Note that this example works with the CH10.MDB Access database on this book's accompanying CD-ROM. Copy the database into another directory because writing to a CD-ROM is somewhat difficult, even for a C# application.

Listing 10.4   Adding data to the database.

```
using System;
using System.Data;
using System.Data.ADO;

public class CH10_4
{
    public static void Main ()
    {
        // Define the connection string
        string strConn =
                "Provider=Microsoft.Jet.OLEDB.4.0;Data Source=CH10.MDB";

        // Define our selection criteria
        string strRec = "Insert Into Contact";
        strRec += " (Name, Address, City, State, ZipCode, Age) ";
        strRec += " VALUES (\"";
```

```
Console.WriteLine("Enter Name: ");
strRec += Console.ReadLine();
strRec += "\",\"";

Console.WriteLine("Enter Address: ");
strRec += Console.ReadLine();
strRec += "\",\"";

Console.WriteLine("Enter City: ");
strRec += Console.ReadLine();
strRec += "\",\"";

Console.WriteLine("Enter State: ");
strRec += Console.ReadLine();
strRec += "\",\"";

Console.WriteLine("Enter Zip Code: ");
strRec += Console.ReadLine();
strRec += "\",";

Console.WriteLine("Enter Age: ");
strRec += Console.ReadLine();
strRec += ");";

Console.WriteLine("Executing command: {0}", strRec );

// Create the connection object, using our connection string
ADOConnection myConn = new ADOConnection(strConn);

// Create the command object from our selection criteria string
ADOCommand myCmd = new ADOCommand( strRec, myConn );

// Try to execute the command
ADODataReader outData = null;
try
{
    // This will do the connection to the database
    myConn.Open();

    // This will run our query and put the result in outData
    myCmd.Execute( out outData );

}
catch ( Exception e )
{
```

```
        Console.WriteLine("Exception {0}", e );
    }
  }
}
```

For more information about working with strings, see Chapter 1.

Nothing surprising is in this example. The interesting aspects are how the SQL insert string is built by appending information a user enters. When you are working with string literals that need to be put in an SQL statement, you should put them in quotes because they may have embedded spaces or other invalid characters. The application prints the string it will use for insertion before running the command so that you can see what it looks like. Here is a sample run of the program:

```
C:\>ch10_4
Enter Name:
Herman Munster
Enter Address:
1313 Mockingbird Lane
Enter City:
Greenville
Enter State:
WI
Enter Zip Code:
13131
Enter Age:
119
Executing command: Insert Into
Contact (Name, Address, City, State, ZipCode, Age
) VALUES ("Herman Munster","1313 Mockingbird
Lane","Greenville","WI","13131",119);
```

If you then view the table in Microsoft Access, you see something similar to the display shown in Figure 10.1.

What happens if you try to insert the same record data twice? The answer, in this case, is that it works fine. In the listing shown in Microsoft Access, the table in question has a defined primary key that is unique. When you insert a new record into the database, it receives a unique key, which is appended to it. For this reason, the database does not care if you put multiple records in with the same data. However, *you* might care. In that case, you need to see if the record is there and either update it or delete it before inserting the new data into the table.

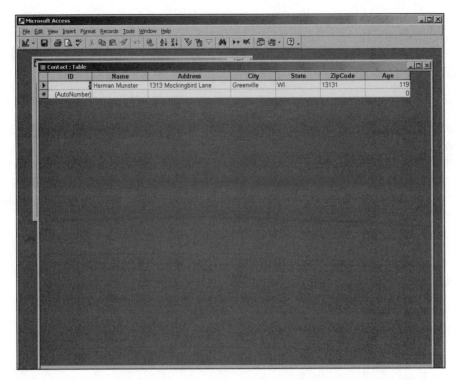

Figure 10.1   The Contact table after its insertion in Microsoft Access.

Deleting Data from the Database

Deleting data is a fact of life for the database programmer. Old data, stale data, data you no longer want—all these conditions require that you be able to remove data from the database. In this example, you look at a simple console application that allows you to find, select, and delete a record from a database, based on user input. This process is interesting because it requires that you do two things: Find a record and then issue a delete command. The delete command (represented by the SQL **Delete** statement) cannot be run while the previous command (**Select**) is being used. This situation avoids the issue of having the data change "out from under" another application while it is reading data from the database.

Listing 10.5 shows the complete application, along with the mini-menuing system for getting user input and the various components for finding, selecting, and deleting the record. Note the use of the named fields to retrieve and display record information for users to verify.

Listing 10.5   Deleting data from the database.

```
using System;
using System.Data;
using System.Data.ADO;

public class CH10_5
{
   public static int GetMenuSelection()
   {
      Console.WriteLine("Please select how you want to find a record:");
      Console.WriteLine("{0} Exit");
      Console.WriteLine("(1) By Name");
      Console.WriteLine("(2) By City" );
      Console.WriteLine("(3) By State");
      int selection = -1;
      do
      {
         Console.WriteLine("\nEnter your Selection: ");
         string s = Console.ReadLine();
         try
         {
             selection = s.ToInt16();
         }
         catch
         {
            selection = -1;
         }
      } while ( selection < 0 || selection > 3 );
      return selection;

   }
   public static void Main ()
   {
      // Define the connection string
      string strConn =
           "Provider=Microsoft.Jet.OLEDB.4.0;Data Source=CH10.MDB";

      // Find out what they want to delete.
      Boolean done = false;

      while ( !done )
      {
         string value = "";
         string strSelect = "";
```

```
switch ( GetMenuSelection() )
{
  case 0:
    done = true;
    break;
  case 1: // Name
    Console.WriteLine("Enter name to find: ");
    value = Console.ReadLine();
    strSelect = "SELECT * from Contact where Name Like \"";
    break;
  case 2: // City
    Console.WriteLine("Enter city to find: ");
    value = Console.ReadLine();
    strSelect="SELECT * from Contact where City Like \"";
    break;
  case 3: // State
    Console.WriteLine("Enter state to find: ");
    value = Console.ReadLine();
    strSelect="SELECT * from Contact where State Like \"";
    break;
}

if ( done )
  break;
strSelect += value;
strSelect += "\";";

// Create the connection object, using our connection string
ADOConnection myConn = new ADOConnection(strConn);

// Create the command object from our selection criteria string
ADOCommand myCmd = new ADOCommand( strSelect, myConn );

// Try to execute the command
ADODataReader outData = null;
try
{
    // This will do the connection to the database
    myConn.Open();

    // This will run our query and put the result in outData
    myCmd.Execute( out outData );

    // See if we got something back
    if ( outData != null )
    {
```

```
while (outData.Read() )
{
    Console.WriteLine( "ID: {0}",
            outData["ID"]);
    Console.WriteLine( "Name: {0}",
            outData["Name"]);
    Console.WriteLine( "Address: {0}",
            outData["Address"]);
    Console.WriteLine( "City: {0}",
            outData["City"]);
    Console.WriteLine( "State: {0}",
            outData["State"]);
    Console.WriteLine( "Zip Code: {0}",
             outData["ZipCode"]);
    Console.WriteLine( "Age: {0}",
             outData["Age"]);

    Console.Write(
        "\nDo you wish to delete this record (y/n):");
    string resp = Console.ReadLine();
    if ( resp == "y" || resp == "Y" )
    {
        int id = (int)outData["ID"];
        outData.Close();

        strSelect = "DELETE from Contact where ID = ";
        strSelect += id;
        strSelect += ";";

        ADOCommand cmd = new
            ADOCommand( strSelect, myConn);
        try
        {
            outData = null;
            cmd.Execute( out outData );
        }
        catch ( Exception e )
        {
            Console.WriteLine(
                "Exception in delete {0}",
                        e);
        }
        break;
    }
}
```

```
          catch ( Exception e )
          {
             Console.WriteLine("Exception {0}", e );
          }
       }
    }
}
```

This sample from the program shows how to utilize the find and delete functions:

```
C:\ >ch10_5
Please select how you want to find a record:
{0} Exit
(1) By Name
(2) By City
(3) By State

Enter your Selection:
1
Enter name to find:
Herman%
ID: 3
Name: Herman Munster
Address: 1313 Mockingbird Lane
City: Waukeegen
State: WI
Zip Code: 13131
Age: 102

Do you wish to delete this record (y/n):y
Please select how you want to find a record:
{0} Exit
(1) By Name
(2) By City
(3) By State

Enter your Selection:
0
```

The interesting part of this example is the use of the percent (%) sign as the wild card. SQL uses the percent sign to mean "match up everything to the sign, and everything else is okay."

Working with Multiple Tables

Being able to get individual pieces of data from a single table in an SQL database is all well and good. Unfortunately, you often need to get more information than is stored in a single table. In this case, you need to "join" multiple tables from the database and extract the fields you want from each table. The SQL language, fortunately, provides this functionality. If SQL can be made to run a query, the ADO.NET classes of C# can be used to get the data back. In this example, you look at how you can work with multiple tables at one time in the SQL database.

For this example, look at the CH10.MDB database, which contains two tables. The first table is the Contact table you used earlier. This Contact table contains customer information about contacts, with data such as the customer's name, address, city, and state. To go with that table, you have a Tax Rate table, which contains information about state tax rates. To join the information and retrieve a given tax rate for a given customer, you need to find the set of all customers for a given state and then match it up with the tax rate for that state. You use a simple SQL statement, as shown in Listing 10.6.

Listing 10.6   Working with multiple tables.

```
using System;
using System.Data;
using System.Data.ADO;

public class CH10_6
{
    public static void Main ()
    {
        // Define the connection string
        string strConn =
            "Provider=Microsoft.Jet.OLEDB.4.0;Data Source=CH10.MDB";

        // Define our selection criteria
        string strRec = "SELECT Contact.State, TaxRate.[Tax Rate] ";
        strRec +=
            "FROM Contact INNER JOIN TaxRate ON Contact.State";
        strRec += " = TaxRate.State ";
        strRec += " WHERE (((Contact.State)=\"WI\"))";

        // Create the connection object, using our connection string
        ADOConnection myConn = new ADOConnection(strConn);

        // Create the command object from our selection criteria string
        ADOCommand myCmd = new ADOCommand( strRec, myConn );
```

```
                    // Try to execute the command
                    ADODataReader outData = null;
                    try
                    {
                            // This will do the connection to the database
                            myConn.Open();

                            // This will run our query and put the result in outData
                            myCmd.Execute( out outData );


                            // See if we got something back
                            if ( outData != null )
                            {
                                    while (outData.Read() )
                                    {
                                            Console.WriteLine( "State: {0}", outData["State"]);
                                            Console.WriteLine( "Rate: {0}", outData["Tax Rate"]);
                                    }
                            }

                    }
                    catch ( Exception e )
                    {
                            Console.WriteLine("Exception {0}", e );
                    }
            }
    }
```

In this particular case, you have hard-coded the state to be Wisconsin (WI). If you run this program against the database, which contains information for contacts in Wisconsin as well as the tax rate there, you see the following output:

```
C:\ >ch10_6
State: WI
Rate: 6
```

As you can see, the join query works just fine. You could, in fact, output the name of the customer, by selecting the **Name** field in the output. If you do, you see that the two tables are, in fact, joined. If you modify this query

```
// Define our selection criteria
string strRec = "SELECT Contact.Name, Contact.State, TaxRate.[Tax Rate] ";
strRec += "FROM Contact INNER JOIN TaxRate ON Contact.State";
strRec += " = TaxRate.State ";
strRec += " WHERE (((Contact.State)=\"WI\"))";;
```

and then modify the output to contain this name

```
Console.WriteLine( "State: {0}", outData["State"]);
Console.WriteLine( "Rate: {0}", outData["Tax Rate"]);
Console.WriteLine( "Name: {0}", outData["Name"]);
```

the new output from the program contains the name of the person in the state—in this case, Ralph Smith:

```
C:\ >ch10_6
State: WI
Rate: 6
Name: Ralph Smith
```

Using a Stored Procedure

Stored procedures are a better way to complete commonly requested tasks for a database. A *stored* procedure allows you to precompile a commonly run SQL statement and keep it within the database. The stored procedure also allows you to "hide" the implementation of a given query from the calling application, which permits you to change the underlying data structures in the database quickly and easily without having to modify programs that use the data. For example, if you define a stored procedure that returns a given set of data and simply give the stored procedure name to the programmer who needs that information, you could completely change the way in which the data is stored in various tables, as long as the stored procedure returns the same information in the same way.

In this example, you look at a simple stored procedure—one that simply returns information from the database without needing any input from the calling application. These types of stored procedures are useful for requests made for reports or other static requests. Listing 10.7 shows a simple stored procedure call for the CH10.MDB database, which returns information you had previously retrieved using a static SQL statement. Notice that the code now contains no SQL commands.

Listing 10.7   Using a stored procedure.

```
using System;
using System.Data;
using System.Data.ADO;

public class CH10_7
{
    public static void Main ()
    {
```

```
// Define the connection string
string strConn =
        "Provider=Microsoft.Jet.OLEDB.4.0;Data Source=CH10.MDB";

// Define our selection criteria
string strRec = "FindWITaxRate";

// Create the connection object, using our connection string
ADOConnection myConn = new ADOConnection(strConn);

// Create the command object from our selection criteria string
ADOCommand myCmd = new ADOCommand( strRec, myConn );
myCmd.CommandType = CommandType.StoredProcedure;

// Try to execute the command
ADODataReader outData = null;
try
{
    // This will do the connection to the database
    myConn.Open();

    // This will run our query and put the result in outData
    myCmd.Execute( out outData );


    // See if we got something back
    if ( outData != null )
    {
        while (outData.Read() )
        {
            // Get the out parameters
            Console.WriteLine("name = {0}",
                outData["Name"]);
            Console.WriteLine("name = {0}",
                outData["Tax Rate"]);

        }
    }

}
catch ( Exception e )
{
    Console.WriteLine("Exception {0}", e );
}
}
}
```

Running this little program (programlet?) results in the following output from the application:

```
C:\ >ch10_7
name = Ralph Smith
name = 6
```

As you can see, it is the equivalent of previous examples in this chapter and executes the SQL statement:

```
SELECT Contact.Name, TaxRate.[Tax Rate]
FROM Contact INNER JOIN TaxRate ON Contact.State = TaxRate.State
WHERE (((Contact.State)="WI"));
```

Simply calling the **FindWITaxRate** command is certainly much easier than entering all this SQL gobbledygook into your program.

Related solution:	Found on page:
Using an Indexer	77

Setting Parameters for a Stored Procedure

You should write more generalized stored procedures for your applications than you have explored in the previous examples in this chapter. For example, although you can have a stored procedure that looks up a tax rate for a specific state in the database, having that state hard-coded into the stored procedure means that you need to write 50 similar procedures to get all the states. Worse, you then have to select which procedure to call based on which state you are interested in. If you could simply tell the stored procedure up front which state you want and have it make that state identifier part of the query it runs, your life would certainly be much easier. That would make a stored procedure more like a function call, which is really what it is.

The SQL language, fortunately, allows you to define stored procedures that can accept parameters. These parameters can be used within the procedure to select only the data you want. In Listing 10.8, you explore the idea of passing parameters to a stored procedure. Note the use of the string indexer to obtain the column names you want from the database row.

Listing 10.8   Setting parameters for a stored procedure.

```
using System;
using System.Data;
using System.Data.SQL;
using System.Data.ADO;

public class CH10_8
{
    public static void Main ()
    {
        // Define the connection string
        string strConn =
                "Provider=Microsoft.Jet.OLEDB.4.0;Data Source=CH10.MDB";

        // Define our selection criteria
        string strRec = "FindTaxRateForState";
        strRec += " 'WI'";

        // Create the connection object, using our connection string
        ADOConnection myConn = new ADOConnection(strConn);

        // Create the command object from our selection criteria string
        ADOCommand myCmd = new ADOCommand( strRec, myConn );
        myCmd.CommandType = CommandType.StoredProcedure;

        // Try to execute the command
        ADODataReader outData = null;
        try
        {
            // This will do the connection to the database
            myConn.Open();

            // This will run our query and put the result in outData
            myCmd.Execute( out outData );

            // See if we got something back
            if ( outData != null )
            {
                while (outData.Read() )
                {
                    // Get the out parameters
                    Console.WriteLine("name = {0}", outData["Name"]);
                    Console.WriteLine("name = {0}", outData["Tax Rate"]);
                }
```

```
        }
    }
    catch ( Exception e )
    {
        Console.WriteLine("Exception {0}", e );
    }
    }
}
```

If you were to run this application, you would see the same expected result you got in the previous hard-coded version of the stored procedure call. That is, the output of this little program is:

```
C:\ >ch10_8
name = Ralph Smith
name = 6
```

So what is the difference between the hard-coded version of the stored procedure and this one? The answer is that you are passing in a parameter that can be modified in the calling application without requiring the rewriting of the stored procedure. Because database administrators are generally fairly picky (and justifiably so) about who messes around with their databases, being able to change what is returned in the application instead of having to change the actual database is a much better idea.

Using Database Transactions

The transaction is the basic lifeblood of the database system. *Transactions* permit you to group a series of events into a single atomic unit, all of which must either work or not work. Transactions exist because sometimes you must perform more than one operation at a time on a database, and you must be sure that the database remains consistent during the entire process, even if one of those operations fails. Imagine that you are working with a banking transaction. You might allow a user to post several deposits and then several withdrawals and then more deposits. If, however, the withdrawal was properly posted and the deposit was not, the user would have a check bounce even when he had done nothing wrong. For this reason, the entire set of operations must be considered atomic.

The ADO.NET system in C# provides built-in functionality for transactions, as you see in this example. If you do not specifically request a transaction, the system wraps into a single transaction all the operations you perform between the open function of a database and the close function of that database. However, you can override this functionality by starting and stopping your transactions when you want. This ability allows you to commit certain actions, for example, and roll back certain other actions.

In Listing 10.9, you see a simple program that allows you to add records to the Contact table of the CH10.MDB Access file on the accompanying CD-ROM. You can specifically start and stop transactions and then view the results in the database itself. Try adding a few records, committing the transaction, and then adding a few more records and rolling back the transaction. You see that the database is updated exactly as you would expect.

Listing 10.9   Using database transactions.

```
using System;
using System.Data;
using System.Data.SQL;
using System.Data.ADO;

public class CH10_4
{
    public static void Main ()
    {
        // Define the connection string
        string strConn =
            "Provider=Microsoft.Jet.OLEDB.4.0;Data Source=CH10.MDB";

        ADOCommand myCmd;
        // Create the connection object, using our connection string
        ADOConnection myConn = new ADOConnection(strConn);
        // This will do the connection to the database
        myConn.Open();
        ADOCommand myCommand = new ADOCommand();

        // Begin the transaction.
        myConn.BeginTransaction();

        bool done = false;

        do
        {
            Console.WriteLine("(A) Add Record");
            Console.WriteLine("(C) Commit Changes");
            Console.WriteLine("(R) Rollback Changes");
            Console.WriteLine("(E) Exit");
```

```
string s = Console.ReadLine();
switch ( s[0] )
{
   case 'A':
   case 'a':

      // Define our selection criteria
      string strRec ="Insert Into Contact (";
      strRec+="(Name, Address, City, State, ZipCode, Age);"
      strRec += " VALUES (\"";

      Console.WriteLine("Enter Name: ");
      strRec += Console.ReadLine();
      strRec += "\",\"";

      Console.WriteLine("Enter Address: ");
      strRec += Console.ReadLine();
      strRec += "\",\"";

      Console.WriteLine("Enter City: ");
      strRec += Console.ReadLine();
      strRec += "\",\"";

      Console.WriteLine("Enter State: ");
      strRec += Console.ReadLine();
      strRec += "\",\"";

      Console.WriteLine("Enter Zip Code: ");
      strRec += Console.ReadLine();
      strRec += "\",";

      Console.WriteLine("Enter Age: ");
      strRec += Console.ReadLine();
      strRec += ");";

      Console.WriteLine("Executing command: {0}", strRec );

      // Create the command object from our selection string
      myCmd = new ADOCommand( strRec, myConn );

      // Try to execute the command
      ADODataReader outData = null;
      try
      {
```

```
                // This will run our query
                myCmd.Execute( out outData );
            }
            catch ( Exception e )
            {
                Console.WriteLine("Exception {0}", e );
            }
            break;

        case 'C':
        case 'c':

                myConn.CommitTransaction();
                myConn.BeginTransaction();
            break;
        case 'R':
        case 'r':
                myConn.RollbackTransaction();
                myConn.BeginTransaction();
                break;
        case 'E':
        case 'e':
                myConn.CommitTransaction();
                done = true;
                break;
        }

    } while ( !done );

    }
}
```

Writing to an XML File

XML (Extensible Markup Language) is the core of many of the new .NET features. XML is a standard way of embedding information in a text stream so that it can be read and interpreted by a variety of systems. Any file in standard XML format can be read and parsed into objects with elements, attributes, and data. Because XML is an important part of the .NET strategy, the C# system provides, not surprisingly, objects to work with XML.

In this example, you look at how you can write out an XML file containing information you want to save. You create the skeleton of an XML file and then populate it with elements passed in by a user. Attributes for these elements are set,

and in ways you can easily understand. Finally, you look at the resulting file and
what it all means. Listing 10.10 shows the code you can use to generate an XML
file from user input.

Listing 10.10   Writing to an XML file.

```
using System;
using System.Xml;

public class CH10_10
{
    public static void Main(string[] args)
    {
        // Create an XML writer.
        XmlTextWriter myXmlTextWriter = new
            XmlTextWriter("ch10_10.xml", null);

        myXmlTextWriter.Formatting = Formatting.Indented;
        myXmlTextWriter.WriteStartDocument(false);
        myXmlTextWriter.WriteDocType("ch10_10", null, null, null);
        myXmlTextWriter.WriteComment
          ("This file represents some user data");

        for ( int i=0; i<args.Length; ++i )
        {
            myXmlTextWriter.WriteStartElement(args[i]);
            myXmlTextWriter.WriteStartElement("entry", null);
            myXmlTextWriter.WriteAttribute("date","Today");
            myXmlTextWriter.WriteAttribute("reason","Because");
            myXmlTextWriter.WriteAttribute("ID", i.ToString());
            myXmlTextWriter.WriteEndElement();
        }
        // Commit the data
        myXmlTextWriter.Flush();
        myXmlTextWriter.Close();
    }
}
```

As you can see, the process is not complicated. You open the XML file using the
XMLTextWriter class, set some formatting options, and then write out to the
file using simple streaming methods of the class. For each element you want to
write out to the class, you first start the element (using the **StartElement** method)
and then write out the individual attributes, if any, of the class using the
WriteAttribute method. Finally, you close off an element using the **EndElement**
method. When you have finished working with the file, first flush out the data to
disk using the **Flush** method, and then close the file using the **Close** method. It's
that simple.

As an example, look at this run of the program and its resulting output:

```
C:\>ch10_10 element1

C:\>type ch10_10.xml
<?xml version="1.0" standalone="no"?>
<!DOCTYPE ch10_10>
<!--This file represents some user data-->
C:\matt\C#>ch10_10 element1

C:\matt\C#>type ch10_10.xml
<?xml version="1.0" standalone="no"?>
<!DOCTYPE ch10_10>
<!--This file represents some user data-->
<element1>
  <entry date="Today" reason="Because" ID="0"/>
</element1>
```

You see how to read this file in the next section.

Reading from an XML File

In the preceding section, you explored the notion of saving data in XML format, the core format for the .NET system. In this example, you look at how to read from an XML file you either wrote or were given by someone else. Reading an XML file is a matter of parsing the individual elements and putting them together into a rational order. To do this, you have to work from the type of elements you are reading. Fortunately, the XML parser in C# makes this process easy, as you see in this example.

In Listing 10.11, you see a simple program that accepts as input the name of an XML file. The file is then parsed using the **XmlTextReader** class and the individual elements displayed. The important elements—the **Element** type, **Attribute** type, and **Document** type—are displayed for users to view.

Listing 10.11   Reading from an XML file.

```
using System;
using System.Xml;

public class CH10_11
{
    public static void Main(string[] args)
```

```
        {

        XmlTextReader reader = new XmlTextReader (args[0]);

        while (reader.Read())
        {
            switch (reader.NodeType)
            {
                case XmlNodeType.Element: // The node is an Element
                    Console.WriteLine("Element: " + reader.Name);
                    while (reader.MoveToNextAttribute()) // Read attributes
                        Console.WriteLine("    Attribute: [" +
                            reader.Name + "] = '"
                                + reader.Value + "'");
                break;
                case XmlNodeType.DocumentType: // The node is a DocumentType
                    Console.WriteLine("Document: " + reader.Value);
                    break;
                case XmlNodeType.Comment:
                    Console.WriteLine("Comment: " + reader.Value);
                    break;
            }
        }

        reader.Close();
    }
}
```

Related solution:	Found on page:
Enumerating Files in a Directory	325

Serializing in XML

XML is a structured storage mechanism that is a series of objects, with attributes of those objects stored within it. That description sounds much like the description of an object-oriented system, and for this reason XML is an ideal way to save object-oriented information to persistent storage. The process of saving an object to a persistent storage device, such as a hard drive, is known as *serializing*. Serializing using XML for an object is particularly useful because you can then use the XML reader and writer classes of C# to restore or save an object in your application whenever you want.

You can use XML in two ways to save and restore data objects in your application. Which one you choose depends on what your application looks like because the objects are either internal or external choices. The first way in which you can save and restore data objects is to create an XML Schema Definition (XSD) for the class and use the XSD.exe tool to save and load them in a program. Although the directions for this process are fairly straightforward, they don't help much when you are working with a C# application rather than with a Web application. External tools just add complexity and require new programs to be distributed with the program. By building in the ability to save and load objects directly from your application into that application, you avoid the overhead and complexity of administrative tools.

The second way in which you can serialize an object in XML is to use the writer and reader classes for XML to output and input the object in the form you want to use. This method is less general, but much more useful in your application. You can apply your own versioning information, for example, as well as work with the data fields in the way your program needs them rather than have to load the entire object at one time.

Listing 10.12 shows a simple program that contains an object (**MyObject**) that "knows" how to save and restore itself from an XML file. As you can see from the code listing, the object is loaded only from the portion of the file it understands, so you can store multiple types of objects in a single file and have each of them load itself properly.

Listing 10.12   Serializing in XML.

```
using System;
using System.Xml;

public class MyObject
{
    int x;
    int y;
    double z;
    string name;

    public MyObject()
    {
        x = 10;
        y = 20;
        z = 35.5;
        name = "This is a test";
    }
    public void Save(XmlTextWriter tw)
```

```
{
    tw.WriteStartElement("MyObject", null);
    tw.WriteAttribute("Version", "1.0");
    tw.WriteAttribute("X", x.ToString() );
    tw.WriteAttribute("Y", y.ToString() );
    tw.WriteAttribute("Z", z.ToString() );
    tw.WriteAttribute("Name", name );
}
public void Initialize()
{
    x = 0;
    y = 0;
    z = 0;
    name = "";
}


public void Read(XmlTextReader reader)
{
    double versionId = 0;


    while (reader.MoveToNextAttribute()) // Read attributes
    {
        Console.WriteLine("Attribute: {0}", reader.Name );
        if ( reader.Name == "Version" )
        {
            versionId = reader.Value.ToDouble();
        }
        if ( reader.Name == "X" )
        {
            x = reader.Value.ToInt16();
        }
        if ( reader.Name == "Y" )
        {
            y = reader.Value.ToInt16();
        }
        if ( reader.Name == "Z" )
        {
            z = reader.Value.ToDouble();
        }
        if ( reader.Name == "Name" )
        {
            name = reader.Value;
        }
    }
}
```

```
        public void Dump()
        {
            Console.WriteLine("X = {0}", x );
            Console.WriteLine("Y = {0}", y );
            Console.WriteLine("Z = {0}", z );
            Console.WriteLine("Name = {0}", name );
        }
    }


    public class CH10_10
    {
        public static void Main(string[] args)
        {
            if ( args[0] == "Write")
            {
                // Create an XML writer.
                XmlTextWriter myXmlTextWriter = new
                    XmlTextWriter ("ch10_12.xml", null);

                // Write the header
                myXmlTextWriter.Formatting = Formatting.Indented;
                myXmlTextWriter.WriteStartDocument(false);
                myXmlTextWriter.WriteDocType("ch10_12", null, null, null);
                myXmlTextWriter.WriteComment("Save Some Objects");


                // Create an object
                MyObject myO = new MyObject();
                myO.Save( myXmlTextWriter );

                // Commit the data
                myXmlTextWriter.Flush();
                myXmlTextWriter.Close();
            }
            else
              if ( args[0] == "Read" )
              {
                    XmlTextReader reader = new XmlTextReader (args[1]);

                    while (reader.Read())
                    {
                        switch (reader.NodeType)
                        {
                            case XmlNodeType.Element: // The node is an Element
```

```
                        if ( reader.Name == "MyObject")
                        {
                            MyObject mo = new MyObject();
                            mo.Initialize();
                            mo.Dump(); // To show it is empty
                            mo.Read( reader );
                            mo.Dump();
                        }
                        break;
                    case XmlNodeType.DocumentType:
                        Console.WriteLine("Document: " + reader.Value);
                        break;
                    case XmlNodeType.Comment:
                        Console.WriteLine("Comment: " + reader.Value);
                        break;
                }
            }

            reader.Close();
        }
    }
}
```

Look at the output from this program when it is first run to save the object and
then to load it from the stored file:

```
C:\ >ch10_12 Read ch10_12.xml
Document: <!DOCTYPE ch10_12>
Comment: Save Some Objects
X = 0
Y = 0
Z = 0
Name =
Attribute: Version
Attribute: X
Attribute: Y
Attribute: Z
Attribute: Name
X = 10
Y = 20
Z = 35.5
Name = This is a test
```

The file itself, after the object is serialized to it, looks like this:

```
<?xml version="1.0" standalone="no"?>
<!DOCTYPE ch10_12>
<!--Save Some Objects-->
<MyObject Version="1.0" X="10" Y="20" Z="35.5" Name="This is a test"/>
```

As you can see, saving and restoring objects in XML is quite easy and is something that makes a great deal of sense in most applications. One warning, however, is that the objects in XML are stored in plain-text mode and can be read or modified by an external program. XML is therefore a poor way to store unencrypted passwords.

Saving a Dataset as XML

In this chapter, I have discussed working with databases and data sets and working with XML files. It would make sense, therefore, to be able to save data sets that have been retrieved from a database and store them as XML files. Naturally, the C# CLR classes permit you to do this quite easily. In this example, you take a look back at a way of getting information from a database and then apply your new knowledge of working with XML files to save it.

Listing 10.13 shows the code you work with to get the database data and save it as XML data. Note that this example works with the Northwind database, which ships standard with Visual Basic and other Visual Studio languages.

Listing 10.13   Saving a dataset as XML.

```
using System;
using System.Data;
using System.Data.ADO;
using System.Xml;

public class CH10_2
{
    public static void Main ()
    {
        // Define the connection string
        string strConn =
            "Provider=Microsoft.Jet.OLEDB.4.0;Data Source=NWIND.MDB";

        // Define our selection criteria
        string strRec ="SELECT EmployeeID, FirstName,";
```

```
        strRec += " LastName, Title FROM Employees";
        strRec += " ORDER BY Last Name";

        // Create the connection object, using our connection string
        ADOConnection myConn = new ADOConnection(strConn);

        // Create the command object from our selection criteria string
        ADODataSetCommand myCmd = new ADODataSetCommand( strRec, myConn );

        try
        {
            // This will do the connection to the database
            myConn.Open();

            DataSet myDataSet = new DataSet();
            myDataSet.Tables.Add("Employees");
            myCmd.FillDataSet(myDataSet,"Employees");

            myDataSet.WriteXmlSchema("ch10_13.xml");
            myDataSet.WriteXml("ch10_13.xml");

        }
        catch ( Exception e )
        {
            Console.WriteLine("Exception {0}", e );
        }
    }
}
```

Chapter 11

Graphics

In Depth

When you are working with an operating system, such as Windows, that is based on a graphical user interface (GUI), you are naturally confronted with the problem of completing graphical tasks. Working with graphics in the Windows world involves such tasks as drawing lines, arcs, and figures, as you would expect. However, it also involves less obvious tasks, like putting images on the screen and displaying text in fancy fonts. Although all these tasks come under the heading of "working with graphics," they are rarely considered that way by the average programmer. The C# system in .NET supports a wide variety of graphics functionality, including putting images into controls easily. Fonts, colors, lines, and figures are all easily displayed on the screen and manipulated just as they were in the "good old days" of Windows programming, when the only available options were the Windows API functions.

You will find differences between the graphics system of the older versions of Windows and that of .NET. For one thing, the graphical interface in C# is much easier to use and is much more consistent than the old-style device context functions of Windows. Rather than have to worry about getting and releasing device contexts, you now work with a graphics object that contains all the functionality as a series of methods that can be used to change the display. Colors and fonts are now properties of the controls they affect rather than strange and arbitrary Windows messages that are sent to handlers for the controls. Although these changes are all for the best, they can cause difficulty if you are accustomed to working with the old-style programming interface. For this reason, I walk you through the graphics system in C# step-by-step, looking at how it is all put together and how you can use it to your best advantage.

The first step on your tour of the graphics system in C# is with the GDI+ library. If you are an old-time Windows programmer, you are probably accustomed to working with the Graphics Device Interface (GDI). This system was created to abstract (get away from) the work of displaying graphics on various graphics devices, such as monitors and printers. In "classic" Windows programming, the GDI was reached by retrieving a handle to a device context (known as an HDC) and passing that handle to various functions to perform such actions as drawing lines or displaying text on the screen. The problem was always that the number of device context handles was limited on the system. Forgetting to release a handle was a common problem in Windows programming and often led to system slowdowns at best—and system crashes at worst.

The GDI+ Interface

The GDI+ interface is a change from the old GDI functionality of Windows and from the GDI functionality of earlier versions of C# and the CLR. Rather than assign properties to each and every element you want to change in the graphics system, you instead utilize those properties to a **Graphics** object method. For example, if you are accustomed to working with the old-style GDI, you might write:

```
Graphics g = new Graphics();
g.Font = new Font("Times New Roman", 22);
g.ForeColor = new Color(Color.Blue);
g.BackColor = new Color(Color.White);
g.DrawString("Hello world", 0, 0 );
```

In the old-style Windows programming, this block of code would look something like this:

```
HDC hDC = GetDC();
SelectObject(hDC, &Font);
TextOut (hdc, 0, 0, "Hello world", strlen("Hello world"));
```

In the new GDI, however, the code looks like this:

```
Graphics g = new Graphics();
g.DrawString("Hello world", new Font("Times New Roman", 22),
             new SolidBrush( new Color(Color.Blue)), 0, 0 );
```

The most important thing to notice about this particular block is that you don't pay much attention to the objects you pass in after you are done with them. You don't need to free up a device context handle or delete the font object or worry about the brush object you are passing into the **DrawString** method. All these tasks are done automatically by the garbage-collection system, at an appropriate time in the application. This feature is by far one of the most useful about working with C#. You lose the danger of leaking resources and causing dangerous system memory leaks.

The GDI+ classes "live" in the **System.Drawing**, **System.Drawing.2D**, **System.Drawing.Imaging**, and **System.Drawing.Text** namespaces and are contained in the System.Drawing.DLL reference library. By including this reference in your project in Visual Studio.NET, you have access to all the drawing functionality that is inherent in the C# development system.

The Graphics Object

The core of the graphics functionality in C# is provided by the **Graphics** class. It contains all the methods you need in order to render images; draw lines, arcs, or figures; or display text on the screen. As you see a bit later in this chapter, this class also contains all the functionality needed to do graphics transformation, which is necessary for such tasks as rotating text displays or rotating 3D objects on the screen.

You create a graphics object by instantiating an object of the **Graphics** class. Use the following single line of code:

```
Graphics g = new Graphics();
```

A *graphics object* is simply a "surface" on which you can render text, graphics, colors, and fonts. Rather than use the old style of selecting the objects you want to use "into" the graphics device, you now simply use the properties you want to use in the method calls you make to the object. For example, you could create a line on a graphics display by using this code:

```
Graphics g = new Graphics();
Pen aPen = new Pen(Color.Blue);
Point startPoint = new Point(0,0);
Point endPoint = new Point(100,100);
g.DrawLine( aPen, startPoint, endPoint);
```

This snippet of code creates a new graphics object, creates a new blue pen, and draws a line from **0,0** to **100,100** in the current graphics coordinate system. When the function that calls this snippet ends, the **Pen**, **startPoint**, and **endPoint** objects (in addition to the **Graphics** object) all simply go away and release the memory associated with them. Unlike with previous Windows programming issues, the window associated with this graphics object is not affected by the object's disappearance.

You can normally create graphics objects in one of three ways:

- You may be given a graphics object as part of a **Paint** event.
- You may create an "off-screen" graphics object so that you can create a bitmap for immediate display on the screen with no flicker or delay.
- You may get a graphics object to use for printing.

You don't really see a difference between drawing on a screen graphics object and a printer graphics object, so I don't talk about the differences between these two approaches. However, some minor changes have taken place for working with off-screen bitmaps. Next, take a look at a simple example of creating such an off-screen bitmap, often called *double buffering* in the graphics world.

This piece of code creates a bitmap and fills it with color. It then draws a text string in the middle of the bitmap:

```
Bitmap theBitmap = new Bitmap(nWidth,nHeight,PixelFormat.Format32bppArgb);
Graphics grfx = Graphics.FromImage(theBitmap);
Font theFont = new Font("MS Sans Serif", 18);
grfx.FillRectangle(new SolidBrush(Color.Blue),
    new Rectangle(0,0,nWidth,nHeight));
grfx.DrawString("I'm an image", theFont,
    new SolidBrush(Color.White), 0, 0);
```

After you have a bitmap, you can do whatever you want with it. As you may recall from Chapter 9, you can display an image, such as a bitmap, in a picture box control. Alternatively, as you see in "Creating a PNG File on the Fly" in the "Immediate Solutions" section later in this chapter, you can save this bitmap to a file in a different format that can be loaded into the C# editor or another application.

A graphics object supports all the functionality you have come to expect in working with GUI-based applications. However, a graphics object by itself is limited in that it doesn't support colors, brushes, or pens. These items make the display exciting for users and attract the human eye (and good reviews) to an application. Take a look at these objects next.

Brushes

The brush is the instrument of choice for anyone wanting to paint the backgrounds of windows or controls. Brushes can also be used to create interesting and beautiful textures for filling in figures displayed on a form. Gradients can be quickly and easily displayed using a brush, making them indispensable for working with form backgrounds and title bars.

C# has two distinct types of brushes, implemented in two separate classes. The first one is the **SolidBrush** class, which implements a brush that is a single, uniform color across its display. For example, to create a brush that is a uniform shade of blue and use it to fill in a rectangle on the drawing surface, you write this code:

```
Graphics g;  // Get a graphics object
SolidBrush sb = new SolidBrush( Color.Blue );
Rectangle r = new Rectangle(0,0,Width,Height);
g.FillRectangle( sb, r );
```

This code fills a rectangle (of size **Width, Height**) with a blue color. Rather than have to create a new brush from scratch each time you want one, you could use the **System** brushes. This collection contains all the standard precreated brushes, requiring no overhead of creation and destruction. You could rewrite the preceding code, therefore, as:

```
Graphics g;  // Get a graphics object
Rectangle r = new Rectangle(0,0,Width,Height);
g.FillRectangle( Brushes.Blue, r );
```

These two pieces of code have exactly the same effect on the screen. The second one is slightly faster because of the lack of overhead of the creation and destruction of the graphics objects. Unless you are creating a large number of brushes and using them in your code, however, you are unlikely to notice any real speed difference. The C# garbage-collection facilities are quite good and hide the overhead time.

In terms of methods, the **Brush** class itself has none to speak of. It has a single public property, **Color**, that represents the color of the solid brush. For methods, the **Brush** class implements all the standard methods of the **Object** class (**Clone** and **Equals**, for example), but none of its own. A brush is a wrapper around a simple Windows brush handle (**HBRUSH**).

The second kind of brush is the textured brush type. These objects—represented by the classes **TextureBrush**, **LinearGradient**, and **PathGradientBrush**—are more interesting than a simple solid brush simply because of all the interesting things you can do with it. The texture brush encapsulates an image, which is used to draw a "texture" on the surface of an area of the screen. The **LinearGradient** and **PathGradientBrush** classes, on the other hand, allow you to draw a gradient on the surface of a figure or form. A *gradient* is a gradual color change from one color to another, which looks like a three-dimensional surface because of its shadow-like color changes.

To create a **TextureBrush** object and use it to fill an area, you need to have an image to work with. For example, to "paint" a bitmap across the background of a form, you could use the following code:

```
Graphics g;
Image i = new Bitmap("myimage.bmp");
TextureBrush tb = new TextureBrush(i);
g.FillRectangle( tb, ClientRectangle);
```

This code results in the image contained in Myimage.bmp being displayed across the background of the form window. You could then mute (soften) the colors of the image by "whitewashing" the image using the **SolidBrush** class:

```
g.FillRectangle( new SolidBrush(Color.FromArgb(180, Color.White)),
        ClientRectangle);
```

The **LinearGradient** brush (which is of type **TexturedBrush**), on the other hand, allows you to define a straight gradient from one side or point in a rectangle to another on the form. Suppose that you want to paint a gradient across the background of a form. You could write this code in the **Paint** handler for the form:

```
LinearGradientBrush lgb = new LinearGradientBrush(
    ClientRectangle, Color.Blue,
    Color.Green, 45, true );
e.Graphics.FillRectangle( lgb, ClientRectangle );
```

The **45** in the constructor call is the angle through which the gradient is drawn. The angle at which the lines pass for the gradient is 45 degrees from the top. The true argument simply indicates that the angle is scalable. Unless you are working with transformations in this graphics display, which I talk about later in this chapter, the scalability means nothing when you are drawing the gradient.

Another kind of textured brush is **PathGradientBrush**. This brush is similar to the **LinearGradientBrush** class, but allows you to do much more complex tasks with the display:

```
using System;
using System.Drawing;
using System.Collections;
using System.ComponentModel;
using System.Windows.Forms;
using System.Data;
using System.Drawing.Imaging;
using System.Drawing.Drawing2D;

namespace CH11_Gradient
{
    public class Form1 : System.Windows.Forms.Form
    {
        private System.ComponentModel.Container components = null;

        public Form1()
        {
            InitializeComponent();
        }
        protected override void Dispose( bool disposing )
        {
            if( disposing )
            {
```

```
        if (components != null)
        {
            components.Dispose();
        }
    }
    base.Dispose( disposing );
}

#region Windows Form Designer generated code
private void InitializeComponent()
{
    this.AutoScaleBaseSize = new System.Drawing.Size(5, 13);
    this.ClientSize = new System.Drawing.Size(768, 533);
    this.Name = "Form1";
    this.Text = "Form1";
    this.Paint += new
            System.Windows.Forms.PaintEventHandler(this.OnPaint);

}
#endregion

[STAThread]
static void Main()
{
    Application.Run(new Form1());
}

private void OnPaint(object sender,
            System.Windows.Forms.PaintEventArgs e)
{
    Rectangle rect = this.ClientRectangle;
    GraphicsPath path = new GraphicsPath(new Point[] {
            new Point(40, 140), new Point(275, 200),
            new Point(105, 225), new Point
                    (190, ClientRectangle.Bottom),
            new Point(50, ClientRectangle.Bottom),
                    new Point(20, 180), },
            new byte[] {
            (byte)PathPointType.Start,
            (byte)PathPointType.Bezier,
            (byte)PathPointType.Bezier,
            (byte)PathPointType.Bezier,
            (byte)PathPointType.Line,
            (byte)PathPointType.Line,
    });
```

```
PathGradientBrush pgb = new PathGradientBrush(path);
pgb.SurroundColors = new Color[] {
    Color.Green,Color.Yellow,Color.Red,
                Color.Blue, Color.Orange, Color.White, };
e.Graphics.FillPath(pgb, path);


    }
  }
}
```

Pens

The pen is the line-drawing tool of the graphics toolbox. Whenever you draw lines, display text, or draw figures on the screen, you are affected by the pen selected to do the job. Pens can be solid, dashed, dotted, or textured (using a **TextureBrush** class type) to display the lines they are used to draw. Whether you're drawing a straight line or an arc, the pen faithfully renders each point along the path of the figure.

Pens have either a color or a texture and a width. You can create a default pen with a single pixel width by using the standard constructor for the pen:

```
Pen p = new Pen(Color.Black);
```

This code creates a pen that draws its lines in black with a width of one pixel across (the default) the drawing surface. On the other hand, you can create a pen three pixels wide by using this line:

```
Pen p1 = new Pen(Color.Black, 3);
```

This line permits you to do some rather fancy drawing on the screen. It also allows you to scale up objects by making them thicker, which makes them appear larger on the screen.

Like the **Brush** classes, the **Pen** classes have a system-wide set of pens that can be used directly in your code without creating them. For example, rather than use the one-pixel black pen shown in the preceding example, you could have used the **Pens.Black** pen, which is already predefined in the C# system.

Another way in which you can use a pen is to initialize it with a brush and a width. Assume that you want to draw a line that is made up of the Clouds.bmp file that is in the Windows directory on your hard drive. You could write the following code, which is on this book's accompanying CD-ROM:

```
Image bmp = new Bitmap("C:\\Windows\\Clouds.bmp");
TextureBrush tb = new TextureBrush( bmp, ClientRectangle);
e.Graphics.DrawLine( new Pen(tb,5),  new Point(0,0), new Point(100,100));
```

This code permits you to draw a line five pixels wide across the form from the point **0,0** to the point **100,100**. The line is made up of the image Clouds.bmp and uses that image to draw the individual segments of the line. This particular functionality is wonderful for drawing such elements as bitmapped status bars, a feature that was particularly attractive in OS/2.

Images

Images are the core of what people think about when they talk about graphics. Unlike pens, brushes, and other graphics tools, images are the part of the system that users generally see the most. In C#, many different image types are supported. BMP, JPEG, PNG, TIFF, and other types of images can be quickly and easily loaded into an **Image** class component and then displayed on the screen in a variety of ways.

To load an image, you can use either the constructor for the image type with the file name, like this

```
Image bmp = new Bitmap("mybitmap.bmp");
```

or the **FromFile** method of the **Image** class to load the image directly from a file at runtime. Here's a simple example of using this method to load an image:

```
Image bmp = Image.FromFile("mybitmap.bmp");
```

The **FromFile** method and the constructor are functionally equivalent.

What is more exciting in C# is that you can save images to a file in a variety of formats. For example, you can load a bitmap and save it as a JPEG image. This complete little program does exactly that:

```
namespace ch11_image
{
    using System;
    using System.Drawing;
    using System.Collections;
    using System.ComponentModel;
    using System.WinForms;
    using System.Data;
    using System.Drawing.Imaging;

    public class Form1 : System.WinForms.Form
    {
        private System.ComponentModel.Container components;
        private System.WinForms.OpenFileDialog openFileDialog1;
```

```
private System.WinForms.Button button2;
private System.WinForms.RadioButton radioButton3;
private System.WinForms.RadioButton radioButton2;
private System.WinForms.RadioButton radioButton1;
private System.WinForms.Button button1;
private ImageFormat fFormat;
private Image fImage;

  public Form1()
  {
      InitializeComponent();
      fFormat = ImageFormat.JPEG;
  }

  public override void Dispose()
  {
      base.Dispose();
      components.Dispose();
  }
  private void InitializeComponent()
  {
    this.components = new System.ComponentModel.Container ();
    this.button1 = new System.WinForms.Button ();
    this.radioButton2 = new System.WinForms.RadioButton ();
    this.radioButton3 = new System.WinForms.RadioButton ();
    this.radioButton1 = new System.WinForms.RadioButton ();
    this.button2 = new System.WinForms.Button ();
    this.openFileDialog1 = new System.WinForms.OpenFileDialog ();
    button1.Location = new System.Drawing.Point (40, 24);
    button1.Size = new System.Drawing.Size (208, 24);
    button1.TabIndex = 0;
    button1.Text = "Load Image";
    button1.Click += new System.EventHandler (this.button1_Click);
    radioButton2.Location = new System.Drawing.Point (56, 112);
    radioButton2.Text = "PNG";
    radioButton2.Size = new System.Drawing.Size (176, 24);
    radioButton2.TabIndex = 2;
    radioButton2.CheckedChanged += new System.EventHandler
            (this.radioButton2_CheckedChanged);
    radioButton3.Location = new System.Drawing.Point (56, 152);
    radioButton3.Text = "TIFF";
    radioButton3.Size = new System.Drawing.Size (176, 24);
    radioButton3.TabIndex = 3;
    radioButton3.CheckedChanged += new System.EventHandler
            (this.radioButton3_CheckedChanged);
```

```
      radioButton1.Location = new System.Drawing.Point (56, 72);
      radioButton1.Text = "JPEG";
      radioButton1.Size = new System.Drawing.Size (176, 24);
      radioButton1.TabIndex = 1;
      radioButton1.CheckedChanged += new System.EventHandler
              (this.radioButton1_CheckedChanged);
      button2.Location = new System.Drawing.Point (40, 200);
      button2.Size = new System.Drawing.Size (208, 24);
      button2.TabIndex = 4;
      button2.Text = "Save Image";
      button2.Click += new System.EventHandler (this.button2_Click);
      this.Text = "Form1";
      this.AutoScaleBaseSize = new System.Drawing.Size (5, 13);
      this.Controls.Add (this.button2);
      this.Controls.Add (this.radioButton3);
      this.Controls.Add (this.radioButton2);
      this.Controls.Add (this.radioButton1);
      this.Controls.Add (this.button1);
   }

   protected void button2_Click (object sender, System.EventArgs e)
   {
      string name = "";
      if ( fFormat == ImageFormat.JPEG )
      {
         name = "myimage.jpg";
      }
      if ( fFormat == ImageFormat.PNG )
      {
         name = "myimage.png";
      }
      if ( fFormat == ImageFormat.TIFF)
      {
         name = "myimage.tif";
      }
      fImage.Save( name, fFormat );
   }

   protected void button1_Click (object sender, System.EventArgs e)
   {
      if ( this.openFileDialog1.ShowDialog() == DialogResult.OK )
      {
         fImage = Image.FromFile( this.openFileDialog1.FileName );
      }
   }
```

```
    protected void radioButton3_CheckedChanged (object sender,
           System.EventArgs e)
    {
       fFormat = ImageFormat.TIFF;
    }


    protected void radioButton2_CheckedChanged (object sender,
         System.EventArgs e)
    {
       fFormat = ImageFormat.PNG;
    }


    protected void radioButton1_CheckedChanged (object sender,
         System.EventArgs e)
    {
       fFormat = ImageFormat.JPEG;
    }

    public static void Main(string[] args)
    {
        Application.Run(new Form1());
    }
  }
}
```

As you can see, you can do an awful lot of work in C# without writing much code. In this case, the vast majority of the code is written for you by the Project Wizard, and the remainder consists mostly of retrieving file names from the user. I tried out this little program on a BMP file that shipped with Windows and saved it in JPEG format. The resulting image was about 10 percent of its original size. *That* is a program worth having.

Transformations

The next graphics subject to consider is transformations. To understand what transformations are, you must first understand the coordinate system used by the GDI+ drawing classes. The GDI+ coordinate system is made up of two views: world view and user view. Normally, these two views are aligned so that the upper-left corner is always 0,0 in either coordinate system. However, before any graphics are drawn, any user-defined transformations are applied and the user coordinate system is shifted by that amount. When the results are applied, they are drawn in world coordinate view, moving the drawing around as the transformations are applied. This system permits you, as a developer, to shift, rotate, and skew the graphics you want displayed on the user's screen.

Three basic types of transformations are allowed in the GDI+ drawing system: **ScaleTransform**, **RotateTransform**, and **TranslateTransform**. Transformations can be applied singly or in multiples for any given display.

The **ScaleTransform** method scales the entire display by a given amount in either the x or y direction or in both directions. To use the **ScaleTransform** method of the graphics object, you simply pass in the x and y adjustments. For example, the following snippet of code scales the display to be twice as high as you originally drew it:

```
g.ScaleTransform( 1, 2 );
```

The **RotateTransform** method simply rotates the graphics display about the origin of the user coordinate system. To rotate the entire drawing 45 degrees about the upper-left corner, for example, add the following line:

```
g.RotateTransform(45);
```

Finally, the **TranslateTransform** method shifts the user coordinate system by a given amount in the directions you specify. You can "pan" around a virtual window, for example, by translating the user coordinate system by a given pan amount. You can also use **TranslateTransform** to shift the axes so that the display moves vertically and/or horizontally. As you can see in "Rotating Fonts" in the "Immediate Solutions" section later in this chapter, this combination is often used to rotate a text string about the center, rather than the upper-left corner, of a window. The general form of the **TranslateTransform** method is:

```
g.TranslateTransform( dx, dy );
```

The **dx** argument can be either positive or negative and represents the amount you want to move the graphical display in the horizontal direction. The **dy** argument, similarly, can be positive or negative and represents the amount you want to move the user coordinate system in the vertical direction.

If you don't understand transformations, don't worry. The default transformations are likely to do everything you need them to do. However, if you are accustomed to working with high-end graphics display engines, the transformations in C#, along with the slew of graphics primitives, will make you think twice before using a third-party drawing library.

Text and Drawing

The final subjects I describe in this chapter are how to display text and graphics primitives. Neither is a complicated affair, but you should understand all the functionality you have at your fingertips when using the GDI+ system. The text-display functions consist of the **Font** object and the text-drawing functions. The graphics primitive functions consist of the **Graphics** class methods to draw lines, arcs, polygons, and other figures.

The powerful **Font** class in the GDI+ library lets you easily select a given font or create your own variation of a font on the fly. For example, to create a font that represents a 45-em (a printer's measure) Arial font, you write the following code:

```
Font f = new Font("Arial", 45);
```

Alternatively, you can be fancy with your fonts and specify virtually every aspect of their display and behavior: Select the **FontStyle** attribute version of the constructor for the **Font** object. For example, this font is in 50-ems Arial style and is also in bold italic style:

```
Font f = new Font("Arial", 45, FontStyle.Bold | FontStyle.Italic );
```

The possible enumerations of the **FontStyle** type are shown in Table 11.1. Most of these values can be OR'd together to form a combination, as shown in this example.

NOTE: *If a font is not installed on the system and that specific font is requested, an exception is thrown.*

To display text, you use the **DrawString** method of the **Graphics** class. This method permits you to display text, position it on the screen, and select its font and color. The general form of the **DrawString** method is

```
g.DrawString( string, font, brush, bounding_rectangle );
```

Table 11.1 Font style enumerations.

Style	Meaning
Bold	A bold (wide) format for the font
Italic	A slanted format for the font
Regular	Normal text for the font
Strikeout	Text with a line through the center of it
Underline	Text that is underlined

where these conditions are true:

- **string** is the string you want to display on the screen.
- **font** is the font object you want to use to display the text string.
- **brush** is the brush object (any of the brush classes I have discussed) used to display the text string.
- **bounding_rectangle** is the area in which you want the text to appear in user coordinates of the form window.

Sometimes, of course, you don't know the bounding rectangle for the string. All you are likely to know is where you want the text to begin on the screen. In these cases, the **Graphics** class provides the **MeasureString** method, which allows you to find the size of a given string using the current settings of the graphics object and the font in which you want the string displayed. The general form of the **MeasureString** method is:

```
SizeF size = g.MeasureString( string, fontToUse );
```

The returned **size** object specifies the width and length of the string for this particular font given the transformations applied to the graphics object at the time the method is called.

Graphic Primitives

The final topic in this section is the list of possible graphic primitives available to you in the **Graphics** class. These primitives form the backbone of the GDI+ methods for rendering graphics for users to view. The primitives are relatively self-explanatory. The complete list of available primitives is shown in Table 11.2.

In addition to simple primitives, a version of each solid-figure-drawing primitive also exists. These methods permit you to draw a rectangle, for example, and fill it with a given color (**FillRectangle**, for example).

Table 11.2   GDI+ graphics methods.

Primitive	Purpose
DrawArc	Draws a segment of a circle
DrawBezier	Draws a curve based on a set of points
DrawBeziers	Draws a series of curves
DrawClosedCurve	Draws a closed curve (the starting point and end point meet) based on an arbitrary set of points
DrawCurve	Draws a simple curve based on a set of points

(continued)

Table 11.2   GDI+ graphics methods *(continued).*

Primitive	Purpose
DrawEllipse	Draws an ellipse (and alternatively a circle)
DrawIcon	Renders an icon on the screen
DrawIconUnstretched	Oddly, stretches an icon to fit user coordinates (and is named Unstretched because the transformation is done based on user requirements rather than on the system)
DrawImage	Draws an image (any **Image**-based class) on the screen
DrawLine	Draws a line between two points
DrawLines	Draws a series of lines, each defined by two points on the screen
DrawPath	Draws a series of lines connected by end points
DrawPie	Draws a pie chart section
DrawPolygon	Draws a closed polygon from a set of points
DrawRectangle	Draws a single rectangle from a set of points
DrawRectangles	Draws a series of rectangles that are all unconnected

Immediate Solutions

Drawing a Simple Pattern on a Form

Sometimes, you want to put a background on a form. You can do this by drawing a bitmap, or perhaps by drawing a simple logo using graphics primitives on the form. In this section, I describe a few ways of doing this, but, for now, concentrate on the graphics primitives. Assume that you work for X Corporation, whose logo is, of course, an X. For this example, therefore, you want to draw a giant X across the background of the form you are working with.

The core task to drawing on a form is in overriding the **Paint** method of the form for your own use. Painting a form is done in response to a **WM_PAINT** message, which is sent from the Windows operating system when the area of the form is uncovered or displayed for the first time. When you do your drawing in the **Paint** method, you guarantee that the form is displayed properly at all times.

Figure 11.1 shows the form you work with in the Form Designer. As you can see, the form is quite simple and contains only a button in its center. No graphics are displayed in Design view because this is a runtime-only display.

Figure 11.2 shows the same form at runtime. As you can see, a giant X is displayed across the center of the form, in the background of the display, behind the button. This figure shows the order in which elements are drawn on a form and allows you to ensure that graphical controls are not overwritten by your own graphical displays.

Figure 11.1   The drawing form at design time.

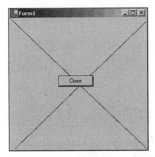

Figure 11.2   The drawing form at runtime.

The code for drawing the giant X is simple, as are most drawing primitives in the C# graphics system. Listing 11.1 shows the entire application, minus the wizard's auto-generated code.

Listing 11.1   Drawing on a form.

```
namespace CH11_1
{
    using System;
    using System.Drawing;
    using System.Collections;
    using System.ComponentModel;
    using System.WinForms;
    using System.Data;

    public class Form1 : System.WinForms.Form
    {
        private System.ComponentModel.Container components;
        private System.WinForms.Button button1;

        public Form1()
        {
            InitializeComponent();
        }

        public override void Dispose()
        {
            base.Dispose();
            components.Dispose();
        }

        private void InitializeComponent()
        {
```

```
            this.components = new System.ComponentModel.Container ();
            this.button1 = new System.WinForms.Button ();
            button1.Location = new System.Drawing.Point (104, 120);
            button1.Size = new System.Drawing.Size (75, 23);
            button1.TabIndex = 0;
            button1.Text = "&Close";
            button1.Click += new System.EventHandler (this.button1_Click);
            this.Text = "Form1";
            this.AutoScaleBaseSize = new System.Drawing.Size (5, 13);
            this.Paint += new System.WinForms.PaintEventHandler
                    (this.Form1_Paint);
            this.Controls.Add (this.button1);
        }

        protected void button1_Click (object sender, System.EventArgs e)
        {
            Close();
        }

        protected void Form1_Paint (object sender,
                System.WinForms.PaintEventArgs e)
        {
            Point p1 = new Point(0,0);
            Point p2 = new Point( Width, Height-20);

            Pen p = new Pen( System.Drawing.Color.Black );

            e.Graphics.DrawLine( p, p1, p2 );

            Point p3 = new Point(Width, 0);
            Point p4 = new Point(0, Height-20);

            e.Graphics.DrawLine( p, p3, p4 );
        }

        public static void Main(string[] args)
        {
            Application.Run(new Form1 ());
        }
    }
}
```

Drawing a Bitmap on a Form

One of the most interesting aspects of Windows is that you can make elements look "pretty." The most exciting thing you can do for users, in terms of static graphics, is to put a background on a form so that that it appears to be a picture postcard. This eye-catching background permits you to show users information in a graphical fashion as well as to simply make the application look better.

In the "bad old days" of Windows programming (the mid 1990s), putting a background on a window was a nightmarish process. You had to trap for several Windows messages, make sure that you had a valid handle to a graphical image, "blit" (copy bitwise) the image on the screen, and then make sure that you didn't overwrite any other controls on the window.

Now that the good times of .NET and C# are here, however, drawing a bitmap as the background of a form has become easy for new applications. As you see in this example, all that is needed to create a form like the one you see in Figure 11.3 is a little bit of code and a little bit of knowledge about how the form system works. In this case, the bit of knowledge is how forms paint themselves and how images are loaded. When a form needs to be painted, it calls the **Paint** method. This method triggers an event, which can be caught in the application program and overridden. As you see in Listing 11.2, painting the image on the form is extremely easy too.

Listing 11.2   Drawing a bitmap on a form.

```
namespace CH11_2
{
    using System;
    using System.Drawing;
    using System.Collections;
    using System.ComponentModel;
```

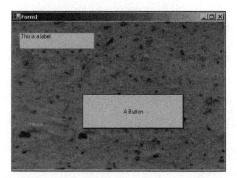

Figure 11.3   A form with a bitmap background.

```
using System.WinForms;
using System.Data;

public class Form1 : System.WinForms.Form
{
    private System.ComponentModel.Container components;
    private System.WinForms.Button button1;
    private System.WinForms.Label label1;
    private Image image;

    public Form1()
    {
        InitializeComponent();

        // Load the image from a file
        image = Image.FromFile("c:\\windows\\Clouds.bmp");
    }

    public override void Dispose()
    {
        base.Dispose();
        components.Dispose();
    }

    private void InitializeComponent()
    {
     this.components = new System.ComponentModel.Container ();
     this.label1 = new System.WinForms.Label ();
     this.button1 = new System.WinForms.Button ();
     label1.Location = new System.Drawing.Point (16, 24);
     label1.Text = "This is a label";
     label1.Size = new System.Drawing.Size (160, 32);
     label1.TabIndex = 0;
     button1.Location = new System.Drawing.Point (152, 152);
     button1.Size = new System.Drawing.Size (216, 72);
     button1.TabIndex = 1;
     button1.Text = "A Button";
     this.Text = "Form1";
     this.AutoScaleBaseSize = new System.Drawing.Size (5, 13);
     this.ClientSize = new System.Drawing.Size (456, 309);
     this.Paint += new System.WinForms.PaintEventHandler
            (this.Form1_Paint);
     this.Controls.Add (this.button1);
     this.Controls.Add (this.label1);
    }
```

```
    protected void Form1_Paint (object sender,
        System.WinForms.PaintEventArgs e)
    {
      e.Graphics.DrawImage( image, e.ClipRectangle );
    }

    public static void Main(string[] args)
    {
        Application.Run(new Form1());
    }
  }
}
```

Displaying a Bitmap in a Form

In the preceding section, you looked at a way to turn a bitmap into the background of a form. In the example in this section, however, you examine how to display a bitmap in a standard fashion. This little example creates a simple bitmap viewer application you can use in your own programs to load and display bitmaps quickly and easily with an absolute minimum of code.

Figure 11.4 shows the form you use for this example. As you can see, the example uses a picture box to display the image and uses a button to allow users to bring

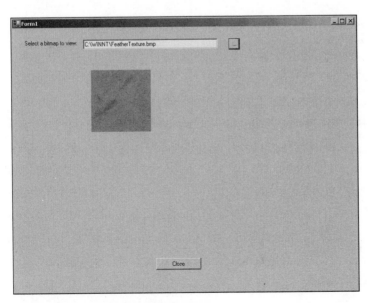

Figure 11.4   The bitmap viewer form.

up an Open File dialog box to select an image to display. All this work is done with just a few lines of code, with the majority of the effort done in the internals of the CLR for C#.

As you can see from the code in Listing 11.3, the code to accomplish this process is simple. All the work of displaying the dialog box and getting the name of the bitmap file name is done in the button handler. Note, however, that this routine does absolutely no filtering or error handling. Both tasks are necessary if you want to convert this example to production-quality code. The private method **ShowBitmap** is used, in a two-step process, to put the image on the screen. First, the image is loaded from the file with the static method **FromFile** of the **Bitmap** class. Next, the image is loaded into the **PictureBox** method by assigning it to the **Image** property of that object. That's all there is to it!

Listing 11.3   Displaying a bitmap in a form.

```
using System;
using System.Drawing;
using System.Collections;
using System.ComponentModel;
using System.Windows.Forms;
using System.Data;

namespace CH11_3
{
    public class Form1 : System.Windows.Forms.Form
    {
        private System.Windows.Forms.Label label1;
        private System.Windows.Forms.TextBox textBox1;
        private System.Windows.Forms.Button button1;
        private System.Windows.Forms.OpenFileDialog openFileDialog1;
        private System.Windows.Forms.PictureBox pictureBox1;
        private System.Windows.Forms.Button button2;
        private System.ComponentModel.Container components = null;

        public Form1()
        {
            InitializeComponent();

        }

        protected override void Dispose( bool disposing )
        {
            if( disposing )
            {
```

```
        if (components != null)
        {
            components.Dispose();
        }
    }
    base.Dispose( disposing );
}

#region Windows Form Designer generated code
private void InitializeComponent()
{
    this.label1 = new System.Windows.Forms.Label();
    this.textBox1 = new System.Windows.Forms.TextBox();
    this.button1 = new System.Windows.Forms.Button();
    this.openFileDialog1 = new System.Windows.Forms.OpenFileDialog();
    this.pictureBox1 = new System.Windows.Forms.PictureBox();
    this.button2 = new System.Windows.Forms.Button();
    this.SuspendLayout();
    this.label1.Location = new System.Drawing.Point(24, 24);
    this.label1.Name = "label1";
    this.label1.Size = new System.Drawing.Size(128, 16);
    this.label1.TabIndex = 0;
    this.label1.Text = "Select a bitmap to view:";
    this.textBox1.Location = new System.Drawing.Point(152, 24);
    this.textBox1.Name = "textBox1";
    this.textBox1.Size = new System.Drawing.Size(288, 20);
    this.textBox1.TabIndex = 1;
    this.textBox1.Text = "textBox1";
    this.button1.Location = new System.Drawing.Point(464, 24);
    this.button1.Name = "button1";
    this.button1.Size = new System.Drawing.Size(24, 23);
    this.button1.TabIndex = 2;
    this.button1.Text = "...";
    this.button1.Click += new
            System.EventHandler(this.button1_Click);
    this.pictureBox1.Location = new System.Drawing.Point(168, 88);
    this.pictureBox1.Name = "pictureBox1";
    this.pictureBox1.Size = new System.Drawing.Size(400, 312);
    this.pictureBox1.TabIndex = 3;
    this.pictureBox1.TabStop = false;
    this.button2.Location = new System.Drawing.Point(304, 480);
    this.button2.Name = "button2";
    this.button2.Size = new System.Drawing.Size(96, 24);
    this.button2.TabIndex = 4;
    this.button2.Text = "&Close";
```

```
                this.button2.Click += new
                        System.EventHandler(this.button2_Click);
                this.AutoScaleBaseSize = new System.Drawing.Size(5, 13);
                this.ClientSize = new System.Drawing.Size(736, 549);
                this.Controls.AddRange(new System.Windows.Forms.Control[] {
                        this.button2,
                        this.pictureBox1,
                        this.button1,
                        this.textBox1,
                        this.label1});
                this.Name = "Form1";
                this.Text = "Form1";
                this.ResumeLayout(false);

        }
        #endregion

        [STAThread]
        static void Main()
        {
            Application.Run(new Form1());
        }
        private void ShowBitmap()
        {
            Image image = Bitmap.FromFile( this.textBox1.Text );
            this.pictureBox1.Image = image;

        }

        private void button1_Click(object sender, System.EventArgs e)
        {
            if ( openFileDialog1.ShowDialog() == DialogResult.OK )
            {
                this.textBox1.Text = this.openFileDialog1.FileName;
                ShowBitmap();
            }
        }

        private void button2_Click(object sender, System.EventArgs e)
        {
            Close();
        }
    }
}
```

Displaying Text

Talking about how to display text might seem odd in a chapter about graphics. In the Windows operating system, however, text is one of the most elegant forms of graphics. In C#, text can easily be displayed using the **Label** class to put text on a form. This class allows you to easily modify, at design time or runtime, the font, color, text, and alignment of the text that is displayed. In this example, you explore how to change these properties and how to make a font-display dialog box that also allows changes to alignment and color.

The core elements of working with text in the C# system are the various text-display components (**RichTextControl** component, **Label** class, and Edit box class, for example) and font components (**FontDialog** class and **Font** class, for example). The color elements are taken care of by the **ForeColor** and **BackColor** properties of the components and by the **ColorDialog** component. Putting all these elements together allows you to control virtually all displayable attributes of your text on the Windows form.

Figure 11.5 shows the form you use to display the textual elements of this example. Because the figure is in black-and-white, you cannot see the colors involved, of course, although the examples on this book's accompanying CD-ROM permit you to play with those as well.

Listing 11.4 shows the code you work with for this form. Compile and run the example, and then play with it. You can change the alignments by clicking on the three radio buttons on the form that control text alignment. You can change the color or font by clicking on either of those buttons and selecting the color or font from the standard dialog boxes that pop up. Note that in this example you have dragged and dropped two dialog boxes to the form. They don't appear visible at design time, but they are there.

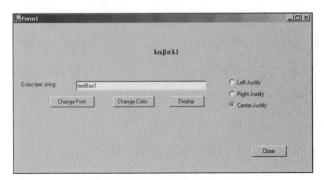

Figure 11.5　The text display form.

Listing 11.4   Displaying text.

```
using System;
using System.Drawing;
using System.Collections;
using System.ComponentModel;
using System.Windows.Forms;
using System.Data;

namespace ch11_4
{
    public class Form1 : System.Windows.Forms.Form
    {
        private System.Windows.Forms.Label label1;
        private System.Windows.Forms.Label label2;
        private System.Windows.Forms.TextBox textBox1;
        private System.Windows.Forms.Button button1;
        private System.Windows.Forms.Button button2;
        private System.Windows.Forms.Button button3;
        private System.Windows.Forms.FontDialog fontDialog1;
        private System.Windows.Forms.RadioButton radioButton1;
        private System.Windows.Forms.RadioButton radioButton2;
        private System.Windows.Forms.RadioButton radioButton3;
        private System.Windows.Forms.Button button4;
        private System.Windows.Forms.ColorDialog colorDialog1;
        private System.ComponentModel.Container components = null;

        public Form1()
        {
            InitializeComponent();
        }

        protected override void Dispose( bool disposing )
        {
            if( disposing )
            {
                if (components != null)
                {
                    components.Dispose();
                }
            }
            base.Dispose( disposing );
        }

        #region Windows Form Designer generated code
        private void InitializeComponent()
```

```
{
    this.label1 = new System.Windows.Forms.Label();
    this.label2 = new System.Windows.Forms.Label();
    this.textBox1 = new System.Windows.Forms.TextBox();
    this.button1 = new System.Windows.Forms.Button();
    this.button2 = new System.Windows.Forms.Button();
    this.button3 = new System.Windows.Forms.Button();
    this.fontDialog1 = new System.Windows.Forms.FontDialog();
    this.radioButton1 = new System.Windows.Forms.RadioButton();
    this.radioButton2 = new System.Windows.Forms.RadioButton();
    this.radioButton3 = new System.Windows.Forms.RadioButton();
    this.button4 = new System.Windows.Forms.Button();
    this.colorDialog1 = new System.Windows.Forms.ColorDialog();
    this.SuspendLayout();
    this.label1.Location = new System.Drawing.Point(56, 40);
    this.label1.Name = "label1";
    this.label1.Size = new System.Drawing.Size(544, 40);
    this.label1.TabIndex = 0;
    this.label1.Text = "label1";
    this.label1.TextAlign =
            System.Drawing.ContentAlignment.MiddleLeft;
    this.label2.Location = new System.Drawing.Point(16, 120);
    this.label2.Name = "label2";
    this.label2.Size = new System.Drawing.Size(104, 24);
    this.label2.TabIndex = 1;
    this.label2.Text = "Enter text string:";
    this.textBox1.Location = new System.Drawing.Point(136, 120);
    this.textBox1.Name = "textBox1";
    this.textBox1.Size = new System.Drawing.Size(280, 20);
    this.textBox1.TabIndex = 2;
    this.textBox1.Text = "textBox1";
    this.button1.Location = new System.Drawing.Point(80, 152);
    this.button1.Name = "button1";
    this.button1.Size = new System.Drawing.Size(96, 23);
    this.button1.TabIndex = 3;
    this.button1.Text = "&Change Font";
    this.button1.Click += new
            System.EventHandler(this.button1_Click);
    this.button2.Location = new System.Drawing.Point(336, 152);
    this.button2.Name = "button2";
    this.button2.TabIndex = 4;
    this.button2.Text = "&Display";
    this.button2.Click += new
            System.EventHandler(this.button2_Click);
    this.button3.Location = new System.Drawing.Point(512, 256);
    this.button3.Name = "button3";
```

```
this.button3.TabIndex = 5;
this.button3.Text = "&Close";
this.button3.Click += new
        System.EventHandler(this.button3_Click);
this.radioButton1.Font =
        new System.Drawing.Font("Microsoft Sans Serif", 8F);
this.radioButton1.Location = new System.Drawing.Point(464, 112);
this.radioButton1.Name = "radioButton1";
this.radioButton1.TabIndex = 6;
this.radioButton1.Text = "Left Justify";
this.radioButton1.CheckedChanged +=
        new System.EventHandler(this.radioButton1_CheckedChanged);
this.radioButton2.Location = new System.Drawing.Point(464, 136);
this.radioButton2.Name = "radioButton2";
this.radioButton2.TabIndex = 7;
this.radioButton2.Text = "Right Justify";
this.radioButton2.CheckedChanged +=
        new System.EventHandler(this.radioButton2_CheckedChanged);
this.radioButton3.Location = new System.Drawing.Point(464, 160);
this.radioButton3.Name = "radioButton3";
this.radioButton3.TabIndex = 8;
this.radioButton3.Text = "Center Justify";
this.radioButton3.CheckedChanged +=
        new System.EventHandler(this.radioButton3_CheckedChanged);
this.button4.Location = new System.Drawing.Point(216, 152);
this.button4.Name = "button4";
this.button4.Size = new System.Drawing.Size(88, 23);
this.button4.TabIndex = 9;
this.button4.Text = "Change Color";
this.button4.Click += new
        System.EventHandler(this.button4_Click);
this.AutoScaleBaseSize = new System.Drawing.Size(5, 13);
this.ClientSize = new System.Drawing.Size(640, 309);
this.Controls.AddRange(new System.Windows.Forms.Control[] {
        this.button4,
        this.radioButton3,
        this.radioButton2,
        this.radioButton1,
        this.button3,
        this.button2,
        this.button1,
        this.textBox1,
        this.label2,
        this.label1});
this.Name = "Form1";
```

```
   this.Text = "Form1";
   this.ResumeLayout(false);

}
#endregion

[STAThread]
static void Main()
{
   Application.Run(new Form1());
}

private void button3_Click(object sender, System.EventArgs e)
{
   Close();
}

private void button1_Click(object sender, System.EventArgs e)
{
   if ( this.fontDialog1.ShowDialog() == DialogResult.OK )
   {
      this.label1.Font = this.fontDialog1.Font;
   }
}

private void radioButton1_CheckedChanged(object sender,
         System.EventArgs e)
{
   this.label1.TextAlign =
         System.Drawing.ContentAlignment.MiddleLeft;
}

private void radioButton2_CheckedChanged(object sender,
         System.EventArgs e)
{
   this.label1.TextAlign =
         System.Drawing.ContentAlignment.MiddleRight;
}

private void radioButton3_CheckedChanged(object sender,
         System.EventArgs e)
{
   this.label1.TextAlign =
         System.Drawing.ContentAlignment.MiddleCenter;
}
```

```
private void button2_Click(object sender, System.EventArgs e)
{
    this.label1.Text = this.textBox1.Text;
}

private void button4_Click(object sender, System.EventArgs e)
{
    if ( this.colorDialog1.ShowDialog() == DialogResult.OK )
    {
        this.label1.ForeColor = this.colorDialog1.Color;
    }
}
}
}
```

Related solution:	Found on page:
Working with an Event Source	205

Drawing from User Input

One of the most famous examples in the MFC tutorial collection is Scribble. This example permits you to draw on a window using the mouse by holding down the left mouse button and moving the mouse around in the window. There is no reason that you can't do the same thing in C#. In fact, you do that in this example, to show how much easier it is to draw in C# using the Windows forms subsystem than it ever was in MFC. The Scribble tutorial in MFC was several dozen pages long and had a few hundred lines of code. As you see in this example, the equivalent in C# is quite small.

Figure 11.6 shows the form as it appears after you have drawn on it. The form itself is simply a blank canvas to which you add some event handlers. The events you need to capture are **MouseDown**, **MouseUp**, **MouseMove**, and **Paint**. Anything else is unnecessary.

Listing 11.5 shows the code used in this example. As you can see, there really isn't much to it. The curious thing is in how you make the drawing appear on the screen. In C#, you have no direct way to draw on a form outside the **Paint** handler. This handler is called whenever the form is obscured or the program or user requests a refresh of the display. Unlike MFC, which permits you to draw anywhere but then makes all the graphics disappear when you refresh the form, C# prefers the more consistent approach.

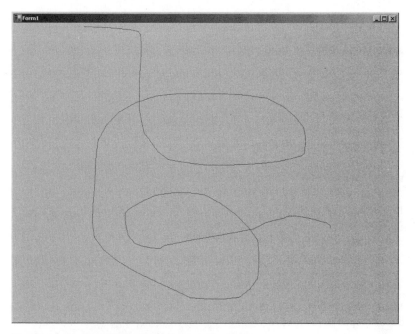

Figure 11.6   The C# Scribble form with drawing.

How does this process work? It's simple: In the **MouseDown** and **MouseMove** event handlers, you collect in an array list—part of the **System.Collections** namespace—all the points the mouse moves through. The **Refresh** method of the form is used to force it to repaint itself. When the repaint event happens, the **OnPaint** method is called. In the **OnPaint** method, you simply "walk" through the array of points, drawing a line between each set. Finally, in the **OnMouseUp** event, you stop collecting points so that the user can quit drawing. In this setup, you can draw only a continuous line, not a series of discrete ones. That would require a collection of arrays rather than a single one.

Listing 11.5   Drawing from user input.

```
using System;
using System.Drawing;
using System.Collections;
using System.ComponentModel;
using System.Windows.Forms;
using System.Data;

namespace ch11_5
{
    public class Form1 : System.Windows.Forms.Form
    {
```

```
private System.ComponentModel.Container components = null;
private Boolean fMouseDown;
private ArrayList fPoints;

public Form1()
{
   InitializeComponent();
   fPoints = new ArrayList();
}

protected override void Dispose( bool disposing )
{
   if( disposing )
   {
      if (components != null)
      {
         components.Dispose();
      }
   }
   base.Dispose( disposing );
}

#region Windows Form Designer generated code
private void InitializeComponent()
{
   this.AutoScaleBaseSize = new System.Drawing.Size(5, 13);
   this.ClientSize = new System.Drawing.Size(824, 621);
   this.Name = "Form1";
   this.Text = "Form1";
   this.MouseDown += new
      System.Windows.Forms.MouseEventHandler(this.OnMouseDown);
   this.MouseUp += new
      System.Windows.Forms.MouseEventHandler(this.OnMouseUp);
   this.Paint += new
      System.Windows.Forms.PaintEventHandler(this.OnPaint);
   this.MouseMove += new
      System.Windows.Forms.MouseEventHandler(this.OnMouseMove);
}
#endregion

[STAThread]
static void Main()
{
   Application.Run(new Form1());
}
```

```csharp
private void OnMouseDown(object sender,
                System.Windows.Forms.MouseEventArgs e)
{
    fMouseDown = true;

    // Clear the array of points
    fPoints.Clear();

    // Add a new point
    Point p = new Point();
    p.X = e.X;
    p.Y = e.Y;
    fPoints.Add( p );
}

private void OnMouseMove(object sender,
                System.Windows.Forms.MouseEventArgs e)
{
    if ( fMouseDown )
    {
        // Add a new point to the array
        Point p = new Point();
        p.X = e.X;
        p.Y = e.Y;
        fPoints.Add( p );

        // And redraw
        this.Refresh();

    }

}

private void OnMouseUp(object sender,
                System.Windows.Forms.MouseEventArgs e)
{
    // Add this point
    Point p = new Point();
    p.X = e.X;
    p.Y = e.Y;
    fPoints.Add( p );

    // Redraw
    this.Refresh();
```

```
                  // And stop collecting points
                  fMouseDown = false;


               }

            private void OnPaint(object sender,
                        System.Windows.Forms.PaintEventArgs e)
            {
               // Move to the first point
               System.Collections.IEnumerator myEnumerator =
                   fPoints.GetEnumerator();
               Pen pen1 = new Pen(Color.FromArgb (150, Color.Purple));
               if ( myEnumerator.MoveNext() )
               {
                  Point p1 = (Point)myEnumerator.Current;
                  while ( myEnumerator.MoveNext() )
                  {
                     Point p2 = (Point)myEnumerator.Current;
                     e.Graphics.DrawLine(pen1, p1, p2);
                     p1 = p2;
                  }
               }
            }
         }
      }
```

Related solution:	Found on page:
Formatting a Rich Edit Control Text String	378

Changing the Font in Controls

One helpful aspect of the C# CLR components is that they are mostly consistent. The same properties exist in virtually all the controls, at least where it makes sense for them to exist. **Color**, **Font**, **Size**—all these properties can be found in any component that has a visible appearance and text. Obviously, an invisible component doesn't need color or font properties. Size means nothing when you are talking about a component that isn't visible, such as a font or color dialog box embedded in a form. As you see in this example, sometimes the properties don't work quite the way you might expect.

In this example, you explore how to change the fonts of various standard controls in the C# CLR system. Figure 11.7 shows the form you work with. As you can

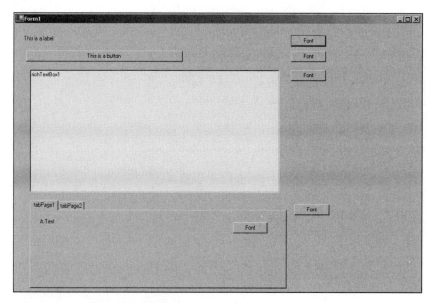

Figure 11.7   The font change form.

see, it contains various components, from a label to a tabbed page, with several items in between. The Font buttons that appear next to each component are used to change the font for that particular component and, in theory, no others. If you play with the form, however, you find that this statement is not necessarily true in all components. For example, changing the font on the tab control changes all the tab pages, and changing the font on a single tab page changes the fonts on only the controls embedded on that page, not on the tabs themselves.

Listing 11.6 shows the code needed to modify the fonts at runtime. As you can see, the process is straightforward and consistent. The only issue is that things don't always happen the way you expect.

Listing 11.6   Changing the font in controls.

```
using System;
using System.Drawing;
using System.Collections;
using System.ComponentModel;
using System.Windows.Forms;
using System.Data;

namespace CH11_6
{
    public class Form1 : System.Windows.Forms.Form
    {
```

```
private System.Windows.Forms.Label label1;
private System.Windows.Forms.Button button1;
private System.Windows.Forms.FontDialog fontDialog1;
private System.Windows.Forms.Button button2;
private System.Windows.Forms.Button button3;
private System.Windows.Forms.RichTextBox richTextBox1;
private System.Windows.Forms.Button button4;
private System.Windows.Forms.TabControl tabControl1;
private System.Windows.Forms.TabPage tabPage1;
private System.Windows.Forms.TabPage tabPage2;
private System.Windows.Forms.Button button5;
private System.Windows.Forms.Label label2;
private System.Windows.Forms.Button button6;
private System.ComponentModel.Container components = null;
public Form1()
{
    InitializeComponent();
}
protected override void Dispose( bool disposing )
{
    if( disposing )
    {
        if (components != null)
        {
            components.Dispose();
        }
    }
    base.Dispose( disposing );
}

#region Windows Form Designer generated code
private void InitializeComponent()
{
    this.label1 = new System.Windows.Forms.Label();
    this.button1 = new System.Windows.Forms.Button();
    this.fontDialog1 = new System.Windows.Forms.FontDialog();
    this.button2 = new System.Windows.Forms.Button();
    this.button3 = new System.Windows.Forms.Button();
    this.richTextBox1 = new System.Windows.Forms.RichTextBox();
    this.button4 = new System.Windows.Forms.Button();
    this.tabControl1 = new System.Windows.Forms.TabControl();
    this.tabPage1 = new System.Windows.Forms.TabPage();
    this.tabPage2 = new System.Windows.Forms.TabPage();
    this.button5 = new System.Windows.Forms.Button();
    this.label2 = new System.Windows.Forms.Label();
```

```
this.button6 = new System.Windows.Forms.Button();
this.tabControl1.SuspendLayout();
this.tabPage1.SuspendLayout();
this.SuspendLayout();
this.label1.Location = new System.Drawing.Point(16, 24);
this.label1.Name = "label1";
this.label1.Size = new System.Drawing.Size(528, 23);
this.label1.TabIndex = 0;
this.label1.Text = "This is a label";
this.button1.Location = new System.Drawing.Point(592, 24);
this.button1.Name = "button1";
this.button1.TabIndex = 1;
this.button1.Text = "Font";
this.button1.Click += new
        System.EventHandler(this.button1_Click);
this.button2.Font = new
        System.Drawing.Font("Microsoft Sans Serif", 8F);
this.button2.Location = new System.Drawing.Point(24, 56);
this.button2.Name = "button2";
this.button2.Size = new System.Drawing.Size(336, 23);
this.button2.TabIndex = 2;
this.button2.Text = "This is a button";
this.button3.Location = new System.Drawing.Point(592, 56);
this.button3.Name = "button3";
this.button3.TabIndex = 3;
this.button3.Text = "Font";
this.button3.Click += new
        System.EventHandler(this.button3_Click);
this.richTextBox1.Location = new System.Drawing.Point(32, 96);
this.richTextBox1.Name = "richTextBox1";
this.richTextBox1.Size = new System.Drawing.Size(536, 256);
this.richTextBox1.TabIndex = 4;
this.richTextBox1.Text = "richTextBox1";
this.button4.Location = new System.Drawing.Point(592, 96);
this.button4.Name = "button4";
this.button4.TabIndex = 5;
this.button4.Text = "Font";
this.button4.Click += new
        System.EventHandler(this.button4_Click);
this.tabControl1.Controls.AddRange(new
    System.Windows.Forms.Control[] {
        this.tabPage1,
        this.tabPage2} );
this.tabControl1.Location = new System.Drawing.Point(32, 368);
this.tabControl1.Name = "tabControl1";
```

```
this.tabControl1.SelectedIndex = 0;
this.tabControl1.Size = new System.Drawing.Size(552, 184);
this.tabControl1.TabIndex = 6;
this.tabPage1.Controls.AddRange(new
        System.Windows.Forms.Control[] {
            this.button6,  this.label2});
this.tabPage1.Location = new System.Drawing.Point(4, 22);
this.tabPage1.Name = "tabPage1";
this.tabPage1.Size = new System.Drawing.Size(544, 158);
this.tabPage1.TabIndex = 0;
this.tabPage1.Text = "tabPage1";
this.tabPage2.Location = new System.Drawing.Point(4, 22);
this.tabPage2.Name = "tabPage2";
this.tabPage2.Size = new System.Drawing.Size(544, 158);
this.tabPage2.TabIndex = 1;
this.tabPage2.Text = "tabPage2";
this.button5.Location = new System.Drawing.Point(600, 376);
this.button5.Name = "button5";
this.button5.TabIndex = 7;
this.button5.Text = "Font";
this.button5.Click += new
        System.EventHandler(this.button5_Click);
this.label2.Location = new System.Drawing.Point(16, 16);
this.label2.Name = "label2";
this.label2.TabIndex = 0;
this.label2.Text = "A Test";
this.button6.Location = new System.Drawing.Point(432, 24);
this.button6.Name = "button6";
this.button6.TabIndex = 1;
this.button6.Text = "Font";
this.button6.Click += new
        System.EventHandler(this.button6_Click);
this.AutoScaleBaseSize = new System.Drawing.Size(5, 13);
this.ClientSize = new System.Drawing.Size(872, 557);
this.Controls.AddRange(new System.Windows.Forms.Control[] {
        this.button5, this.tabControl1,  this.button4,
        this.richTextBox1, this.button3,  this.button2,
        this.button1,  this.label1});
this.Name = "Form1";
this.Text = "Form1";
this.tabControl1.ResumeLayout(false);
this.tabPage1.ResumeLayout(false);
this.ResumeLayout(false);
}
```

```
#endregion
[STAThread]
static void Main()
{
    Application.Run(new Form1());
}
private void button1_Click(object sender, System.EventArgs e)
{
    if ( this.fontDialog1.ShowDialog() == DialogResult.OK )
    {
        this.label1.Font = this.fontDialog1.Font;
    }
}
private void button3_Click(object sender, System.EventArgs e)
{
    if ( this.fontDialog1.ShowDialog() == DialogResult.OK )
    {
        this.button2.Font = this.fontDialog1.Font;
    }
}
private void button4_Click(object sender, System.EventArgs e)
{
    if ( this.fontDialog1.ShowDialog() == DialogResult.OK )
    {
        this.richTextBox1.Font = this.fontDialog1.Font;
    }
}
private void button5_Click(object sender, System.EventArgs e)
{
    if ( this.fontDialog1.ShowDialog() == DialogResult.OK )
    {
        this.tabControl1.Font = this.fontDialog1.Font;
    }
}
private void button6_Click(object sender, System.EventArgs e)
{
    if ( this.fontDialog1.ShowDialog() == DialogResult.OK )
    {
        this.tabPage1.Font = this.fontDialog1.Font;
    }
}
}
}
```

11. Graphics

Rotating Text

Once upon a time, rotating fonts was a well-known and well-understood issue in working with the graphical display in Windows. Programmers simply stole a piece of code that worked to rotate a TrueType font and then used that code to display the rotated text on their window displays. The methodology was simple: The font had properties named **Escapement** and **Orientation**, which were used to rotate the text displayed in that font by an arbitrary number of degrees. Many programmers jumped on that bandwagon and then moved to C#, only to discover that the **Font** class has no such properties. What is a programmer to do?

The good news is that rotating text and any other sort of object in C# is easier than it used to be. The bad news is that the way in which you rotate text is not readily apparent. In this example, you look at a way to rotate text by an arbitrary angle, regardless of the font family and type used to display it. Figure 11.8 shows the result of the font rotation form in action. The buttons at the bottom of the form are used to control the angle at runtime.

The code to perform the translations is shown in Listing 11.7. Let's take a look at the code first and then discuss how it works. Note the shaded portion of the listing—that's the code you look at.

Listing 11.7   Rotating text.

```
using System;
using System.Drawing;
using System.Collections;
```

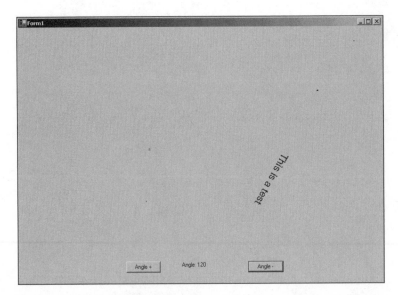

Figure 11.8   The font rotation form.

```
using System.ComponentModel;
using System.Windows.Forms;
using System.Data;

namespace ch11_7
{
    public class Form1 : System.Windows.Forms.Form
    {
        private System.ComponentModel.Container components = null;
        private System.Windows.Forms.Button button1;
        private System.Windows.Forms.Button button2;
        private System.Windows.Forms.Label label1;
        private float fAngle;

        public Form1()
        {
            InitializeComponent();

            fAngle = 0;
        }
        protected override void Dispose( bool disposing )
        {
            if( disposing )
            {
                if (components != null)
                {
                    components.Dispose();
                }
            }
            base.Dispose( disposing );
        }

        #region Windows Form Designer generated code
        private void InitializeComponent()
        {
            this.button1 = new System.Windows.Forms.Button();
            this.button2 = new System.Windows.Forms.Button();
            this.label1 = new System.Windows.Forms.Label();
            this.SuspendLayout();
            this.button1.Location = new System.Drawing.Point(232, 488);
            this.button1.Name = "button1";
            this.button1.TabIndex = 0;
            this.button1.Text = "Angle +";
            this.button1.Click += new
                    System.EventHandler(this.button1_Click);
            this.button2.Location = new System.Drawing.Point(496, 488);
            this.button2.Name = "button2";
```

```
            this.button2.TabIndex = 1;
            this.button2.Text = "Angle -";
            this.button2.Click += new
                    System.EventHandler(this.button2_Click);
            this.label1.Location = new System.Drawing.Point(352, 488);
            this.label1.Name = "label1";
            this.label1.TabIndex = 2;
            this.label1.Text = "Angle: 0";
            this.AutoScaleBaseSize = new System.Drawing.Size(5, 13);
            this.ClientSize = new System.Drawing.Size(784, 533);
            this.Controls.AddRange(new System.Windows.Forms.Control[] {
                                                    this.label1,
                                                    this.button2,
                                                    this.button1});
            this.Name = "Form1";
            this.Text = "Form1";
            this.Paint +=
                    new System.Windows.Forms.PaintEventHandler(this.OnPaint);
            this.ResumeLayout(false);

        }
        #endregion
        [STAThread]
        static void Main()
        {
            Application.Run(new Form1());
        }


        void DrawRotatedString(Graphics g, string text, Font font, Brush br,
            Rectangle rect, StringFormat format, float angle)
        {
            Point center = new Point(rect.X+rect.Width/2,
                rect.Y+rect.Height/2);
            g.TranslateTransform(center.X, center.Y);
            g.RotateTransform(angle);
            rect.Offset(-center.X, -center.Y);

            g.DrawString(text, font, br, rect, format);
            g.ResetTransform();
        }


        private void OnPaint(object sender,
                System.Windows.Forms.PaintEventArgs e)
        {
            // Create the font.
            Font f = new Font("MS Sans Serif", 16);
```

```
        Rectangle layoutRect = new
                Rectangle( new Point(Width/2, Height/2),
                new Size(200,100));

        string text = "This is a test";

        // Get the format
        StringFormat fmt = new StringFormat();

        // Draw the text
        DrawRotatedString( e.Graphics, "This is a test", f,
            new SolidBrush(Color.Blue), layoutRect, fmt, fAngle);
    }

    private void button1_Click(object sender, System.EventArgs e)
    {
        fAngle += 10;
        this.label1.Text = "Angle: " + fAngle;
        this.Refresh();
    }

    private void button2_Click(object sender, System.EventArgs e)
    {
        fAngle -= 10;
        this.label1.Text = "Angle: " + fAngle;
        this.Refresh();
    }
  }
}
```

To work with rotations, translations, or other movements in the graphics system, you use the transformation objects. In this example, you first use the **TranslateTransform** method to move the center of rotation to the center of the text string. This step is needed because rotation takes place in the upper-left corner of the transform area. You need to move the rectangle center to this point, so you translate it to that region. After the rectangle has been translated, you simply rotate the rectangle about that point by using the **RotateTransform** method with the angle the user specifies. In the case of positive angles, the text string is rotated clockwise (to the right); in the case of negative angles, the text string is rotated counterclockwise (to the left). In either case, after the transformation is complete, you draw the text string and reset all the transformations to their defaults by using the **ResetTransform** method.

NOTE: *Because the transformation process applies to the drawing of the individual pixels on the screen, you can use this same method for rotating lines, shapes, or anything else that can be rendered in a form window.*

---

11. Graphics

Creating a PNG File on the Fly

The PNG format is a neutral standard for use on the Internet. Unlike the JPEG or GIF formats, PNG is not owned or operated by any company, making it perfect for sending images across the Internet for sharing with others. The PNG compression ratio makes it an excellent choice for working with images in low-bandwidth environments, such as dial-up modem access to the Internet. Not surprisingly, Microsoft has built PNG support into C#.

When you think of graphics files, you generally think of disk files that contain precreated images you can load into your applications. This statement doesn't have to be true, however, because you can generate graphics on the fly and save them to disk for use in either your own applications or others. After all, paint programs do it all the time—why shouldn't you be able to? In C#, by using the classes of the CLR, you can easily this functionality to your own programs. In this example, you create a graphics image, store it to a disk file, and then load it into a standard **PictureBox** control to show that everything is working properly.

Figure 11.9 shows the form you work with for this example. As you can see, the form contains a picture box and three buttons for use in generating the graphics image, loading it from disk, and closing the application.

How do you generate the graphic and save it? Listing 11.8 shows the code needed to create a dynamic graphic and save it to a file. As you can see, it is not a particularly complicated affair.

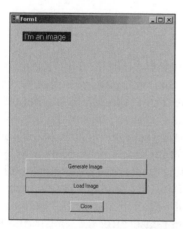

Figure 11.9   The dynamic graphics form.

Listing 11.8   Creating a PNG file on the fly.

```
using System;
using System.Drawing;
using System.Collections;
using System.ComponentModel;
using System.Windows.Forms;

using System.Data;
using System.Drawing.Imaging;

namespace CH11_8
{
    public class Form1 : System.Windows.Forms.Form
    {
        private System.Windows.Forms.Button button1;
        private System.Windows.Forms.Button button2;
        private System.Windows.Forms.Button button3;
        private System.Windows.Forms.PictureBox pictureBox1;
        private System.ComponentModel.Container components = null;

        public Form1()
        {
            InitializeComponent();
        }
        protected override void Dispose( bool disposing )
        {
            if( disposing )
            {
                if (components != null)
                {
                    components.Dispose();
                }
            }
            base.Dispose( disposing );
        }

        #region Windows Form Designer generated code
        private void InitializeComponent()
        {
            this.button1 = new System.Windows.Forms.Button();
            this.button2 = new System.Windows.Forms.Button();
            this.button3 = new System.Windows.Forms.Button();
            this.pictureBox1 = new System.Windows.Forms.PictureBox();
            this.SuspendLayout();
            this.button1.Location = new System.Drawing.Point(32, 280);
            this.button1.Name = "button1";
```

```
            this.button1.Size = new System.Drawing.Size(264, 32);
            this.button1.TabIndex = 0;
            this.button1.Text = "Generate Image";
            this.button1.Click += new
                System.EventHandler(this.button1_Click);
            this.button2.Location = new System.Drawing.Point(32, 320);
            this.button2.Name = "button2";
            this.button2.Size = new System.Drawing.Size(264, 32);
            this.button2.TabIndex = 1;
            this.button2.Text = "Load Image";
            this.button2.Click += new
                System.EventHandler(this.button2_Click);
            this.button3.Location = new System.Drawing.Point(128, 368);
            this.button3.Name = "button3";
            this.button3.TabIndex = 3;
            this.button3.Text = "&Close";
            this.button3.Click += new
                System.EventHandler(this.button3_Click);
            this.pictureBox1.Location = new System.Drawing.Point(24, 16);
            this.pictureBox1.Name = "pictureBox1";
            this.pictureBox1.Size = new System.Drawing.Size(272, 240);
            this.pictureBox1.TabIndex = 4;
            this.pictureBox1.TabStop = false;
            this.AutoScaleBaseSize = new System.Drawing.Size(5, 13);
            this.ClientSize = new System.Drawing.Size(352, 405);
            this.Controls.AddRange(new System.Windows.Forms.Control[] {
                this.pictureBox1,
                this.button3,
                this.button2,
                this.button1});
            this.Name = "Form1";
            this.Text = "Form1";
            this.ResumeLayout(false);

        }
        #endregion
        [STAThread]
        static void Main()
        {
            Application.Run(new Form1());
        }

        private void button3_Click(object sender, System.EventArgs e)
        {
            Close();
        }
```

```
private void button1_Click(object sender, System.EventArgs e)
{
    // Initialize the graphic objects we need
    Bitmap theBitmap = null;
    Graphics grfx = null ;

    try
    {
        Font theFont = new Font("MS Sans Serif", 12);

        // Calculate the size of the string.
        theBitmap = new Bitmap(1,1,PixelFormat.Format32bppArgb);

        // Create the graphics object so we can draw
        grfx = Graphics.FromImage(theBitmap);

        // Build the width of the image from the string
        SizeF stringSize =
            grfx.MeasureString("I'm an Image!", theFont);
        int nWidth = (int)stringSize.Width;
        int nHeight = (int)stringSize.Height;
        grfx.Dispose();
        theBitmap.Dispose();

        // Re-create it with the right dimensions
        theBitmap = new
                Bitmap(nWidth,nHeight,PixelFormat.Format32bppArgb);
        grfx = Graphics.FromImage(theBitmap);
        grfx.FillRectangle(new SolidBrush(Color.Blue),
        new Rectangle(0,0,nWidth,nHeight));

        grfx.DrawString("I'm an image", theFont,
                new SolidBrush(Color.White), 0, 0);
        theBitmap.Save("c:\\matt\\c#\\ch11_8.png", ImageFormat.Png);
    }
    catch (Exception exc)
    {
        MessageBox.Show(this, exc.ToString());
    }
    finally
    {
        if (grfx != null)
        grfx.Dispose();
        if (theBitmap != null)
        theBitmap.Dispose();
    }
}
```

```
private void button2_Click(object sender, System.EventArgs e)
{
    // Load the image from the file into the picture box
    this.pictureBox1.Image =
        Image.FromFile("c:\\matt\\c#\\ch11_8.png");
}
}
}
```

Chapter 12

Threads

In Depth

When you think of an application, you might be reminded of a tapestry: All the little pieces of the tapestry are made up of individual components in your application source code. The tapestry itself is the final, beautiful piece of art your users will admire and use to decorate their walls. Okay, maybe you don't want your application decorating a wall—"That's shelfware" is an awful thing to say about a program. However, the analogy still holds true. A program is a tapestry, and it is made up of individual weavings. These weavings are built around threads, just as they are in a real tapestry.

In this chapter, I discuss the concept of threads and multithreading in applications. The first question that comes to mind, of course, is "What is a thread?" A *thread* is (from the perspective of the machine's CPU, not of the user) a single unit of program execution. A thread cannot be interrupted by anything at a lower level and does not contain smaller units of execution (except, of course, for individual program statements).

If one thread is in a program, as in the old MS-DOS applications, that's a *single-threaded* application. If, on the other hand, a number of different threads are doing different tasks in the application, it's a *multithreaded* application. The latter subject is what you tackle in this chapter.

What Is Multithreading?

Now that you know the definition of multithreading, what does it mean to an application programmer? On modern computer equipment, threading is the most efficient way to do more than one thing at a time. Unless you have multiple processors, no chance exists of the machine doing two or more tasks at exactly the same time; with fast processors and efficient time-slicing algorithms, however, a machine can appear to work on numerous different tasks—even within a single application—at the same instant. Obviously, this feature has tremendous potential for programmers because you often want to do tasks simultaneously. First, let's examine the types of cases under which you might want to use a multithreaded application.

Why Would You Want to Use Threading in Your Application?

Suppose that a program needs to search for data in response to a user query. Smart soul that you are, you want to do a little background work each time a user starts a search. For example, you might want to know if all the databases you access during your search will be available when the user clicks the Search button on your form. Perhaps you want to see what she has searched for in the past so that you can see whether that information applies to the current search criteria.

The first option that might come to mind is some sort of polling loop that calls an idle function when the user is not pressing keys to enter search criteria. Given the time that it takes the average person to type a search string, and the speed of modern computers, this idea might not be a bad one. After all, you can do a great deal in those milliseconds between keystrokes. The problem is that after your application has started querying a database, the search virtually cannot stop until the function you use to query the database has finished.

"Okay," you may say, "I'll write an asynchronous routine that sends a message to the application whenever a database is available." This process is in keeping with the whole Windows messaging system, and it works fine. After trying to debug your application crashes, which were caused by too many tasks going on at the same time, however, you find that it just isn't worth it. Of course, an easier way exists: a background thread.

In any case where you are considering some sort of a polling or idle loop, you should reexamine the code and see if a separate thread would be a better idea, particularly if the background process has nothing to do with the foreground, or GUI, process. These kinds of situations are designed for a multithreaded solution.

Another tailor-made situation for a multithreaded application is that of a socket-based server. You have requests coming in, and messages going out, to multiple clients at the same time. Although you could potentially service each customer on a first-in, first-out basis, this strategy would lead to timeouts and other problems when the returned data got very large. Instead, having a separate thread handling each request makes more sense, where the only one paying a penalty for using a large reply is the one that made the request for it.

You probably have more reasons to use a second, third, or fourth thread in your applications than you have reasons not to use them. The one problem with multithreading applications is that they need to be designed from the ground up to be multithreaded. Adding threading to a program that was not intended to be multithreaded from the start is difficult and dangerous.

How Do You Use Threading in Your Application?

Obviously, you must understand the critical issues in working with threading before you can start working with threads in your own applications. Let's start with the simple tasks, like starting and stopping a thread, and then move on to the more complicated issues in working with threaded applications.

To run a thread, you need a thread procedure. Next, you must create the thread object. When a thread starts, this procedure is called to do the actual work of the thread. When the procedure terminates, the thread stops. Therefore, your thread procedure needs to have a looping mechanism built into it in order to continue processing in the background. Take a look at a simple example of a thread procedure that simply prints a message to the console every second:

```
protected void ThreadFunc()
{
    Boolean done = false;
    int counter = 0;
    while ( !done )
    {
        Thread.Sleep(1000);
        counter ++;
        Console.WriteLine("Counter: {0}", counter);
    }
}
```

This procedure does what you expect: It runs forever, printing a counter whenever the sleep function returns, which is every second. You have no way to terminate this thread from inside the function, nor does it check for an outside force that might exit the loop. Obviously, this situation is not ideal for a normal thread. The problem is that when the remainder of the application terminates, this thread continues to run, which, for one thing, makes recompiling an application very hard because Windows does not allow you to write to the executable file while the program is still running. Windows considers a program to still be running whenever a single thread is open.

Assume, for the moment, that this situation is what you want and that you don't mind that this thread would run forever. How do you go about launching this thread from within the remainder of your application code? The following code snippet illustrates how to create a thread and then start it running:

```
Thread fThread = new Thread( new ThreadStart(ThreadFunc) );
fThread.Start();
```

Running the thread involves two parts: First, you must create a new **Thread** object. The constructor for the **Thread** class takes a single argument, a **ThreadStart** object. The **ThreadStart** object is a delegate that is invoked when the **Start** method is called for the **Thread** object. The second part, therefore, consists of starting up the **Thread** object by calling that **Start** method.

After you call the **Start** method of the class, the thread starts itself and the thread procedure starts running. You see this process happen if you compile the complete console thread application shown here:

```
using System;
using System.Threading;

namespace Ch12ThreadConsole
{
   class Class1
   {
      protected static void ThreadFunc()
      {
         Boolean done = false;
         int counter = 0;
         while ( !done )
         {
            Thread.Sleep(1000);
            counter ++;
            Console.WriteLine("Counter: {0}", counter);
         }
      }

      static void Main(string[] args)
      {
         Thread fThread = new Thread( new ThreadStart(ThreadFunc) );
         fThread.Start();
      }
   }
}
```

A few parts of this application are interesting. First, notice that in order to use the threading classes in your application, you need to include the **System.Threading** class library as a reference to your application. Fortunately, the threading classes are found in the System.DLL library, so you do not need to include any new DLLs in your link line. The second interesting aspect is that the threading procedure has been modified slightly from the first time you saw it. Notably, the **static** keyword was introduced to make this a static method of the class. This step is necessary because the **Main** function of the class does not create an object to use with the method. However, it also points out an interesting aspect of working with threads: Unlike in Windows C++ programming, you can use an object method as a thread procedure. That is, if you had left off the **static** keyword, you could have rewritten the **Main** function as follows:

```
static void Main(string[] args)
{
    Class1 c1 = new Class1();
    Thread fThread = new Thread( new ThreadStart(c1.ThreadFunc) );
    fThread.Start();
}
```

Why is this possibility important? Normally, in a Windows application, you could not reach any class-level properties or methods of an object from within a thread function because the thread function is just that—a function. In C#, however, the thread procedure can be either a static method (function) or a true class method. In the latter case, the method would have access to any class-level variables it needed at runtime. As you see in just a few pages, this concept could have important ramifications in how you design thread procedures.

Of course, a static method would have access to the static class variables of the class in which it is created as well as of any other class. However, that is often not what is needed to make everything work properly.

Here is the output from this console application when you run it from the command line:

```
C:\ >Ch12ThreadConsole
Counter: 1
Counter: 2
Counter: 3
Counter: 4
Counter: 5
Counter: 6
^C
```

As you can see, to stop the application and the thread, you need to kill the program by using the Ctrl+C keyboard combination. This technique obviously is not the ideal way to work with an application. There must be an easier way to stop a thread after it is running. But how?

Let's look at two possible ways in which you can shut down an application thread while it is running: The first method takes advantage of the fact that a thread procedure can be a true method of a class, and the second uses the more generic approach associated with the threading library.

First, you need to modify the little console application to use more class-level information. Then, you need to create a way to stop the thread externally from the thread procedure. To do this, you allow the user to enter a command to stop the program. In this case, to keep the process simple, you just have the user enter anything and press Enter. This action causes a class-level variable to change its state, which is reflected in the thread procedure. To do this, you change the thread procedure to use a class-level variable rather than a local variable. Here's the modified console application:

```
using System;
using System.Threading;

namespace Ch12ThreadConsole
{
    class Class1
    {
        Boolean bDone = false;
        protected void ThreadFunc()
        {
            int counter = 0;
            while ( !bDone )
            {
                Thread.Sleep(1000);
                counter ++;
                Console.WriteLine("Counter: {0}", counter);
            }
        }

        static void Main(string[] args)
        {
            Class1 c1 = new Class1();
            Thread fThread = new Thread( new ThreadStart(c1.ThreadFunc) );
            fThread.Start();
            Console.Write(
                "Enter a string and press return to stop the app: ");
            string s = Console.ReadLine();
            c1.bDone = true;
        }
    }
}
```

The important changes to the program are shown in the shaded sections of the code. Now, when you run the program, pressing Enter terminates the thread and shuts down the application. Give it a try, and you'll see that it works as advertised.

This approach has a slight snag, however. What happens if multiple threads are running with the same procedure? This approach is perfectly acceptable in C#, and it happens frequently in such events as socket applications. For example, the **Main** function could have the following lines of code in it rather than simply one set:

```
Thread fThread1 = new Thread( new ThreadStart(c1.ThreadFunc) );
FThread1.Start();
Thread fThread2 = new Thread( new ThreadStart(c1.ThreadFunc) );
FThread2.Start();
Thread fThread3 = new Thread( new ThreadStart(c1.ThreadFunc) );
FThread3.Start();
```

This example is obviously not what you would normally do in an application because all three threads would simply print information to the console. In fact, if you run this little application, modified with the three threads rather than one, you see the following output to the console:

```
C:\ >Ch12ThreadConsole
Enter a string and press return to stop the app: Counter: 1
Counter: 1
Counter: 1
Counter: 2
Counter: 2
Counter: 2
Counter: 3
Counter: 3
Counter: 3

Counter: 4
Terminating
Counter: 4
Terminating
Counter: 4
Terminating
```

NOTE: *I added a* **Terminating** *statement at the end of the thread procedure so that you can see when tasks are ending and in what order. The remainder of the program is the same, however.*

The problem is that you might not want to kill all the threads at one time. Perhaps you want to kill only one of them in response to a user action. Suppose that you have a background search thread that can be used for a variety of tasks. One search thread runs at all times, looking for common words to index; another search thread checks for copyright violations in typed text; and a third thread runs a user search for keywords in some text. If you simply shut down all the tasks, you are likely ending a thread that still needs to run. So the question is "How do you stop a single thread you know about in an application?"

The answer lies in the **Abort** and **Interrupt** methods of the **Thread** class. These two methods can be used to stop a thread, either instantly or in a slightly more gentle fashion. The methods are called in the **Thread** handling function. For example, you can add the following code in the **Main** function to stop the threads when a user presses a key:

```
static void Main(string[] args)
{
    Class1 c1 = new Class1();
    Thread fThread1 = new Thread( new ThreadStart(c1.ThreadFunc) );
    fThread1.Start();
    Thread fThread2 = new Thread( new ThreadStart(c1.ThreadFunc) );
    fThread2.Start();
    Thread fThread3 = new Thread( new ThreadStart(c1.ThreadFunc) );
    fThread3.Start();
    while ( c1.bDone == false )
    {
        Console.Write("Enter a string and press return to stop the app: ");
        string s = Console.ReadLine();
        if ( s == "1" )
            fThread1.Abort();
        if ( s == "2" )
            fThread2.Abort();
        if ( s == "3" )
            fThread3.Abort();
        if ( s == "a" || s == "A" )
            c1.bDone = true;
    }
}
```

When you run the program now, it loops around, asking what you want to kill each time. Pressing the numbers 1 through 3 terminates each thread. Pressing the A key terminates all remaining threads and terminates the application. This solution is obviously better than simply killing all the threads at one time.

The **Interrupt** method is similar, but a bit different. It sends an interrupt exception to the thread. The actual exception that is sent, **ThreadInterrupted-Exception**, can be caught by the underlying thread procedure and either handled or allowed to kill the thread. If you modify the preceding code to use the **Interrupt** method rather than the **Abort** method, you see that it can have the same effect.

Background Threads

If you have worked in the programming world for some time, you have heard of a *background* thread. This thread runs at a lower priority and in a different process than the main GUI of the application. Background threads are excellent for performing tasks that do not need to be done immediately and that you don't want to have to wait for when you want them done. A background thread is a good choice for doing look-aheads in searching (checking for things a user hasn't yet asked for, but is likely to) or for cleaning out files when they are no longer needed. Background threads are also ideal for program-level garbage collection, such as eliminating temporary files and directories that were created during a process in the program.

Fortunately, C# makes converting a thread into a background thread particularly easy: All you need to do is modify a single property of the thread object, **IsBackground**, and set it to true. Background threads working in C# applications have a number of issues you need to be aware of, however. For one thing, you cannot directly work with data references outside the process in which the thread is operating. Because the GUI elements of C# operate in their own process, therefore, you can't talk directly to a GUI element, such as a list box, from within a background thread.

How Do You Communicate with a Thread?

How do you go about talking to a background thread from a GUI element and vice versa? The answer lies in the **MethodInvoker** delegate entity. This delegate allows you to move data back and forth between various processes without crashing your application or the thread in which you are working. To use the **MethodInvoker** delegate, you need three items:

- A background thread from which to create the delegate
- A class-level method with which to interface the thread and the foreground visual elements
- A visual element in your application that can be updated

Here's a simple example of using a background thread to talk to a foreground visual element. You look at this example more closely in "Talking to Visual Elements from a Background Thread" in the "Immediate Solutions" section later in this chapter. Assume that a foreground element is a label and that you want to update the text on this label whenever the thread is running. To do this, you first create a background thread:

```
Thread fThread = new Thread( new ThreadStart(ThreadFunc) );
FThread.IsBackground = true;
fThread.Start();
```

Note that you have set the **IsBackground** property to true so that this thread is a background thread. Next, you need the method for working with this background thread—its processing function. Within this processing function, you create a delegate that permits you to talk to another method in the class, which updates the label:

```
public void ThreadProc()
{
   try
   {
      MethodInvoker mi = new MethodInvoker(this.UpdateLabel);
      while (true)
      {
         bCounter ++;
         this.BeginInvoke (mi);
         Thread.Sleep(500) ;
      }
   }
   catch (ThreadInterruptedException e)
   {
      Console.WriteLine("Interruption Exception in Thread: {0}", e );
   }
   catch (Exception we)
   {
      Console.WriteLine("Exception in Thread: {0}", we );
   }
}
```

You must complete two tasks in this procedure:

- Create a new delegate that can communicate with the method—in this case, **UpdateLabel**.
- Call the **Invoke** method of the delegate whenever you want the update to take place.

Finally, you need the update function, which is simple. Here is the code you might use:

```
public void UpdateLabel()
{
   label1.Text = bCounter.ToString();
}
```

Of course, the **bCounter** variable has to be a class-level variable so that it can be read from either the background thread or the foreground thread. Because these variables exist in the object itself, they are automatically marshaled across from one process to another (pointers and data are moved so that they retain the same values) and allow either method to work with them.

How Do You Close Down a Threaded Application?

In this chapter, I've discussed how an application does not completely shut down while an active thread is running. In many cases, however, that active thread can't simply run its course and terminate before the program shuts down. A thread used to poll a given hardware device, for example, needs to run until it is terminated, not when the need for its services run out—because they never will. In this case, you need to be sure that all the threads in your applications terminate.

The best place to terminate all the threads in an application is in the **Dispose** method of the class that created the threads in the first place. The best way to do this task is simply to keep track of all the threads you create in an application in an array. Then this array can be processed in the **Dispose** method, as shown in this code snippet:

```
protected override void Dispose( bool disposing )
{
    if( disposing )
    {
        if (components != null)
        {
            components.Dispose();

            for ( int i=0; i<fThreadList.Count; ++i )
            {
                Thread fThread = (Thread)fThreadList[ i ];
                fThread.Abort();
            }
        }
    }
    base.Dispose( disposing );
}
```

Concurrency

When someone talks about multithreading applications, the first caution flag that always jumps into anyone's mind is the issue of concurrency. Although it's useful to have a program that does many tasks at the same time, it is also often dangerous. For example, if multiple tasks try to delete the same block of memory at the same time, a problem will certainly occur. To solve this issue, C# introduces the concept of critical sections and locking.

A *critical* section, in programming parlance, is one that can be entered by only a single process at a time. You can think of this concept as a gate that cuts down the width of a multilane road to a single lane for a brief period. Obviously, if lots of traffic is on the road, the gate leads to severe backups in the rest of the traffic. So it is with critical sections. You must take care to lock up only the smallest portion of the code you need to protect in a program.

Critical Sections and Locking

C# addresses the issue of critical sections through the **lock** statement. This statement ensures that the code that follows it, whether it's a single line or a block of C# statements, is executed by a maximum of a single process at a time. You look at the **lock** statement in some detail in "Synchronizing Multiple Threads" in the "Immediate Solutions" section later in this chapter; for now, however, just look at why you might want one.

Consider the following block of code. You are incrementing an index value, checking it, and then using it to index into an array. Seems like a simple enough piece of code, doesn't it?

```
index ++;
if ( index > MaxIndex )
    return;
int nValue = Values[index];
```

You would not normally think that this piece of code could cause any problems. After all, you checked the index value before you used it to index into the array, right? Now consider what happens when a hundred threads are running this same piece of code, entering into it at different times. One of the threads might be on the index increment statement, and the other might be on the retrieval of the indexed value statement.

What do you suppose happens if the index happens to be **MaxIndex** when it enters the second thread-processing function? The answer is simple: The index is incremented by the second thread processing function, and then the function returns because it has reached its maximum. No problem? Big problem. The problem occurs when the first thread, which has just seen its index incremented, tries to access the data in the **Values** array. The index is now too big, and an exception is thrown, probably crashing the application. That's not exactly what you had in mind, and the exception is hard to track down when you're debugging the code.

How can you fix this particular problem? The answer lies in the aforementioned **lock** statement. All you need to do is modify the code so that it looks like this:

```
int nValue = 0;
lock
{
    index ++;
    if ( index > MaxIndex )
        return;
    nValue = Values[index];
}
// Do whatever
```

Now, whenever the code reaches the **lock** statement, the second thread processing function is "locked out" and cannot increment the index again before the first processing function has finished accessing the data. This process makes the block of code *atomic*, which mean that it executes all at once or not at all.

That pretty much sums up the threading library in C# and how it is used. Threading is an extremely important and powerful function in programming and one you should strongly consider in your own applications. At this point, turn your attention to the "Immediate Solutions" section of this chapter, where you can get some full code examples of the tasks I have talked about in this chapter.

Immediate Solutions

Creating a New Thread

Creating a thread is the first step in creating multiple threaded applications. Fortunately, creating threads in C# is not particularly difficult. The process is reasonably straightforward, as you see in this example. First, you create a **Thread** object. The constructor for the **Thread** object accepts a single argument, which is the function you want to call for processing the thread. The second step is to call the **Start** method of the **Thread** object to get everything going.

Within the thread-handling function is where all the action is. This normal C# method, static or otherwise, is used to process the information for the thread.

NOTE: *If this method exits, the thread ends. You must stay inside this method until you are ready to exit your thread. You normally do this via some sort of loop construct.*

Figure 12.1 shows the form you use to create a thread. The button at the top of the form is used to start a new thread and is disabled as soon as the thread is started. The label is used to display status information to indicate that the thread is really running. As you see from the code, this label counter is updated each second. Finally, the Close button is used to stop the thread and terminate the application.

Listing 12.1 shows the code for the Create Thread application. As you can see, there isn't much to the process. You start the thread, and it runs. Other than that, the main work is done in the threading function itself.

Listing 12.1   Creating a new thread.

```
using System;
using System.Drawing;
using System.Collections;
using System.ComponentModel;
```

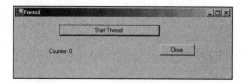

Figure 12.1   The create thread form.

```
using System.Windows.Forms;
using System.Data;
using System.Threading;

namespace Ch12_1.cs
{
    public class Form1 : System.Windows.Forms.Form
    {
        private System.Windows.Forms.Button button1;
        private System.Windows.Forms.Button button2;
        private System.ComponentModel.Container components = null;
        private System.Windows.Forms.Label label1;
        private Thread fThread = null;

        public Form1()
        {
            InitializeComponent();
        }
        protected override void Dispose( bool disposing )
        {
            if( disposing )
            {
                if (components != null)
                {
                    components.Dispose();
                }
            }
            base.Dispose( disposing );
        }

        #region Windows Form Designer generated code
        private void InitializeComponent()
        {
            this.label1 = new System.Windows.Forms.Label();
            this.button1 = new System.Windows.Forms.Button();
            this.button2 = new System.Windows.Forms.Button();
            this.SuspendLayout();
            this.label1.Location = new System.Drawing.Point(72, 64);
            this.label1.Name = "label1";
            this.label1.TabIndex = 3;
            this.label1.Text = "Counter: 0";
            this.button1.Location = new System.Drawing.Point(96, 16);
            this.button1.Name = "button1";
            this.button1.Size = new System.Drawing.Size(216, 23);
            this.button1.TabIndex = 0;
            this.button1.Text = "Start Thread";
```

```
   this.button1.Click += new
            System.EventHandler(this.button1_Click);
   this.button2.Location = new System.Drawing.Point(312, 56);
   this.button2.Name = "button2";
   this.button2.TabIndex = 2;
·  this.button2.Text = "Close";
   this.button2.Click += new
            System.EventHandler(this.button2_Click);
   this.AutoScaleBaseSize = new System.Drawing.Size(5, 13);
   this.ClientSize = new System.Drawing.Size(464, 125);
   this.Controls.AddRange(new System.Windows.Forms.Control[] {
            this.label1,
            this.button2,
            this.button1});
   this.Name = "Form1";
   this.Text = "Form1";
   this.Load += new System.EventHandler(this.Form1_Load);
   this.ResumeLayout(false);

}
#endregion
[STAThread]
static void Main()
{
   Application.Run(new Form1());
}

private void button2_Click(object sender, System.EventArgs e)
{
   if ( fThread != null )
      fThread.Abort();
   Close();
}

protected void ThreadFunc()
{
   Boolean done = false;
   int counter = 0;
   while ( !done )
   {
      Thread.Sleep(1000);
      counter ++;
      this.label1.Text = "Counter: " + counter;
   }
}
```

```
private void button1_Click(object sender, System.EventArgs e)
{
    // Don't allow them to do this more than once
    button1.Enabled = false;
    fThread = new Thread( new ThreadStart(ThreadFunc) );
    fThread.Start();
}
}
}
```

Related solution:	Found on page:
Creating a Collection	25

Killing a Thread

Of course, if you can start a thread, you probably want to know how to stop a thread. Although a thread normally terminates itself when some terminating condition is reached in its processing function, this statement is not always universally true. For example, a background thread might sort a file of entries. If a user decides to delete the file, you want the background thread to stop processing the entries. You can accomplish this task in a variety of ways, from setting a global variable to sending a message to a specific item in a form. However, the easiest way to kill a running thread is to simply get hold of the thread object representing that particular thread running in the application and to abort it.

In this example, you look at exactly how to go about tracking threads and killing them off when you want. The form shown in Figure 12.2 has two buttons: a Start button and a Stop button. Each click of the Start button creates a new thread and increments a label on the form. Each click of the Stop button terminates the last thread started and decrements the label on the form.

As you can see in Listing 12.2, the threads all use the same thread function to process themselves: They all enter and exit this particular function at any given time, with no assurances about which ones might be in there when you happen to

Figure 12.2   The thread start and thread stop form.

check. For this reason, any operation in this method must be atomic. You cannot do something, therefore, that could take multiple steps or use local variables to track your progress. This is not to say that all threads need to be created with a single thread function. In fact, you could create a number of different thread functions and use the one that is appropriate to a given operation when you create that particular thread. In this case, however, watching the multiple threaded application gives a good indication of the speed change that occurs in multiple thread processing when you use a single function.

Listing 12.2   Starting and stopping a thread.

```csharp
using System;
using System.Drawing;
using System.Collections;
using System.ComponentModel;
using System.Windows.Forms;
using System.Data;
using System.Threading;


namespace ch12_2
{
   public class Form1 : System.Windows.Forms.Form
   {
      private System.Windows.Forms.Button button1;
      private System.Windows.Forms.Button button2;
      private System.Windows.Forms.Label label1;
      private System.Windows.Forms.Label label2;
      private System.Windows.Forms.Label NumThreads;
      private System.Windows.Forms.Label Counter;
      private int                 fCounter;
      private ArrayList           fThreadList;

      private System.ComponentModel.Container components = null;

      public Form1()
      {
         InitializeComponent();
         fThreadList = new ArrayList();
      }

      protected override void Dispose( bool disposing )
      {
         if( disposing )
         {
            if (components != null)
            {
               components.Dispose();
```

```
                for ( int i=0; i<fThreadList.Count; ++i )
                {
                    Thread fThread = (Thread)fThreadList[ i ];
                    fThread.Abort();
                }


            }
        }
        base.Dispose( disposing );
    }

    #region Windows Form Designer generated code
    private void InitializeComponent()
    {
        this.button1 = new System.Windows.Forms.Button();
        this.button2 = new System.Windows.Forms.Button();
        this.label1 = new System.Windows.Forms.Label();
        this.label2 = new System.Windows.Forms.Label();
        this.NumThreads = new System.Windows.Forms.Label();
        this.Counter = new System.Windows.Forms.Label();
        this.SuspendLayout();
        this.button1.Location = new System.Drawing.Point(32, 104);
        this.button1.Name = "button1";
        this.button1.TabIndex = 0;
        this.button1.Text = "&Start";
        this.button1.Click += new
                System.EventHandler(this.button1_Click);
        this.button2.Location = new System.Drawing.Point(136, 104);
        this.button2.Name = "button2";
        this.button2.Size = new System.Drawing.Size(88, 24);
        this.button2.TabIndex = 1;
        this.button2.Text = "&Stop";
        this.button2.Click += new
                System.EventHandler(this.button2_Click);
        this.label1.Location = new System.Drawing.Point(32, 40);
        this.label1.Name = "label1";
        this.label1.Size = new System.Drawing.Size(152, 16);
        this.label1.TabIndex = 2;
        this.label1.Text = "Number of Threads Running:";
        this.label2.Location = new System.Drawing.Point(32, 64);
        this.label2.Name = "label2";
        this.label2.Size = new System.Drawing.Size(100, 16);
        this.label2.TabIndex = 3;
        this.label2.Text = "Counter:";
        this.NumThreads.Location = new System.Drawing.Point(192, 40);
        this.NumThreads.Name = "NumThreads";
```

```
        this.NumThreads.Size = new System.Drawing.Size(64, 16);
        this.NumThreads.TabIndex = 4;
        this.Counter.Location = new System.Drawing.Point(192, 64);
        this.Counter.Name = "Counter";
        this.Counter.Size = new System.Drawing.Size(64, 16);
        this.Counter.TabIndex = 5;
        this.AutoScaleBaseSize = new System.Drawing.Size(5, 13);
        this.ClientSize = new System.Drawing.Size(272, 165);
        this.Controls.AddRange(new System.Windows.Forms.Control[] {
                this.Counter,
                this.NumThreads,
                this.label2,
                this.label1,
                this.button2,
                this.button1});
        this.Name = "Form1";
        this.Text = "Form1";
        this.ResumeLayout(false);

    }
#endregion
[STAThread]
static void Main()
{
    Application.Run(new Form1());
}
protected void ThreadFunc()
{
    Boolean done = false;
    while ( !done )
    {
        Thread.Sleep(1000);
        fCounter ++;
        this.Counter.Text = fCounter.ToString();
    }
}
private void button1_Click(object sender, System.EventArgs e)
{
    Thread fThread = new Thread( new ThreadStart(ThreadFunc) );
    fThread.Start();
    fThreadList.Add( fThread );

    this.NumThreads.Text = fThreadList.Count.ToString();
}
private void button2_Click(object sender, System.EventArgs e)
{
```

```
                    // Stop the last one.
                    Thread fThread = (Thread)fThreadList[ fThreadList.Count - 1 ];
                    fThread.Abort();
                    fThreadList.Remove( fThread );
                    this.NumThreads.Text = fThreadList.Count.ToString ();


            }
        }
    }
```

Notice the use of **ArrayList** to keep track of the threads running in the process. When you are done with a thread, you call the **Abort** method to kill it off and then remove it from the tracking list with the **Remove** call to the **ArrayList** object. This allows the garbage-collection mechanism to take care of the used-up thread. In addition, notice that the **Dispose** method has been modified to kill off any active threads when the form is closed. This modification is important because a process that contains any active threads does not terminate by itself. As a result, the executable does not close itself down.

TIP: *If you are debugging a multithreaded application and the Visual Studio tool suddenly does not allow you to create a new version of it during the link process, the most likely explanation is that a copy of the program is running that still has an active thread. Bring up the Task Manager application, and look under the Process (not Application) tab to find a process with the same name as your program. Kill the process, and your program terminates.*

You must make sure that you are not trying to do something that is unsafe in a multithreaded application with multiple threads, such as delete an object in a thread function when you are done with it. If the thread function was reentrant and there were multiple threads, the object could be deleted before you finished using it in another thread. This warning applies only to global (or class-level) objects, of course. Local objects can be created and are allocated only to the stack of the thread itself.

Background Processing in a Thread

Sometimes, having a thread that runs in the background of an application is useful. This type of thread is not affected by the shutdown of the execution engine, nor is it subject to priority problems with other foreground threads. You have many reasons to have background threads, but you will also have issues with them. Threads may not affect items that exist in another thread. For example, in a **WinForms** application, a background thread cannot easily reach a visual component on the form because that component exists in another thread. Background threads can access class-level variables because they exist in the same space. In the example in this section, you look at how to create a background thread and how to use it to update variables that can be checked in the main application.

Figure 12.3 shows the form you use for this example. This form contains a button to start the thread and one to update the value that the thread function is slowly manipulating in the background. The form has two labels: one for information and one to store the value on the screen. Try the application, and start the thread. Then, regularly click the update button to see if the thread is still running in the background. You will notice no slowdown in processing, as you might with a foreground thread.

Listing 12.3 shows the code for the background thread form-processing example. As you can see, not much work is involved in working with threads—foreground or background. In this case, you are primarily manipulating the **IsBackground** property of the thread to indicate to the runtime system that this thread should be running in the background of the process space.

Listing 12.3   Background processing in a thread.

```
using System;
using System.Drawing;
using System.Collections;
using System.ComponentModel;
using System.Windows.Forms;
using System.Data;
using System.Threading;

namespace ch12_3
{
    public class Form1 : System.Windows.Forms.Form
    {
        private System.Windows.Forms.Label label1;
        private System.Windows.Forms.Button button1;
        private System.Windows.Forms.Label ValueLabel;
        private System.Windows.Forms.Button button2;
        private System.ComponentModel.Container components = null;
        private Thread fThread;
        private int    fValue;
```

Figure 12.3   The background thread form.

```
public Form1()
{
    InitializeComponent();

    fValue = 0;

}

protected override void Dispose( bool disposing )
{
    if( disposing )
    {
        if (components != null)
        {
            components.Dispose();
        }
    }
    base.Dispose( disposing );
}

#region Windows Form Designer generated code
private void InitializeComponent()
{
    this.label1 = new System.Windows.Forms.Label();
    this.button1 = new System.Windows.Forms.Button();
    this.ValueLabel = new System.Windows.Forms.Label();
    this.button2 = new System.Windows.Forms.Button();
    this.SuspendLayout();
    this.label1.Location = new System.Drawing.Point(24, 32);
    this.label1.Name = "label1";
    this.label1.Size = new System.Drawing.Size(80, 16);
    this.label1.TabIndex = 0;
    this.label1.Text = "Value of Data:";
    this.button1.Location = new System.Drawing.Point(232, 32);
    this.button1.Name = "button1";
    this.button1.TabIndex = 1;
    this.button1.Text = "&Update";
    this.button1.Click += new
            System.EventHandler(this.button1_Click);
    this.ValueLabel.Location = new System.Drawing.Point(120, 32);
    this.ValueLabel.Name = "ValueLabel";
    this.ValueLabel.TabIndex = 2;
    this.button2.Location = new System.Drawing.Point(104, 88);
    this.button2.Name = "button2";
    this.button2.RightToLeft =
            System.Windows.Forms.RightToLeft.No;
```

```
        this.button2.Size = new System.Drawing.Size(96, 23);
        this.button2.TabIndex = 3;
        this.button2.Text = "Start Thread";
        this.button2.Click += new
                System.EventHandler(this.button2_Click);
        this.AutoScaleBaseSize = new System.Drawing.Size(5, 13);
        this.ClientSize = new System.Drawing.Size(336, 141);
        this.Controls.AddRange(new System.Windows.Forms.Control[] {
                this.button2,
                this.ValueLabel,
                this.button1,
                this.label1});
        this.Name = "Form1";
        this.Text = "Form1";
        this.ResumeLayout(false);

    }
    #endregion

    [STAThread]
    static void Main()
    {
        Application.Run(new Form1());
    }
    private void ThreadProc()
    {
        while ( fValue < 1000 )
        {
            Thread.Sleep(1000);
            fValue ++;
        }
    }

    private void button2_Click(object sender, System.EventArgs e)
    {
        fThread = new Thread(new ThreadStart(ThreadProc));
        fThread.IsBackground = true;
        fThread.Start();

    }

    private void button1_Click(object sender, System.EventArgs e)
    {
        this.ValueLabel.Text = fValue.ToString ();
    }
  }
}
```

Talking to Visual Elements from a Background Thread

One problem with working with threads is that a background thread cannot "talk" to any visual elements that exist in the main GUI thread, because talking to objects across thread boundaries is forbidden. The reasons are obvious: Because a thread has its own process space, the address of an object in one thread is not useful as an address in another thread. As a result, trying to access that object in another process space results in a program crash from an unhandled exception. Because this isn't something you want to do, C# provides a mechanism for working with cross-thread process issues.

The **BeginInvoke** method of the **MethodInvoker** delegate is used within a thread process to call another process method. These methods are threadsafe and can be used even in a multithreaded environment. In the example in this section, you see exactly how to go about using them this way.

Figure 12.4 shows the form you use for this example. As you can see, the form contains buttons to start and stop the thread and a progress bar control to display the results of background processing.

The code for this little task is shown in Listing 12.4. Notice the shaded lines; these code blocks are used to do the job. First, you see how the thread is created. Note that the background flag is used to ensure that the thread is not running in the same process as the main window form. Next, look at how the **MethodInvoker** delegate is used to connect the background process with the foreground control.

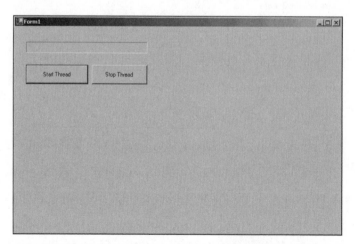

Figure 12.4   The background thread processing form.

Listing 12.4 Talking to a visual element in a background thread.

```csharp
using System;
using System.Drawing;
using System.Collections;
using System.ComponentModel;
using System.Windows.Forms;
using System.Data;
using System.Threading;

namespace Ch12_4
{
   public class Form1 : System.Windows.Forms.Form
   {
      private System.Windows.Forms.ProgressBar progressBar1;
      private System.Windows.Forms.Button button1;
      private System.Windows.Forms.Button button2;
      private Thread fThread = null;
      private System.ComponentModel.Container components = null;

      public Form1()
      {
         InitializeComponent();
      }

      protected override void Dispose( bool disposing )
      {
         if (fThread != null)
         {
            fThread.Interrupt();
            fThread = null;
         }

         if( disposing )
         {
            if (components != null)
            {
               components.Dispose();
            }
         }
         base.Dispose( disposing );
      }

      #region Windows Form Designer generated code
      private void InitializeComponent()
      {
         this.progressBar1 = new System.Windows.Forms.ProgressBar();
```

```csharp
      this.button1 = new System.Windows.Forms.Button();
      this.button2 = new System.Windows.Forms.Button();
      this.SuspendLayout();
      this.progressBar1.Location = new System.Drawing.Point(24, 32);
      this.progressBar1.Name = "progressBar1";
      this.progressBar1.Size = new System.Drawing.Size(264, 23);
      this.progressBar1.TabIndex = 0;
      this.button1.Location = new System.Drawing.Point(24, 80);
      this.button1.Name = "button1";
      this.button1.Size = new System.Drawing.Size(136, 40);
      this.button1.TabIndex = 1;
      this.button1.Text = "Start Thread";
      this.button1.Click += new
            System.EventHandler(this.button1_Click);
      this.button2.Location = new System.Drawing.Point(168, 80);
      this.button2.Name = "button2";
      this.button2.Size = new System.Drawing.Size(120, 40);
      this.button2.TabIndex = 2;
      this.button2.Text = "Stop Thread";
      this.button2.Click += new
            System.EventHandler(this.button2_Click);
      this.AutoScaleBaseSize = new System.Drawing.Size(5, 13);
      this.ClientSize = new System.Drawing.Size(704, 429);
      this.Controls.AddRange(new System.Windows.Forms.Control[] {
            this.button2,
            this.button1,
            this.progressBar1});
      this.Name = "Form1";
      this.Text = "Form1";
      this.ResumeLayout(false);

   }
   #endregion

   [STAThread]
   static void Main()
   {
      Application.Run(new Form1());
   }

   private void UpdateProgress()
   {
      if (progressBar1.Value == progressBar1.Maximum)
      {
         progressBar1.Value = progressBar1.Minimum ;
```

```
         }
         progressBar1.PerformStep() ;
      }


      public void ThreadProc()
      {

         try
         {
            MethodInvoker mi = new MethodInvoker(this.UpdateProgress);
            while (true)
            {
               this.BeginInvoke(mi);
               Thread.Sleep(500) ;
            }
         }
         catch (ThreadInterruptedException e)
         {
            Console.WriteLine(
               "Interruption Exception in Thread: {0}",
                     e );
         }
         catch (Exception we)
         {
            Console.WriteLine("Exception in Thread: {0}", we );
         }
      }

      private void button1_Click(object sender, System.EventArgs e)
      {
         // Start the background thread
         fThread = new Thread(new ThreadStart(ThreadProc));
         fThread.IsBackground = true;
         fThread.Start();


      }

      private void button2_Click(object sender, System.EventArgs e)
      {
         fThread.Interrupt();
         fThread = null;
      }
   }
}
```

Synchronizing Multiple Threads

One problem with having multiple threads accessing the same data at the same time is that synchronization problems can occur. A synchronization problem happens when two threads hit the same piece of data at the same time, without regard for the business rules that might apply to that piece of data. A good example is the banking industry: When a transaction is in progress, it must run to completion. If I want to add a certain amount to an account and then withdraw an amount based on that addition, the addition must finish before the withdrawal can take place.

In this example, you look at what happens if you allow multiple threads to modify the same piece of data in a single object, both with and without synchronization. Listing 12.5 shows the simple console application that illustrates this point.

Listing 12.5   Synchronizing multiple threads.

```
using System;
using System.Threading;


namespace Ch12_5
{
    class Account
    {
        int fBalance;
        Boolean fLocks;

        Random r = new Random();

        internal Account(Boolean useLocks, int initial)
        {
            fBalance = initial;
            fLocks = useLocks;
        }

        internal int DoTransaction(Boolean doLock, int amount)
        {

            if (fBalance < 0)
            {
                throw new Exception("Negative fBalance");
            }
            if ( doLock )
            {
                lock (this)
                {
                    if (fBalance >= amount)
```

```
            {
                Thread.Sleep(5);
                fBalance = fBalance - amount;
                return amount;
            }
            else
            {
                return 0; // transaction rejected
            }
        }
    }
    else
    {
        if (fBalance >= amount)
        {
            Thread.Sleep(5);
            fBalance = fBalance - amount;
            return amount;
        }
        else
        {
            return 0; // transaction rejected
        }
    }
}

internal void DoTransactions()
{
    for (int i = 0; i < 100; i++)
    {
        DoTransaction(fLocks, r.Next(-50, 100));
    }
}
}

class CH12_5
{

    static Thread[] threads = new Thread[10];

    public static void Main(string[] args)
    {
        Boolean doLock = false;

        if ( args[0] == "lock" )
            doLock = true;
```

```
            else
               doLock = false;

            Account acc = new Account (doLock, 0);

            for (int i = 0; i < 10; i++)
            {
               Thread t = new Thread(new ThreadStart(acc.DoTransactions));
               threads[i] = t;
            }

            for (int i = 0; i < 10; i++)
            {
               threads[i].Start();
            }
      }
   }
}
```

If you run this application with the command line ch12_5 lock, you see no output from the program, which indicates that no exceptions were thrown and the account balanced properly without "going negative." If, on the other hand, you run the program with the command line ch12_5 nolocks, you see the following output:

```
Unhandled Exception:Unhandled Exception:
        System.Exception: Negative fBalance
   at Ch12_5.Account.DoTransaction(Boolean doLock, Int32 amount)
      in c:\matt\c#\ch12_5\class1.cs:line 24
   at Ch12_5.Account.DoTransactions() in c:\matt\c#\ch12_5\class1.cs:
     line 61
System.Exception: Negative fBalance
   at Ch12_5.Account.DoTransaction(Boolean doLock, Int32 amount) in
c:\matt\c#\c
h12_5\class1.cs:line 24
   at Ch12_5.Account.DoTransactions() in c:\matt\c#\ch12_5\class1.cs:
line 61
System.Exception: Negative fBalance
```

As you can see, the **lock** statement in this code is the difference between the two situations. What does the **lock** statement do? It prevents multiple threads from accessing the block that modifies the **fBalance** field. Because only one thread at a time can enter that block, the code works the way you would expect: It modifies the balance for that particular transaction and continues. If you do not stop the second thread (and all other threads) from entering that block, several threads at a time can modify the second thread. Each thread thinks that the balance is still positive before that thread acts, but each thread-processing function completes the action on a different balance, which causes the problem.

Listing All Threads for a Process

One helpful quality of the diagnostic class library in the .NET CLR framework is being able to look at the internals of a running system. Because I am discussing threads and processes, it makes sense to show you how to write a simple diagnostic application that lets you look at the running threads in a process and see what sorts of information you can retrieve from those threads. You may often be surprised by the total number of threads that are running for any given process. Although you might believe that it might have only a single foreground thread and maybe a background thread that deals with loading and unloading modules, nothing could be further from the truth, as you see in this application.

Figure 12.5 shows the form you use in this application. This simple form allows you to see the machine name, as the system knows it, as well as a list of the processes running on your local machine. When you select a process from the list of running processes, the second list view is populated with the running threads in that application. In this particular example, you are showing only a fraction of the information available to you about a thread—and you could learn much more. A more complete application would show everything possible about a running thread.

Listing 12.6 shows the code for the thread monitoring application. Note that this program does not monitor in real-time: It shows a static view of the threads at the time it is launched. As a result, by the time you do something with a process, it might not be there any more. Let the buyer beware. Also, don't be concerned

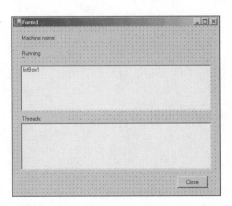

Figure 12.5   The thread monitor application.

about the length of the application. Look at the shaded parts—they are the important pieces. The remainder is simply the GUI code needed to make it all work.

Listing 12.6   Listing all threads for a process.

```
namespace Ch12_6
{
    using System;
    using System.Drawing;
    using System.Collections;
    using System.ComponentModel;
    using System.Windows.Forms;
    using System.Data;
    using System.Diagnostics;

    /// <summary>
    ///     Summary description for Form1.
    /// </summary>
    public class Form1 : System.Windows.Forms.Form
    {
        /// <summary>
        ///     Required designer variable.
        /// </summary>
        private System.Windows.Forms.ColumnHeader VirtualMemory;
        private System.Windows.Forms.ColumnHeader Priority;
        private System.Windows.Forms.ColumnHeader Id;
        private System.Windows.Forms.Label machinename;
        private System.Windows.Forms.Button button1;
        private System.Windows.Forms.Label label3;
        private System.Windows.Forms.ListBox listBox1;
        private System.Windows.Forms.Label label2;
        private System.Windows.Forms.Label label1;
        private System.Windows.Forms.ListView listView1;
        private System.Windows.Forms.ColumnHeader ThreadID;
        private System.Windows.Forms.ColumnHeader ThreadPriority;
        private System.Windows.Forms.ColumnHeader ProcessorTime;
        private ArrayList sProcIds;

        public Form1()
        {
            InitializeComponent();

            sProcIds = new ArrayList();

            // First, fill in the machine name
            machinename.Text = Process.GetCurrentProcess().MachineName;
```

```
    // Now, load the processes
    Process[] sProcess = Process.GetProcesses();
    foreach( Process p in sProcess )
    {
        listBox1.Items.Add( p.ProcessName );
        sProcIds.Add( p.Id );
    }
}
public override void Dispose()
{
    base.Dispose();
}
private void InitializeComponent()
{
 this.label1 = new System.Windows.Forms.Label();
 this.label2 = new System.Windows.Forms.Label();
 this.label3 = new System.Windows.Forms.Label();
 this.machinename = new System.Windows.Forms.Label();
 this.ThreadPriority = new System.Windows.Forms.ColumnHeader();
 this.ThreadID = new System.Windows.Forms.ColumnHeader();
 this.VirtualMemory = new System.Windows.Forms.ColumnHeader();
 this.listBox1 = new System.Windows.Forms.ListBox();
 this.listView1 = new System.Windows.Forms.ListView();
 this.ProcessorTime = new System.Windows.Forms.ColumnHeader();
 this.Priority = new System.Windows.Forms.ColumnHeader();
 this.Id = new System.Windows.Forms.ColumnHeader();
 this.button1 = new System.Windows.Forms.Button();
 this.SuspendLayout();
 this.label1.Location = new System.Drawing.Point(16, 16);
 this.label1.Name = "label1";
 this.label1.Size = new System.Drawing.Size(88, 16);
 this.label1.TabIndex = 0;
 this.label1.Text = "Machine name:";
 this.label2.Location = new System.Drawing.Point(16, 48);
 this.label2.Name = "label2";
 this.label2.Size = new System.Drawing.Size(100, 16);
 this.label2.TabIndex = 1;
 this.label2.Text = "Running Processes:";
 this.label3.Location = new System.Drawing.Point(16, 184);
 this.label3.Name = "label3";
 this.label3.Size = new System.Drawing.Size(100, 16);
 this.label3.TabIndex = 3;
 this.label3.Text = "Threads:";
 this.machinename.Location = new System.Drawing.Point(128, 16);
 this.machinename.Name = "machinename";
 this.machinename.Size = new System.Drawing.Size(100, 16);
```

```
            this.machinename.TabIndex = 6;
            this.ThreadPriority.Text = "Priority";
            this.ThreadID.Text = "Thread ID";
            this.VirtualMemory.Text = "Virtual Mem";
            this.listBox1.Location = new System.Drawing.Point(16, 80);
            this.listBox1.Name = "listBox1";
            this.listBox1.Size = new System.Drawing.Size(408, 95);
            this.listBox1.TabIndex = 2;
            this.listBox1.SelectedIndexChanged += new
                    System.EventHandler(this.SelectItemHandler);
            this.listView1.Columns.AddRange(new
                    System.Windows.Forms.ColumnHeader[] {
                        this.ThreadID,
                        this.ThreadPriority,
                        this.ProcessorTime});
            this.listView1.Location = new System.Drawing.Point(16, 200);
            this.listView1.Name = "listView1";
            this.listView1.Size = new System.Drawing.Size(408, 97);
            this.listView1.TabIndex = 7;
            this.ProcessorTime.Text = "Processor Time";
            this.ProcessorTime.Width = 90;
            this.Priority.Text = "Priority";
            this.Id.Text = "ID";
            this.Id.Width = 20;
            this.button1.Location = new System.Drawing.Point(352, 312);
            this.button1.Name = "button1";
            this.button1.Size = new System.Drawing.Size(64, 24);
            this.button1.TabIndex = 5;
            this.button1.Text = "Close";
            this.button1.Click += new
                        System.EventHandler(this.button1_Click);
            this.AutoScaleBaseSize = new System.Drawing.Size(5, 13);
            this.ClientSize = new System.Drawing.Size(440, 349);
            this.Controls.AddRange(new System.Windows.Forms.Control[] {
                                        this.listView1,
                                        this.machinename,
                                        this.button1,
                                        this.label3,
                                        this.listBox1,
                                        this.label2,
                                        this.label1});
            this.Name = "Form1";
            this.Text = "Form1";
            this.ResumeLayout(false);
        }
```

```
protected void SelectItemHandler (object sender, System.EventArgs e)
{
    int idx = this.listBox1.SelectedIndex;
    // Get the threads for this process ID
    Process proc = Process.GetProcessById( (int)sProcIds[ idx ] );
    ProcessThreadCollection procThreads = proc.Threads;
    this.listView1.View = System.Windows.Forms.View.Details;
    this.listView1.Items.Clear();
    int nRow = 0;
    foreach ( ProcessThread pt in procThreads )
    {
        string priority = "Normal";
        switch ( (int)proc.BasePriority )
        {
            case 8:
                priority = "Normal";
                break;
            case 13:
                priority = "High";
                break;
            case 24:
                priority = "Real Time";
                break;
            case 4:
            default:
                priority = "Idle";
                break;
        }
        this.listView1.Items.Add( pt.Id.ToString() );
        this.listView1.Items[nRow].SubItems.Add( priority );
        this.listView1.Items[nRow].SubItems.Add(
                pt.UserProcessorTime.ToString() );
        nRow ++;
    }
}

protected void button1_Click (object sender, System.EventArgs e)
{
    Close();
}
public static void Main(string[] args)
{
    Application.Run(new Form1());
}
}
}
```

When you run the application, you see a display such as the one shown in Figure 12.6. Selecting a process from the process list, such as the one for the Ch12_6 code (this application), displays a list of threads like the one shown in Figure 12.7. As you can see, a .NET C# application has dozens of threads.

NOTE: *The diagnostic code in some of the C# beta releases apparently have some bugs. For example, I could not display the machine name on some machines, no matter what I tried.*

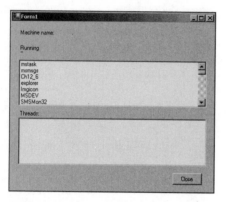

Figure 12.6   The running Ch12_6 application.

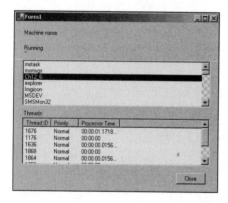

Figure 12.7   Threads for the CH12_6 application process.

Chapter 13

Components

In Depth

When you hear the word *component*, you might think of a black box or a $500 toilet seat or a stereo piece, such as a turntable. A *component* is simply a building block for creating a finished product. Components are used to solve a specific need in building, such as a junction box in an electrical design. In the software world, components are also black boxes. Components in a software design still solve a specific need, containing functionality to perform a given set of related tasks. In this chapter, you look at how to create your own components in C# and how to use the capabilities of the new Visual Studio.NET and the Common Language Runtime (CLR) to leverage the built-in functionality in your custom components.

Component-Based Design

When you discuss components, you usually refer to the new component-based design, or CBD. What does CBD entail and why is it important to you as a developer? CBD forms the whole basis for drag-and-drop programming in C# and Visual Studio.NET. Because of the capabilities of components, you can select the functionality you want in your application, select the components that best serve that functionality, and drop them onto forms to create the overall package you want to offer to users.

When you talk about components, you usually think of visual elements, such as list boxes and tab sheets, that can be dragged onto a form and used directly to display information or retrieve input from users. In fact, components need not be visual, nor must they even interface with users. Some components are entirely internal to the application and are never seen. Examples of these types of components are database interface components and timers.

What attributes does something have to have to qualify as a component? Essentially, any object or set of classes can be a component if it:

- Is completely self-contained
- Solves a specific need
- Can be removed and replaced by another component that provides the same interface

Self-contained means that the component is really a "black box": You don't need to know how it works, nor do you need to include anything else to make it work. You may have to link in additional libraries for a component, but you should never have to do any other work to have a usable component in your system. Self-contained components are important because they promote reuse while limiting the copying of code between applications. If a component is reusable at the binary level (a library or COM object), only a single copy of the source code exists for that component. Contrast that with the notion of a class in C++, which is copied from project to project and modified in each one. What you end up with is a dozen copies of the same code, slightly different and impossible to maintain together.

A component also solves a specific need, which means that components are not generalized bodies of code. When you select a given component to use in your system, you want it to solve a specific problem you are having. For example, you might select a list box component to display a list of items for users to view. You would not expect that list box component to do something else, like go out to the Internet and search for stock quotes. The advantage of single-need components is obvious: By solving a specific need, the component can be small, portable, and more reusable than general-purpose code, which would need to be modified via a cut-and-paste operation.

The third element in determining whether something is a true component is being able to "unplug" it from your application and replace it with another component that does the same thing. This factor might not appear obvious because anything can be removed and replaced in an application. However, imagine for a moment that an entire application is filled with list boxes. Suddenly, your boss comes along and decides that you should be able to not only display items in a list but also select and modify the color of each item in each list box. If you can find a component that implements a colorized list box (yes, they do exist), you can simply replace each instance of the **ListBox** component name in your application with the **ColorListBox** name. Because the base functionality of the component and its interfaces is the same, you can be assured that it will all work fine.

Advantages of Components

Now that you understand what a component is, and how you can identify one, why would you care about having a component-based application? What advantages do components have over other bodies of code? The answer lies in three words: portability, extensibility, and replaceability. These three concepts help you understand why component-based design is much more than simply a neat idea. The CBD concept allows you to create applications quickly and to maintain those applications effectively.

Portability

The first, and possibly most, important reason to use components is their *portability*, which means that they can easily be moved from one application to another with no source code modifications. Portability also means that components are reusable. Because you do not need to make extensive modifications to your application to use a component, you don't need to worry about the work involved in including it in your application. This concept is important because the more work needed to use a body of code, such as initialization work and cleanup work, the less likely a programmer will use that code in his project. If code is not reused, it is essentially wasted.

When you create or use a component, that component is responsible for initializing itself properly with intelligent defaults. The more intelligent the set of defaults you select when creating the component, the more likely the component will be reused. In addition, by selecting intelligent defaults, you can have a component that drops right into any application in which it is needed, with a minimum of work on the part of users. This increases its reuse, which in turn increases the amount of portability in the system.

Extensibility

The second important attribute of a component is extensibility. To be *extensible* means that the component can be used as the basis for new components that allow for more or varied functionality that the original designer never envisioned. The reason that extensibility is important is that it is often difficult to see what might be important in the future. The easiest way to show you what I am talking about is to illustrate a real-world example of component extensibility.

When the edit box was created, it was a marvel of functionality and coding. You could drop an edit box onto a dialog box (as forms were then known) and interface with it simply. You could get back the text that was typed into the edit box. You could set the text that initially appeared in the edit box. You could even restrict the length of input into the edit box at design time so that users could enter only a fixed number of characters at runtime. The edit box was a wonderful thing at a time when you normally had to write from scratch any visual element you wanted to use in a Windows application.

As time went by, however, the edit box became more and more limited in its application. Users wanted to be able to have the system automatically complete their entries. Programmers wanted to be able to filter out invalid characters before they were ever entered. Imagine having a Social Security number edit box that allows only nine digits and automatically formats the entered data in the proper ### - ## - #### format. All these concepts were important to users, who were accustomed to paper forms that helped them to understand what sort of data they were supposed to enter.

The answer to all these problems turned out to be the "masked edit" control for Windows. This control, built on the framework of the edit control, allowed you to do much more with input from users. You could trap input on a character-by-character basis. You could validate input in a given "mask" that defined exactly what characters could be in which places in the input string. All this new functionality was simply "grafted on" to the existing edit control, making a new component in its place.

Components have come a long way since the days of the original Windows edit control and masked edit control. Versions of the edit control can now modify the text color or autocomplete entries or even allow for the incremental searching of databases. Yet all these components are built on the back of the original, innocent little edit control. This is the classic example of successful extensible components.

Replaceability

The third attribute of a successful component is that it is replaceable. A component is the ultimate example of Plug and Play systems. You should be able to simply "unplug" a component that implements a given set of methods and properties and replace it with another component that performs the same set of functionality. In the example I have been discussing, the masked edit control is a drop-in replacement for the edit control, when it became obvious that it needed additional functionality. Because the two components had the same basic set of functionality built into them, you could use a masked edit control in place of a "standard" edit control without modifying the code for the component in the least.

One thing that makes this situation possible is the interface concept. Similar to the COM concept of the same name, an interface defines a set of functionality and an API for accessing that functionality in the application. In the case of edit controls, the functionality was the ability to set and retrieve the text in the edit box at runtime or design time. The added ability to set a mask for the input did not change this basic functionality; the edit component still retrieved the data from the edit box and just happened to include in the returned string any mask characters that could not be entered, such as the hyphens in the Social Security number. When the edit control was enhanced, additional functionality was added for programmers who did not want the returned string to contain the mask characters. Developers could—but weren't required to—use additional functionality, preserving backward compatibility.

The Windows world contains many examples of extensions of existing controls to add new functionality on top of existing functionality. When you think about it, the tree and list view controls are nothing more than extended list box controls. The tab control is simply an enhanced version of the label control. Although not all these controls appear to be the same, they are just evolutionary adaptations of existing controls to fit newer needs in the development world.

C# Controls

Although this background discussion is interesting, how does it apply to the C# programming language? Of course, C# permits you to create components. In fact, it makes the process of creating them extremely easy, using the integrated wizards of Visual Studio.NET. Take a few moments to look at how components and custom controls are implemented in C# and what the functionality available to you to create these types of components look like.

All the basic functionality of a generic control comes from the **UserControl** class in the CLR. The **UserControl** class contains most of the basic functionality you would need in order to implement your own controls in the C# system. The **UserControl** class contains properties that would apply to any control, such as **Width**, **Height**, **Size**, and **Location**, all of which define where on the screen the control appears. The class also contains properties for such properties as **TabIndex** and **TabStop**, which define whether users can press Tab to use the control and in what order the control appears on the tab list.

Table 13.1 shows some common **UserControl** properties and their meanings. This list is by no means exhaustive, but it does show you the sorts of things that are available to you.

Table 13.1   UserControl properties.

Property	Specifies
AllowDrop	Whether this component supports drag-and-drop
BackColor	The background color to use when painting this control
Bottom	The bottom position (y coordinate) of this component
Bounds	The window coordinates of this control on the screen
CanFocus	Whether this control can receive input focus
CanSelect	Whether this control can be selected with the mouse
Cursor	The cursor to be displayed when the mouse is within the control border
Dock	Which side of the container for this control it docks with
Enabled	Whether this control is enabled or disabled
Font	The font used by default to display text for this control
ForeColor	The foreground (text) color for use in painting this control

(continued)

Table 13.1 UserControl properties *(continued)*.

Property	Specifies
Handle	The underlying window handle for this control for use with Windows API functions and third-party libraries
Height	The height of the control in pixels
Left	The left side (x coordinate) of the control
Location	The upper-left corner of the control in window coordinates
Parent	The parent control (owner) for this control
Right	The right side (x-coordinate) of the control
Size	The height and width of the control
TabIndex	The order in which this control is moved to via the tab key
TabStop	Whether the tab stops at this control on the form
Top	The top coordinate (y-coordinate) of the control
Visible	Whether this control is visible to users
Width	The width in pixels of the control

What Makes Up a Component?

Now that you know the basis for a component, the next question is "What makes up a component from the perspective of the application developer?" The answer consists of three elements: functionality in the form of methods, customizability in the form of properties, and extensibility in the form of events. Let's take a look at each one of these and see how to implement them in a C# control.

Methods

As you have seen, a *method* in a C# object is simply a function that can be invoked either from within the object or from an external source. The difference lies in the scope of the method. If the method is declared to be private, or protected, only those objects of the same class can call the method. If, on the other hand, the method is declared to be public, anyone can call the method from any object. An example is probably easier to understand. This class snippet has two methods:

```
class FooObject
{
    private int GetX() { return fX; };
    public void setX(int _x) { fX = _x; };
};
```

The **GetX** method returns to the caller the current value of the internal member variable **fX**. Because the method is declared as private, however, this method can be used internally only by objects of class **FooObject**. Suppose that you have another object of a different class, such as **Bar**, as in this example:

```
Int aFunction()
{
    Bar s = new Bar();
    FooObject fo = new FooObject();
    int i = fo.GetX();
}
```

This code generates a compile-time error because the function **aFunction** is not an internal method of the **FooObject** class and therefore does not have access to the private methods of the **FooObject** class.

Methods provide functionality to perform an action within controls. For example, you might have a method to print the status of a given control. If a control implements a Social Security masked edit entry, as I have discussed, a method of that control might return the prefix value (the first three digits) of the Social Security the user entered.

Properties

A *property* is an intrinsic value within an object. Properties represent elements of the object that can be modified or read from the outside world. A property might represent, for example, the color of the text in a label. Alternatively, a property might represent the style of a bar graph, defining whether the graph is displayed in three dimensions. Properties provide the ability to customize an object.

In terms of the C# language, a property can be readable, writeable, or both. Properties are implemented via two different methods within the class: a **set** method, which writes to the internal property member variable, and a **get** method, which retrieves the internal member variable. Here's a simple example of a class that implements both a **set** method and a **get** method for an integer property:

```
class FooObject
{
    private int fX;
    public int X
    {
        get() { return fX; };
        set() { fX=value; };
    }
}
```

First, you see that you define an internal member variable named **fX**. This variable is declared as private so that a user can directly modify it. Next, the property declaration defines an externally available property named **X**, which has both a **set** method allowing a user to modify it and a **get** method allowing her to retrieve the value of the property.

Why did the language implementers choose to use **set** and **get** methods for properties rather than simply allow direct access to the internal member variables? The answer lies in the fact that you can choose whether to modify the values of the internal variables in the **set** methods of the property. Suppose that a property can assume the values from 1 to 10. This property is implemented as an integer value (which is probably a mistake), which allows the user to pass in any valid integer value. You could then write for this property a **set** method that looks like this:

```
public int X
{
    set()
    {
        if ( value > 0 && value <= 10 )
            fX = value;
    }
};
```

In this example, if the external user passes in an invalid value, the member variable is not modified and therefore does not receive an invalid setting. This situation avoids nasty problems in debugging applications later on. That explains the rationale for the **set** method. But why would you want to have a **get** method as well? Honestly, for only one reason—so that you can create properties that cannot be read. Why would you want such a thing? Imagine a system that must keep track of the amount of taxes due to the government. This type of system exists in Europe, where countries such as Italy require that a special chip be placed in point-of-sale devices to track the amount of tax paid. You can write to the chip, but cannot read back from the chip to see what the current value is. This arrangement ensures that you pay the right amount in taxes.

Events

To modify the behavior of a component at runtime, you need to be able to know what is going on in the component at any given time. For example, if you want to be able to screen out certain keystrokes in an edit control, you need to know when a user enters a keystroke into the edit control in the first place. The mechanism for doing this is the *event*.

Events provide a feedback mechanism for your application from the component. For example, the list box control in C# contains events for when a user selects a new item or when the mouse is clicked in the list box. These events allow you to do something about occurrences when they happen. Imagine, in a list box, that you want to change the text of a label control in response to a user's clicking a different item. You "catch" the event and update the text when you receive notification that she has clicked a different element in the list box.

Events are made up of two components. From the control side, a delegate represents the method by which the event is fired when the control deems that the time is appropriate. On the application side, an event handler catches the event firing. Suppose that you want to fire an event when a given value in the system changes. You could have a delegate that looks like this:

```
public delegate Boolean ValueChangedEventHandler(int nValue);
```

Within the component, then, you have defined a delegate event that can be used with this delegate. For example, you might define a handler that can be used from the external world and that looks like this:

```
public event ValueChangedEventHandler Changed;
```

To fire the event from within the component, you simply invoke the delegate if it has been set. Because the delegate takes the index of the new selection index for the component, you invoke it by doing something like this:

```
if ( Changed )
    Changed( newIndex );
```

The other side of the issue is receiving the event on the application side. When a user changes the index of the list box, the event is fired from the list box and sent to something in the application. What is that "something"? The answer is an *event handler*, which is nothing more than a method in the application that has the same signature as the required delegate. So, an event handler for the selection change might look something like this:

```
private bool OnChanged( int nIndex )
{
    MessageBox.Show( this, "New Index!" + nIndex );
    return true;
}
```

In this event handler, of course, you aren't doing anything other than displaying the new index for the list box that was set. But how do you connect this event handler to the event itself? To connect a method as an event handler, you just do this:

```
this.component.Changed += new
    obj.CompoundControl.ValueChangedEventHandler(OnChanged);
```

In this example, the component is the component on the form from which you want to receive messages about events. The **obj** variable is the actual form object you want to work with. The **OnChanged** method is the method you want called when the event is fired. That's all that is required to get an event and handle it in your own code.

Components with GUI Segments

Components can be virtually any sort of element, from simple COM components that interact with dedicated devices or data stores to complicated GUI displays that put a complete interface in front of users. When you are working with simple components, all you need to do is implement the functionality you want to work with. However, when you work with GUI components, a bit more is involved in the process.

When you want to display an object on the face of your component, you must paint the object, just as you would in any standard Windows application. If you have worked with the MFC programming interface or any of the other Windows programming libraries, you are probably accustomed to painting objects by overriding the **OnPaint** method or handling a WM_PAINT message. The situation is just slightly different in the CLR world, when you're working with C# components. Fortunately, that slight difference makes things easier, not more difficult.

Although C# allows you to override methods that are defined in base classes, such as the **RichControl** class that makes up the basis of custom controls, the preferred method for working with classes is to implement event handlers for events. The painting method of C# is no different in this respect.

To add a paint handler to a component, simply select the component in the Properties window and select the Events tab. Then select the **Paint** event and enter the handler name you want to create. In this example, you use the **OnPaint** method name to create a new handler for painting the control:

```
this.Paint += new
    System.Windows.Forms.PaintEventHandler(this.OnPaint);
```

After you have defined your **Paint** handler, the next issue is implementing the functionality of the handler. You can do pretty much anything you want to do in a **Paint** handler. Note, however, that only those items drawn in the **Paint** handler are persistent for the control. You can draw on the screen whenever you want, but unless the drawing is in a **Paint** handler, the drawing disappears when the window or control is covered up and then uncovered.

Here's a simple example of a component that draws on its surface. The surface of a control is called the *component*. The **Graphics** component is passed to your handler as a part of the arguments to the handler, as shown here. In this example, you are simply displaying the system time in long format (hours, minutes, and seconds) on the **Graphics** canvas:

```
private void OnPaint(object sender,
    System.Windows.Forms.PaintEventArgs e)
{
    // Get the time in system format.
    System.DateTime dt = System.DateTime.Now;

    // Get the text that represents that time
    String Text = dt.ToLongTimeString();

    e.Graphics.DrawString(Text, Font, new SolidBrush (ForeColor),
        ClientRectangle);
}
```

The other aspect to a GUI component is dealing with user input. Fortunately, this process is essentially the same as painting. You simply pick the event you want to handle, such as a user pressing the mouse button in your control. Then you handle it by adding an event handler to process that event. To illustrate this process, the following complete component allows you to use some of the functionality of the Scribble application from MFC and Visual Basic. This application allows users to move the mouse down on the control, move the mouse around, and have a line drawn from the start point to the end point:

```
using System;
using System.Collections;
using System.ComponentModel;
using System.Drawing;
using System.Data;
using System.Windows.Forms;

namespace ch13_paint
{
    public class ScribbleComponent : System.Windows.Forms.UserControl
    {
        private System.ComponentModel.Container components = null;
        private System.Drawing.Point fStartPoint;
        private System.Drawing.Point fEndPoint;

        public ScribbleComponent()
        {
            // This call is required by the Windows.Forms Form Designer.
            InitializeComponent();
```

```
        fStartPoint = new System.Drawing.Point();
        fEndPoint = new System.Drawing.Point();
    }
    protected override void Dispose( bool disposing )
    {
        if( disposing )
        {
            if(components != null)
            {
                components.Dispose();
            }
        }
        base.Dispose( disposing );
    }

    #region Component Designer generated code
    private void InitializeComponent()
    {
        //
        // ScribbleComponent
        //
        this.Name = "ScribbleComponent";
        this.Paint += new
            System.Windows.Forms.PaintEventHandler(this.OnPaint);
        this.MouseMove += new
            System.Windows.Forms.MouseEventHandler(this.OnMouseMove);
        this.MouseDown += new
            System.Windows.Forms.MouseEventHandler(this.OnMouseDown);

    }
    #endregion

    private void OnMouseMove(object sender,
        System.Windows.Forms.MouseEventArgs e)
    {
        fEndPoint.X = e.X;
        fEndPoint.Y = e.Y;
        Refresh();

    }

    private void OnMouseDown(object sender,
        System.Windows.Forms.MouseEventArgs e)
    {
        fStartPoint.X = e.X;
        fStartPoint.Y = e.Y;
    }
```

```
private void OnPaint(object sender,
     System.Windows.Forms.PaintEventArgs e)
{
    Pen p = new Pen( System.Drawing.Brushes.Blue, 1 );
    e.Graphics.DrawLine( p,
        fStartPoint, fEndPoint );


}
    }
}
```

With the information you garner in this section, you should have all the background you need to create amazing components for use in the C# system. By utilizing the other information in this book, such as databases and graphics, you can create components that can do almost anything users need them to do. You can then bundle functionality into your components to do specialized processing for your own company applications.

Immediate Solutions

Creating a New Control

One of the most useful features of the new C# language is its reliance on prebuilt components, or controls, that can do a specific task. These controls allow the same drag-and-drop design process that C# provides in the Visual Studio.NET environment. Unfortunately, those controls are not always enough to do what you want them to do. Microsoft has done an excellent job of building a solid foundation of controls on which you can base most applications. When you need a specialized control, however, you are not likely to find it in the CLR library.

Given the number of different industries that use software to solve their problems, building specialized components into the system for all of them is simply impossible. Imagine trying to create specialized components that work with both the banking world and the world of Hollywood movies. Doesn't seem likely, does it? Unless, of course you consider the specialized accounting objects that Hollywood uses to make hit movies seem to lose money. That, of course, is a joke. Nobody would really want to lose money. And they certainly wouldn't use a specialized component to do it. But if they did want to create a component to do that, C# would certainly be the best language for it.

Because you have no simple way to make sure that controls exist for all possible cases, the designers of C# realized that they would need a way for application programmers to develop their own controls that would fit into specialized systems. The Visual Studio.NET system provides a simple way to create new controls in your application and, as you see in later examples, ways to share those controls with other applications. In this example, you create a simple digital clock you can use to display the time in your own application. Using this control, you no longer have to update some clock display in an idle loop of your program.

Figure 13.1 shows a form displaying the clock control running in an application. You can see that the clock displays the simple time, in a standard format for the region. If you run the program from the enclosed CD-ROM, you see that the clock does, in fact, update itself once per second.

Listing 13.1 shows the code needed to implement the control itself. Note that this is only the control itself. This code does not use the control or load it into a form. That task is shown next.

Figure 13.1   The clock control in action.

Listing 13.1   The clock control code.

```
using System;
using System.Collections;
using System.ComponentModel;
using System.Drawing;
using System.Data;
using System.Windows.Forms;

namespace CH13_1
{
    public class DigitalClock : System.Windows.Forms.UserControl
    {
        private System.Windows.Forms.Timer timer1;
        private System.ComponentModel.IContainer components;

        public DigitalClock()
        {
            // This call is required by the Windows.Forms Form Designer.
            InitializeComponent();

        }
        protected override void Dispose( bool disposing )
        {
            if( disposing )
            {
                if(components != null)
                {
                    components.Dispose();
                }
            }
            base.Dispose( disposing );
        }
```

```
#region Component Designer generated code
private void InitializeComponent()
{
    this.components = new System.ComponentModel.Container();
    this.timer1 = new System.Windows.Forms.Timer(this.components);
    this.timer1.Enabled = true;
    this.timer1.Interval = 1000;
    this.timer1.Tick += new System.EventHandler(this.OnTick);
    this.Name = "DigitalClock";
    this.Paint += new
        System.Windows.Forms.PaintEventHandler(this.OnPaint);
}
#endregion

private void OnPaint(object sender,
                  System.Windows.Forms.PaintEventArgs e)
{
    // Get the time in system format.
    System.DateTime dt = System.DateTime.Now;

    // Get the text that represents that time
    String Text = dt.ToLongTimeString();

    e.Graphics.DrawString(Text, Font, new SolidBrush (ForeColor),
        ClientRectangle);
}
private void OnTick(object sender, System.EventArgs e)
{
    this.Refresh();
}
    }
}
```

By compiling this code into your application, you can load the clock control into your application. Loading that control into your own form, however, requires that you do some things by hand. Listing 13.2 shows all the code needed to load the control into a form. The changes needed are shown in the highlighted sections.

Listing 13.2 The clock form code.

```
using System;
using System.Drawing;
using System.Collections;
using System.ComponentModel;
using System.Windows.Forms;
using System.Data;
```

```
namespace CH13_1
{
    public class Form1 : System.Windows.Forms.Form
    {
        private System.ComponentModel.Container components = null;
        private System.Windows.Forms.Label label1;

        private CH13_1.DigitalClock clock;

        public Form1()
        {
            InitializeComponent();
        }

        protected override void Dispose( bool disposing )
        {
            if( disposing )
            {
                if (components != null)
                {
                    components.Dispose();
                }
            }
            base.Dispose( disposing );
        }

        #region Windows Form Designer generated code
        private void InitializeComponent()
        {
            this.label1 = new System.Windows.Forms.Label();
            this.SuspendLayout();
            this.label1.Location = new System.Drawing.Point(16, 24);
            this.label1.Name = "label1";
            this.label1.Size = new System.Drawing.Size(128, 16);
            this.label1.TabIndex = 0;
            this.label1.Text = "Clock:";

            this.clock = new CH13_1.DigitalClock();
            this.clock.Location = new System.Drawing.Point(16,50);
            this.clock.Name = "clock";
            this.clock.Size = new System.Drawing.Size(128, 80);
            this.clock.TabIndex = 1;
            this.AutoScaleBaseSize = new System.Drawing.Size(5, 13);
            this.ClientSize = new System.Drawing.Size(292, 273);
            this.Controls.AddRange(new System.Windows.Forms.Control[] {
                            this.label1,
                            this.clock});
```

```
        this.Name = "Form1";
        this.Text = "Form1";
        this.Load += new System.EventHandler(this.Form1_Load);
        this.ResumeLayout(false);


    }
    #endregion

    [STAThread]
    static void Main()
    {
        Application.Run(new Form1());
    }
}
}
```

Using an Existing Control

One problem with having controls is that they tend to accumulate in projects, never to be reused. In earlier releases of Windows and such languages as C++, this problem was serious because you had no easy way to bring these controls into your new projects, which meant that they went unused. Project settings required tweaking, include files needed to be manipulated, and libraries had to be included in order to make things work. This situation was often so frustrating that people would simply rewrite the controls or, worse, copy them into the project—leading to multiple copies of the same code in different places.

Of course, when the code was fixed in one project, it would never be fixed in another. This situation led to even more baffling problems when the same bug was reported in multiple systems, but fixed in only one or two. Later on, maintenance programmers did not understand why the same control would behave differently in two different places. Only by tracking through any version control (if any existed) could the issue be resolved, which led to many frustrated programmers and lots of duplicated code.

The new Visual Studio.NET has an option to create a control library. By using these libraries, which are maintained and used by the .NET framework, the code can reside in a single place and be used by multiple projects. Better, because the libraries themselves are copied into a project, you have no need to worry about a binary incompatibility when a library is updated. Of course, you then have the problem of having multiple copies of the binary code, but that is a vast improvement over having multiple copies of the source.

Figure 13.2   The custom control shown from a control library.

In the example in this section, you create a control library to implement a custom control in C#. That library is then referenced and used by a project that uses the control in a form. The control itself, as shown in Figure 13.2, simply displays a text string. In this case, the infamous "Hello World" string is shown.

The code to implement this simple control is simple, as shown in Listing 13.3. Note that you must first create a control library (the one in this project is called Ch13_3Lib), which contains this control.

Listing 13.3   The control code.

```
using System;
using System.Collections;
using System.ComponentModel;
using System.Drawing;
using System.Data;
using System.Windows.Forms;

namespace CH13_2Lib
{
    public class UserControl1 : System.Windows.Forms.UserControl
    {
        private System.ComponentModel.Container components = null;

        public UserControl1()
        {
            InitializeComponent();
        }
        protected override void Dispose( bool disposing )
        {
            if( disposing )
            {
                if( components != null )
                    components.Dispose();
            }
```

```
      base.Dispose( disposing );
   }


   #region Component Designer generated code
   private void InitializeComponent()
   {
      this.Name = "UserControl1";
      this.Paint += new
         System.Windows.Forms.PaintEventHandler(this.OnPaint);

   }
   #endregion

   private void OnPaint(object sender,
            System.Windows.Forms.PaintEventArgs e)
   {
      e.Graphics.DrawString( "Hello world", Font,
            new SolidBrush(Color.Blue), ClientRectangle );
   }
 }
}
```

As you can see, the code is not particularly complex. You add a single event handler for the **Paint** event and add some code to that handler to display the text string in the client rectangle of the control. Take a look at Listing 13.4, which shows the code needed to use this control in a separate project. This standard Windows application project was created with Visual Studio.NET. Note that you added the CH13_2Lib.DLL file as a reference via the Add Reference tool.

Listing 13.4   The project using a control library.

```
using System;
using System.Drawing;
using System.Collections;
using System.ComponentModel;
using System.Windows.Forms;
using System.Data;
using CH13_2Lib;

namespace Ch13_2
{
   public class Form1 : System.Windows.Forms.Form
   {
      private System.ComponentModel.Container components = null;
      private System.Windows.Forms.Label label1;
      private CH13_2Lib.UserControl1 control1;
```

```
        public Form1()
        {
            InitializeComponent();
        }
        protected override void Dispose( bool disposing )
        {
            if( disposing )
            {
                if (components != null)
                {
                    components.Dispose();
                }
            }
            base.Dispose( disposing );
        }

        #region Windows Form Designer generated code
        private void InitializeComponent()
        {
            this.control1 = new CH13_2Lib.UserControl1();
            this.label1 = new System.Windows.Forms.Label();
            this.SuspendLayout();
            //
            // control1
            //
            this.control1.Location = new System.Drawing.Point(32, 48);
            this.control1.Name = "control1";
            this.control1.Size = new System.Drawing.Size(80, 24);
            this.control1.TabIndex = 0;
            this.label1.Location = new System.Drawing.Point(32, 24);
            this.label1.Name = "label1";
            this.label1.Size = new System.Drawing.Size(144, 24);
            this.label1.TabIndex = 1;
            this.label1.Text = "Custom Control:";
            this.AutoScaleBaseSize = new System.Drawing.Size(5, 13);
            this.ClientSize = new System.Drawing.Size(292, 273);
            this.Controls.AddRange(new System.Windows.Forms.Control[] {
                    this.label1,
                    this.control1});
            this.Name = "Form1";
            this.Text = "Form1";
            this.ResumeLayout(false);

        }
```

```
    #endregion
    [STAThread]
    static void Main()
    {
        Application.Run(new Form1());
    }
  }
}
```

The highlighted lines show the code you must add to the project to make the new control work in the project. As you can see, the code is not terribly complicated. After you have added the lines, you can then modify the code via the Form Designer, just as if you had placed the control on the form via the drag-and-drop method. For now, you cannot do this directly.

TIP: For more information about properties, see Chapter 3.

Related solution:	Found on page:
Using Events with Form Objects	285

Creating a Property for a Component

Creating a new control for use in your application is always helpful. Unfortunately, if that control is not configurable, you cannot use it in many applications. The method the C# system provides for configuring controls is the property. I talked a little about properties in Chapter 3. In this instance, you want to add to the control a property that someone can configure at either design time or runtime.

For this example, you turn to the tried-and-true digital clock control. In this case, however, you want to allow users to configure the control to display time in either the short format or the long format. The short format does not contain the seconds portion of the time, and the long format does. For now, that is the only real difference between the two formats. Figure 13.3 shows the clock component displayed using the short time format, which is a change from the last time you used this particular control.

Listing 13.5 shows the code that is needed to create this control. The highlighted section of code shows the property you have added and how it is used in the control to configure the display of the time text.

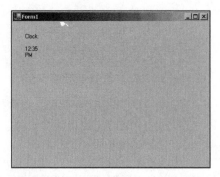

Figure 13.3   The clock control using the short time format.

Listing 13.5   The clock control with properties code.

```
using System;
using System.Collections;
using System.ComponentModel;
using System.Drawing;
using System.Data;
using System.Windows.Forms;

namespace CH13_3
{
    public class DigitalClockWithProperties :
              System.Windows.Forms.UserControl
    {
        private System.ComponentModel.IContainer components;
        private System.Windows.Forms.Timer timer1;

        public enum TimeFormat
        {
            ShortForm = 1,
            LongForm  = 2
        };
        private TimeFormat fFormat;

        public TimeFormat Format
        {
            get
            {
                return fFormat;
            }
            set
            {
                fFormat = value;
            }
        }
```

```
public DigitalClockWithProperties()
{
    // This call is required by the Windows.Forms Form Designer.
    InitializeComponent();
}
protected override void Dispose( bool disposing )
{
    if( disposing )
    {
        if(components != null)
        {
            components.Dispose();
        }
    }
    base.Dispose( disposing );
}

#region Component Designer generated code
private void InitializeComponent()
{
    this.components = new System.ComponentModel.Container();
    this.timer1 = new System.Windows.Forms.Timer(this.components);
    //
    // timer1
    //
    this.timer1.Enabled = true;
    this.timer1.Interval = 1000;
    this.timer1.Tick += new System.EventHandler(this.OnTick);
    //
    // DigitalClockWithProperties
    //
    this.Name = "DigitalClockWithProperties";
    this.Paint += new
            System.Windows.Forms.PaintEventHandler(this.OnPaint);
}
#endregion

private void OnPaint(object sender,
            System.Windows.Forms.PaintEventArgs e)
{
    // Get the time in system format.
    System.DateTime dt = System.DateTime.Now;

    // Get the text that represents that time
    String Text = "";
    switch ( fFormat )
    {
```

13. Components

```
            case TimeFormat.LongForm:
                Text = dt.ToLongTimeString();
                break;
            case TimeFormat.ShortForm:
                Text = dt.ToShortTimeString();
                break;
        }

    e.Graphics.DrawString(Text, Font, new SolidBrush (ForeColor),
        ClientRectangle);

    }

    private void OnTick(object sender, System.EventArgs e)
    {
        Refresh();
    }
  }
}
```

One other helpful part of this example is that it shows how to use an enumeration as a property. Note that C# makes no distinction between enumerations and any other sort of data type. You can therefore easily create properties that users can understand how to use rather than have strange hard-coded numbers.

Creating a Read-Only Property for a Component

Sometimes, it is useful to be able to have properties for a control or component that are accessed from the outside world, but can't be modified by the application developer, such as internal status elements that can be read but not changed externally. In the C# world, these elements are known as *read-only* properties. In this example, you explore how to create a read-only property and make a component that is nonvisual.

Creating a read-only property for a component is not difficult. Because properties are implemented with **set** and **get** methods to modify and retrieve the property value, simply omitting the **set** method makes the property read-only. Likewise, a property can omit a **get** property and become write-only. This process might seem strange, but it is needed by some real-world applications.

Figure 13.4 shows the form you use to test the component you create in the example in this section. Listing 13.6 shows the control code to implement your simple component, and Listing 13.7 shows the added code for the form to test the new

Figure 13.4   The **TimerCounter** form.

component. The control simply increments an internal counter for each passing second. A developer could use this component to see how long something is taking or to test something that requires an incrementing value.

In the code listing, notice that the highlighted segment shows how to create the read-only property. As an experiment, you might try assigning something to the property in your application code, just to see what the compiler says.

Listing 13.6   The read-only property control.

```
using System;
using System.Collections;
using System.ComponentModel;
using System.Drawing;
using System.Data;
using System.Windows.Forms;

namespace C13_4
{
    public class TimerCounter : System.Windows.Forms.UserControl
    {
        private System.Windows.Forms.Timer timer1;
        private System.ComponentModel.IContainer components;
        private int fCounter = 0;
        public int Counter
        {
            get
            {
                return fCounter;
            }
        }

        public TimerCounter()
        {
            // This call is required by the Windows.Forms Form Designer.
            InitializeComponent();
        }
        protected override void Dispose( bool disposing )
        {
```

```
            if( disposing )
            {
               if(components != null)
               {
                  components.Dispose();
               }
            }
            base.Dispose( disposing );
         }

         #region Component Designer generated code
         private void InitializeComponent()
         {
            this.components = new System.ComponentModel.Container();
            this.timer1 = new System.Windows.Forms.Timer(this.components);
            this.timer1.Enabled = true;
            this.timer1.Interval = 1000;
            this.timer1.Tick += new System.EventHandler(this.OnTick);
            this.Name = "TimerCounter";

         }
         #endregion

         private void OnTick(object sender, System.EventArgs e)
         {
            fCounter++;
         }
      }
   }
```

Listing 13.7   The TimerCounter test form.

```
using System;
using System.Drawing;
using System.Collections;
using System.ComponentModel;
using System.Windows.Forms;
using System.Data;

namespace C13_4
{
   public class Form1 : System.Windows.Forms.Form
   {
      private System.Windows.Forms.Label label1;
      private System.Windows.Forms.Label CounterLabel;
      private System.Windows.Forms.Button Update;
```

```
private System.ComponentModel.Container components = null;
private C13_4.TimerCounter counter;

public Form1()
{
    InitializeComponent();
    counter = new C13_4.TimerCounter();
}
protected override void Dispose( bool disposing )
{
    if( disposing )
    {
        if (components != null)
        {
            components.Dispose();
        }
    }
    base.Dispose( disposing );
}

#region Windows Form Designer generated code
private void InitializeComponent()
{
    this.label1 = new System.Windows.Forms.Label();
    this.CounterLabel = new System.Windows.Forms.Label();
    this.Update = new System.Windows.Forms.Button();
    this.SuspendLayout();
    this.label1.Location = new System.Drawing.Point(32, 24);
    this.label1.Name = "label1";
    this.label1.Size = new System.Drawing.Size(48, 23);
    this.label1.TabIndex = 0;
    this.label1.Text = "Counter: ";
    this.CounterLabel.Location = new System.Drawing.Point(96, 24);
    this.CounterLabel.Name = "CounterLabel";
    this.CounterLabel.Size = new System.Drawing.Size(32, 23);
    this.CounterLabel.TabIndex = 1;
    this.Update.Location = new System.Drawing.Point(80, 72);
    this.Update.Name = "Update";
    this.Update.TabIndex = 2;
    this.Update.Text = "Update";
    this.Update.Click += new System.EventHandler(this.Update_Click);
    this.AutoScaleBaseSize = new System.Drawing.Size(5, 13);
    this.ClientSize = new System.Drawing.Size(224, 133);
    this.Controls.AddRange(new System.Windows.Forms.Control[] {
            this.Update,
            this.CounterLabel,
            this.label1});
```

```
            this.Name = "Form1";
            this.Text = "Form1";
            this.ResumeLayout(false);


        }
        #endregion
        [STAThread]
        static void Main()
        {
            Application.Run(new Form1());
        }
        private void Update_Click(object sender, System.EventArgs e)
        {
            CounterLabel.Text = counter.Counter.ToString();
        }
    }
}
```

Creating an Event for a Component

The process of communicating between a custom component and the application in which it resides is done via events and event handlers. In this example, you look at a few new examples, from creating a compound component from other individual components to creating an event for a component and handling it in the main form.

TIP: *For more information about delegates, see Chapter 5.*

To create a component event, you need to understand how to work with delegates. As I discussed in Chapter 5, a *delegate* is a conduit from one piece of the software to another. For events, delegates represent the "pipe" that the event source uses to communicate with the event handler. In this case, the custom component is the event source, and the form in which it resides is the event handler.

C# and the CLR allow for the creation of compound components. Assume that you have a rather consistent need for a component to enter a person's name and address. You could create a small form that does this and use it repeatedly. Alternatively, you could create a simple component that contains just the fields you want and then embed that component in all the forms that use it. By creating intelligent events for this small component, you would have a single reusable component that could be dragged and dropped onto each form. Reusing a component is useful because it looks, acts, and responds the same way to a user each time it is used, no matter what form it might be on. Additionally, of course, you save space by having only one copy of the code in your source application.

In this example, you create a simple compound component (how's that for an oxymoron?) that has a label and a drop-down combo box. The small component is shown in Figure 13.5. No figure exists for the form itself because it doesn't have anything else on it. The code for the component is shown in Listing 13.8.

TIP: *In the highlighted section of the code, notice how you create a delegate for the event and then use that delegate to communicate with the form.*

Listing 13.8   Creating an event for a component.

```
using System;
using System.Collections;
using System.ComponentModel;
using System.Drawing;
using System.Data;
using System.Windows.Forms;

namespace CH13_5
{
    public class CompoundControl : System.Windows.Forms.UserControl
    {
        // Allow a handler for the event
        public delegate Boolean ValueChangedEventHandler(int nValue);

        private System.Windows.Forms.Label label1;
        private System.Windows.Forms.ComboBox comboBox1;
        private System.ComponentModel.Container components = null;
        public event ValueChangedEventHandler Changed;

        public CompoundControl()
        {
```

Figure 13.5   The compound component.

```
        // This call is required by the Windows.Forms Form Designer.
        InitializeComponent();
    }
    protected override void Dispose( bool disposing )
    {
        if( disposing )
        {
            if(components != null)
            {
                components.Dispose();
            }
        }
        base.Dispose( disposing );
    }

    #region Component Designer generated code
    private void InitializeComponent()
    {
        this.comboBox1 = new System.Windows.Forms.ComboBox();
        this.label1 = new System.Windows.Forms.Label();
        this.SuspendLayout();
        this.comboBox1.DropDownWidth = 121;
        this.comboBox1.Items.AddRange(new object[] {
            "New York",
            "Colorado",
            "California",
            "Florida",
            "Georgia",
            "New Mexico"});
        this.comboBox1.Location = new System.Drawing.Point(24, 48);
        this.comboBox1.Name = "comboBox1";
        this.comboBox1.Size = new System.Drawing.Size(200, 21);
        this.comboBox1.TabIndex = 1;
        this.comboBox1.Text = "comboBox1";
        this.comboBox1.SelectedIndexChanged += new
            System.EventHandler(this.OnSelectionIndexChange);
        this.label1.Location = new System.Drawing.Point(16, 24);
        this.label1.Name = "label1";
        this.label1.TabIndex = 0;
        this.label1.Text = "Select An Entry";
        this.Controls.AddRange(new System.Windows.Forms.Control[] {
            this.comboBox1,
            this.label1});
        this.Name = "CompoundControl";
        this.Size = new System.Drawing.Size(240, 96);
```

```
        this.ResumeLayout(false);
    }
    #endregion

    private void OnSelectionIndexChange(object sender,
            System.EventArgs e)
    {
        if (Changed != null)
            Changed( this.comboBox1.SelectedIndex);
    }
  }
}
```

Notice in this example how you pass through the event from the base control to the parent form. In this case, the base control notifies you via your own delegate handler that a user has changed the selection on the combo box. You then pass this event along in a more customized approach to the parent form. Take a look at Listing 13.9, which shows how the parent form works with the event and displays its own message box when the event is fired.

Listing 13.9   The parent form of the compound component.

```
using System;
using System.Drawing;
using System.Collections;
using System.ComponentModel;
using System.Windows.Forms;
using System.Data;

namespace CH13_5
{
    public class Form1 : System.Windows.Forms.Form
    {
        private System.ComponentModel.Container components = null;
        private CH13_5.CompoundControl compoundcomponent1 = null;

        public Form1()
        {
            InitializeComponent();
        }
        protected override void Dispose( bool disposing )
        {
            if( disposing )
            {
                if (components != null)
                {
```

```
                    components.Dispose();
            }
        }
        base.Dispose( disposing );
    }

    #region Windows Form Designer generated code
    private void InitializeComponent()
    {
        this.compoundcomponent1 = new CH13_5.CompoundControl();
        this.compoundcomponent1.Location = new
                System.Drawing.Point(24,50);
        this.compoundcomponent1.Name = "compound1";
        this.compoundcomponent1.Size = new System.Drawing.Size(250,100);
        this.compoundcomponent1.TabIndex = 1;
        this.compoundcomponent1.Changed += new
            CH13_5.CompoundControl.ValueChangedEventHandler(OnChanged);

        this.components = new System.ComponentModel.Container();
        this.Size = new System.Drawing.Size(300,300);
        this.Text = "Form1";
        this.Controls.AddRange(new System.Windows.Forms.Control[]
        {
            this.compoundcomponent1,
        });
    }
    #endregion

    private bool OnChanged( int nIndex )
    {
        MessageBox.Show( this, "New Index!" + nIndex );
        return true;
    }

    [STAThread]
    static void Main()
    {
        Application.Run(new Form1());
    }
}
}
```

If you run this little form program and change the combo box selection at runtime, you see a display that looks like the one shown in Figure 13.6. It shows you that all the delegate and event handler processes have worked as advertised.

Figure 13.6   Showing the combo box selection change.

Dragging and Dropping in a Component

The ability to drag-and-drop components is one hallmark of Windows applications. Users are accustomed to working with Windows and being able to simply drag information from one application to another. You might, for example, take an item from one list box or list view and move it to another list box or list view in the application by selecting it, dragging it over to the other list view, and then releasing the mouse button.

This example shows how to do this in your own application. As you can see in Figure 13.7, the form has two simple list view components. You can move items from the first list view to the second list view by simply dragging and dropping them. The system then adds the item to the second list box and removes it from the first.

Listing 13.10 shows the code that performs the drag-and-drop operation. The highlighted elements in the listing show the items you have to add and the events that need to be handled for this form.

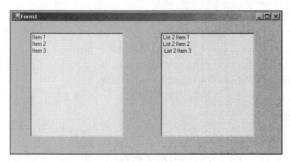

Figure 13.7   The drag-and-drop list view form.

Listing 13.10   Dragging and dropping in a component.

```
using System;
using System.Drawing;
using System.Collections;
using System.ComponentModel;
using System.Windows.Forms;
using System.Data;

namespace CH13_6
{
    public class Form1 : System.Windows.Forms.Form
    {
        private System.Windows.Forms.ListView listView1;
        private System.Windows.Forms.ListView listView2;
        private System.ComponentModel.Container components = null;

        public Form1()
        {
            InitializeComponent();
        }
        protected override void Dispose( bool disposing )
        {
            if( disposing )
            {
                if (components != null)
                {
                    components.Dispose();
                }
            }
            base.Dispose( disposing );
        }

        #region Windows Form Designer generated code
        private void InitializeComponent()
        {
            System.Windows.Forms.ListViewItem listViewItem1 = new
                    System.Windows.Forms.ListViewItem("List 2 Item 1");
            System.Windows.Forms.ListViewItem listViewItem2 = new
                    System.Windows.Forms.ListViewItem("List 2 Item 2");
            System.Windows.Forms.ListViewItem listViewItem3 = new
                    System.Windows.Forms.ListViewItem(" List 2 Item 3");
            System.Windows.Forms.ListViewItem listViewItem4 = new
                    System.Windows.Forms.ListViewItem("Item 1");
            System.Windows.Forms.ListViewItem listViewItem5 = new
                    System.Windows.Forms.ListViewItem("Item 2");
```

```
System.Windows.Forms.ListViewItem listViewItem6 = new
        System.Windows.Forms.ListViewItem("Item 3");
this.listView2 = new System.Windows.Forms.ListView();
this.listView1 = new System.Windows.Forms.ListView();
this.SuspendLayout();
this.listView2.AllowDrop = true;
listViewItem1.UseItemStyleForSubItems = false;
listViewItem2.UseItemStyleForSubItems = false;
listViewItem3.UseItemStyleForSubItems = false;
this.listView2.Items.AddRange(new
    System.Windows.Forms.ListViewItem[]
{
        listViewItem1,
        listViewItem2,
        listViewItem3});
this.listView2.Location = new System.Drawing.Point(320, 24);
this.listView2.Name = "listView2";
this.listView2.Size = new System.Drawing.Size(200, 216);
this.listView2.TabIndex = 1;
this.listView2.View = System.Windows.Forms.View.List;
this.listView2.DragDrop += new
    System.Windows.Forms.DragEventHandler(this.OnDragDrop);
this.listView2.DragEnter += new
        System.Windows.Forms.DragEventHandler(this.OnDragEnter);
this.listView1.AllowDrop = true;
listViewItem4.UseItemStyleForSubItems = false;
listViewItem5.UseItemStyleForSubItems = false;
listViewItem6.UseItemStyleForSubItems = false;
this.listView1.Items.AddRange(new
        System.Windows.Forms.ListViewItem[]
{
    listViewItem4,
    listViewItem5,
    listViewItem6});
this.listView1.Location = new System.Drawing.Point(40, 24);
this.listView1.Name = "listView1";
this.listView1.Size = new System.Drawing.Size(200, 216);
this.listView1.TabIndex = 0;
this.listView1.View = System.Windows.Forms.View.List;
this.listView1.ItemDrag +=
    newSystem.Windows.Forms.ItemDragEventHandler(
        this.OnItemDrag);
this.AutoScaleBaseSize = new System.Drawing.Size(5, 13);
this.ClientSize = new System.Drawing.Size(576, 273);
this.Controls.AddRange(new System.Windows.Forms.Control[] {
        this.listView2,
        this.listView1});
```

577

```
            this.Name = "Form1";
            this.Text = "Form1";
            this.ResumeLayout(false);


        }
        #endregion

        [STAThread]
        static void Main()
        {
            Application.Run(new Form1());
        }


        private void OnItemDrag(object sender,
                    System.Windows.Forms.ItemDragEventArgs e)
        {
            string s = e.Item.ToString();
            // Start the Drag operation
            DoDragDrop(s, DragDropEffects.Copy | DragDropEffects.Move);
        }
        private void OnDragEnter(object sender,
                    System.Windows.Forms.DragEventArgs e)
        {
            if (e.Data.GetDataPresent(DataFormats.Text))
                e.Effect = DragDropEffects.Copy;
            else
                e.Effect = DragDropEffects.None;
        }


        private void OnDragDrop(object sender,
                    System.Windows.Forms.DragEventArgs
                            e)
        {
            string typestring = "Type";
            string s = e.Data.GetData(typestring.GetType()).ToString();
            string orig_string = s;
            // Parse out the type information
            s = s.Substring(s.IndexOf(":")+1).Trim();
            s = s.Substring(1,s.Length-2);


            // First, add it to our list box
            this.listView2.Items.Add( s );


            // Find it in the first list box
            IEnumerator enumerator = listView1.Items.GetEnumerator();
            int whichIdx = -1;
```

```
        int idx = 0;
        while ( enumerator.MoveNext() )
        {
            string s2 = enumerator.Current.ToString();
            if ( s2.Equals(orig_string) )
            {
                whichIdx = idx;
                break;
            }
            idx ++;
        }
        this.listView1.Items.RemoveAt( whichIdx );


    }
  }
}
```

Versioning a Component

One major interest in the .NET world is being able to version a component so that only the correct version is used. How do you set the version information for a component? The answer, it turns out, is quite easy. Simply modify a single file in your project, and your component will have the version you want. Listing 13.11 shows the listing of the AssemblyInfo.cs file, which shows the changes you would make to change from the default 1.0 version to a new version number.

Listing 13.11   Versioning a component.

```
using System.Reflection;
using System.Runtime.CompilerServices;

//
// General information about an assembly is controlled through the
// following set of attributes. Change these attribute values to modify
// the information associated with an assembly.
//
[assembly: AssemblyTitle("")]
[assembly: AssemblyDescription("")]
[assembly: AssemblyConfiguration("")]
[assembly: AssemblyCompany("")]
[assembly: AssemblyProduct("")]
[assembly: AssemblyCopyright("")]
[assembly: AssemblyTrademark("")]
[assembly: AssemblyCulture("")]
```

```
//
// Version information for an assembly consists of the following four
// values:
//
//      Major Version
//      Minor Version
//      Build Number
//      Revision
//
// You can specify all the values, or you can default the Revision
// and Build Numbers by using the '*' as shown below:

[assembly: AssemblyVersion("3.5.*")]


//
// To sign your assembly, you must specify a key to use. Refer to the
// Microsoft .NET Framework documentation for more information on
// assembly signing.
//
// Use the attributes below to control which key is used for signing.
//
// Notes:
//    (*) If no key is specified, the assembly is not signed.
//    (*) KeyName refers to a key that has been installed in the Crypto
//        Service Provider (CSP) on your machine. KeyFile refers to a file
//        which contains a key.
//    (*) If the KeyFile and the KeyName values are both specified, the
//        following processing occurs:
//        (1) If the KeyName can be found in the CSP, that key is used.
//        (2) If the KeyName does not exist and the KeyFile does exist,
//            the key in the KeyFile is installed into the CSP and used.
//    (*) To create a KeyFile, you can use the sn.exe (Strong Name)
//        utility. When specifying the KeyFile, the location of the KeyFile
//        should be relative to the project output directory, which is
//        %Project Directory%\obj\<configuration>. For example, if your
//        KeyFile is located in the project directory, you would specify
//        the AssemblyKeyFile attribute as
//        [assembly: AssemblyKeyFile("..\\..\\mykey.snk")]
//    (*) Delay Signing is an advanced option. See the Microsoft .NET
//        Framework documentation for more information on this.
//
[assembly: AssemblyDelaySign(false)]
[assembly: AssemblyKeyFile("")]
[assembly: AssemblyKeyName("")]
```

That sums up the component development aspects of C#. I hope that you got from this chapter a good overview of how you can use the language to extend your own applications. Remember, though, that components are useful only if they are reused. You should therefore work to devise and implement components that can be used over and over. This capability is one of the few forms of immortality available to you in the programming world, so take advantage of it.

Chapter 14

Miscellaneous Areas

In Depth

Whenever you discuss any new language, some areas don't seem to fit into neat little categories. This catch-all chapter deals with many of these issues. You will almost certainly face these real problems when you're working in C#, but they do not fit nicely into one of the other categories that make up the other chapters in the book.

Printing

One thing most programs require is some way to print data. In spite of all your attempts to create a paperless office, you still require paper in order to make the business world work. Whether it is printing an email message so that you can keep a copy in your filing cabinet or printing a report so that it can be mailed to a client, the issue of printing is still one that will be with us for a long time. The C# support library, of course, contains support for printing.

If you want to simply print a file, the following code does most of the work. Let's look at the code first and then take a look at how it all works:

```
try
{
    streamToPrint = new StreamReader (filePath);
    try
    {
        printFont = new Font("Arial", 10);
        PrintDocument pd = new PrintDocument();
        pd.PrintPage += new PrintPageEventHandler(PrintPage);
        pd.Print ();
    }
    finally
    {
        streamToPrint.Close() ;
    }
}
catch(Exception ex)
{
    MessageBox.Show("An error occurred printing the file - " +
            ex.Message);
}
```

This particular chunk of code uses a delegate to handle the printing of each page of the file. The print handler (named **PrintPage**, in this case) does the printing of each chunk of file. This handler might look something like the following example:

NOTE: *This is only a code snippet. For the complete print handler, see the "Immediate Solutions" section, later in this chapter.*

```
private void PrintPage(object sender, PrintPageEventArgs ev)
{
    float lpp = 0 ;
    float yPos =  0 ;
    int count = 0 ;
    float leftMargin = ev.MarginBounds.Left;
    float topMargin = ev.MarginBounds.Top;
    String line=null;

    // Lines per page
    lpp = ev.MarginBounds.Height  / printFont.GetHeight(ev.Graphics) ;

    while (count < lpp && ((line=streamToPrint.ReadLine()) != null))
    {
        yPos = topMargin + (count * printFont.GetHeight(ev.Graphics));

        ev.Graphics.DrawString (line, printFont, Brushes.Black,
                leftMargin, yPos, new StringFormat());

        count++;
    }

    if (line != null)
        ev.HasMorePages = true ;
    else
        ev.HasMorePages = false;
}
```

As you can see, this routine steps through the lines in the file one at a time. When this routine has printed enough lines to fill a page, it terminates itself. If lines remain to be printed, the handler indicates to the print system that the routine should be called an additional time. If no lines are left, the handler terminates by setting the **HasMorePages** flag of the event argument to false.

The job of rendering the text to the physical printer and controlling the font and color that are displayed is left to the C# system. The skeleton shown here can be used to display any information.

14. Miscellaneous Areas

Extending Classes

C# is, at its heart, an object-oriented language designed from the ground up to implement and espouse object-oriented concepts. One core function of an object-oriented language is its ability to extend the core functionality of the base classes in your own applications. You can extend classes in one of two ways.

The first way you can extend a class in C# or in any other object-oriented language is the most familiar: inheritance. Inheritance allows you to add your own functionality on top of the public interface to a class. In addition, in certain cases, you can modify the behavior of the existing functionality.

If a method is defined as virtual in C++, you can override that method in your derived class. You override a method by simply adding a method of the same name and signature. For example, in C++, if you had a method like this:

```
virtual void DoSomething( int iValue );
```

Now, if you implement in your derived class a method with the same name and signature, this method overrides the function in the base class. Any method or function that made a call to the **DoSomething** method of a pointer to the derived class calls the method you wrote rather than the one written by the base class programmer.

In C#, you cannot simply override a base class method by naming it the same as the base class method name. You must use the **override** keyword, introduced in Chapter 2. If, for example, you have a method defined in the base class as

```
public virtual void setAge(int age);
```

and you want to override this method in a derived class, you would write:

```
override public void setAge(int age)
```

NOTE: *In either case, the derived method is called whenever an object of the derived class is called. All this information is covered in Chapter 2.*

The second way in which you can extend an existing class is necessary when the class being extended is **sealed**. A *sealed* class cannot be inherited from. Although you should not use this technique in your own base classes without a good reason, the designers of the Common Language Runtime (CLR) chose this technique in many instances. Their reasons are varied, but usually the implementers felt that the classes would be complete and would cause problems only if modified.

How can you modify a sealed class? The answer lies in another object-oriented technique: *encapsulation.* By placing an instance of the base class within a new wrapper, you can allow access to the functionality of the base class as well as add new functionality of your own in your inherited class. I discuss an example of extending the sealed string class in "Extending the String Class" in the "Immediate Solutions" section later in this chapter.

Help

No discussion of application development would be complete without a discussion of the help system. As you may know, the Windows help system was originally a proprietary format that used such specialized tools as the Help Compiler to build files from a collection of different input sources. Later, HTML help files were introduced along with extensions that allowed for indexing and searching these HTML files. Both help file formats are still allowed in the Windows operating system, allowing for both forward and backward compatibility.

The C# CLR supports both help file formats through a single interface. As the developer, you can then worry more about the content and functionality of your help files and less about their format. All this functionality is supported through the **System.Help** namespace. The **Help** class methods are shown in Table 14.1.

You use the functions by simply specifying the command you want to issue and any information you need to include to execute that command. You can use these four commands:

- COMMAND_CONTENTS
- COMMAND_FIND
- COMMAND_INDEX
- COMMAND_TOPIC

You can use each of these possible commands with the **ShowHelp** method of the class. For example, to show the contents for the xyz.chm file (a new-style HTML file), you use the following command:

```
ShowHelp( this, "xyz.chm" );
```

Table 14.1 The Help class methods.

Method	Purpose
ShowHelp	Displays the contents of a help file in various ways
ShowHelpIndex	Displays the index for a given help file
ShowPopup	Displays a help page as a small pop-up window

The **this** argument is the window control you want to use as the parent of the Help file. This window receives any messages from the Help file, if any are embedded in it. The second argument is simply the name of the help file. This method is overloaded so that you can do other things with the same method. For example, to display the same help file, but with the topic **topic1**, you use this format:

```
ShowHelp( this, "xyz.chm", "topic1");
```

To bring up the search page for the specified help file, you use this version of the command:

```
ShowHelp( this, "xyz.chm", COMMAND_FIND, nil);
```

The **COMMAND_CONTENTS, COMMAND_FIND**, and **COMMAND_INDEX** commands have no arguments to pass to this method. For the **COMMAND_TOPIC** command, you pass in the name of the topic you want to display. As you can see, working with the help system in C# is not difficult.

NOTE: When I was experimenting with the various commands in the final beta version of the C# CLR, the **COMMAND_FIND** command did not appear to work for HTML files. This problem may or may not be fixed by the time the final version is released.

System Trays

The final "other" topic I discuss in this chapter is the system tray, or notification tray, as it is now called. Whatever its name, the *system tray* is the small area of icons displayed along with the clock in the bottom corner of the taskbar in the Windows system area.

Working with the system tray is quite easy in the C# CLR, as long as you remember that Microsoft has renamed the tray. The **NotifyIcon** class is used to manage the whole process of displaying and working with the system tray area for a given application.

To use the **NotifyIcon** component, you first drag and drop a component of the **NotifyIcon** class to your form. Two properties are important to use in this component: **Icon**, which contains the icon to display in the system tray, and **ContextMenu**, which contains the small popup menu that is used when a user right-clicks on the icon in the tray.

If you just want to work with the notification icons, the only thing you need to do from that point is to respond to the context menu selections. You do this in the standard way, by creating a context menu and double-clicking the menu item you want to handle in your form. When the user selects that item from the notify icon, your form handler is called, and you can perform whatever actions you want.

Many programmers use tray icons to give users the ability to hide or show the main program window. Another possible action allows users to shut down the program. The reasons for these particular commands are apparent. If your window is buried under many other windows, you want to free up screen real estate to be able to work with other programs. If too many windows are open, you want to hide the ones you aren't working with, but not shut down those applications. On the other hand, you may not want to load the window for a given application and then find the Close button for it. Right-clicking on the icon for the program and selecting Exit is easier.

TIP: *A complete example of working with the system tray is in the "Immediate Solutions" section, later in this chapter.*

Immediate Solutions

Printing a Text Box

One of the most helpful things about C# is how simple it is to create items, like notepads for your application. You can put a rich text edit box on your form and allow users to enter whatever data they want in whatever format they want. One addition you can make to this type of notepad utility is the printing capability for those notes. Users can then edit notes and print them so that they can keep a permanent record of them without fear of being away from their computer. In this example, you look at how to print the contents of a text edit box.

Figure 14.1 shows the form you use in this example. As you can see, the form contains only the rich edit box and two buttons that are visible to users. In addition, a print dialog box component on the form is not visible to users. Print dialog components are visible only at design time. They must be shown explicitly at runtime in a separate dialog window.

Listing 14.1 shows the code needed to implement the printing of the text box for this application. As you can see, you start the process of printing in the button handler for the Print button. This process kicks off the rest of the print system. Note the highlighted code in the listing—this code is directly involved in the printing process.

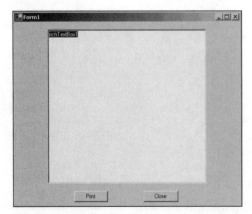

Figure 14.1   The text box print form.

Listing 14.1   The print process application.

```
using System;
using System.Drawing;
using System.Collections;
using System.ComponentModel;
using System.Windows.Forms;
using System.Data;

namespace CH14_1
{
    public class Form1 : System.Windows.Forms.Form
    {
        private System.Windows.Forms.RichTextBox richTextBox1;
        private System.Windows.Forms.Button button1;
        private System.Windows.Forms.Button button2;
        private System.ComponentModel.Container components = null;
        private System.Windows.Forms.PrintDialog printDialog1;
        private System.Drawing.Printing.PrintDocument
            ThePrintDocument = null;
        private System.IO.StringReader myStringReader = null;

        public Form1()
        {
            InitializeComponent();
            ThePrintDocument = new System.Drawing.Printing.PrintDocument();
        }
        protected override void Dispose( bool disposing )
        {
            if( disposing )
            {
                if (components != null)
                {
                    components.Dispose();
                }
            }
            base.Dispose( disposing );
        }

        #region Windows Form Designer generated code
        private void InitializeComponent()
        {
            this.richTextBox1 = new System.Windows.Forms.RichTextBox();
            this.button1 = new System.Windows.Forms.Button();
            this.button2 = new System.Windows.Forms.Button();
            this.printDialog1 = new System.Windows.Forms.PrintDialog();
```

```
            this.SuspendLayout();
            this.richTextBox1.Location = new System.Drawing.Point(72, 16);
            this.richTextBox1.Name = "richTextBox1";
            this.richTextBox1.Size = new System.Drawing.Size(344, 320);
            this.richTextBox1.TabIndex = 0;
            this.richTextBox1.Text = "richTextBox1";
            this.button1.Location = new System.Drawing.Point(128, 352);
            this.button1.Name = "button1";
            this.button1.TabIndex = 1;
            this.button1.Text = "&Print";
            this.button1.Click += new
                System.EventHandler(this.button1_Click);
            this.button2.Location = new System.Drawing.Point(280, 352);
            this.button2.Name = "button2";
            this.button2.TabIndex = 2;
            this.button2.Text = "&Close";
            this.button2.Click += new
                System.EventHandler(this.button2_Click);
            this.AutoScaleBaseSize = new System.Drawing.Size(5, 13);
            this.ClientSize = new System.Drawing.Size(488, 381);
            this.Controls.AddRange(new System.Windows.Forms.Control[] {
                this.button2,
                this.button1,
                this.richTextBox1});
            this.Name = "Form1";
            this.Text = "Form1";
            this.ResumeLayout(false);
        }
        #endregion
        [STAThread]
        static void Main()
        {
            Application.Run(new Form1());
        }


        private void button2_Click(object sender, System.EventArgs e)
        {
            Close();
        }


        private void button1_Click(object sender, System.EventArgs e)
        {
            ThePrintDocument.PrintPage += new
                System.Drawing.Printing.PrintPageEventHandler(PrintPage);
            printDialog1.Document = ThePrintDocument;
            string strText = this.richTextBox1.Text;
```

```
        myStringReader = new System.IO.StringReader(strText);
        if (printDialog1.ShowDialog() == DialogResult.OK)
        {
            this.ThePrintDocument.Print();
        }
    }
    protected void PrintPage (object sender,
            System.Drawing.Printing.PrintPageEventArgs ev)
    {
        float linesPerPage = 0;
        float yPosition = 0;
        int count = 0;
        float leftMargin = ev.MarginBounds.Left;
        float topMargin = ev.MarginBounds.Top;
        string line = null;
        Font printFont = this.richTextBox1.Font;
        SolidBrush myBrush = new SolidBrush(Color.Black);
        linesPerPage = ev.MarginBounds.Height /
            printFont.GetHeight(ev.Graphics);
        while(count < linesPerPage &&
            ((line=myStringReader.ReadLine()) != null))
        {
            yPosition = topMargin + (count *
                printFont.GetHeight(ev.Graphics));
            ev.Graphics.DrawString(line, printFont, myBrush, leftMargin,
                    yPosition, new StringFormat());
            count++;
        }
        if  (line != null)
            ev.HasMorePages = true;
        else
            ev.HasMorePages = false;

        myBrush.Dispose ();
    }

  }
}
```

In this example, when a user selects the Print button, the print process begins. The print document is set up to use the page-printing function as its delegate to the print process. The common print dialog box is displayed so that users can get information, such as which printer to use and which format to employ. Finally, the **Print** method of your document is invoked, which calls the **PrintPage** function repeatedly until no more text is available to print.

Implementing Print Preview

The common print dialog box is used for a variety of reasons. You can use it to gather information about the printing process from the user as well as to select which printer to use or how many copies to print. However, as you see in the example in this section, the print dialog boxes have another use: Print Preview can be implemented using the Print Preview dialog box. Let's take a look at how to do this.

Figure 14.2 shows the form you use for this application. It looks similar to the form you used in the printing example, but this time it contains a Preview button rather than a Print button. When the program is run and text is entered into the rich text edit box, the resulting print preview dialog box is displayed with that text in it.

Listing 14.2 shows the code necessary to implement the print preview process. Let's take a look at the code first and then worry about how it all works.

Listing 14.2   The print preview application.

```
using System;
using System.Drawing;
using System.Collections;
using System.ComponentModel;
using System.Windows.Forms;
using System.Data;

namespace CH14_2
{
    public class Form1 : System.Windows.Forms.Form
    {
```

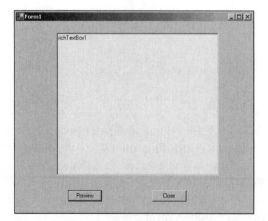

Figure 14.2   The print preview text box program.

```csharp
private System.Windows.Forms.RichTextBox richTextBox1;
private System.Windows.Forms.Button button1;
private System.Windows.Forms.Button button2;
private System.ComponentModel.Container components = null;
private System.Drawing.Printing.PrintDocument
        ThePrintDocument = null;
private System.IO.StringReader myStringReader = null;

public Form1()
{
   InitializeComponent();

   ThePrintDocument = new System.Drawing.Printing.PrintDocument();
}
protected override void Dispose( bool disposing )
{
   if( disposing )
   {
      if (components != null)
      {
         components.Dispose();
      }
   }
   base.Dispose( disposing );
}

#region Windows Form Designer generated code
private void InitializeComponent()
{
   this.richTextBox1 = new System.Windows.Forms.RichTextBox();
   this.button1 = new System.Windows.Forms.Button();
   this.button2 = new System.Windows.Forms.Button();
   this.SuspendLayout();
   this.richTextBox1.Location = new System.Drawing.Point(88, 24);
   this.richTextBox1.Name = "richTextBox1";
   this.richTextBox1.Size = new System.Drawing.Size(352, 296);
   this.richTextBox1.TabIndex = 0;
   this.richTextBox1.Text = "richTextBox1";
   this.button1.Location = new System.Drawing.Point(112, 352);
   this.button1.Name = "button1";
   this.button1.TabIndex = 1;
   this.button1.Text = "&Preview";
   this.button1.Click += new
           System.EventHandler(this.button1_Click);
```

```
        this.button2.Location = new System.Drawing.Point(296, 352);
        this.button2.Name = "button2";
        this.button2.TabIndex = 2;
        this.button2.Text = "&Close";
        this.button2.Click += new
                System.EventHandler(this.button2_Click);
        this.AutoScaleBaseSize = new System.Drawing.Size(5, 13);
        this.ClientSize = new System.Drawing.Size(512, 397);
        this.Controls.AddRange(new System.Windows.Forms.Control[] {
                    this.button2,
                    this.button1,
                    this.richTextBox1});
        this.Name = "Form1";
        this.Text = "Form1";
        this.ResumeLayout(false);

    }
    #endregion
    [STAThread]
    static void Main()
    {
        Application.Run(new Form1());
    }

    private void button2_Click(object sender, System.EventArgs e)
    {
        Close();
    }

    protected void PrintPage (object sender,
            System.Drawing.Printing.PrintPageEventArgs ev)
    {
        float linesPerPage = 0;
        float yPosition = 0;
        int count = 0;
        float leftMargin = ev.MarginBounds.Left;
        float topMargin = ev.MarginBounds.Top;
        string line = null;
        Font printFont = this.richTextBox1.Font;
        SolidBrush myBrush = new SolidBrush(Color.Black);

        linesPerPage = ev.MarginBounds.Height /
                printFont.GetHeight(ev.Graphics);
```

```
        while(count < linesPerPage &&
            ((line=myStringReader.ReadLine()) != null))
        {
            yPosition = topMargin + (count *
                printFont.GetHeight(ev.Graphics));
            ev.Graphics.DrawString(line, printFont, myBrush, leftMargin,
                yPosition, new StringFormat());
            count++;
        }

        if  (line != null)
            ev.HasMorePages = true;
        else
            ev.HasMorePages = false;

        myBrush.Dispose();
    }

    private void button1_Click(object sender, System.EventArgs e)
    {
        ThePrintDocument.PrintPage += new
            System.Drawing.Printing.PrintPageEventHandler(PrintPage);
        try
        {
string strText = this.richTextBox1.Text;
            myStringReader = new System.IO.StringReader(strText);
            PrintPreviewDialog printPreviewDialog1 = new
                PrintPreviewDialog();
            printPreviewDialog1.Document = this.ThePrintDocument ;
            printPreviewDialog1.BorderStyle = FormBorderStyle.Fixed3D ;
            printPreviewDialog1.ShowDialog();
        }
        catch(Exception exp)
        {
            System.Console.WriteLine(exp.Message.ToString());
        }
    }
    }
}
```

When you run the program and enter some text into the rich text edit box, clicking the Preview button results in a display much like the one shown in Figure 14.3. You see the complete dialog box, with no extra effort on your part, which is obviously an added benefit of working with C#!

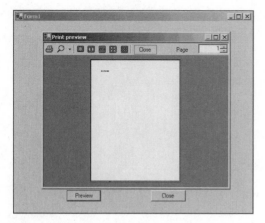

Figure 14.3   The print preview dialog box.

Writing Secure Mobile Code

The C# system was built from the ground up to be secure for users and programmers. A system can not only be assured that it will not be allowed to do something wrong, but can also force the rest of the application to not be allowed to break something the user is worried about. In this example, you look at how to use the security system in a mobile application.

As you can see in Figure 14.4, the form you use to emulate a mobile code application contains radio buttons to either allow or deny access to a specific file on disk. If a user selects the radio button to allow access and then clicks the Open a File button, nothing bad happens. If, on the other hand, the user checks the radio button to deny access to the file and selects the Open button, a security exception is generated.

The code for this application is shown in Listing 14.3. As you can see, the code makes use of the C# security components to either allow or deny permissions to a specific file. Other alternatives exist, such as allowing or denying access to specific environment variables or even directories.

Figure 14.4   The secure-file form.

Listing 14.3   Writing secure code.

```
using System;
using System.Drawing;
using System.Collections;
using System.ComponentModel;
using System.Windows.Forms;
using System.Data;
using System.Security;
using System.IO;
using System.Security.Permissions;

namespace CH14_3
{
   public class Form1 : System.Windows.Forms.Form
   {
      private System.Windows.Forms.Button button1;
      private System.Windows.Forms.RadioButton radioButton1;
      private System.Windows.Forms.RadioButton radioButton2;
      private System.Windows.Forms.Button button2;
      private System.ComponentModel.Container components = null;
      private Boolean fAllowWrite = true;

      public Form1()
      {
         InitializeComponent();
      }
      protected override void Dispose( bool disposing )
      {
         if( disposing )
         {
            if (components != null)
            {
               components.Dispose();
            }
         }
         base.Dispose( disposing );
      }

      #region Windows Form Designer generated code
      private void InitializeComponent()
      {
         this.button1 = new System.Windows.Forms.Button();
         this.radioButton1 = new System.Windows.Forms.RadioButton();
         this.radioButton2 = new System.Windows.Forms.RadioButton();
         this.button2 = new System.Windows.Forms.Button();
         this.SuspendLayout();
         this.button1.Location = new System.Drawing.Point(48, 96);
```

```
        this.button1.Name = "button1";
        this.button1.Size = new System.Drawing.Size(192, 24);
        this.button1.TabIndex = 0;
        this.button1.Text = "Open a File";
        this.button1.Click += new
                System.EventHandler(this.button1_Click);
        this.radioButton1.Location = new System.Drawing.Point(40, 16);
        this.radioButton1.Name = "radioButton1";
        this.radioButton1.Size = new System.Drawing.Size(184, 24);
        this.radioButton1.TabIndex = 1;
        this.radioButton1.Text = "Allow Permission to Temp";
        this.radioButton1.CheckedChanged += new
            System.EventHandler(this.radioButton1_CheckedChanged);
        this.radioButton2.Location = new System.Drawing.Point(40, 56);
        this.radioButton2.Name = "radioButton2";
        this.radioButton2.Size = new System.Drawing.Size(176, 24);
        this.radioButton2.TabIndex = 2;
        this.radioButton2.Text = "Deny Permission to Temp";
        this.radioButton2.CheckedChanged += new
             System.EventHandler(this.radioButton2_CheckedChanged);
        this.button2.Location = new System.Drawing.Point(96, 136);
        this.button2.Name = "button2";
        this.button2.TabIndex = 3;
        this.button2.Text = "&Close";
        this.button2.Click += new
                System.EventHandler(this.button2_Click);
        this.AutoScaleBaseSize = new System.Drawing.Size(5, 13);
        this.ClientSize = new System.Drawing.Size(292, 181);
        this.Controls.AddRange(new System.Windows.Forms.Control[] {
                this.button2,
                this.radioButton2,
                this.radioButton1,
                this.button1});
    this.Name = "Form1";
    this.Text = "Form1";
    this.ResumeLayout(false);
}
#endregion
[STAThread]
static void Main()
{
    Application.Run(new Form1());
}

private void radioButton1_CheckedChanged(object sender,
        System.EventArgs e)
{
```

```
            fAllowWrite = true;
        }

        private void radioButton2_CheckedChanged(object sender,
                System.EventArgs e)
        {
            fAllowWrite = false;
        }

        private void button2_Click(object sender, System.EventArgs e)
        {
            Close();
        }

        private void button1_Click(object sender, System.EventArgs e)
        {
            PermissionSet ps = new
                PermissionSet (
                    System.Security.Permissions.PermissionState.None);

            ps.AddPermission(

                new FileIOPermission(FileIOPermissionAccess.Read |

                FileIOPermissionAccess.Write | FileIOPermissionAccess.Append,

                "c:\\temp\\temp.txt"));

            if ( fAllowWrite == false  )
                ps.Deny();
            else
                ps.Assert();

            FileStream fs = new FileStream(@"c:\temp\temp.txt" ,
                    FileMode.OpenOrCreate, FileAccess.Write);
            StreamWriter m_streamWriter = new StreamWriter(fs);

            // Write to the file using StreamWriter class
            m_streamWriter.BaseStream.Seek(0, SeekOrigin.End);
            m_streamWriter.Write("Test");
        }
    }
}
```

Related solution:	Found on page:
Creating a Derived Class	57

Extending the String Class

The core of C# is an object-oriented language. One hallmark of an object-oriented language is being able to extend that language through inheritance, which, unfortunately, is not always directly possible. For example, you might believe that you could create a "better" string class in C# by extending the base string class by writing something like this:

```
public class SuperString : string
{
}
```

Unfortunately, this example does not work because **string** is a sealed class. The **sealed** keyword in C# means that no one can derive a new class from this existing class. Why would you want to seal a class? The most basic reason is to avoid causing problems in existing functionality. If you allow someone to derive from a basic class, such as **string**, and that derived class creates a serious problem, that problem is propagated into the lower levels of the C# CLR code.

Sealing a class is a serious decision, and one you should think seriously about before you implement it. In your own code, unless you have an overwhelmingly good reason to seal a class, you should not do it. None of this advice, however, solves your problem. How do you create a "super-**string**" class? The answer lies not in inheritance, but in another object-oriented concept: encapsulation. Listing 14.4 shows the super-**string** class, implementing three Visual Basic functions: Mid, Right, and Left.

Listing 14.4   The super-string class.

```
using System;

namespace CH14_4
{
    public class SuperString
    {
        private string fString;

        public SuperString()
        {
            fString = "";
        }
        public SuperString( string inStr )
        {
            fString = inStr;
        }
```

```csharp
public string ToStr()
{
    return fString;
}
// Return the rightmost n characters
public string Right( int nChars )
{
    if ( nChars > fString.Length )
        return fString;

    string s = "";
    for ( int i=fString.Length-nChars; i<fString.Length; ++i )
        s += fString[i];
    return s;
}
public string Left( int nChars )
{
    if ( nChars > fString.Length )
        return fString;
    string s = "";
    for ( int i=0; i<nChars; ++i )
        s += fString[i];
    return s;
}
public string Mid( int nStart, int nEnd )
{
    if ( nStart < 0 || nEnd > fString.Length )
        return fString;
    if ( nStart > nEnd )
        return "";

    string s = "";
    for ( int i=nStart; i<nEnd; ++i )
        s += fString[i];
    return s;
}
}

class Class1
{
    static void Main(string[] args)
    {
        SuperString s = new SuperString("Hello world");
        System.Console.WriteLine("s = {0}", s.ToStr() );
        System.Console.WriteLine("Right 3 = [{0}]", s.Right(3));
        System.Console.WriteLine("Left 6 = [{0}]", s.Left(6));
```

```
            System.Console.WriteLine("Mid 2,4 = [{0}]", s.Mid(2,4));
        }
    }
}
```

When you run this little console application to test the super **string** class, you get the following output :

```
C:\CH14_4\bin\Debug>ch14_4
s = Hello world
Right 3 = [rld]
Left 6 = [Hello ]
Mid 2,4 = [ll]
```

As you can see, the class does the equivalent of the Visual Basic string class, as it was advertised to do. This technique, of encapsulating an existing class and adding to it is powerful; you can use it with any existing component, whether or not that component is sealed in C#.

Displaying Help for Your Application

One of the best things you can do for users is to give them the ability to get help in your program when they need it. Normally, you do this via some sort of a help menu that links directly to a series of help files. In the newer Windows operating systems, help files can be in either classic format (.hlp or .chm files) or the new HTML help (.html) format. The C# CLR system provides interfaces so that you need not know which kind of help file you are working with.

In Figure 14.5, you can see the form you use to explore the help system in C#. The form allows you to select a help file to browse, and then can bring up either the main contents page of the help file or the index into that help file.

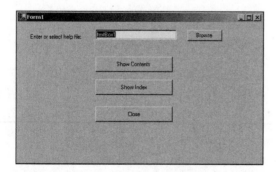

Figure 14.5   The help file viewer form.

The code to show the help files is shown in Listing 14.5. As you can see, the code is not terribly complicated. You simply use the functionality provided by the system **Help** class to do all the work.

Listing 14.5   Displaying help for your application.

```csharp
using System;
using System.Drawing;
using System.Collections;
using System.ComponentModel;
using System.Windows.Forms;
using System.Data;

namespace CH14_5
{
    public class Form1 : System.Windows.Forms.Form
    {
        private System.Windows.Forms.Label label1;
        private System.Windows.Forms.TextBox textBox1;
        private System.Windows.Forms.Button button1;
        private System.Windows.Forms.OpenFileDialog openFileDialog1;
        private System.Windows.Forms.Button button2;
        private System.Windows.Forms.Button button3;
        private System.Windows.Forms.Button button4;
        private System.ComponentModel.Container components = null;

        public Form1()
        {
            InitializeComponent();
        }
        protected override void Dispose( bool disposing )
        {
            if( disposing )
            {
                if (components != null)
                {
                    components.Dispose();
                }
            }
            base.Dispose( disposing );
        }

        #region Windows Form Designer generated code
        private void InitializeComponent()
        {
            this.label1 = new System.Windows.Forms.Label();
            this.textBox1 = new System.Windows.Forms.TextBox();
```

```
this.button1 = new System.Windows.Forms.Button();
this.openFileDialog1 = new System.Windows.Forms.OpenFileDialog();
this.button2 = new System.Windows.Forms.Button();
this.button3 = new System.Windows.Forms.Button();
this.button4 = new System.Windows.Forms.Button();
this.SuspendLayout();
this.label1.Location = new System.Drawing.Point(24, 24);
this.label1.Name = "label1";
this.label1.Size = new System.Drawing.Size(128, 23);
this.label1.TabIndex = 0;
this.label1.Text = "Enter or select help file:";
this.textBox1.Location = new System.Drawing.Point(168, 16);
this.textBox1.Name = "textBox1";
this.textBox1.Size = new System.Drawing.Size(176, 20);
this.textBox1.TabIndex = 1;
this.textBox1.Text = "textBox1";
this.button1.Location = new System.Drawing.Point(368, 16);
this.button1.Name = "button1";
this.button1.TabIndex = 2;
this.button1.Text = "&Browse";
this.button1.Click += new
        System.EventHandler(this.button1_Click);
this.button2.Location = new System.Drawing.Point(168, 72);
this.button2.Name = "button2";
this.button2.Size = new System.Drawing.Size(168, 32);
this.button2.TabIndex = 3;
this.button2.Text = "Show Contents";
this.button2.Click += new
        System.EventHandler(this.button2_Click);
this.button3.Location = new System.Drawing.Point(168, 120);
this.button3.Name = "button3";
this.button3.Size = new System.Drawing.Size(168, 32);
this.button3.TabIndex = 4;
this.button3.Text = "Show Index";
this.button3.Click += new
        System.EventHandler(this.button3_Click);
this.button4.Location = new System.Drawing.Point(168, 176);
this.button4.Name = "button4";
this.button4.Size = new System.Drawing.Size(168, 32);
this.button4.TabIndex = 5;
this.button4.Text = "&Close";
this.button4.Click += new
        System.EventHandler(this.button4_Click);
this.AutoScaleBaseSize = new System.Drawing.Size(5, 13);
this.ClientSize = new System.Drawing.Size(528, 293);
```

```
        this.Controls.AddRange(new System.Windows.Forms.Control[] {
                this.button4,
                this.button3,
                this.button2,
                this.button1,
                this.textBox1,
                this.label1});
        this.Name = "Form1";
        this.Text = "Form1";
        this.ResumeLayout(false);

    }
    #endregion
    [STAThread]
    static void Main()
    {
        Application.Run(new Form1());
    }

    private void button1_Click(object sender, System.EventArgs e)
    {
        if ( this.openFileDialog1.ShowDialog() == DialogResult.OK )
        {
            this.textBox1.Text = this.openFileDialog1.FileName;
        }
    }

    private void button4_Click(object sender, System.EventArgs e)
    {
        Close();
    }

    private void button2_Click(object sender, System.EventArgs e)
    {
        Help.ShowHelp(this, this.textBox1.Text );
    }

    private void button3_Click(object sender, System.EventArgs e)
    {
        Help.ShowHelpIndex(this, this.textBox1.Text);
    }
}
}
```

14. Miscellaneous Areas

Figure 14.6   Displaying a help file.

As an example, when you run the program and select one of the help files in the Windows system directory, you see a display much like the one shown in Figure 14.6. In this case, you elect to view the index of the help file.

Related solution:	*Found on page:*
Adding a Menu to a Form	297

Creating a Menu "On the Fly"

You might think of a menu as a static element for a given window or form. Menus exist to allow you to get to certain functionality within the program. Having menus add new functionality as they run seems to make little sense because that information needs to be thought out in advance. This statement is untrue, however: A dynamic menu system often makes sense.

The first case in which a dynamic menu system makes perfect sense is in a configurable system that allows users to determine what functionality they need access to. Few applications do this now, primarily because the notion of a configurable menu seems to be one that has not yet been integrated into system design. The reason may have been the difficulty with which programming handled dynamic menus.

The second case in which dynamic menus are used is much more common: a recent file list for an application. Alternatively, a list of recent commands might be displayed. In either case, the menus must be updated at runtime for users and those menu items handled by the application after the item is added. In this example, you explore this second case with a small program that adds items to the menu dynamically and then process those items to understand how to work with them.

Figure 14.7 shows the form you use to create the new menu items. As you can see, it contains a single main menu and two buttons. The first button adds new items to the main menu as a recent file list. The second button simply closes down the application. After a menu item has been added to the main menu, selecting that item displays a message to indicate that it has been processed and to show which menu item was selected.

Listing 14.6 shows the code necessary to implement the dynamic menu process. The important new functionality is shown in shaded areas. Let's take a look at the code first, and then examine what is going on.

Listing 14.6   Creating a menu on the fly.

```
using System;
using System.Drawing;
using System.Collections;
using System.ComponentModel;
using System.Windows.Forms;
using System.Data;

namespace CH14_6
{
    public class Form1 : System.Windows.Forms.Form
    {
        private System.Windows.Forms.MainMenu File;
        private System.Windows.Forms.MenuItem menuItem1;
        private System.Windows.Forms.MenuItem menuItem2;
        private System.Windows.Forms.MenuItem menuItem3;
        private System.Windows.Forms.Button button1;
        private System.Windows.Forms.Button button2;
```

Figure 14.7   The dynamic menu form.

```csharp
       private System.ComponentModel.Container components = null;
       private int nIndex = 0;

       public Form1()
       {
          InitializeComponent();
       }
       protected override void Dispose( bool disposing )
       {
          if( disposing )
          {
             if (components != null)
             {
                components.Dispose();
             }
          }
          base.Dispose( disposing );
       }

       #region Windows Form Designer generated code
       private void InitializeComponent()
       {
          this.File = new System.Windows.Forms.MainMenu();
          this.menuItem1 = new System.Windows.Forms.MenuItem();
          this.menuItem2 = new System.Windows.Forms.MenuItem();
          this.menuItem3 = new System.Windows.Forms.MenuItem();
          this.button1 = new System.Windows.Forms.Button();
          this.button2 = new System.Windows.Forms.Button();
          this.SuspendLayout();
          this.File.MenuItems.AddRange(new
                System.Windows.Forms.MenuItem[] {
                      this.menuItem1});
          this.menuItem1.Index = 0;
          this.menuItem1.MenuItems.AddRange(new
                System.Windows.Forms.MenuItem[]
                {
                      this.menuItem2,
                      this.menuItem3});
          this.menuItem1.Text = "File";
          this.menuItem2.Index = 0;
          this.menuItem2.Text = "&Close";
          this.menuItem2.Click += new
                System.EventHandler(this.menuItem2_Click);
          this.menuItem3.Index = 1;
          this.menuItem3.Text = "E&xit";
          this.button1.Location = new System.Drawing.Point(40, 208);
```

```
        this.button1.Name = "button1";
        this.button1.TabIndex = 0;
        this.button1.Text = "&Add";
        this.button1.Click += new
                System.EventHandler(this.button1_Click);
        this.button2.Location = new System.Drawing.Point(176, 208);
        this.button2.Name = "button2";
        this.button2.TabIndex = 1;
        this.button2.Text = "&Close";
        this.button2.Click += new
                System.EventHandler(this.button2_Click);
        this.AutoScaleBaseSize = new System.Drawing.Size(5, 13);
        this.ClientSize = new System.Drawing.Size(292, 273);
        this.Controls.AddRange(new System.Windows.Forms.Control[] {
                this.button2,
                this.button1});
        this.Menu = this.File;
        this.Name = "Form1";
        this.Text = "Form1";
        this.ResumeLayout(false);

    }
#endregion
    [STAThread]
    static void Main()
    {
        Application.Run(new Form1());
    }

    private void button2_Click(object sender, System.EventArgs e)
    {
        Close();
    }

    private void menuItemHandler(object sender, System.EventArgs e)
    {
        MessageBox.Show(this, "Menu Handler Called");
        MenuItem mi = (MenuItem)sender;
        MessageBox.Show(this, "Menu Item: " + mi.Text);
    }

    private void button1_Click(object sender, System.EventArgs e)
    {
        // Create a new menu item
        MenuItem mi = new MenuItem("File "+(nIndex+1), new
```

```
                    EventHandler(menuItemHandler) );
        this.menuItem1.MenuItems.Add( mi );
        nIndex ++;
    }

    private void menuItem2_Click(object sender, System.EventArgs e)
    {
        Close();
    }
  }
}
```

When a user of the form clicks the Add button, the program creates a new **MenuItem** object. This item contains the text of the menu item itself, which is simply a text string of the form File xx, where xx is an incremented number. The second shaded area is the handler for the menu item, which you notice is always the same internal method of the class.

Creating a Utility Console Application

Although you might think that C# is primarily good for writing Windows forms applications, a whole other world of applications can be written. Like its predecessors C and C++, C# is excellent for writing utility applications that can be used to help you in your development effort.

When you are trying to decipher a proprietary data format that you or others have created, you often need to see the actual data. Unfortunately, it is often in a binary format, making it impossible for you to print the data. A hex dump program then becomes valuable: It outputs the data in the file in hexadecimal format, regardless of whether the data can be printed. In the example in this section, you create a simple hex dump utility you can use to view your own data files.

Listing 14.7 shows the hex dump program you use to dump data files. As you can see, this pure console application contains no GUI element. All data is written to the console, allowing you to dump files and redirect the output to a file. These elements are useful when you are continually examining a file's contents.

Listing 14.7   The hex dump program.

```
using System;
using System.IO;

namespace CH14_7
{
```

```
class Class1
{
    public static string Pad( string s, int len )
    {
        string temp = s;
        for ( int i=s.Length; i<len; ++i )
            temp = "0" + temp;
        return temp;
    }
    static void Main(string[] args)
    {
        StreamReader sr = null;

        // Verify we received an argument to dump
        if ( args.Length < 1 )
        {
            System.Console.WriteLine("Usage: ch14_7 <filename>");
            return;
        }
        try
        {
            // Try to open the file
            sr = new StreamReader( args[0] );
        }
        catch ( Exception e )
        {
            System.Console.WriteLine("Error opening file {0}", e);
            return;
        }
        string line = "";
        int nCounter = 0;
        int nOffset = 0;
        while ( (line = sr.ReadLine()) != null )
        {

            for ( int i=0; i<line.Length; ++i )
            {
                int c = (int)line[i];
                string fmt = String.Format("{0:x}", c);

                // Pad the format out to 2 digits
                if ( fmt.Length == 1 )
                    fmt = Pad(fmt, 2);

                // If we are at a 16 byte boundary, write it out
                if ( nOffset % 16 == 0 )
```

```
            {
                string offsetFmt = nOffset.ToString();

                System.Console.Write(Pad(offsetFmt,5)+": ");
            }

            // Output the space between characters
            System.Console.Write(fmt + " ");
            if ( nCounter == 15 )
            {
                System.Console.Write("\n");
                nCounter = 0;
            }
            else
                nCounter ++;
            // Increment the line offset
            nOffset ++;
        }
    }
  }
 }
}
```

If you then compile and run this program on itself, the output looks something like the following text. Note that only a few lines of the output are shown, to give you an idea of what it looks like without taking up too much book space:

```
C:\CH14_7\bin\Debug>ch14_7 ..\..\class1.cs
00000: 75 73 69 6e 67 20 53 79 73 74 65 6d 3b 75 73 69
00016: 6e 67 20 53 79 73 74 65 6d 2e 49 4f 3b 6e 61 6d
00032: 65 73 70 61 63 65 20 43 48 31 34 5f 37 7b 09 63
00048: 6c 61 73 73 20 43 6c 61 73 73 31 09 7b 09 09 70
00064: 75 62 6c 69 63 20 73 74 61 74 69 63 20 73 74 72
00080: 69 6e 67 20 50 61 64 28 20 73 74 72 69 6e 67 20
00096: 73 2c 20 69 6e 74 20 6c 65 6e 20 29 09 09 7b 09
00112: 09 09 73 74 72 69 6e 67 20 74 65 6d 70 20 3d 20
00128: 73 3b 09 09 09 66 6f 72 20 28 20 69 6e 74 20 69
00144: 3d 73 2e 4c 65 6e 67 74 68 3b 20 69 3c 6c 65 6e
00160: 3b 20 2b 2b 69 20 29 09 09 09 09 74 65 6d 70 20
00176: 3d 20 22 30 22 20 2b 20 74 65 6d 70 3b 09 09 09
00192: 72 65 74 75 72 6e 20 74 65 6d 70 3b 09 09 7d 09
```

As you can see, each character in the file is displayed in hexadecimal format, as advertised.

Running Another Program from Your Own

Have you ever wanted to launch a utility application from within your own program? For example, wouldn't it be nice to allow users to launch Notepad to edit a text file you have created? Or perhaps to allow users to select a file to edit and then launch a program to modify that file? The ability to start a program and pass it arguments from within your own application exists in the CLR class **Process**. In the example in this section, you look at how to use the **Process** class to launch programs and pass them arguments.

Figure 14.8 shows the form you use to examine the **Process** class. Selecting the first two buttons simply launches applications (Notepad and Solitaire, for example). Entering a file name path in the text box and selecting the third button launches Notepad to edit the file you have selected.

The code to do all this is shown in Listing 14.8. As you can see, there really isn't much to the program. The bulk of the work is done by the **Process.Start** method of the CLR.

Listing 14.8   Running another program from your own.

```
using System;
using System.Drawing;
using System.Collections;
using System.ComponentModel;
using System.Windows.Forms;
using System.Data;
using System.Diagnostics;

namespace CH14_8
{
    public class Form1 : System.Windows.Forms.Form
    {
        private System.Windows.Forms.Button button1;
        private System.Windows.Forms.Button button2;
```

Figure 14.8   The program launch form.

```
private System.Windows.Forms.Button button3;
private System.Windows.Forms.TextBox textBox1;
private System.Windows.Forms.Button button4;
private System.ComponentModel.Container components = null;

public Form1()
{
   InitializeComponent();
}
protected override void Dispose( bool disposing )
{
   if( disposing )
   {
      if (components != null)
      {
         components.Dispose();
      }
   }
   base.Dispose( disposing );
}


#region Windows Form Designer generated code
private void InitializeComponent()
{
   this.button1 = new System.Windows.Forms.Button();
   this.button2 = new System.Windows.Forms.Button();
   this.button3 = new System.Windows.Forms.Button();
   this.textBox1 = new System.Windows.Forms.TextBox();
   this.button4 = new System.Windows.Forms.Button();
   this.SuspendLayout();
   this.button1.Location = new System.Drawing.Point(56, 24);
   this.button1.Name = "button1";
   this.button1.Size = new System.Drawing.Size(168, 32);
   this.button1.TabIndex = 0;
   this.button1.Text = "Run Notepad";
   this.button1.Click += new
           System.EventHandler(this.button1_Click);
   this.button2.Location = new System.Drawing.Point(56, 80);
   this.button2.Name = "button2";
   this.button2.Size = new System.Drawing.Size(168, 40);
   this.button2.TabIndex = 1;
   this.button2.Text = "Run Solitaire";
   this.button2.Click += new
           System.EventHandler(this.button2_Click);
   this.button3.Location = new System.Drawing.Point(56, 144);
```

```
       this.button3.Name = "button3";
       this.button3.Size = new System.Drawing.Size(168, 40);
       this.button3.TabIndex = 2;
       this.button3.Text = "Launch With Args";
       this.button3.Click += new
                System.EventHandler(this.button3_Click);
       this.textBox1.Location = new System.Drawing.Point(56, 192);
       this.textBox1.Name = "textBox1";
       this.textBox1.Size = new System.Drawing.Size(168, 20);
       this.textBox1.TabIndex = 3;
       this.textBox1.Text = "textBox1";
       this.button4.Location = new System.Drawing.Point(192, 240);
       this.button4.Name = "button4";
       this.button4.TabIndex = 4;
       this.button4.Text = "Close";
       this.button4.Click += new
                System.EventHandler(this.button4_Click);
       this.AutoScaleBaseSize = new System.Drawing.Size(5, 13);
       this.ClientSize = new System.Drawing.Size(292, 273);
       this.Controls.AddRange(new System.Windows.Forms.Control[] {
                this.button4,
                this.textBox1,
                this.button3,
                this.button2,
                this.button1});
       this.Name = "Form1";
       this.Text = "Form1";
       this.ResumeLayout(false);

   }
   #endregion
   [STAThread]
   static void Main()
   {
      Application.Run(new Form1());
   }
   private void button1_Click(object sender, System.EventArgs e)
   {
      Process.Start("notepad.exe", "");
   }

   private void button2_Click(object sender, System.EventArgs e)
   {
      Process.Start("sol.exe", "");
   }
```

```
private void button3_Click(object sender, System.EventArgs e)
{
    Process.Start("notepad.exe", this.textBox1.Text );
}

private void button4_Click(object sender, System.EventArgs e)
{
    Close();
}
}
}
```

Creating a System Tray Icon for Your Application

System tray icons were a new concept in Windows 95. These little icons sat in the small tray in the corner of your taskbar, giving you immediate access to certain functionality within the program. You could, for example, show or hide the program window or activate the most commonly used functions of your applications. Tray icons commonly allowed users to close an application, open a specific input file, or start up a music program. In any case, the icons themselves allowed you to keep a utility program running but not visible on the screen and to bring up the window for the application only when it was needed. This feature saved valuable screen real estate and still permitted users to know that applications were running and available.

The C# CLR took the system tray icon into account when it was built. If you have been using an earlier beta of the C# system, or if you were looking for a class named **SystemTray**, you find that it does not exist. In the current CLR, the class is referred to as a **NotifyIcon** object, to better model the real use of these trays.

Figure 14.9 shows the form you use for this example. Two nonvisible components are on the form: the **NotifyIcon** component and the **ContextMenu** component. The **NotifyIcon** component is used for the handling and display of the icon, and ContextMenu is attached to the **NotifyIcon** component to handle the pop-up menu that is displayed when you right-click on the icon in the system tray.

The code to implement the pop-up menu is shown in Listing 14.9. As you can see, the majority of the work is done by the CLR functions. Functionality is available to make the main form visible or invisible and to make the tray icon visible or not visible.

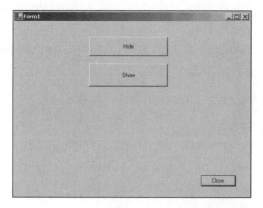

Figure 14.9 The system tray manager form.

Listing 14.9 Creating a system tray icon for your application.

```
using System;
using System.Drawing;
using System.Collections;
using System.ComponentModel;
using System.Windows.Forms;
using System.Data;

namespace CH14_9
{
   public class Form1 : System.Windows.Forms.Form
   {
      private System.Windows.Forms.NotifyIcon notifyIcon1;
      private System.Windows.Forms.ContextMenu contextMenu1;
      private System.Windows.Forms.MenuItem menuItem1;
      private System.Windows.Forms.Button button1;
      private System.Windows.Forms.Button button2;
      private System.Windows.Forms.Button button3;
      private System.Windows.Forms.MenuItem menuItem2;
      private System.Windows.Forms.MenuItem menuItem3;
      private System.ComponentModel.IContainer components;

      public Form1()
      {
         InitializeComponent();
      }
      protected override void Dispose( bool disposing )
      {
         if( disposing )
         {
```

```
            if (components != null)
            {
                components.Dispose();
            }
        }
        base.Dispose( disposing );
    }

    #region Windows Form Designer generated code
    private void InitializeComponent()
    {
        this.components = new System.ComponentModel.Container();
        System.Resources.ResourceManager resources = new
                System.Resources.ResourceManager(typeof(Form1));
        this.notifyIcon1 = new
                System.Windows.Forms.NotifyIcon(this.components);
        this.contextMenu1 = new System.Windows.Forms.ContextMenu();
        this.menuItem1 = new System.Windows.Forms.MenuItem();
        this.button1 = new System.Windows.Forms.Button();
        this.button2 = new System.Windows.Forms.Button();
        this.button3 = new System.Windows.Forms.Button();
        this.menuItem2 = new System.Windows.Forms.MenuItem();
        this.menuItem3 = new System.Windows.Forms.MenuItem();
        this.SuspendLayout();
        // This line associates the context menu with the icon
        this.notifyIcon1.ContextMenu = this.contextMenu1;
        this.notifyIcon1.Icon =
            ((System.Drawing.Icon)
                (resources.GetObject("notifyIcon1.Icon")));
        this.notifyIcon1.Text = "Tray Icon";
        this.notifyIcon1.Visible = true;
        this.contextMenu1.MenuItems.AddRange(new
                System.Windows.Forms.MenuItem[] {
                    this.menuItem1,
                    this.menuItem2,
                    this.menuItem3});
        this.menuItem1.Index = 0;
        this.menuItem1.Text = "Exit";
        this.menuItem1.Click += new
                System.EventHandler(this.menuItem1_Click);
        this.button1.Location = new System.Drawing.Point(400, 320);
        this.button1.Name = "button1";
        this.button1.TabIndex = 0;
        this.button1.Text = "Close";
        this.button1.Click += new
                System.EventHandler(this.button1_Click);
```

```
            this.button2.Location = new System.Drawing.Point(160, 32);
            this.button2.Name = "button2";
            this.button2.Size = new System.Drawing.Size(168, 40);
            this.button2.TabIndex = 1;
            this.button2.Text = "Hide";
            this.button2.Click += new
                    System.EventHandler(this.button2_Click);
            this.button3.Location = new System.Drawing.Point(160, 88);
            this.button3.Name = "button3";
            this.button3.Size = new System.Drawing.Size(168, 48);
            this.button3.TabIndex = 2;
            this.button3.Text = "Show";
            this.button3.Click += new
                    System.EventHandler(this.button3_Click);
            this.menuItem2.Index = 1;
            this.menuItem2.Text = "Hide";
            this.menuItem2.Click += new
                    System.EventHandler(this.menuItem2_Click);
            this.menuItem3.Index = 2;
            this.menuItem3.Text = "Show";
            this.menuItem3.Click += new
                    System.EventHandler(this.menuItem3_Click);
            this.AutoScaleBaseSize = new System.Drawing.Size(5, 13);
            this.ClientSize = new System.Drawing.Size(504, 365);
            this.Controls.AddRange(new System.Windows.Forms.Control[] {
                    this.button3,
                    this.button2,
                    this.button1});
            this.Name = "Form1";
            this.Text = "Form1";
            this.ResumeLayout(false);

}
#endregion
[STAThread]
static void Main()
{
    Application.Run(new Form1());
}

private void menuItem1_Click(object sender, System.EventArgs e)
{
    Close();
}
```

```
private void button1_Click(object sender, System.EventArgs e)
{
   Close();
}

private void button2_Click(object sender, System.EventArgs e)
{
   notifyIcon1.Visible = false;
}

private void button3_Click(object sender, System.EventArgs e)
{
   notifyIcon1.Visible = true;
}

private void menuItem2_Click(object sender, System.EventArgs e)
{
   this.Visible = false;
}

private void menuItem3_Click(object sender, System.EventArgs e)
{
   this.Visible = true;
}
   }
}
```

Index

B

W

X

Expand your .NET development knowledge with these reference guides from Coriolis Technology Press!

What's on the CD-ROM

The *C# Black Book*'s companion CD-ROM contains elements specifically selected to enhance the usefulness of this book, including:

- *The .NET SDK*—The SDK features:
  - The complete CLR class library
  - The most current version of the command-line C# compiler
  - Complete debugging libraries and symbol files
  - Documentation for the .NET class libraries
  - Complete example applications ready to compile and run
  - Up-to-date documentation for the .NET system

Note: This program was reproduced by The Coriolis Group under a special arrangement with Microsoft Corporation. For this reason, The Coriolis Group is responsible for the product warranty and for support. If your diskette is defective, please return it to The Coriolis Group, which will arrange for its replacement. PLEASE DO NOT RETURN IT TO MICROSOFT CORPORATION. Any product support will be provided, if at all, by The Coriolis Group. PLEASE DO NOT CONTACT MICROSOFT CORPORATION FOR PRODUCT SUPPORT. End users of this Microsoft program shall not be considered "registered owners" of a Microsoft product and therefore shall not be eligible for upgrades, promotions or other benefits available to "registered owners" of Microsoft products.

Please note that Coriolis is providing the .NET SDK under license from Microsoft Corporation. While we are happy to assist you with defective, damaged, or unusable CDs, we are unable to address any technical or product support issues associated with the Microsoft SDK.

- *Source code for the book's projects*—You can adapt these real-world programs based on your needs:
  - A complete Scribble application in C#
  - A complex Hex dump application
  - Illustrations of an image-viewing application

Note: *The following software (not included on this CD-ROM) is required to complete the projects in this book:*

- Visual Studio.NET (Visual Studio 7.0)

System Requirements

Software Requirements

- Your operating system must be Windows ME, Windows NT 4, Windows 2000, or Windows XP.
- You must have Internet Explorer 5.5 or higher to view some of the newer documentation.

Hardware

- An Intel (or equivalent) Pentium 300MHz processor is the minimum platform required; an Intel (or equivalent) Pentium 500MHz processor is recommended.
- 64MB of RAM is the minimum requirement. 128MB is the minimum amount you should consider.
- The .NET CLR requires approximately 200MB of disk storage space.
- A color monitor (256 colors) is recommended.